CODING STREAMS OF LANGUAGE

TECHNIQUES FOR THE SYSTEMATIC CODING OF TEXT, TALK, AND OTHER VERBAL DATA

Practices & Possibilities

Series Editors: Nick Carbone and Mike Palmquist

Series Associate Editors: Katie McWain, Karen-Elizabeth Moroski, and Aleashia Walton

The Practices & Possibilities Series addresses the full range of practices within the field of Writing Studies, including teaching, learning, research, and theory. From Joseph Williams' reflections on problems to Richard E. Young's taxonomy of "small genres" to Adam Mackie's considerations of technology, the books in this series explore issues and ideas of interest to writers, teachers, researchers, and theorists who share an interest in improving existing practices and exploring new possibilities. The series includes both original and republished books. Works in the series are organized topically.

The WAC Clearinghouse, Colorado State University Open Press, and University Press of Colorado are collaborating so that these books will be widely available through free digital distribution and low-cost print editions. The publishers and the series editors are committed to the principle that knowledge should freely circulate. We see the opportunities that new technologies have for further democratizing knowledge. And we see that to share the power of writing is to share the means for all to articulate their needs, interest, and learning into the great experiment of literacy.

Other Books in the Series

Ellen C. Carillo, *A Guide to Mindful Reading* (2017)
Lillian Craton, Renée Love & Sean Barnette (Eds.), *Writing Pathways to Student Success* (2017)
Charles Bazerman, *Involved: Writing for College, Writing for Your Self* (2015)
Adam Mackie, *New Literacies Dictionary: Primer for the Twenty-first Century Learner* (2011)
Patricia A. Dunn, *Learning Re-abled: The Learning Disability Controversy and Composition Studies* (2011)
Richard E. Young, *Toward A Taxonomy of "Small" Genres and Writing Techniques for Writing Across the Curriculum* (2011)
Joseph M. Williams, *Problems into PROBLEMS: A Rhetoric of Motivation* (2011)
Charles Bazerman, *The Informed Writer: Using Sources in the Disciplines* (2011)

CODING STREAMS OF LANGUAGE

TECHNIQUES FOR THE SYSTEMATIC CODING OF TEXT, TALK, AND OTHER VERBAL DATA

Cheryl Geisler

Simon Fraser University

Jason Swarts

North Carolina State University

WAC Clearinghouse
wac.colostate.edu
Fort Collins, Colorado

University Press of Colorado
upcolorado.com
Louisville, Colorado

The WAC Clearinghouse, Fort Collins, Colorado 80523

University Press of Colorado, Louisville, Colorado 80027

ISBN 978-1-64215-023-0 (PDF) | 978-1-64215-024-7 (ePub) | 978-1-60732-730-1 (pbk.)

Printed in the United States of America

Library of Congress Cataloging-in-Publication Data

Names: Geisler, Cheryl, author. | Swarts, Jason, 1972– author.
Title: Coding streams of language : techniques for the systematic coding of text, talk, and other verbal data
| Cheryl Geisler, Simon Fraser University ; Jason Swarts, North Carolina State University.
Description: Fort Collins, CO : The WAC Clearinghouse, [2019]
| Series: Practices and possibilities | Includes bibliographical references and index.
Identifiers: LCCN 2019017157 | ISBN 9781607327301 (pbk : alk. paper) | ISBN 9781642150247 (epub) | 9781642150230 (PDF)
Subjects: LCSH: Content analysis (Communication)—Data processing. | Communication—Methodology.
Classification: LCC P93 .G35 2019 | DDC 302.2—dc23
LC record available at https://lccn.loc.gov/2019017157

Copyeditor: Don Donahue
Designer: Mike Palmquist
Series Editors: Nick Carbone and Mike Palmquist
Series Associate Editors: Katie McWain, Karen-Elizabeth Moroski, and Aleashia Walton

The WAC Clearinghouse supports teachers of writing across the disciplines. Hosted by Colorado State University, and supported by the Colorado State University Open Press, it brings together scholarly journals and book series as well as resources for teachers who use writing in their courses. This book is available in digital formats for free download at wac.colostate.edu.

Founded in 1965, the University Press of Colorado is a nonprofit cooperative publishing enterprise supported, in part, by Adams State University, Colorado State University, Fort Lewis College, Metropolitan State University of Denver, Regis University, University of Colorado, University of Northern Colorado, University of Wyoming, Utah State University, and Western Colorado University.

Contents

Procedures ix

Acknowledgments xv

Chapter 1. An Introduction to Coding Streams of Language 3

Some Preliminaries 3
Our Core Commitments 9
Using This Book 13
Our Aspirations 21
Selected Studies Using Coding 22
For Further Reading 23

Chapter 2. Designing the Analysis 25

Writing Memos 25
Designing the Analysis 28
Focusing on a Phenomenon 30
Constructing a Descriptive Framework 34
Building in Contrasts for Comparison 40
Sampling Streams of Language 41
Choosing a Sampling Strategy 47
Acquiring the Data 50
Cleaning the Data 56
Setting Up The Data 62
Setting Up a Data Table 64
Selected Studies Using Sampling 65
For Further Reading 65

Chapter 3. Segmenting the Data 67

Introduction to Segmenting 67
Basic Units of Language 73

Units in Conversation 82
Units in Text 86
Other Selective Units 88
Segmenting the Data 93
Moving the Segmented Data 103
Issues in Segmenting 107
Selected Studies Using Segmentation 110
For Further Reading 111

Chapter 4. Coding the Data 113
Concepts in Coding 113
Coding the World of Discourse 115
Getting Ready to Code 119
Deciding on a Coding Framework 124
Using a Coding Scheme 125
Revising a Coding Scheme 127
Techniques for Inspecting Coding 135
Techniques for Automated Coding 138
Nested Coding 148
Enumerative Coding Schemes 148
Selected Studies Using Procedural Coding 152
Selected Studies Using Automated Coding 152
For Further Reading 153

Chapter 5. Achieving Reliability 155
Introduction to Reliability 155
Measures of Intercoder Agreement 160
Selecting Data for Second Coding 172
Managing the Second Coding 174
Calculating Item-by-Item Agreement 177

Revising Your Analytic Procedures 194
Finalizing Reliability. 200
Selected Studies Reporting Reliability 201
For Further Reading. 201

Chapter 6. Seeing Patterns of Distribution 203
Introduction to Patterns of Distribution 203
Building a Frequency Table 208
Graphing Distribution 212
Interpreting Patterns of Distribution 215
Refining Patterns across the Built-In Contrast 222
Refining Patterns Across Codes 231
Limitations on Combining Codes 233
Selected Studies Using Frequency Distributions 234
For Further Reading. 234

Chapter 7. Exploring Patterns Across Dimensions 235
Dimensions 235
Contingency Tables 238
Graphing Dimensions 245
Characterizing Dimensions. 255
Checking Patterns across Contrast. 261
Checking Patterns across Dimensions. 266
Checking Patterns across Data Streams. 271
Putting It All Together 275
Selected Studies Exploring Patterns across Dimensions 277

Chapter 8. Following Patterns over Time. 279
Time 279
Indexing in Time 280
Aggregating in Time. 292

Selected Studies Examining Temporal Patterns 307
For Further Reading 307

Chapter 9. Evaluating Significance 309
Significance and Surprise 309
Significance Tests for Coded Verbal Data 313
Assessing Your Data 321
Choosing Your Significance Test(s) 323
The χ^2 Test of Goodness of Fit 327
The χ^2 Test of Homogeneity 332
The χ^2 Test of Independence 339
One-Factor Multinomial Logistic Regression 344
Two-Factor Multinomial Logistic Regression 352
For Further Reading 359

Chapter 10. Writing the Analysis 361
Sorting 362
Reflecting 366
Ordering 367
Detailing 368
Areas for Detailing 371
Locating Detail 381
Writing the Draft 385
Selected Studies Using Details 390
For Further Reading 391

Procedures: Excel

Excel Procedure 2.1: Creating a Memo 26
Excel Procedure 2.2: Generating a Random Sample in Excel. 45
Excel Procedure 2.3: Setting up a Data Workbook 63
Excel Procedure 2.4: Creating a Table of Contents for the Workbook 64
Excel Procedure 3.1: Moving & Numbering Comprehensively Segmented Data into Excel 103
Excel Procedure 3.2. Numbering and Moving Selective Segments in Excel. 105
Excel Procedure 4.1: Linking to Coding Scheme in Excel 122
Excel Procedure 4.2: Assigning a Code in Excel 126
Excel Procedure 4.3: Creating a Code in Excel. 129
Excel Procedure 4.4: Re-coding Data in Excel 131
Excel Procedure 4.5: Adding a Dimension in Excel. 133
Excel Procedure 4.6: Inspecting by Code in Excel. 137
Excel Procedure 4.7: Automated Coding in Excel 146
Excel Procedure 4.8: Nested Coding in Excel. 149
Excel Procedure 5.1: Preparing Excel Data for Second Coding 175
Excel Procedure 5.2: Putting the Two Codings Side by Side 177
Excel Procedure 5.3: Checking Item-by-Item Agreement. 178
Excel Procedure 5.4: Calculating Simple Agreement in Excel 182
Excel Procedure 5.5: Making a Table of Agreements & Disagreements for Excel Data 184
Excel Procedure 5.6: Formatting a Table of Agreements & Disagreements for Excel Data 185
Excel Procedure 5.7: Using GraphPad's Online Calculator for Cohen's Kappa for Excel Data 187
Excel Procedure 5.8: Converting Codes to Numeric Values for Excel Data. 190

Excel Procedure 5.9: Saving to Alternative File Formats for Excel Data. . . . 190
Excel Procedure 6.1: Naming Data in Excel 209
Excel Procedure 6.2: Making a Frequency Table in Excel. 209
Excel Procedure 6.3: Creating a Distribution Graph for Excel Data 213
Excel Procedure 6.4: Collapsing across Streams in Excel 224
Excel Procedure 6.5: Calculating Averages in Excel 227
Excel Procedure 6.6: Combining Codes in Excel. 232
Excel Procedure 7.1: Naming the Data Ranges for Each Dimension 240
Excel Procedure 7.2: Setting Up a Core Contingency Table 240
Excel Procedure 7.3: Filling Core Contingency Tables 241
Excel Procedure 7.4: Creating a Block Chart 246
Excel Procedure 7.5: Rotating a Block Chart in Excel 249
Excel Procedure 7.6: Creating Clustered Categories in a Block Chart 253
Excel Procedure 7.7: Summing Overall Frequencies 258
Excel Procedure 7.8: Selecting Non-Adjacent Data for Graphing 261
Excel Procedure 7.9: Formatting a Graph Axis. 269
Excel Procedure 8.1: Giving a Numeric Value to Codes for a Temporal Index in Excel 284
Excel Procedure 8.2: Making & Formatting a Temporal Index in Excel. . . . 285
Excel Procedure 8.3: Exploring Verbal Data with a Temporal Index in Excel 290
Excel Procedure 8.4: Marking the Aggregate Borders in Excel 295
Excel Procedure 8.5: Numbering the Aggregate Units in Excel. 296
Excel Procedure 8.6: Subtotaling by Aggregate Unit. 297
Excel Procedure 8.7: Making an Aggregate Temporal Graph in Excel 299
Excel Procedure 9.1: Calculating a Goodness of Fit χ^2 Test in Excel. 330
Excel Procedure 9.2: Calculating a χ^2 Test of Homogeneity in Excel 333
Excel Procedure 9.3: Calculating a χ^2 Test of Independence in Excel 340
Excel Procedure 10.1: Viewing Memos in Excel. 363
Excel Procedure 10.2: Exploring Detail in Full Context 383

Procedures: MAXQDA

MAXQDA Procedure 2.1: Creating a Memo 27
MAXQDA Procedure 2.2: Reviewing a Memo 27
MAXQDA Procedure 2.3: Setting Up a Document System 62
MAXQDA Procedure 3.1: Importing Comprehensively Segmented Data . . 104
MAXQDA Procedure 3.2: Importing Selectively Segmented Data 107
MAXQDA Procedure 4.1: Linking to Your Coding Scheme in MAXQDA . . 123
MAXQDA Procedure 4.2: Assigning a Code in MAXQDA 127
MAXQDA Procedure 4.3: Creating a Code in MAXQDA 129
MAXQDA Procedure 4.4: Re-coding Data in MAXQDA 132
MAXQDA Procedure 4.5: Collapsing Coding Categories in MAXQDA . . . 132
MAXQDA Procedure 4.6: Adding a Dimension in MAXQDA 134
MAXQDA Procedure 4.7: Inspecting by Code in MAXQDA 137
MAXQDA Procedure 4.8: Automated Coding in MAXQDA 147
MAXQDA Procedure 4.9: Nested Coding in MAXQDA 150
MAXQDA Procedure 5.1: Preparing MAXQDA Data for Second Coding 176
MAXQDA Procedure 5.2: Putting the Two Codings Side by Side 179
MAXQDA Procedure 5.3: Checking Item-by-Item Agreement 181
MAXQDA Procedure 5.4: Calculating Simple Agreement 183
MAXQDA Procedure 5.5: Making a Table of Agreements & Disagreements 186
MAXQDA Procedure 5.6: Formatting a Table of Agreements & Disagreements 186
MAXQDA Procedure 5.7: Using GraphPad's Online Calculator for Cohen's Kappa 188
MAXQDA Procedure 5.8: Converting Codes to Numeric Values 192
MAXQDA Procedure 5.9: Saving to Alternative File Formats 192
MAXQDA Procedure 6.1: Making a Frequency Table in MAXQDA 211

MAXQDA Procedure 6.2: Creating a Distribution Graph in MAXQDA. . . 214
MAXQDA Procedure 6.3: Creating Distribution Graphs with a Common Scale . . . 214
MAXQDA Procedure 6.4: Collapsing across Streams in MAXQDA . . . 225
MAXQDA Procedure 6.5: Calculating Averages in MAXQDA. . . 228
MAXQDA Procedure 6.6: Combining Codes in MAXQDA . . . 232
MAXQDA Procedure 7.1: Creating a Contingency Table with Two Dimensions . . . 243
MAXQDA Procedure 7.2: Creating a Contingency Table with One Dimension . . . 244
MAXQDA Procedure 7.3: Making a Block Chart from MAXQDA Data . . . 247
MAXQDA Procedure 7.4: Rotating a Block Chart for MAXQDA Data . . . 249
MAXQDA Procedure 7.5: Creating Clustered Categories in a Block Chart . . . 254
MAXQDA Procedure 7.6: Summing Overall Frequencies . . . 258
MAXQDA Procedure 8.1: Ordering Codes for a Temporal Index in MAXQDA . . . 286
MAXQDA Procedure 8.2: Creating a Temporal Index in MAXQDA. . . 286
MAXQDA Procedure 8.3: Exploring Verbal Data Associated with a Temporal Index . . . 291
MAXQDA Procedure 8.4: Marking the Aggregate Borders in MAXQDA . . . 300
MAXQDA Procedure 8.5: Creating and Moving the MAXQDA codeline into Excel . . . 301
MAXQDA Procedure 8.6: Moving the MAXQDA codeline into a new Excel worksheet . . . 301
MAXQDA Procedure 8.7: Marking the Aggregate Borders in Excel . . . 302
MAXQDA Procedure 8.8: Reformat the MAXQDA codeline in Excel . . . 303
MAXQDA Procedure 8.9: Subtotaling by Aggregate Unit . . . 304
MAXQDA Procedure 8.10: Making an Aggregate Temporal Graph in Excel . . . 304
MAXQDA Procedure 10.1: Selecting Memos in MAXQDA. . . 364
MAXQDA Procedure 10.2: Exploring Detail in Full Context . . . 383

Procedures: Other

Procedure 2.1: Locating Keywords with AntConc 33
Procedure 2.2: Exploring the Data with Clusters 33
Procedure 2.3: Exploring Data with N-Grams 33
Procedure 2.4: Cleaning a Transcript Using Find and Replace in Microsoft Word 59
Procedure 2.5: Using Wildcards in Microsoft Word 59
Procedure 2.6: Using Macros to Assist Multi-step Segmentation in Microsoft Word 62
Procedure 3.1: Segmenting Using Comprehensive Units 94
Procedure 3.2: Segmenting Conversational Data 95
Procedure 3.3: Using a Style to Format your Data 102
Procedure 4.1: Adding a Stop List in AntConc 139
Procedure 4.2: Generating Keywords in AntConc 141
Procedure 4.3: Examining Keywords in Context 142
Procedure 4.4: Examining a List of Keywords in Context 142
Procedure 4.5: Examining Keyword Custers 143
Procedure 4.6: Automated Coding in Microsoft Word 145
Procedure 5.1: Using the ReCal2 Calculator for Cohen's Kappa & Krippendorff's Alpha 191
Procedure 9.1: Calculating a Goodness of Fit χ^2 Test with an Online App 331
Procedure 9.2: Calculating a χ^2 Test of Homogeneity with an Online App 335
Procedure 9.3: Calculating a χ^2 Test of Independence with an Online App 342
Procedure 9.4: Preparing the Data for a One-Factor Multinomial Regression 346
Procedure 9.5: Running a One-Factor Multinomial Regression 347

Procedure 9.6: Preparing the Data for a Two-Factor Multinomial Regression 354
Procedure 9.7: Running a Two-Factor Multinomial Regression with Interaction 355
Procedure 9.8: Running a Two-Factor Multinomial Regression without Interaction 356

Acknowledgments

So much has changed in the analysis of language since I published *Analyzing Streams of Language* more than 15 years ago. Blogging was hot; Facebook had just launched. YouTube, Twitter, Instagram were all yet to come. As a result of these and other developments, more and more texts are circulating. And under the umbrella of text analytics, more and more tools have been developed to deal with the onslaught and opportunity such big data affords.

What has not changed is my passion for uncovering the often hidden processes that make up "hand coding"—the use of human coders to interpret and categorize streams of language. While hand coding is not sufficient for dealing with big data sets, it is still a fundamental tool. No analysis that deals with language in its full complexity can ignore the essential role of humans as interpreters of language, what language means and what language does in the world. That is what this book is about.

I have too many people to thank for contributions that have lead to this new and much expanded book, but I must begin by acknowledging my coauthor & colleague, Jason Swarts, Professor of Technical Communication at North Carolina State University. It is gratifying to see a former student grow a research program beyond its roots, but it is also a pleasure to be able to still see those roots. Jason is a wonderful collaborator: He has kept me on my toes and has always delivered. Without him, this book would not be.

I also have to acknowledge the confidence and deepening friendship of Christiane Donahue at Dartmouth College. Her invitation to teach language coding as part of the Dartmouth Summer Seminar for Composition Research for almost a decade has provided me with the opportunity to interact with scholars from all over the world, to puzzle through interesting data sets, and to explore and articulate emerging procedures. The Dartmouth Seminar is certainly the world in which this book has come to be. Thanks to Christiane and Dartmouth partcipants!

The regular and invigorating conversations that I have had over the years with Bill Hart-Davidson of Michigan State & Dave Kaufer of Carnegie Mellon have kept emerging methods for language analysis on my intellectual front burner. Trying to understand the deep structure of their efforts in a rhetorical approach to machine learning (Bill) and dictionary-based text analysis (Dave) has been crucial to understanding the key role that hand coding should continue to play in emerging methods. I thank them both for not running the other way when they saw me coming!

To Emily Griffiths from Statistics at NC State, I give a special thanks for patience and insight as we worked on statistical analysis for coded verbal data. She went above and beyond what normally gets called consulting, working through the application of logistic regression and then deploying it in an appropriate web-based tool.

Both Jason and I would like to thank Mike Palmquist, founding editor of the WAC Clearinghouse. Mike was the one who got what we wanted for *Coding Streams of Language*, our commitment to making the book available digitally at no cost to scholars around the world and across the fields as well as supporting embedded links to a updated digital resources including our own YouTube channel. Analytic methods are evolving at a rapid rate and the WAC Clearinghouse publishing collaborative with its new section on scholarly and research practices is a perfect environment for this book.

Finally, I want to acknowledge my family. Mark has believed in me and supported my work in innumerable and uncountable ways. Naomi & Bella have taken pleasure in my accomplishments as well as expected me to do more. I love you all.

– Cheryl Geisler, Vancouver, 2019

As little as two years ago, I did not envision myself writing a contribution to the acknowledgments page for this major update and expansion of Cheryl's 2004 book, *Analyzing Streams of Language*. Until that point, it was a book that I used but not one that I thought I would ever contribute to. My scholarship has been shaped by the lessons given in this book because I had the good fortune to work with Cheryl while I was a doctoral student at Rensselaer Polytechnic from 1998–2002, but I am grateful now for the chance to have collaborated with my mentor and friend on this project.

I also want to acknowledge all of the graduate students at NC State University who have taken the course that I developed around the techniques outlined in this book. A number of excellent projects have arisen from these techniques and each of those classes and projects has helped refine my understanding of how to apply the analytic techniques and how to develop explanations, exercises, and examples that convey the lessons of this analytic method more intuitively. Without a doubt, those years of classroom-based user testing have had a positive impact on the materials in this book.

Finally, I would like to acknowledge the input of the participants from the Dartmouth Summer Seminar for Composition Research. Since 2016, I have been a faculty mentor at the summer seminar and as sections of this book have been written, Cheryl and I have tested them out with the seminar participants. The content has only improved as a result of those interactions. Thank you to the many participants and to Christiane Donahue for organizing the seminar.

– Jason Swarts, Raleigh, 2019

CODING STREAMS OF LANGUAGE

TECHNIQUES FOR THE SYSTEMATIC CODING OF TEXT, TALK, AND OTHER VERBAL DATA

Chapter 1. An Introduction to Coding Streams of Language

In this chapter, we provide you with an introduction to coding streams of language. Beginning with a rationale for coding language, we also detail our commitments on several methodological issues. We then explain how to use this book, inviting you to adapt it in whole or in part to develop an appropriate analytic workflow, to choose your tools, and to follow its procedures. We close by articulating our aspirations, the challenges we have tried to address, and the sometimes technical quandries on which we have tried to provide some guidance. For those readers familiar with the 2004 *Analyzing Streams of Language*, we have also included a list of what is new.

Some Preliminaries

What Coding Is

Coding is the analytic task of placing non-numeric data into descriptive categories, assigning them to *codes*. The data that we will be concerned with coding in this book is *verbal data*, data in the form of words that usually combine to make up what we like to call a *stream of language*, a stream that we as readers or writers, listeners or speakers experience as a flow over time. When we code verbal data, we analyze this flow, breaking it up into a categorical array, using a set of codes. We do this analysis to answer research questions, to better understand what the language is saying, doing, or revealing about the participants or about the situation in which the language has been used.

Any kind of verbal data can be coded. Varying in length, verbal data include the single word responses participants give in questionnaires, the quick posts that participants make in response to news articles, the full texts published in books, articles, and essays—and anything in between. Verbal data may come from conversations that need to be transcribed in order to be analyzed. Or they may come in print form, which may need to be scanned and converted using optical character recognition (OCR). And, increasingly, verbal data come in digital form, harvested from the web, sent in tweets, or published in digital databases. In most of these cases, verbal data are copious; words come fast and cheap in many contexts. They tell us a lot about what is going on, but we need to work to understand their underlying patterns. This is the work of coding streams of language.

Usually when we refer to coding, we are referring to an analytic process guided by a set of procedures—a procedural coding scheme—that tells the analyst how to categorize a segment of verbal data by defining and illustrating the use of each coding category. This is the primary kind of coding we deal with in this book. But we will also introduce readers to two other kinds of coding: automated coding, which uses digital searches to automatically identify members of a coding category, and enumerative coding schemes, which list all of the members of its coding categories. As we shall see in Chapter 4, these three kinds of coding can be used on their own or in combination.

■ Methodological Approaches to Verbal Data Analysis

Because verbal data are so ubiquitous, many different methodological approaches have been developed to deal with them. Figure 1.1 shows one attempt at displaying complex relationships among these approaches. While coding is an analytic technique used in many fields, it has primarily been developed in the field of communication studies under the term *content analysis* and in the social sciences, more broadly, under the term *qualitative research*.

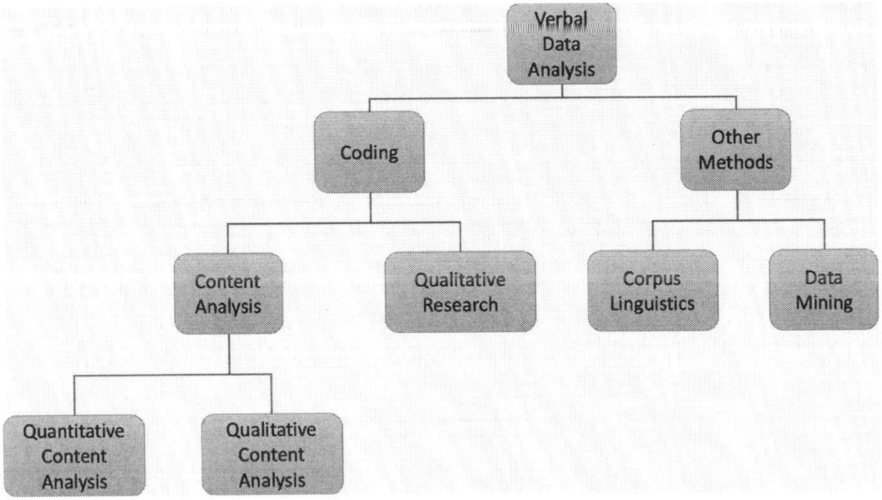

Figure 1.1: Taxonomy of approaches to verbal data analysis.

Traditional quantitative content analysis attempts to remove interpretation from coding. Often used for studies of media coverage, it provides coders with procedures using exact word matches or unambiguous judgments and uses quantification to look at overall patterns. By contrast, qualitative researchers, including those using qualitative content analysis, take an approach that is more interpretative. Many researchers adopt a qualitative approach as part of the process of choosing a CAQDAS (Computer-Aided Qualitative Data Analysis Software) tool such as Nvivo or Atlas.ti. Most though not all qualitative approaches to coding take a code as you go approach, and some, but not all, eschew any kind of quantification. In *Coding Streams of Language*, we take an interpretive approach to coding; that said, our commitment to being systematic and exploring patterns through numbers places us among the growing number of researchers taking a mixed-methods approach, which we discuss more fully in a later section.

Other methods for verbal data analysis exist that do not use coding. Approaches taken by corpus linguists, for example, focus on analyzing large sets of texts, often using some variety of grammatical or semantic tagging. In Chapter 2 on Designing the Analysis and in Chapter 4 on Coding Data, we suggest ways that one kind of corpus tool, AntConc, can be used to explore and automatically code data.

Finally, emerging methods for data mining have been introduced to deal with large sets of verbal data. Using algorithmic rather than interpretive approaches, many big data approaches have little use for interpretation. But those who use machine learning methods to duplicate human judgment will often begin their work with the kind of coding we pursue.

The Important Role Coding Plays in Many Fields

We come to the coding of verbal data from the allied fields of writing studies and technical communication. No one should be surprised to find these language-intensive fields relying on a method that deals with verbal data. As we noted elsewhere (Geisler, 2018), coding is a key analytic method in writing studies and technical communication, being used in 44% of the research reports published in 2015 and 2016. These reports used a wide range of data. For example, Breuch et al. (2016) coded interview data from hospital patients and their families for recurring themes. Martinez et al. (2015) coded video data for the cognitive activities students used while writing syntheses.

Coding plays an important role in a far wider range of fields than this brief sample of studies might suggest. Any field that deals with humans as social beings, that collects naturally occurring language data or elicits such data from participants, will find a use for coding:

- In applied linguistics, Wyrley (2010) used coding to study communication practices in radiotherapy.
- In education, Stevenson (2013) used coding to study the linguistic strategies used by fifth grade bilingual students in science.
- In engineering education, Richter and Paretti (2009) used coding to analyze how engineering students reacted to multidisciplinary design.
- In information science, Nobarany and Booth (2014) used coding to examine the use of politeness strategies in open peer review.
- In human-computer interaction, Friess (2012), used coding to study the use of personas in software design.

- In legal studies, Jameson, Sohan, and Hodge (2014) used coding to better understand turning points in mediation.
- In environmental studies, Thompson (2005) used coding to examine the kinds of issues that were discussed in newspaper articles about a proposed off-shore wind power project.
- In public health, Banna et al. (2016) used coding to make a cross-culture comparison of ideas about healthy eating among Chinese and American undergraduate students.
- In operations management, Mugurusi and Bals (2016) use coding to study the stages of an offshoring strategy adopted by a purchasing and supply organization.

When to Code Verbal Data—Or Not

The coding we introduce in *Coding Streams of Language* is best used when three conditions hold:

1. You are looking for recurrent phenomena within and across streams of language.
2. You are interested in understanding underlying patterns of doing and meaning in these streams.
3. You and your co-researchers have sufficient intuitions about these streams to place them into appropriate coding categories.

Let's take a look at these conditions one at a time.

First, coding is a procedure designed to detect recurrent patterns in a stream of language. If you are looking for phenomena that occurs rarely, the procedural coding we recommend in *Coding Streams of Language* would be more complex than the rewards would justify. For example, if you are looking for the turning point in a conversation, and you expect there to be, at most, one turning point or perhaps none at all in a given stream, you may be better off using a careful close reading to find it. You might still find useful some of the techniques we describe in Chapter 4 for creating an explicit definition for yourself and your readers, but the other procedures described in this book would be more than you need.

Second, the analytic work we recommend in *Coding Streams of Language* is designed to examine the underlying patterns of meaning and doing, the ways with words of which participants may be largely be unaware. If, however, you are not concerned with the ways specific words and phrases are deployed and responded to, if you only want to identify the places in which certain topics are discussed, then you may only need to use a more simple topical coding (Geisler, 2018; Saldaña, 2016).

Finally, procedural coding, the primary method described in *Coding Streams of Language*, is designed to guide coders intuitions toward appropriate coding decisions. As we describe more full in Chapter 4, in some situations, no one outside of the context in which a stream was originally produced may have good intuitions about what the language means or how it works. The level of jargon and specialized knowledge may simply prevent outsiders from understanding what is going on from what is being said. If, for example, your verbal stream is in a language you do not understand, you obviously won't have the intuitions to code it.

But even if you fully understand the language of a verbal stream, you may not have the intuitions to code it appropriately. In this situation, you have two options. One option is to invite an informant, someone who is familiar with the context of production, to work with you as a coder. Another option is to use the enumerative coding, as described in Chapter 4, in which you list all of the possible words or phrases that you include within a coding category. An enumerative coding scheme has the benefit both of being transparent to your readers and of helping them to better understand intuitively what you intend.

To summarize, we invite you to use the procedures in *Coding Streams of Language* to code verbal data when you are looking for recurrent and underlying patterns in streams of language and about which you or your co-researchers have adequate intuitions.

The Patterns Revealed by Coding

As we discuss in this book, coding can be used to examine three basic kinds of patterns. The simplest pattern is the one-dimensional analysis we describe in Chapter 6, which asks how verbal data is distributed across a set of coding categories, often across a built-in contrast. Banna et al. (2016), for example, used a built-in contrast across Chinese and American undergraduates to notice differences in the ways they thought about healthy eating. Based on these distributional differences, Banna and colleagues recommended different public health strategies be used in these two communities.

Verbal data that have been coded with more than one coding scheme can be looked at multidimensionally, as we introduce in Chapter 7. Jameson et al. (2014), for example, analyzed conversational interactions that occurred during mediation along two distinct dimensions. First, they coded the precipitants leading to turning points in negotiations, points in which the relationship between the disputants seem to change. Second, they coded for negotiation outcome. This allowed Jameson and colleagues to look for relationships between the two dimensions, the kind of precipitants used, and the outcomes of the mediation. Based on the relationships they saw, they suggested ways that mediators could be more helpful.

The third pattern that can be revealed by coding is temporal. As we acknowledge in Chapter 8, temporal analysis deserves to be used more often for what it shows us about streams of language. Mugurusi and Bals (2016) use a kind of temporal analysis to show how the dimensions of Centralization, Participation, Formalization, Standardization, and Specialization changed over four phases in the offshoring process. The authors concluded that the offshoring process may be more disjointed and non-linear than current models in operations management would suggest.

Our Core Commitments

We bring to the task of coding streams of language a set of commitments that we'd like to put on the table from the start. They have served as our points of departure for the process and procedures that you will find in the rest of the book. In this section, we make these commitments explicit not so much to argue for them but so that you can judge for yourself.

Commitment to Being Procedural

Coding Streams of Language is fundamentally a procedural guide. That is, it provides you with a set of step-by-step procedures for coding and then analyzing verbal data. We anticipate that, as you grow in experience, you will modify, extend, and even discard these procedures. But our intention is to provide you a very clear basis with which to begin.

You will find that most of this procedural knowledge has not been documented elsewhere. Instead, it most often handed down mentor to student during office hours or shared peer to peer in late night sessions. The trouble with these practices is that they tend to keep cultural knowledge about analysis within a closed inner circle. Not only does this seem unfair to us, but it also keeps these procedures out of the light of day. So we put our procedures out there for you to see, use, question, and refine.

Commitment to the Systematicity of Coding

Coding Streams of Language aims to help you produce a systematic analysis. To be systematic means to follow some articulate orderly procedure. It does not mean you have abandoned intuition—more about this later—but it does mean that you have tried as far as possible to create an analysis that can be replicated: that the coding decisions you make today will be the ones that you agree with tomorrow; that the coding decisions your co-researchers make will be more or less the ones that you would make.

The commitment to systematicity lies behind the importance we give to segmenting verbal data in advance of coding it. And, as we introduce in Chapter 3, choosing the right unit for segmentation is key to developing a coding scheme that works. The commitment to systematicity also lies behind our emphasis on reliability. In Chapter 5 we describe how having someone else try to code your data and then comparing it to your own coding is the eye-opening key to developing a good coding scheme.

Commitment to the Design of Analysis

Coding Streams of Language urges you to design your analysis. Verbal data tends to pile up and overwhelm the best of us. Stepping back to consider how you will design your analysis can help you get a handle on what can otherwise be an enormous task.

In Chapter 2, we suggest that you begin with some initial explorations, sharpening your intuitions about what looks interesting. Then we give you some options on sampling your data, using your research questions to pick out a manageable subset of your data for further in-depth analysis. And finally, we recommend that you build your analysis around a built-in contrast, looking not only at data that you think should reveal the phenomenon in which you are interested, but also at data in which you expect the phenomenon to be absent. Sometimes the best way to know what you're looking for it to see its absence.

Commitment to the Complexity of Language

Coding Streams of Language takes a rhetorical approach to coding. That is, it acknowledges the complexity of language use. It considers not just what language says—that is, its topics—but also what language does. It assumes that language is more than just a vessel for content, more than a series of topics; that it *does* as well as *means*.

Acknowledging the complexity of language also requires us to forgo the expectation that any coding scheme can be absolutely unambiguous. Language will always require the interpretive powers of a language user. Coding does not replace the human coder but provides a guide to our intuitions. The role that context plays in developing these intuitions is inescapable. What words and phrases mean in one context might be quite different in another context. Coding depends, however, on the idea that these intuitions can be developed using a full coding scheme as we discuss in Chapter 4.

A Commitment to Mixed Methods

In *Coding Streams of Language*, we take a mixed-methods approach to the analysis of verbal data. Adapting the terminology introduced by Vogt et al. (2014), the workflow we advocate moves from coding in words to an analysis that combines qualitative (words), quantitative (numbers), and graphic (charts) representations. Like many mixed-methods researchers, we no longer find it useful to see qualitative and quantitative approaches as opposing methodologies, but rather prefer to see them as constituting a useful set of tools (Sandelowski et al., 2009).

Nevertheless, our commitment to mixed methods has lead us to adopt the standard of mutual exclusivity for coding. Mutual exclusivity refers to the requirement that each segment of data should be assigned to one and only one code. Mutual exclusivity is often seen as one of the major dividing practices between qualitative and quantitative approaches to coding. Examined more closely, however, we have found that these two analytic traditions are often closer than we might expect because language is inherently multidimensional.

In practical terms, multidimensionality often means that an analyst considering how to code a piece of language often sees multiple ways to code it. This will be true whether one is approaching coding from the perspective of content analysis, in which the goal is to create mutually exclusive categories, or from the perspective of qualitative analysis, in which double coding is not uncommon. Our method for dealing with the tendency to double code is to dimensionalize the data. As we describe in Chapter 4, rather than seeing the inclination to double code as arising from irreconcilable options, we can turn it into an invitation to develop mutually exclusive codes in different dimensions.

Our commitment to mixed methods also keeps us open with respect to research designs. We agree with Vogt et al. (2014), that the choice of analytic methods is not predetermined by the design of your study. Whether you have collected data in the context of a tightly-controlled experimental investigation or as a result of an extended stay in the field, as long as you have verbal data, you can code it and analyze it following the procedures we lay out in this book.

Using This Book

We have organized the material in this book to support your coding work in three distinct ways: first, with a distinctive workflow, second, with a distinctive set of tools, and finally, with a distinctive set of procedures. We briefly introduce each of these below.

The Workflow

In keeping with its procedural nature, *Coding Streams of Language* is organized around a workflow that you can adopt in part or whole for your analytic endeavors. A bird's eye view is shown in Figure 1.2. The first five components, shown in green in the figure, take you through the heart of coding and conclude with your having a set of data coded with a reliable coding scheme. The next three components, shown in blue, provided techniques for visualizing the patterns revealed by this coding. And the final two components, shown in orange, include ways to check the significance of those patterns and detail their results for readers.

We have made this book available in whole or by chapter to allow you to adopt this entire workflow or to pick and choose depending on your needs, interests and the state of your investigation. Below, we describe what is covered in each chapter so that you may target your reading.

Chapter 2: Designing the Analysis

If you are just beginning your project, with some data in mind but not yet collected, or with some data collected but not yet analyzed, you may want to start with Designing the Analysis in Chapter 2. Chapter 2 will suggest ways to focus on a specific phenomenon, articulate research questions, and develop a strategy for sampling from what may be a large universe of potential data.

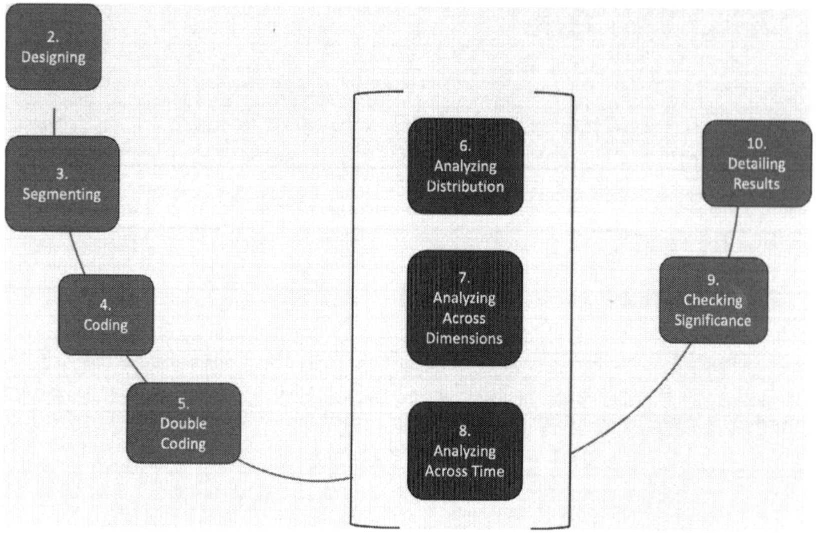

Figure 1.2: The workflow in Coding Streams of Language.

Chapter 3: Segmenting

If you have data in hand and some idea of what you are interested in, start with *Segmenting* in Chapter 3. A necessary precursor to coding, segmenting involves dividing your stream of language into units appropriate to the phenomenon in which you are interested. In this chapter, we provide a range of options for segmenting not discussed elsewhere in the literature, including basic grammatical units common to all language, more specific units characteristic of conversation and written texts, and interesting linguistic features such as indexicals, personal pronouns, modals, and metadiscourse.

Chapter 4: Coding the Data

Once you have segmented data in hand, you will want to turn to *Coding the Data* in Chapter 4. There you will learn about the components of a full procedural coding scheme and be guided through the iterative process of building one. Chapter 4 also introduces techniques for automated and enumerative coding as well as ways these can be combined.

Chapter 5: Achieving Reliability

If you have already coded your data, you may want to consider Chapter 5 on *Achieving Reliability*. To insure that you have a coding scheme that makes sense and is consistent, Chapter 5 suggests you invite a second coder to code using your coding scheme, check for intercoder agreement, and then use the results to improve your coding scheme. By the end of this chapter, you should have a set of data coded with a reliable coding scheme.

Chapter 6: Seeing Patterns of Distribution

Chapter 6 is the first of three dealing with seeing patterns in data that have been fully coded. Include *Seeing Patterns of Distribution* in your workflow in order to detect patterns in the way that your data is distributed among the categories of a single coding scheme. In the process, you will learn how to build a frequency table and distribution graphs like those shown in Figure 1.3.

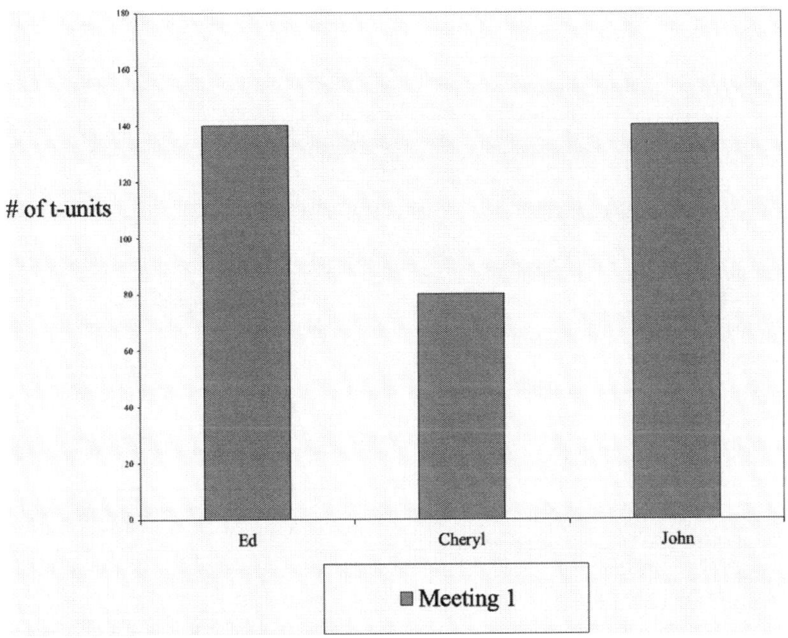

Figure 1.3: A sample distribution graph.

Chapter 7: Exploring Patterns Across Dimensions

If you have coded your data using more than one coding scheme, you may want to explore the relationships among the schemes. How does the pattern revealed in one dimension relate to patterns in a second dimension? Chapter 7, *Exploring Patterns Across Dimensions*, walks you through building contingency tables and block charts like that shown in Figure 1.4, as well as making stepwise comparisons of the dimensional patterns to check their relationships.

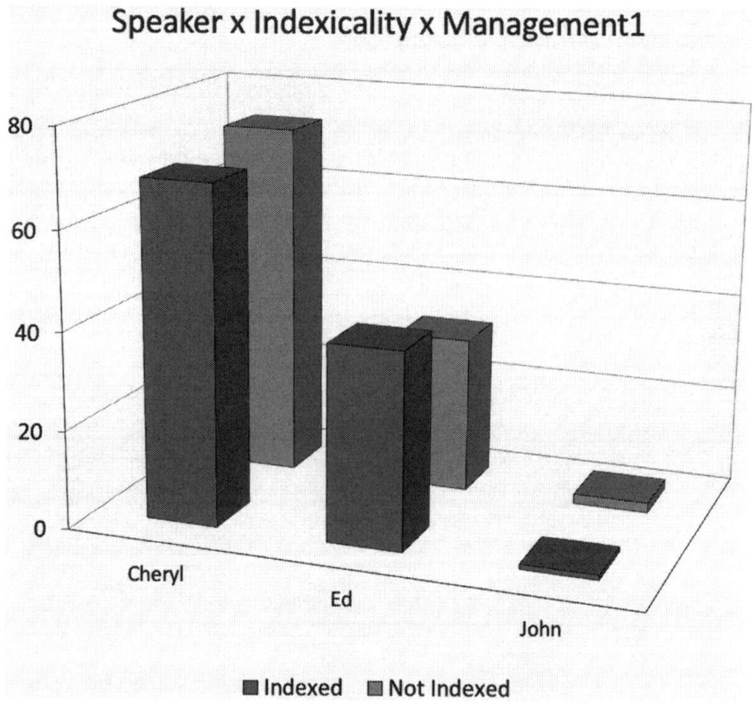

Figure 1.4: A sample block chart.

Chapter 8: Following Patterns over Time

If you want to understand the way that a stream of language unfolds over time or to compare two or more different streams of language, you may find Chapter 8 on temporal analysis useful. Coded verbal data that has been taken from intact cultural artifacts—complete texts, full conversations, an extended thread, and so on—often exhibit a distinctive temporal shape like the one shown in Figure 1.5. *Following Patterns over Time* will help you to uncover and understand these temporal shapes.

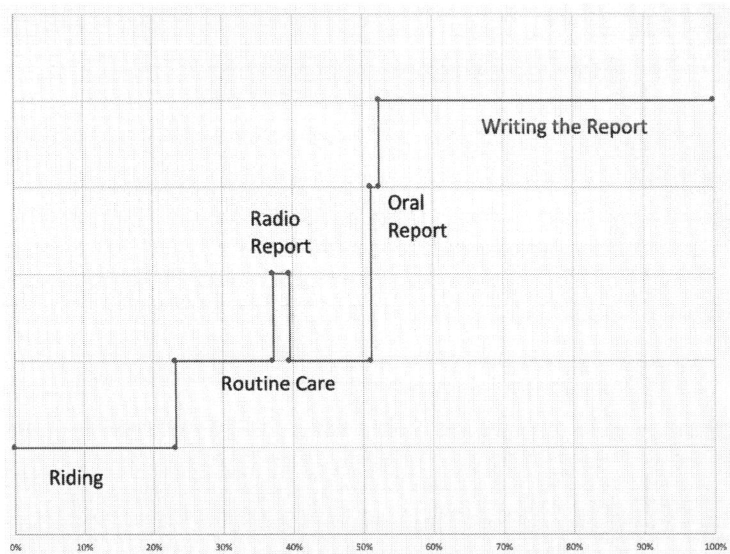

Figure 1.5: A sample temporal index showing the use of language in an ambulance run.[1]

Chapter 9: Evaluating Significance

If you have noticed interesting differences in the distribution of coding categories across your data, you may want to better assess their significance. Are these differences big enough to matter? *Evaluating Significance* shows you how to compare the actual distribution of your data across coding categories with the distribution that would be expected if these differences were not significant. Not all researchers will want or need to measure significance, but Chapter 9 provides some techniques for those who do.

---

1 Adapted from Geisler & Munger (2001).

Chapter 10: Detailing the Analysis

If you have coded your data and analyzed its patterns, you will want to find the best way to communicate the results to your readers. In Chapter 10, we show you how to make the link between the overall patterns you have uncovered and the details of language use. Use *Detailing the Analysis* to make the language patterns come alive for your readers.

The Tools

In 2004, Geisler published *Analyzing Streams of Language* using procedures in Microsoft Excel. For *Coding Streams of Language*, we have made significant updates to these procedures as well as added a second set of procedures using MAXQDA, a Computer Assisted Qualitative Data Analysis Software (CAQDAS) package. We have also incorporated some useful procedures using Microsoft Word and AntConc, a concordance program. We do not assume any working knowledge of these software packages on our readers' part in advance of trying out the procedures, although we do recommend using a free trial to get comfortable.

Microsoft Excel is the traditional tool used for coding verbal data (Geisler, 2004). Although most people think of it as a quantitative tool, Excel can function as a database manager, functionality that is important to coding. Many academics have access to Excel through their university's educational program for Microsoft Office, but if one were to buy an individual educational license to use it off-line for a year, the cost would be around $150 US. It runs on both Windows and Mac platforms,[2] and you can use it to accomplish all of the work in *Coding Streams of Language*.

MAXQDA, our second major tool, is one of a growing class of CAQDAS tools that support mixed-methods analysis. Developed in 1989 by Udo Kuckartz to deal with political discourse, it is supported by VERBI GmbH out of Berlin, Germany. It is one of the oldest CAQDAS programs and has a strong reputation as an efficient and responsive tool (Schmeider, 2014; Silver & Lewins, 2017). It can also be expensive unless you're a student. A single license for

[2] Readers who prefer to use Google sheets will find that most of the procedures in this book appear to be adaptable to this tool, although we have not tested this directly.

a regular user is over $500 USD, but students can get access for two years for under $100. We particularly like MAXQDA for its ease of use, use of color, and easy integration with Excel. It does not do everything we include in *Coding Streams of Language*, but it does many things superbly. And it is relatively easy, when necessary, to move into Excel to complete tasks. Our procedures provide you with explicit directions for managing this integration.

In *Coding Streams of Language*, we have created procedures that stay faithful to our commitments to approach coding systematically and with respect for language complexity. Neither Excel nor MAXQDA were designed for this task. Each is a general purpose tool that we have adapted to our needs, sometimes easily and sometimes by using complex workarounds (see Geisler, 2018). We invite you to extend, modify, and reinvent our procedures and, by all means, share them with us at https://wac.colostate.edu/books/practice/codingstreams/.

The Procedures

Procedures have been formatted to facilitate their use. Excel procedures always appear first with the parallel MAXQDA procedure(s) following. Other procedures in tools like Microsoft Word and AntConc will be found interspersed throughout the chapters.

Procedures appear in a distinctive typeface with numbered steps, are numbered and labeled, and have their own table of contents at the front of the book. All of these formatting conventions are designed to make them easy to find and follow. We often find ourselves paging to a specific procedure to remember "how do I do that?" We anticipate you will too.

Screencasts on YouTube

Every procedure in this book has a screencast video where you can watch the procedure in action. The URL following the procedure name is a direct link to the appropriate YouTube video playlist. If you are reading a chapter electronically, click on the link to access the chapter playlist and then choose the video from that list. If you are using this book in print, you can go to our website at https://wac.colostate.edu/books/practice/codingstreams/ for the links or go to our YouTube channel at https://www.youtube.com/channel/UCYi7qEAnSOvkMzCMogMkW5g/playlists.

Technical Questions and Where to Find the Answers

The following list includes technical questions that many readers are searching for. It is both more fine-grained and less comprehensive than the chapter-by-chapter summary we provided earlier. If you're looking for something specific and slightly complicated, we expect you will be able to find it here.

How do I decide what to code?	Chapter 2
How do I choose the right unit to segment my data?	Chapter 3
How can I easily number my segments?	Excel Procedure 3.1 & 3.2
How can I automatically code my data?	Excel Procedure 4.7 & MAXQDA Procedure 4.8
How much of my data do I have to double code?	Chapter 5
How much agreement is enough agreement?	Chapter 5
Which reliability test should I use?	Chapter 5
How do I check intercoder agreement?	Excel Procedure 5.3 & MAXQDA Procedure 5.3
How do I calculate interrater reliability?	Excel Procedure 5.7, Excel Procedure 5.1, MAXQDA Procedure 5.7 & Procedure 5.1
How do I make a frequency table?	Excel Procedure 6.2 & MAXQDA Procedure 6.1
How do I make a pivot table?	Excel Procedure 5.5
How do I make a distribution graph for a single coding dimension?	Excel Procedure 6.3 and MAXQDA Procedure 6.2
How do I make a contingency table?	Excel Procedures 7.1, 7.2, and 7.3

How do I make a block chart to see the relationships across two dimensions?	Excel Procedure 7.4
How do I make a temporal graph to see distribution over time?	Excel Procedure 8.2 and MAXQDA Procedure 8.2
How do I calculate subtotals for aggregates?	Excel Procedure 8.6
Is a chi-square test enough?	Chapter 9
How do I calculate chi-square?	Chapter 9

What's New since 2004 *Analyzing Streams of Language*

For readers who are using *Analyzing Streams of Language*, here is what is new in *Coding Streams of Language*:

- All procedures in Excel have been updated. Data summarizing the use of pivot tables and countifs functions have been included.
- Procedures for using Computer-Aided Qualitative Data Analysis Software (CAQDAS) have been included using MAXQDA.
- Screencasts have been created for all procedures and are available at our YouTube channel at https://www.youtube.com/channel/UCYi7qEAnSOvkMzCMogMkW5g/playlists.
- Procedures are more explicit and easier to find.
- Memoing as a way to reflect and document your analytic process has been included.
- The use of a concordance program, AntConc, for data exploration is explained.
- Conceptual discussions of major issues in coding open each chapter.

Our Aspirations

Our hope for this volume in its entirety and in each chapter individually is to guide you through the process of doing verbal data analysis. In the end, we would like each reader to reach a point of comfort and proficiency with the concepts and techniques outlined in this book to conduct good research and to pass along those skills and perspectives to others.

One way that we aim to address this grand ambition is to provide you with a method for doing verbal data analysis that has plenty of conceptual and procedural scaffolding. We do not assume that you have knowledge of coding and analysis or that you are beginning from anywhere other than square one. Our aim is to help you develop your own analysis, develop a robust and reliable coding scheme, analyze coding patterns in your data, and then link those patterns back to the scholarly or professional conversations you participate in.

A related aim is to provide you with a comprehensive and systematic approach to studying verbal data analysis that makes its analytic assumptions plain. We invite you to reflect on those assumptions and recognize the way that the analytic techniques we describe derive from those assumptions. As your needs warrant, we want you to reflect on your own assumptions and then adapt and extend the techniques to your research situation. The procedures discussed in this book are extensible.

Above all, our aim is to make this method of verbal data analysis accessible to a broad range of scholars in rhetoric and writing studies while at the same time reaching out to scholars in other fields who may be grappling with streams of verbal data without a clear notion of how to derive meaning from those streams in a way that is disciplined, systematic, and reliable.

■ Selected Studies Using Coding

Banna, J. C., Gililand, B., Keefe, M. & Zheng, D. (2016). Cross-cultural comparison of perspectives on healthy eating among Chinese and American undergraduate students. *BMC Public Health*. Retrieved from https://bmcpublichealth.biomedcentral.com/articles/10.1186/s12889-016-3680-y.

Breuch, L. K., Bakke, A., Thomas-Pollei, K., Mackey, L. E. & Weinert, C. (2016). Toward audience involvement: Extending audiences of written physician notes in a hospital setting. *Written Communication, 33(4)*, 418–451.

Friess, E. (2012). Personas and decision making in the design process: An ethnographic case study. *Proceedings of the SIGCHI Conference on Human Factors in Computing Systems, USA,* 1209–1218.
Jameson, J. K., Sohan, D. & Hidge, J. (2014). Turning points and conflict transformation in mediation. *Negotiation Journal, 30(2),* 209–229.
Martínez, I., Mateos, M., Martín, E. & Rijlaarsdam, G. (2015). Learning history by composing synthesis texts: Effects of an instructional programme on learning, reading and writing processes, and text quality. *Journal of Writing Research, 7(2),* 275–302.
Mugurisi, G. & Bals, L. (2017). A processual analysis of the purchasing and supply organization in transition: The impact of offshoring. *Operations Management Research, 10(1–2),* 64–83.
Ngai, C. S. B. & Jin., Y. (2016). The effectiveness of crisis communication strategies on Sina Weibo in relation to Chinese publics' acceptance of these strategies. *Journal of Business and Technical Communication, 30(4),* 451–494.
Nobarany, S. & Booth, K. S. (2015). Use of politeness strategies in signed open peer review. *Journal of the Association for Information Science and Technology, 66*(5), 1048–1064.
Stevenson, A. (2013). How fifth grade Latino/a bilingual students use their linguistic resources in the classroom and laboratory during science instruction. *Cultural Studies of Science Education, 8(4),* 973–989.
Thompson, R. (2005). Reporting offshore wind power: Are newspapers facilitating informed debate? *Coastal Management, 33(3),* 242–262.
Wyrley, B. (2010). "Talking technical": Learning how to communicate as a health care professional. *South African Linguistics and Applied Language Studies, 28*(3), 209–218.
Richter, D. M. & Paretti, M. C. (2009). Identifying barriers to and outcomes of interdisciplinarity in the engineering classroom, *European Journal of Engineering Education, 34(1),* 29–45.

■ For Further Reading

Geisler, C. (2004). *Analyzing streams of language: Twelve steps to the systematic coding of text, talk and other verbal data.* London: Pearson/Longman.
Geisler, C. (2018). Coding for language complexity: The interplay among methodological commitments, tools, and workflow in writing research. *Written Communication* 35(2), 215–249.
Saldaña, J. (2016). *The coding manual for qualitative researchers* (3rd ed.). Los Angeles: Sage.

Sandelowski, M., Voils, C. I. & Knafl, G. (2009). On quantitizing. *Journal of Mixed Method Research* 3(3), 208–222.
Shuy, R. (2018). What are "allness terms"? *The Chronicle of Higher Education*. Retrieved from https://www.chronicle.com/blogs/linguafranca/2018/10/08/what-are-allness-terms/.
Vogt, W. P., Vogt, E. R., Gardner, D. C. & Haeffele, L. M. (2014). *Selecting the right analyses for your data: Quantitative, qualitative, and mixed methods.* New York: Guilford Press.

Chapter 2. Designing the Analysis

> In this chapter, you will develop a design to guide your analysis. Based on what you know of your phenomenon, either from a literature review or from exploration at the site, you will build a framework to determine what is of interest and how to study it. You will articulate your questions, build a descriptive framework, decide how to focus your analysis, build in a contrast for comparison, and then make decisions about how to sample cases.

Writing Memos

Throughout the book we will be asking you to document your thoughts, analyses, and investigations using a memo-writing process. As Saldaña (2009) discusses, there are many different purposes and occasions for writing memos, but what they have in common is reflection. A memo is a conversational moment with yourself, an opportunity to take stock of how your analysis is taking shape. At various moments, you can use memos to reflect on emerging themes, patterns in the data, potential points of significance in the analysis, problems, and solutions. Eventually, memos can lead you to an analytic design, a coding scheme, or an analysis.

Throughout this chapter and all chapters in this book, we will offer you memo prompts to document your analytic process. The prompts will include questions that we find helpful to consider, whether to make decisions about the study design, to remind yourself of methodological choices, to make educated guesses about analysis, or to begin drafting part of your final write up. Of course you should also memo yourself at any point and on any question or thought that seems important.

Aside from options supported by Excel and MAXQDA (see Excel Procedure 2.1 and MAXQDA Procedures 2.1 and 2.2), the simplest approach would be to start a word processing document and keep your memos in a single file. Divide your memos into sections, using subheadings that correspond to the "Write a Memo" sections that you find in this chapter and throughout the book (e.g., Memo 2.1 Descriptive Framework). Another option for writing memos could be to create a file folder with subfolders that correspond to different phases of the verbal data analysis process (e.g., design of analysis, sampling, coding, analysis). If you are inclined, a more creative option would be to memo with a tool like WordPress, which allows you to insert labels to use for filtering memos at a later point.

Excel Procedure 2.1: Creating a Memo

https://bit.ly/2kL7ATv

1. Place your cursor in the cell to which you want to add a memo.
2. Select **Insert** > **New Comment**.
3. Resize the comment field to give yourself a visible field on which to write.
4. Write your memo and press enter to finish.
5. Mouse over the cell to see the memo.

MAXQDA Procedure 2.1: Creating a Memo

https://bit.ly/2kL7ATv

If you intend to use MAXQDA for your later analysis, you may use its free memo function to document your analytic processes. Unlike other memos in MAXQDA, free memos are not associated with specific locations in your data, but are general to your project as a whole. Once you create a free memo on some aspect of your analytic process, you can easily locate it, update it, and export it to be included in a later description of your methods.

1. Select **New Free Memo** from the **Analysis** menu in the toolbar.
2. Select a memo type, if desired (see Figure 2.1).

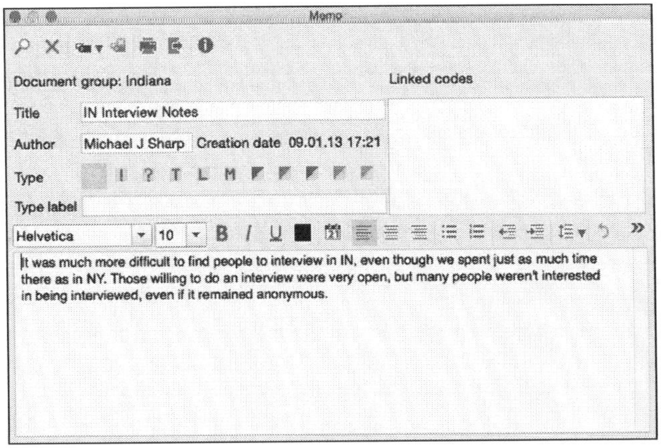

Figure 2.1: Writing a memo in MAXQDA.

3. Give your memo a title and write your thoughts.

MAXQDA Procedure 2.2: Reviewing a Memo

1. Open the **Overview of Memos** command by clicking on the **Overview of Memos** icon in the toolbar.
2. Click on the left-most table column to sort by type.
3. Click a specific memo to open and edit its contents.
4. If desired, click the **Export** icon to export your memo content to either an .rtf or an .HTML file.

Designing the Analysis

To get at the importance of an analytic design for doing verbal data analysis, it can be helpful to start with a polarized picture of different research approaches. In an over-simplified world, there are two kinds of research approaches: quantitative and qualitative. Each carries its own analytic assumptions that, in turn, shape how researchers envision their phenomena of study, ask questions, and decide how to acquire data.

Quantitative studies are largely based on empirical data about phenomena that researchers assume to be real and "out there" in the world. Quantitative researchers design their research by defining an object or problem to study, framing it in terms of a theory and associated variables, and testing it in some way, whether through an experimental or survey design. This approach sets constraints on the kinds of questions to be answered and the kind of data to be used in answering them.

Qualitative studies are also based on empirical data about phenomena in the world. However, those phenomena are taken to be constructed rather than objectively real. In this sense, constructed is commonly understood to mean constituted in and constitutive of a discourse. In other words, qualitative researchers study the discourses through which phenomena come to be (see Berger & Luckmann, 1991). For example, studying the phenomenon of online social activism might entail looking not only at the comments from community organizers who see their actions as social activism but also at other discourses that portray the same activities as civic disruption. A qualitative researcher designs her analysis to be exploratory, inductive, and emergent, and these qualities are reflected in more open-ended research questions whose answers require rich information gathered through case studies, ethnographies, and other descriptive studies. As a result, the scope and amount of data collected can be vast, often more than can be used productively.

The verbal data studies discussed in this book take a middle road and reflect more of a mixed-methods approach. Studies of verbal data are empirical and focused on the discourses that constitute or are associated with the phenomena we wish to study. However, we attempt to apply an analytic framework that allows us to ask more precise questions and make judicious selections of data that are sensible within that analytic frame. The result is that a mixed-methods approach benefits from the analytic constraint of quantitative approaches while utilizing a data source that supports a more nuanced understanding of our phenomena. Yet to achieve this benefit of a mixed-methods approach, a clear analytic design is a necessity.

More is at stake in designing an analysis than just identifying a phenomenon of study. How you choose which streams of language to analyze and how you construct the comparative frameworks in which the analysis takes place will form the foundation of your study's credibility and applicability. You must be able to explain how the streams you have selected are related to the questions that drive your study. You must be able to articulate your process of sampling. And, in most cases, you must show how the comparisons you make are meaningful and relevant to the issues at hand. To meet these challenges, you must design your analysis.

Much of the advice in this chapter can be employed at one of two stages in a project. A first point comes when you have gathered your data and need to develop a strategy to direct your analysis. The data you have gathered may be comprehensive. Perhaps you have tried, to the best of your ability, to collect all texts and to tape record all interactions. Or the data may come from a preexisting archive, whether it be the paper archives of a historical collection or the electronic archives of a chat room. In all these examples, you have more data than you can possibly analyze in a reasonable period of time. You may focus your analysis by examining your data through a theoretical frame.

Another possible point for using the advice in this chapter follows an exploration of the data, a time when you have entered into a situation, become familiar with it, and seen something interesting. At that point you have developed a sense of what is interesting and worth exploring as well as an appreciation of what that data looks like and where it can be found. At this point, you may construct a design using the techniques in this chapter in order to guide your data collection. This kind of early design will not relieve you of the need to refocus your design when you come to the stage of data analysis, but it may considerably reduce the amount of data you face when analysis time rolls around.

Focusing on a Phenomenon

Before designing the analysis, you need to focus in on an object or phenomenon of study. Sometimes a phenomenon of study will present itself vividly and the exigence and audience for the study will be immediately apparent. Other times, a phenomenon of study might start from something that you have read or may arise out of an inkling that something interesting is going on at some site. Spending some time up front, focusing on what you are interested in studying, can help you develop a more focused analysis. There are two common and productive ways of focusing a study: reviewing the literature and exploring a site.

Reviewing the Literature

For many researchers, the phenomena they study arise from their review of the literature. You might start with some ideas of what you want to study, but the shape and significance of those ideas will come into focus as you situate a phenomenon in the literature of your field.

By reviewing the literature on or related to your phenomenon of interest, you gain awareness of it as a theoretical phenomenon: something to which others in your field have previously attached ideas and beliefs in an attempt to explain that phenomenon and articulate principles about it. This theoretical framework becomes clearer as you read the conversations that have helped define the phenomenon you want to study. A review of the literature can tell you the questions that others have asked about the phenomenon, the settings in which they have studied it, and questions that remain unanswered. Knowing what has been said already can help you determine what still needs to be said and how to talk about the results of your research in a way that fits into the conversations that people are already having about it.

Ideally, your review of the literature should allow you to do what John Swales (1990) called "create a research space" where the purpose is to:

- state why the phenomenon is important and worth studying,
- establish what is known or understood about the phenomenon, and
- articulate what is unknown or uncertain about the phenomenon.

Your contribution will be to occupy the space that you created by identifying what is unknown and uncertain. For example, if you are interested in studying legal mediation practices, a review of the literature might point to questions about the effectiveness of different strategies that you could test or observe in existing data. By reviewing the literature, you will have also acquired a sense of how to think about your phenomenon, including concepts, theories, heuristics or other analytic frames that you can develop, extend, or refute for your analysis.

Exploring the Data and Site

A second approach to focusing on a phenomenon of study is to explore it. While it is important to appreciate your phenomenon of study theoretically, you also need to build an empirical appreciation. Unlike the theoretical frame that you build through a review of the literature, an empirical frame is built up through experiences with the phenomenon and the sites where it is found. What does the data sound like? How is it received? How is it used? How formal or informal is it? There are no practical limits to the amount of exploration you can do.

It is possible to explore a site of research before identifying a phenomenon of interest or before situating that phenomenon in the literature. In this free exploration, your goal is to explore because your intuition tells you that something might be important or interesting. For example, in Jason's study of user forum traffic for open source science software, he noticed that the participants would often preface issues by talking about problems with technologies other than the one the forum was set up to support. These apparent digressions struck him as important to understanding the bigger picture of user support for open source science software. By approaching the study design in this way, you may not know what is going on at the site, what objects are available to study, what comparisons are meaningful, or what might be interesting cases to study. Even so, you could uncover a point of interest that had not previously been anticipated in the literature.

You can also explore a site in a way that is guided by your developing theoretical understanding of your phenomenon. Guided exploration allows you to enter a site with an idea of what you want to look for and what it might mean. Returning to the previous example, Jason recalled literature on networking and technological ecologies which suggested that the apparent digressive conversation about other technologies might, in fact, be sketching a picture of the technology as a collection of networked technologies, where the user problem is not located in any one technology but is instead located across functionally-linked technologies. Your goal would be to observe where your phenomenon occurs, under what conditions and with what participants. This guided exploration will help you develop a sense of how to recognize and measure your phenomenon of interest.

Exploring with AntConc

One way to explore your data that is relatively simple and cost effective is to use any number of concordancing tools for examining the contents of your data. AntConc (http://www.laurenceanthony.net/software/antconc/) is one such tool. While AntConc is relatively simple to learn and use, it is too complicated to explore fully here. Instead, let us suggest two features that would be useful for guided and free exploration of your data: keywords and cluster analysis. We will discuss both tools again in Chapter 4 on coding.

Assuming that you have data in text form, save a portion of that data in a plain text (.txt) format. If your exploration of the data has already pointed to portions of the data that might be interesting to study, save those portions as separate .txt files. What you want are two collections of data: 1) a collection of the entire corpus of data, and 2) a collection of the subset of data that you wish to isolate for further study. For example, you may have data that includes the transcripts of a set of design meetings. All of the transcripts will be your first collection. Your second collection should be a selection of interesting transcripts taken from the entire collection. Procedure 2.1 shows how to carry this out.

Another exploratory analysis that may help you design an analysis is a cluster analysis, or an analysis of phrases and word groupings around a search term (see Procedure 2.2).

A related exploratory analysis is one where you simply want to see the most commonly occurring phrases in your data set (see Procedure 2.3). Here you are exploring units of language that offer slightly more context—just how much is up to you. The N-Grams tool, which is in the same tab as the Cluster

Procedure 2.1: Locating Keywords with AntConc

https://bit.ly/2kL7ATv

1. Select **Settings** > **Tool Preferences** > **Keyword List**.
2. At the bottom of the window you will see an option to upload a directory. Click **Add Directory** and navigate to the folder containing your collection containing all data.
3. When the files appear in the text field, click **Load** and then **Apply**.

This collection will become your reference corpus, the collection of what constitutes normal discourse in this setting. You will use the corpus to compare with the collection of data you set aside as potentially interesting.

4. Click **File** > **Open Dir** and navigate to the folder containing the collection that you want to analyze.
5. Click on the **Word List** tab and click **Start** to create a basic list of words appearing in your data set.
6. Click the **Keyword List** tab then **Start** to see a list of keywords.

The results show you what appear to be keywords in your second collection based on their "unusual frequency" in your data (Scott & Tribble, 2006).

7. Scroll through the keywords to see if some with higher keyness rankings are of interest.

Procedure 2.2: Exploring the Data with Clusters

https://bit.ly/2kL7ATv

1. Click on the **Clusters/N-Grams** tab.
2. Set the **Cluster Size** to the minimum and maximum you want to have returned.
3. In the search field, type a word that you feel is important to your analysis and click **Search**.

AntConc will return a list of phrases in which the searched word appears, sorted by frequency.

4. Click on each result to see the phrase in context.

Procedure 2.3: Exploring Data with N-Grams

https://bit.ly/2kL7ATv

1. From the **Clusters/N-Grams** tab, check the **N-Grams box** and set the **N-Gram size** to the minimum and maximum size N-grams you wish to receive.
2. Click **Start**.
3. Click any N-Gram to view it in a larger context.

tool, allows you to set the "N" or phrase length (e.g., 4-gram, 5-gram) and return a list of phrases within those parameters.

■ Constructing a Descriptive Framework

Having focused your phenomenon, you probably have some sense of what is going on: who's involved, what they do, what resources they have available, and how things shift over time. To design an analysis, you begin by articulating that knowledge through what Miles and Huberman (1994) have called a descriptive framework: The descriptive framework is the first step toward explaining what you think is going on. It is your conceptual representation of the components of the verbal phenomenon you are interested in studying. At the same time, the framework is a decision about which components of that verbal phenomenon are significant for your study.

A few years ago, for example, Cheryl became interested in a senior capstone design course in mechanical engineering. She had explored the course in her role as the director of the writing intensive program of which this course was a part. The descriptive framework in Figure 2.6 is a graphical representation of its weekly events and their participants. Eventually, she had gathered a great deal of data about each of the components of the course:

- For each of fifteen weeks, teams of students met with the instructors in the course for a 1 ½ hour class meeting: she had recorded these class meetings.
- In addition, each team met twice, once with one of the instructors and a second time on their own: she had recorded the team meetings and gathered all of the texts from four of these teams.
- Each student also prepared work on their own. To track this work, she collected process logs from all of the team members. She also met for weekly interviews with a team contact as well as one other team member on a rotating basis.
- Finally, she knew the instructors attended a 1-hour staff meeting each week, in addition to whatever course preparation they did on their

own. She attended and recorded each of these staff meetings and held a longer interview with the instructor at the beginning and end of the course.

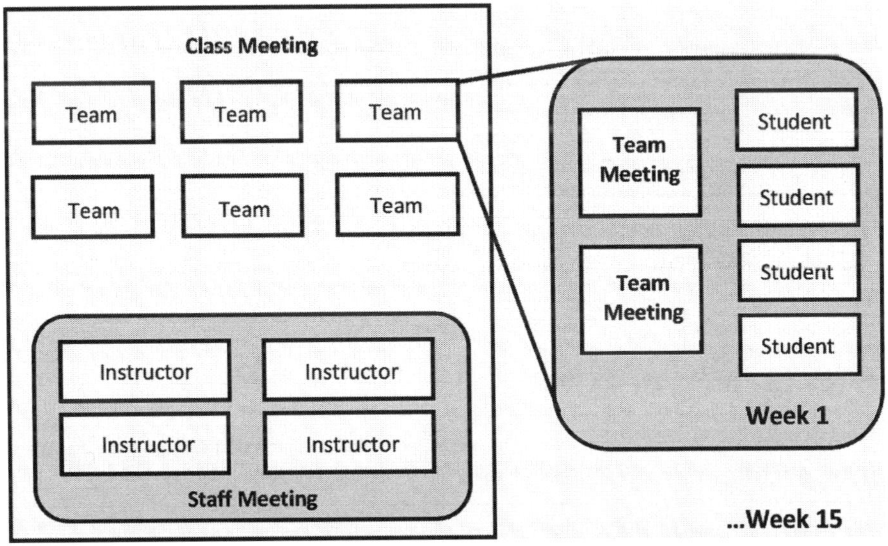

Figure 2.6: A descriptive framework for a capstone design course.

A good descriptive framework will allow you to focus on the major verbal events and their relevant attributes. In the descriptive framework in Figure 2.6, for example, three events have been identified: class meetings, team meetings, and staff meetings.

Second, a good descriptive framework will identify the relevant participants in the events making up the phenomena. In Figure 2.6, for example, we see that students attend the team meetings as well as the class meetings; that instructors join the students in class meetings but also meet on their own in staff meetings.

Third, a good descriptive framework will specify significant relationships among its entities. It will, for example, show the categories of which participants are members—such as the teams in Figure 2.6. It can also indicate other kinds of relationships such as hierarchy, opposition, and association—that an instructor "mentors" a team, that teams "compete" for the best design, that team members may "belong to" the same fraternity.

All of these relationships might be characterized as spatial because they describe the interconnections among various entities in the spatial dimension. In addition, a good descriptive framework will have a temporal dimension. It should, for instance, indicate temporal routines—as Figure 2.6 shows how the class meeting, staff meeting, and team meetings combine to make up a weekly routine that repeats itself fifteen times during the course of a semester. Or, it might describe temporal change—that, for instance, a design team moves through three phases in the course of their work.

A good descriptive framework can also indicate which attributes or characteristics of the data will be of potential interest for your analysis. Attributes about the verbal phenomena might include length of sessions or syntactic complexity in team discussions. Attributes about the participants might include gender, experience, and frequency of contributions. Attributes about the contexts could include access (whether public or private) and location. Any of these attributes could influence your analysis, but not all of them will. Regardless, you should pay attention to the attributes suggested by your framework.

Exercise 2.1: Test Your Understanding

The descriptive framework in Figure 2.6 does a good job of indicating the components that shape the phenomenon. The framework is rather coarse in its depiction, focusing only on the simplest interactions and contexts. It does not focus on more specific spatial relationships between participants (e.g., hierarchy, opposition, affiliation, cooperation) that might be important in understanding the phenomenon. Modify this diagram, available on the book website (https://wac.colostate.edu/books/practice/codingstreams/), to include one or more of these additional relationships.

For Discussion: Is it possible for a descriptive framework to represent all of the relationships in the universe to be studied? If not, how can a researcher choose what to include and what to leave out in her descriptive framework?

Memo 2.1: Descriptive Framework

Construct your own descriptive framework and reflect on the attributes of the participants, settings, relationships, and data that might be significant in understanding your phenomenon.

Articulating Research Questions

At this point in the analytic design, you have learned a bit about your phenomenon by exploring it through the published literature and by examining the site where your phenomenon is found. You have sketched out a descriptive framework that gives a picture of verbal events, participants, relationships, and contexts that make up your phenomenon of interest. In doing so, you have been developing a tacit sense of what you want to study and how. Now is the time to be more explicit about those aims by articulating research questions that will drive your analysis.

Before articulating questions directly, take a moment to think about the aims of your research project. Most research projects have one or more of the following aims: to define or describe something that exists, to describe a relationship between variables, or to understand how one thing causes another. When studying verbal data, your aims will primarily be descriptive because of limitations on the amount and type of data that you can collect and analyze, as well as limitations on the contexts of study, make inferring causal relationships troublesome.

One source of research questions is your own curiosity and need to know. Look at your descriptive framework. What is it you want to know about this phenomenon? Is there something you suspect that is going on here? Is there something you feel a need to know more about? A second important source of questions is the literature you may have studied. What does the literature suggest is going on here? What gaps in the literature can be addressed by an investigation of your phenomenon?

These initial steps should help you arrive at a big research question like "How do students collaborate?" or "How are decisions made?" These large questions are what Creswell calls "grand tour questions" (1994, p. 70) and they are a necessary step in refining a set of research questions that are more directly and concretely answerable. A grand tour question is the overall question that you want to answer, but it is too broad to answer directly. Instead, you must come up with questions that have more concrete outcomes, that in answering you can speak to the grand tour question

In general, there are three kinds of questions that can be answered by the kind of descriptive analysis you will take forward in this book:

Questions of Kind: What kind of thing is this? What is it made up of?

Questions of Association: What is this thing associated with? When this occurs, what occurs with it? What is absent?

Questions of Time: How does this thing vary over time? What are its routines? How does it evolve?

As you articulate these questions, you might be tempted to include a fourth kind of question, a question of cause, to drive your research. Be careful about this. Strictly speaking, descriptive analysis cannot give a definitive answer to questions of causality: did this cause that? But we can make some headway on causality with questions of association—is this associated with that?—because there can be no causality without association. And we can also go some distance toward causality by using questions of time—does this precede that?—because there can be no causality without precedence. Thus, if you find yourself wanting to ask questions of causality, try to rephrase them as questions of association or questions of time.

While questions of kind, association, and time are straightforward in definition, it can be challenging to decide which questions to ask. One approach recommended by Booth, Colomb, and Williams (1995, pp. 39–41) is to begin with a list of every who, what, when, where, and how question you can think of, answers to which would get you closer to answering your grand tour question. Then categorize these questions as shown in Table 2.1.

Table 2.1: Mapping question objectives to question types

Questions defining parts/wholes	Questions of Kind
Questions identifying categories and characteristics	Questions of Kind
Questions about values and uses	Questions of Association
Questions about history and changes	Questions of Time

Memo 2.2: Research Questions

What are your question types and what kind of data would you need to collect in order to answer those questions? How definitively could you answer those questions? Where is that data to be found?

Defining the Focus for Analysis

From the universe of data mapped out by a descriptive framework, you need to select one or more foci for further analysis. The focus defines the object at the center of your research questions as well as the streams of language that you will use in your analysis. For instance, if you want to answer the question, how does a design evolve over time? appropriate answers would involve the object "the design"—thus, "the design" would be your focus.

The kinds of objects you may take as the focus of your analysis can vary considerably. Many analyses take the individual as its focus. Such analysis asks, "What has this individual been doing?" Using a focus on the individuals in the capstone design course, we might decide, for example, to select the following data to analyze:

- all of the texts written by an individual,
- all of the interviews with the individual, and
- all of the contributions the individual made in class and team meetings.

Other analyses focus on certain kinds of events. Such analysis asks, "What happened here?" In the data set for the capstone course, for example, we might focus on the team meeting as an event and pull the following data for analysis:

- transcripts of all of the team meetings,
- selections from interviews in which the team meetings are discussed, and
- all texts used during the team meetings.

And some analyses focus on specific activities that occur in the situation. Such analysis asks, "What gets done here?" It cuts across the individuals and events in a situation and may even involve other quite different situations. In the capstone data, for example, we might focus on the activity of engineering design and select the following data for further analysis:

- all of the texts and sketches that a team constructs for a design,
- all of the segments of team meetings in which the design was discussed,
- all discussions in the staff meetings about students design work in general, or a particular team's design, and
- interviews with the staff member responsible for mentoring the team through their design work.

By choosing a focus for analysis, you make a commitment to analyze a certain phenomenon and to discuss that phenomenon in reporting your results. Such commitments need not be final or exclusive. That is, taking one focus for analysis for your current project does not preclude you looking at the data with a different focus later on. One of the strengths of a approach to research is, in fact, that the data it produces is rich enough to sustain a variety of analyses. Making a choice about focus now just allows you to isolate the streams of language in which you are more likely to find the phenomenon that you want to study.

■ Building in Contrasts for Comparison

Before selecting a sampling scheme, there is one further consideration that is critical to the analytic process: choosing a built-in contrast for comparison. A built-in contrast allows you to examine your focused phenomenon in relationship to other phenomena that you take be *a priori* different and through that comparison to focus attention on qualities of the data that highlight those differences. Such contrasts become essential to shaping the coding and pattern detection we describe in later chapters. As it pertains to sampling, building in a contrast will help you think about what data you need to support the comparative analysis you are building.

It is through your choice of a sampling scheme that you build in the contrast. For example, if you have chosen to analyze a stream of language because you think it offers an idealized look at the phenomenon of interest, search for another stream that has a high probability of not being very good. If you have chosen what you think is a typical stream of language, look at the periphery of your data to search for streams that are less than typical. A failsafe strategy is always to include what appear to be negative streams or atypical streams for analysis.

Ideally, your contrasts come from the same data set as your core data. Streams of language which come from the same data set but exhibit contrast help to define the boundaries of a phenomenon in a way that streams outside of that data set cannot. If, for example, we find the instructors in the capstone course consistently use sketches in ways different from the students, despite sharing a lot of the same context: the same course, the same design project, the same university, even the same field, then we may be on to something.

Contrastive streams may come, as in the comparison of instructors versus students, from variations in the spatial dimension, such as different sections, or the presence of supporting technologies. Do the student teams use different tools when sketching and what variations in the sketches might those tools explain? Other comparisons may be possible by looking for temporal contrasts. For example, do sketches vary significantly from the ill-defined early stages of design to the final stages of specification?

The source of appropriate comparisons often comes from the literature that you used to guide your study. Does the literature take a certain situation as paradigmatic, typical, desirable? Can you build in a contrast with your data set? Or, if such a contrast is not available in your own data, can you find data elsewhere that might make an appropriate comparison? Could we compare, for example, the ways students use sketches to design with the way they are used in the published literature in engineering?

Sampling Streams of Language

Once you have decided on a focus for your analysis and a contrast for comparison, you will need to decide how to sample among the language streams that your site presents. In almost all situations, you will have more than one choice. In the situation diagrammed in Figure 2.6, for example, if you decide to focus on students, which students? If you decide to focus on team meetings, which team? If you decide to focus on a team's design activity, which design? If you decide to focus on a whole course, why this course?

■ Convenience Sampling

One of the most commonly used strategies for sampling streams is also the least defensible: convenience. Using convenience sampling, we might choose a student because he sits next to us. We might choose a set of meetings because they occurred at a time when we can easily attend. We might choose a certain team because we already know some of the members. We might choose this course because it was one we already knew about. Sampling by convenience, as these examples suggest, puts personal considerations ahead of other consideration that might be relevant to your study.

If convenience is your only answer to a question about sampling, you will lose a great deal of credibility and possibly miss out on finding your phenomenon of interest. By the same token, however, convenience is almost never totally irrelevant in the design of a study. If your desired focus is difficult to access for whatever reason, you may need to consider what is possible for you. If access depends upon a history of interaction in a site that is difficult and costly to build, you may want to rely upon rather than abandon what you already have access to.

■ Snowball Sampling

Related to the convenience sample is a snowball sample and next to convenience sampling, it is one of the more popular and widely used techniques. In a snowball sample, you gather the data that you can and then work from those data sources to find other sources. Often this sampling entails working through participants who can introduce you to other participants who are similar. Snowball sampling can be useful if you are studying phenomena that are difficult to locate or are found within populations or settings that are difficult to access. In our example, we could gather a snowball sample by first finding a student team willing to share data with us and then asking them to introduce us to friends and fellow students who might also be willing to participate. As with the convenience sample, the snowball sample has similar limitations, but sometimes the networks of affiliation that participants use to create the snowball sample may be relevant to the analysis.

Typical Case Sampling

Can you pick a stream or streams that are typical in your site: a typical student, a typical team, a typical meeting, a typical course? To use the strategy of typicality you will need to have some kind of data available about the range of relevant variation across streams of language at your site. If most of the teams in the capstone design course, for example, are made up of both men and women, we may want to make sure to pick mixed-gender teams for my cases. Not all variations are relevant, of course: if we find out that most of the students in the course own cats, we may still feel we do not have to worry about whether the students on the team we choose are cat-owners.

Extreme/Deviant Case Sampling

A counter point to the typical-case sample is to choose outliers or extreme cases that show the range of conditions where you would find your phenomenon. Sometimes it can be beneficial to your analysis if you can show how the phenomenon differs from what is typical by examining the unusual circumstances in which it occurs. In the example of the capstone course, one could sample by looking at only the teams with the highest scores or the teams with the lowest scores.

Best Case Sampling

If the phenomenon in which you are interested only occurs in some streams, you may want to employ a sampling strategy that maximizes your chances of finding it. If, for example, you are interested in describing successful design activities, and you know that about a third of the teams in any capstone design course will not be judged successful by their instructors, you may want to try to find a way to sample teams with a high probability of being successful.

Criterion-based Sampling

Best case sampling is a special variety of the more general strategy of criterion-based sampling. With criterion-based sampling, you specify a certain relevant criteria and choose all streams that meet that criteria. If, for example, I want to study mixed-gender communication patterns in student design teams, I might decide to study all of the mixed-gender teams formed in a particular semester at a particular university.

Stratified Sampling

With a stratified sampling strategy, you take advantage of knowing something about the existing variations in a site. If you know, for example, that in a certain site, most design teams are either all male or all female, but that a few are mixed gender, you may want to make sure that you study a certain number of each of these three kinds of teams: male-only, female-only, and mixed. If you know that some design teams succeed and others fail, you may want to make sure to interview students from both types of teams.

Random Sampling

With random sampling, you chose streams based on the patterns established by a randomly generated sequence of numbers. Using a random sampling strategy involves three basic steps (see Excel Procedure 2.2).

Using the example of student teams, we can easily use Excel to build a random sample to include in our analysis. An alternative to working with Excel to generate a random sample is to use an online random value generator, such as Research Randomizer (https://www.randomizer.org/).

Comprehensive Sampling

The final strategy may not seem like a strategy at all yet, in some situations, it is appropriate. In comprehensive sampling, you choose all of the streams available to you in a site. If there are 50 teams, you analyze 50.

Excel Procedure 2.2: Generating a Random Sample in Excel

https://bit.ly/2kL7ATv

1. Open a blank Excel worksheet.
2. In the first column enumerate the universe of samples.

For example, with 50 teams we would type 1–50 in the first column.

3. In the second column type =RAND()
4. Drag this formula down to generate a random number for each sample (See Figure 2.7).

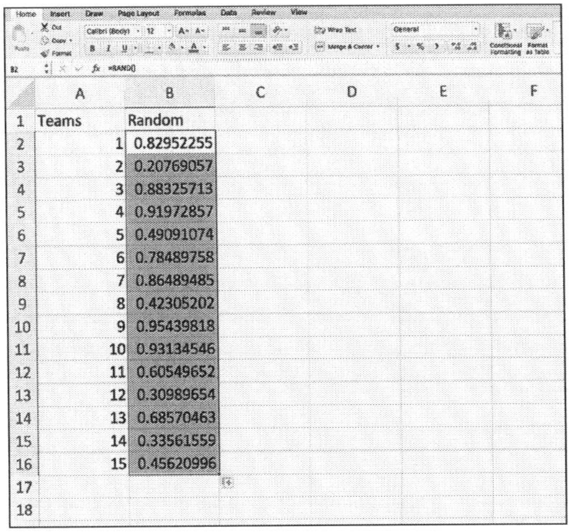

Figure 2.7: Generating a random number for each sample.

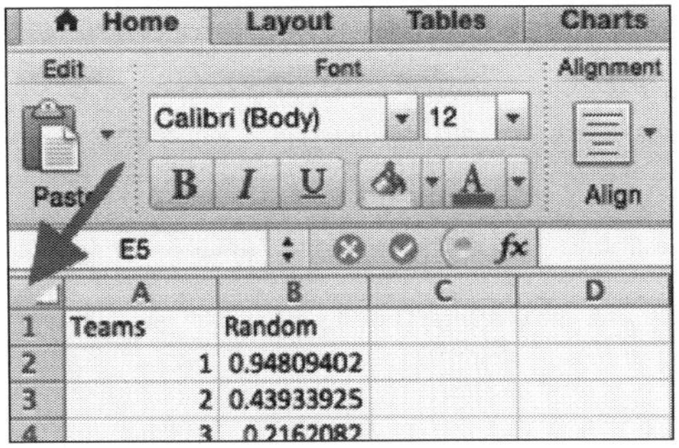

Figure 2.8: Clicking the box where the row and column numbers originate.

5. Select all of the random values and click **Edit** > **Copy** > **Paste Special** and check the option for "values." Click **Okay** to paste the values over the random values.

Cutting and pasting the random numbers as values keeps the numbers the same instead of recalculating new random values.

6. Select the whole worksheet by clicking as shown in Figure 2.8.
7. From the menu bar, choose **Data** > **Sort** and sort by the column containing your random values

To get a sample size of 12 teams, take the first 12 in your sorted list.

Exercise 2.2. Try It Out

#	Gender Composition	Score in Class	Coop
1	Women-Only	2	yes
2	Women-Only	6	no
3	Mixed	18	no
4	Mixed	10	no
5	Women-Only	46	yes
6	Men-only	1	yes
7	Men-only	23	yes
8	Women-Only	1	no
9	Men-only	44	yes
10	Men-only	12	no
11	Women-Only	11	yes
12	Men-only	32	no
13	Men-only	20	yes
14	Men-only	23	no
15	Mixed	36	no
16	Women-Only	11	no
17	Men-only	18	no
18	Mixed	25	yes
19	Women-Only	11	yes
20	Men-only	17	no
21	Men-only	47	yes
22	Men-only	38	no
23	Men-only	3	yes
24	Men-only	30	no
25	Women-Only	12	yes
26	Men-only	17	yes
27	Women-Only	19	no
28	Men-only	35	no
29	Men-only	1	yes
30	Mixed	18	yes
31	Women-Only	14	no
32	Men-only	15	yes
33	Men-only	11	yes
34	Men-only	39	no
35	Mixed	49	yes
36	Men-only	49	no
37	Men-only	14	yes
38	Women-Only	4	no
39	Men-only	34	yes
40	Men-only	43	no
41	Men-only	37	no
42	Women-Only	14	yes
43	Men-only	36	no
44	Men-only	18	no
45	Men-only	8	yes
46	Women-Only	19	yes
47	Women-Only	11	no
48	Mixed	46	no
49	Women-Only	37	no
50	Men-only	44	yes

Figure 2.9: A sample of 50 cases.

Suppose I have gathered data from 50 teams in the order shown in Figure 2.9. Complete the table on the following page, available on the book website (https://wac.colostate.edu/books/practice/codingstreams/) showing the gender characteristics of the following samples:

- A convenience sample of 12.
- A typical case sample of 12, with typicality defined by gender.
- A best-case sample of 12 with "best" defined as top-scoring.
- A criterion-based sample of ten using the criterion of experience.

- A stratified sample of 12 stratified by gender composition.
- A random sampling of 12 (use the following random number sequence: 16, 50, 36, 9, 25, 1, 5, 27, 19, 29 or one you generate on your own using the directions in Excel Procedure 2.2).
- An extreme case of high and low performing.

Kind of Sample	Teams Sampled	# of men-only teams	# of women-only teams	# of mixed-gender teams
Convenience				
Typical				
Best-Case				
Criterion-Based				
Stratified				
Random				
Comprehension				

For Discussion: Given what you find, discuss the benefits and costs of each strategy.

Choosing a Sampling Strategy

Deciding what sampling strategy or combination of strategies to use is more an art than a science. The guiding principle is to choose the strategy that will best support the credibility of your eventual analysis and support your checking of that analysis with contrastive cases. Obviously, for example, if you are concerned with a phenomenon that is not widely encountered, you may want to use some variation of criterion-based sampling. If you wish to describe a best-case phenomenon, it makes sense to use a best-case sampling technique. But if you want to show how a phenomenon is distributed over the range of your data, you would not want to restrict yourself to best cases: a stratified, random, or even comprehensive sample may be best.

Your choice of a sampling strategy should be driven by three concerns. The first is whether the sampling strategy you choose will ensure that you select enough data to observe the phenomenon you are interested in studying. The second is that the sampling strategy corresponds to and represents the larger phenomenon that you are trying to study and draw conclusions about. The third is that the sampling strategy includes cases that productively contrast with those you are interested in analyzing. Sometimes, these goals can be in conflict. For example, if we choose a sampling strategy to maximize chances of seeing a particular design activity, we may end up with a sample that over-represents one kind of student team. However, you may find that it is necessary to weight the sample in order to reveal more of your phenomenon. Just be aware of the potential bias of representation and temper your conclusions accordingly.

To make this discussion of sampling choice less abstract, consider the capstone example again. Suppose we want to describe the ways that sketches are used in the engineering design process. And suppose we choose an example of the use of sketches from the opening lecture by the primary instructor, a lecture which stuck in our mind for the skillful and interesting way that the instructor used sketches.

When we complete the analysis and write up the results for the readers, what could we conclude? Minimally, we could suggest that the patterns in this stream are examples of the kind of patterns that may occur when engineers use sketches to design. If we were to go further, however, and claim that these patterns were somehow typical, somehow best, or somehow characteristic of professional practice, the credibility of our claims would be undermined by our casual approach to the sampling strategy that lead to the stream to begin with, for we had only picked an example that stood out in our minds without considering what made it exemplary—or typical, and so on.

A little more consideration of sampling would have gone a long way toward putting the analysis on more solid ground. We could have, for example, used a comprehensive strategy to select transcripts of all interactions that involved the use of sketches and then tried to describe the stream in relation to that comprehensive sample. We could have done a stratified sample, choosing to look at a some streams produced by students in team meetings compared to streams produced by instructors in class meetings. We could have used a random sample to pick 10 streams of sketch use. Any of these strategies might have put us on more solid ground with respect to the credibility of the results.

The drawback to this approach is that the analysis becomes that much more complex and the analysis is not so sharply focused on the phenomenon that you have an interest in studying. Each approach has its advantages and disadvantages.

The next consideration in choosing a sampling strategy is to be aware of what your selection assumes to be true about your phenomenon and its distribution throughout the setting where it is found. Strategies like a stratified sample or a random sample are systematic approaches, designed to ensure that all data points have equal probability to be selected. These approaches assume that the phenomenon of interest is either equally distributed throughout the data or equally distributed throughout the strata. Non-systematic or purposive sampling assumes that some researcher judgment is required to locate the phenomenon and isolate it for analysis. Since the phenomena tracked in verbal data analysis tend to be exceptional and not random, purposive sampling like best-case, typical-case, and criterion-based sampling may make fair assumptions about the phenomenon you are studying. In any case, the most important lesson is to have an articulated sampling strategy and to be able to explain your strategy to readers in a way that enhances rather than undermines your credibility.

Finally, be sure that your sample allows you the opportunity to select streams that contrast or give negative examples of the kind of phenomenon that you are interested in analyzing. If you want to study high scoring teams and the materials they use to support collaboration be sure to select low scoring teams for comparison.

■ Memo 2.3: Sampling Scheme

Consider two or more sampling schemes and reflect on how those approaches would change the shape of the data you collect. What data will be included and excluded with each sampling scheme? How might your analysis be affected?

Acquiring the Data

Once you have chosen the appropriate unit for your segmentation, you will need to apply it to your data in preparation for coding. Essentially, this will involve five steps that we cover in the rest of this chapter: acquiring the data, cleaning the data, segmenting the data, moving the segmented data into your analytic application, and then labeling the segments.

Your goal in the first step, acquiring the data, is to put the data into the word processing program that you will use for segmentation. In our examples, we will use Microsoft Word for Mac (Version 15.28), which uses a look and feel similar to Microsoft Word for Windows. You may choose to use one of these or any other word processing application.

The Ethics of Acquisition

Before you begin to acquire data, an important consideration in any research project, but especially those that involve streams of verbal data produced by people, are the ethical guidelines that govern how research participants are to be recruited and treated in the course of that research. If you are working in a university context, your institution may already have a research office dedicated to helping you consider the ethical considerations entailed in your research.

Most research offices in the United States that make determinations about human ethics base their guidelines on those recommended in the so-called Belmont Report, which was drafted in 1978, partly in response to the Tuskegee Syphilis Studies. The Belmont Report centers around three basic principles that ought to guide all research:

> **Respect for Persons:** Researchers should respect the autonomy of all research participants. People who are autonomous act in accordance with their own goals and have the right to hold opinions and make decisions in pursuit of those goals. In cases dealing with populations that have their autonomy restricted (e.g., prisoners) it is important for the researcher to allow for special protections from harm.
>
> **Beneficence:** Researchers must take steps to act in the best interests of research participants. This principle asks researchers to consider

a balance between, on the one hand, doing no harm to the research participant and, on the other hand, the prospect of conducting research that provides some larger benefit, even if the research participants themselves are not the direct beneficiaries.

Justice: Researchers must ensure that the risk entailed in participating in a research program does not unfairly burden one particular population, especially if that population is not the direct beneficiary of that positive outcome.

While these principles were largely developed to govern biomedical research, the precepts are written with enough room for broader application to other realms of research involving human participants, including verbal data analysis. As the guidelines pertain to your research project, consider the participants who will be offering their verbal data for your analysis. How aware are they of your analytic intentions and do they know enough about what you are collecting and analyzing to determine whether participation in your study is in accord with their goals? In other words, do your participants have enough information and do they comprehend it well enough to make a decision about whether participation in your study fits with their goals? In the case of accessing publicly available information, how aware are the contributors that their contributions may be used in your analysis? Have you articulated for yourself and for your participants what the purpose and ultimate benefit of your research will be? Will your participants receive some benefit from your research, and if not, will they at least be protected from harm or injury as a result of your research (e.g., can any direct quotes be traced back to participants in some identifiable and damaging way?)

As you can see, applying these ethical principles to research outside the realm of biomedical research requires us to stretch our understanding of concepts like participants, privacy, and benefits. Even so, taking verbal data from face-to-face contexts like classrooms and other kinds of meetings does not present insurmountable obstacles for applying the same basic guidelines for conduct. Looking for verbal data to study on the internet, however, does pose additional problems.

Because it is entirely likely that you may be interested in studying streams of language from online settings, it is useful to broaden our understanding of how general principles of research ethics (such as those found in the Belmont Report) might need to be expanded to address the challenges of doing research online. One assumption of human-subjects research is that the focus of study is human subjects. And in the case of verbal data analysis, this is often the case. However, a human subject on the internet is not so unproblematically defined as in a lab setting. On the internet, human subjects are present as information, registering as potentially personally identifiable information that someone may not be aware they are sharing. What we choose to study can, if we are not careful, capture a wider range of this data than a person might knowingly give. For this reason, we need to exercise a bit more ethical discretion when utilizing what might otherwise seem to be publicly available information on the internet (e.g., online video, forum exchanges, blog posting, tweets, customer reviews, email list contributions, etc.).

The Association of Internet Researchers (AoIR) have developed a heuristic and set of considerations for researchers to use when gathering verbal data found online. Among the considerations one should keep in mind are:

- How is the research context defined? Given that the internet is a collection of specific locales, you ought to be aware of expectations in this context.
- How do you gain access to the research context? Is the context publicly accessible or for members only? How aware are people of your presence?
- What is your ethical stance with regard to the aims of the locale you are accessing and the expectations of participants regarding how their verbal data flows?
- Who is involved in your study and what options do they have for opting in or out?
- What is your object of study and how may that object be traceable to individuals or not (e.g., direct quoting from forum postings).

Ultimately, the AoIR panel suggests that each instance of internet-based research presents its own ethical context and the factors that matter when making an ethical evaluation should be built up from the specifics pertaining to that case, the context of the research, the people directly and indirectly reached, and their expectations about how their verbal data is supposed to be used (see Nissenbaum, 2012).

The internet is an altogether different kind of public space in which the very notion of public and private is complicated. While a forum or email archive might provide you public access to a stream of verbal data, it is an open question whether the people who participated in those exchanges considered their contributions private or public. Early concern over online privacy still rings true today: "the end user can never be sure [. . .] who has access to his or her information, under what conditions and limitations such access is granted, and so on" (Jones, 1994) and even in cases where the law does not specifically prevent information from being made public, it may be the participants' expectations that their contributions were private, and that expectation ought to be respected and balanced against consideration of the benefits that derive from your research. Further complications arise when we consider the various ways that you might recruit participants into a study, especially when you utilize cloud computing resources like file sharing services, online drives, and other resources, in that unintended, private information may very easily be uploaded along with the contributions that participants are aware they are providing.

By all means, do use streams of language data that are accessible on the internet. There is significant good that can come of research on information seeking practices, user assistance, crowdsourcing projects, and other creative projects. However, it is your responsibility as a researcher to be aware of the ethical issues that touch upon the work that you doing.

Please familiarize your self with the Belmont Report guidelines for human subjects research as well as the adaptations recommended for internet-based research as supported by the Association of Internet Researchers (AoIR) and always be sure to submit your research plan to your university's research ethics board to seek guidance and approval before starting.

Transcribing Audio

If you are beginning the acquisition process with audio files, you will need to transcribe them. If you have the budget, you may want to employ someone to transcribe them for you, and there are many services that specialize in transcription that can save you a lot of time. But you should be aware that you will still need to listen to and review the transcripts to correct for errors that result from arcane vocabulary, overlapping speakers, or poor quality recordings. We have done such corrections numerous times in previous projects and can testify to the fact that uncorrected transcriptions can contain so many errors as to make their analysis hardly worthwhile.

Another route you might consider is voice recognition software. Ideally, this kind of software produces a complete transcript from an audio file. While some voice recognition software works well when trained to recognize the voice of a single speaker, it does not yet do well enough with unknown speakers or multiple speakers. For most of the audio data that we encounter, then, the quality will not be adequate.

If you are resigned to making your own transcriptions, you will want to use transcription software that allows you to adjust the speed of playback and automatically rewinds a few second each time you stop to transcribe. If you are transcribing from video, the ability to insert timestamps into your transcript will also be useful to help you sync the transcript with the video. As well, a footpedal can really speed up the transcription process, so if you are considering using one, make sure the transcription software you choose is compatible.

Some qualitative analysis software has transcription functionality built in. The Standard package of MAXQDA, for instance, supports transcription of audio and video and provides automatic timestamping that links to the media from the transcript. If you are using or have access to any CAQDAS package, check to see if it offers transcription functionality.

You may also decide to use stand-alone transcription software. The three applications listed below vary by price and by the kind of features that they offer. Note that the free application, Express Scribe, does not do automatic rewinding.

- Express Scribe (http://www.nch.com.au/scribe/) version free for non-commercial purposes
- Transcribe (http://transcribe.wreally.com) for $20 US a year
- F4transkrip for Windows or F5transkrip for Mac (https://www.audiotranskription.de/english/f4.htm) for about $45 US

Scanning Texts

If you are working with texts on paper—without digital files—you will need to scan them and then convert them into readable form with optical character recognition (OCR). Many higher-end copiers combine scanning and OCR functionality and can process many pages quickly. You may also use a stand-alone scanner; many of these also come with OCR software. Or if you have scanned a small number of texts, you may find that a free online conversion service like Online OCR (http://www.onlineocr.net) will be sufficient to produce readable texts.

Scanning texts can take a lot of time, especially if you have to do optical character recognition as a separate step. For this reason, if you have a lot to scan, you may want to try to organize access to a high end photocopier that can do both at once. And keep in mind that even the best scan will introduce errors that will need to be dealt with using the techniques described in the section on Cleaning the Data.

Exporting PDFs

If you begin your work with files in Adobe PDF form, you will need to convert them to editable documents. To do so, open each file with Adobe Acrobat or Adobe Acrobat Reader and save them as either an .rtf file (preferred) or a .txt file. Again, keep in mind that the conversion will introduce errors that will need to be dealt with using the techniques described in the section on Cleaning the Data.

Memo 2.4: Data Acquisition Process

Describe the format in which your data is now recorded (hand-written or typed or audio-recording? on paper or in electronic form? graphic or text?). What steps will it take to move this data into a word processing application for segmentation? Plan for the resources (people, machines, time) you expect to need in order to carry out this process. Try out the process to see if it works. Document your final data acquisition process.

Cleaning the Data

Transcribing, scanning, and or exporting your data from another form often introduces errors that you will want to correct before segmentation. Sometimes these errors arise from transcription error. More often, they are the result of format conversion errors. In either case, you should clean your data before moving forward with segmentation and further analysis.

Manual Cleaning

Manually cleaning data requires you to read through the data word by word, comparing it to the source data, to insure that it has not been altered in the acquisition process. If you have employed someone to transcribe the data for you, for example, you will want to review the transcript while listening to the audio file. Sometimes transcription errors arise because the discourse is too technical for the transcriptionist. Other times, the voice is too low or distorted for the transcriptionist to make out. Many times this kind of listening can be done in double speed, slowing down only for difficult passages. In any case, it is useful to have someone familiar with the domain and the data to review the transcript and correct for errors and omissions.

In one of our earlier projects, for example, a transcriptionist had recorded a contribution by a speaker in a focus group meeting as shown in the left-hand side of Figure 2.10. The areas highlighted contained transcription errors. The first "talked to" is a mis-transcription; the remaining errors are areas where the transcriptionist could not understand what the speaker was saying. You can see the cleaned up transcript in the right-hand column. Five new phrases have been added that significantly clarify the meaning of the conversational turn. The turn also grew by 24% after cleaning.

If you have acquired your data using optical character recognition (OCR) from a graphics file, you will often find errors from failures in the OCR conversion process. On the left-hand side, Figure 2.11 shows an original graphic file of a text with some highlighting. The conversion produced by OCR is shown on the right-hand side. Many errors have been produced and will need to be cleaned manually.

Actually I had known my advisor before I came here. I had the chance to work with him and also knew my project so when I came here, I just talked to.......... so I also obtained my MS degree from another institution. So nearly ..... so I guess I had ..... so the answer for your question is sometimes my advisor says that... he told me his...... So I had the chance to work on a project but there are some disadvantages, too. Your advisor sees you like a colleague, so sometimes I wanted him to be my only advisor but not be my colleague. ...

Actually I had known my advisor before I came here. I had the chance to work with him and also knew my project so when I came here, I just started working on this topic so I also obtained my MS degree from another institution. So nearly I took like 20 grad level courses so I guess I had ..... enough background so the answer for your question is sometimes my advisor says that... he told me he saw me like his colleagues. So I had the chance to work on a project but there are some disadvantages, too. Your advisor sees you like a colleague, so sometimes I wanted him

Figure 2.10: A conversational turn. The right-hand column shows the transcript before cleaning. The left-hand column shows the turn after cleaning. Five phases have been added and the turn has grown by 24%.

Original tif file

Handheld computers come ready to use out of the box, with all
the software most customers will want already installed, But that hasn't stopped
a small industry from springing up to supply add-on programs. Handhelds have
no disk drives, so loading software requires first copying the program to
a PC, then transferring it to the handheld over your synchronization setup
. Applications for the popular Palm Pilot are by far the most numerous
. If you've added a modem to your Palm, you may want
a good mail program to send and receive messages over the Internet.
My favorite is MultiMail PRO from Actual Software Corp. ($ 29
.95). This program works well with corporate mail systems.
Other choices include HandWEB and HandMAIL from Smartcode Software Inc. or,
if you just want to access an America Online Inc, mail account
, PocketFlash from Power Media (both $ 49.95).
The Palm doesn't make for much of a Web browser, but it
can read text pages if you have the HandWEB browser from Smartcode (
$ 49.95). A better idea is AvantGo Inc.
, from a company of the same name. AvantGo's free reader allows
you to choose from free and subscription `` channels '' and
download pages specially formatted for Palms. Most PC mapping programs now feature
links for handhelds, too. Microsoft Corp.'s Expedia Streets
can download actual maps to Windows CE handhelds, though using them on
the smaller devices can be difficult. Rand McNally & Co. and

OCR Conversion

Handheld computers come ready to use out of the box, with all
the software most customers will want already installed . Nit that hasn't stopped
a small industry from springing up to supply add-on programs . Handhelds have
no disk drives , so loading software requires lust copying the program to
a PC , then transfening it to the handheldyour synchronization setup
. Applications for the popular Palm Pilot gg by far the most
numerous
liza&,agidtd a modem Weaur Palm, monayscat
ivgad mail program to send and receive messages over the
Internet .
My Wag&g MultiMail PRO from Actual Software Corp . ($
29 . 95) .
This program yak well with corporate mail systems .
Other choices include HandWEB and HandMAIL from Smancode Software Inc .
or,
a.50114u wantto access an America Online Inc ,mail account
, PoolutFlash from Power Media (both $ 49 . 95) .
The Palm doesn't make for much of a Web browser int i
=Lind text pages twat= the HandWEB browser from
Smartcode (
$ 49 . 95) . A better idea k AvantGo Inc .

Figure 2.11: A graphic image of a text file with highlighting, shown in the left-hand column, has been read optically to produce the editable text shown in the right hand column. Many errors, shown highlighted, have been introduced by the conversion and will need to be cleaned up before analysis.

Using Find and Replace

One step up from manually cleaning your data is the use of a simple find and replace command in your word processor (see Procedure 2.4). If, for example, you find that a transcriptionist has routinely used an incorrect term, you might use a find and replace command to correct all of the errors at once. Or you could use a global find and replace to change a speaker's actual name to a chosen pseudonym.

Using Regular Expressions

A further step up in ingenuity for cleaning your data involves the use of regular expressions in your Find and Replace commands. Regular expressions are special text strings that create flexibility in search. They are sometimes called wildcards (see Procedure 2.5). For instance, if you want to search for all words starting with "th," you could search for "th*" which uses the wildcard * to match on any string. Many regular expressions exist, but only those shown in Table 2.2 are recognized by Microsoft Word.

To see how you might use regular expressions, consider a search for demonstrative pronouns, a major category of indexicals. You could use four separate searches, one for this, one for that, one for these and one for those, or you could use the single regular expression:

```
<([Tt]h[iaeo][st][e ])>
```

Here the letters in square brackets indicate alternative acceptable matches. The angle brackets limit the search only to words that contain the full expression. [Tt] allows matches for both upper and lower case words starting with t; [iaeo] allows matches on thi . . ., tha . . ., the . . ., and tho . . .; [st] allows matches on this . . ., that . . ., thes . . ., and thos . . .; [e] allows for matches that end after the s (this) or the t (that) or those which take another e (these, those).

Another time you could use regular expressions is to clean up files scraped from the web. You may use regular expressions to find and delete HTML tags with the wildcard search string

```
\<*\>
```

Procedure 2.4: Cleaning a Transcript Using Find and Replace in Word

1. Open your transcript in Microsoft Word.
2. From the Edit menu select **Find** > **Replace**.
3. In the top field, type the character string you want removed and in the bottom field type the character string you want inserted as the replacement.
4. Click **Replace All** to replace all matches at once or **Replace** to replace them one at a time.

Procedure 2.5: Using Wildcards in Microsoft Word

https://bit.ly/2kL7ATv

Open your transcript in Microsoft Word.

1. From the Edit menu, select **Find** > **Advanced Find and Replace**
2. Expand the menu in the lower left of the dialogue box and check the box for **Use Wildcards** (Figure 2.12).
3. Type in the string with the RegEx wildcard in the **Find what** field.
4. Click **Find Next** to see the next match.

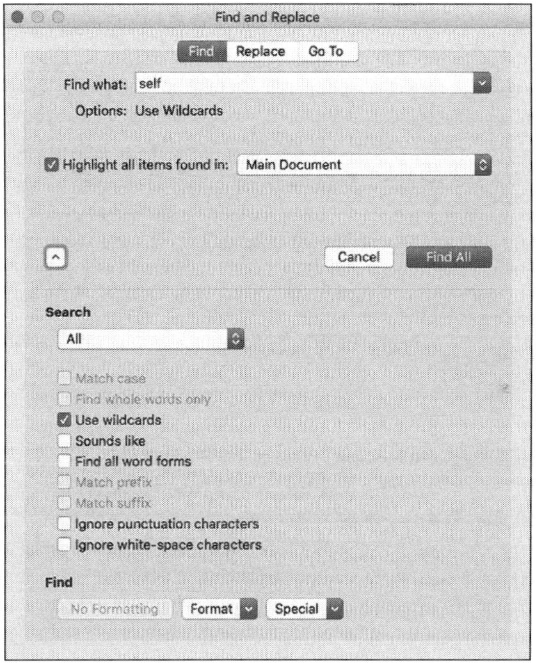

Figure 2.12: Enabling wildcards with find and replace in Microsoft Word.

which will match any HTML tag. To find and delete pairs of HTML tags along with all the characters between them, you can use the regular expression,

\<tag*tag\>

replacing "tag" with the name of the specific tag. To find all style tags, for example, search for

\<style*style\>

With this regular expression, you could find and replace all of the material between an opening style tag and its close with something like a simple paragraph return.

To preserve the content enclosed by the tags, modify the expression to

\<*\>

You may want to consult an excellent guide to using wildcards created by Graham Mayer, *Finding and Replacing Characters Using Wildcards* which can be found at http://word.mvps.org/faqs/general/usingwildcards.htm.

Table 2.2: Regular expressions recognized in Microsoft Word [1]

To find	Use this	For example
Any single character	?	s?t finds "sat" and "set."
Any string of characters	*	s*d finds "sad" and "started."
One of the specified characters	[ ]	w[io]n finds "win" and "won."
Any single character in this range	[-]	[r-t]ight finds "right" and "sight" and "tight." Ranges must be in ascending order.
Any single character except the characters inside the brackets	[!]	m[!a]st finds "mist" and "most" but not "mast."
Any single character except characters in the range inside the brackets	[!x-z]	t[!a-m]ck finds "tock" and "tuck" but not "tack" or "tick." Ranges must be in ascending order.
Exactly n occurrences of a character or expression	{ n}	fe{2}d finds "feed" but not "fed."

To find	Use this	For example
At least n occurrences of a character or expression	{ n,}	fe{1,}d finds "fed" and "feed."
A range of occurrences of a character or expression	{ n, n}	10{1,3} finds "10," "100," and "1000."
One or more occurrences of a character or expression	@	lo@t finds "lot" and "loot."
The beginning of a word	<	<(inter) finds "interesting" and "intercept" but not "splintered."
The end of a word	>	(in)> finds "in" and "within," but not "interesting."

1. Available at https://support.office.com/en-us/article/Find-and-replace-text-or-formatting-in-Word-for-Mac-ac12f262-e3cd-439a-88a0-f5a59875dcea

Using Macros

Before you segment the data, you will often need to clean up the data by removing extraneous carriage returns which could be mistaken for segmentation breaks. Particularly if you have copied electronic interactions to a file, you may find unwanted carriage returns at the end of each line. In texts, you may find unwanted blanks lines (i.e., 2 carriage returns) between each paragraph.

Removing unwanted carriage returns by hand can be tedious in the extreme. In Word, however, you can create a macro to do the task, assign it to a keyboard shortcut and then apply it repeatedly with far less tedium. Basically, you are linking three separate commands together into a sequence which can then be repeated as a single command. The sequence that will remove a carriage return immediately preceding a line break is as follows:

Backspace delete + insert space + move to beginning of next line

You can assign a sequence of segmentation moves to a single macro in Microsoft Word (see Procedure 2.6).

Setting Up The Data

During the analytic process described in this book, you will store and manipulate verbal data as a set of documents. In Excel, each document will be placed in a sheet in a data workbook (see Excel Procedures 2.3 and 2.4). In MAXQDA, each document will be imported into a Document System (see MAXQDA Procedure 2.3).

Note: You should not import any data into EXCEL or MAXQDA until it has been segmented as discussed in Chapter 3.

Procedure 2.6: Using Macros to Assist Multi-step Segmentation in Word

https://bit.ly/2kL7ATv

1. Open your transcript in Microsoft Word.
2. From the Tools menu, select **Macro** > **Record New Macro**.
3. Give the macro a name (spaces not allowed).
4. Click on the keyboard icon to assign the macro to a keystroke.
5. Type the keystroke combination you wish to use.

   For example: Cntrl+Option+J.
6. Click **OK** to start recording.

The only indication you will have that a macro is recording is the change in the shape of your cursor.

7. Perform the action you wish to assign to the macro.
8. Return to the **Tool** menu, select **Macro** > **Stop Recording**.
9. Return to the transcript and press the keystroke assigned to your macro to use throughout.

MAXQDA Procedure 2.3: Setting Up a Document System

https://bit.ly/2kL7ATv

The Document System window is usually found in the upper left-hand side of the MAXQDA interface.

1. To import data into the document system, choose **Documents** > **Import Document(s)**
2. Navigate to the data file you want to import and click **Open**.

The file will be imported as a document and appear in your document system window.

Excel Procedure 2.3: Setting up a Data Workbook

https://bit.ly/2kL7ATv

When you open Excel, it will provide you with a workbook with a set of empty worksheets as shown in Figure 2.13.

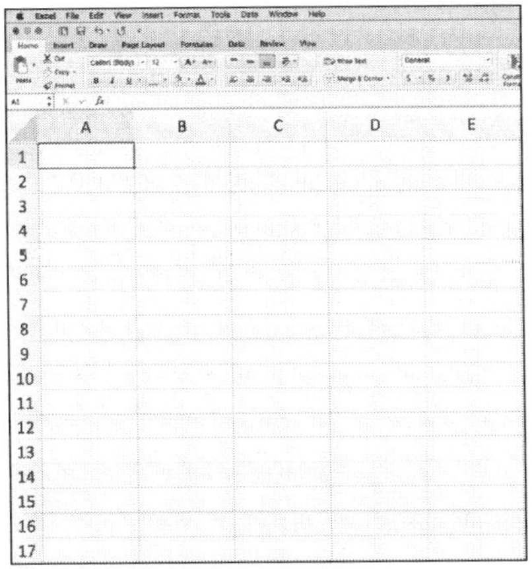

Figure 2.13: An empty Excel workbook.

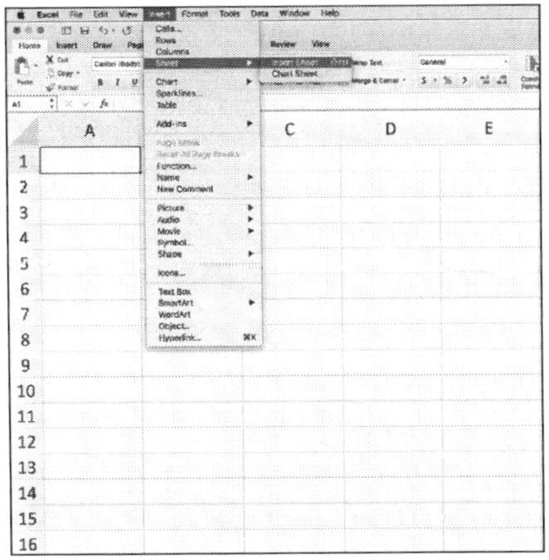

Figure 2.14: Inserting a new worksheet.

1. To add additional worksheets, choose **Worksheet** > **Insert** as shown in Figure 2.14.
2. For each worksheet choose a one-word name that will help you remember its contents (e.g., Design1).

Choosing a one-word name for each sheet will make it possible to use named data ranges that will simplify later analytic processes. Get in the habit of naming a worksheet as soon as you create it in order to save yourself much confusion later on.

3. To name a worksheet, select **Name** > **Define Name** from the **Insert** menu, as shown in Figure 2.15.
4. Type in the name you have chosen.

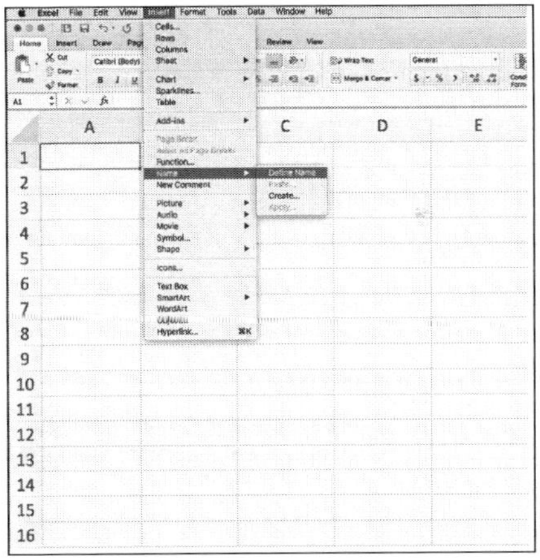

Figure 2.15: Naming a worksheet.

Setting Up a Data Table

A Data Table catalogs all of the data available to you in your data set. This established the universe of data available for possible analysis. As the sample table in Figure 2.16 suggests, it includes the following kinds of information:

- The type of data, listed in columns across the top
- The dates of collection/recording/publishing, listed in rows down the side
- The weeks/months of the projects, numbered.
- The data label: e.g., Technical Meeting #1
- The accession number: This might be the number of the tape on which it was recorded, the document number under which it was filed, the name of the computer file in which it is stored.

Excel Procedure 2.4: Creating a Table of Contents for the Workbook

https://bit.ly/2kL7ATv

One of the best ways to manage your workbook is to create a special worksheet that serves as a table of contents for the rest of the data workbook.

1. Open a blank Excel worksheet.
2. Rename the worksheet TOC.
3. Write a header for the first three columns:
   - Worksheet
   - Date Created
   - Description
4. Place your cursor in the cell with the first worksheet name.
5. From the Insert menu, select **Hyperlink** > **Webpage** or **File** > **Select**.
6. Navigate to the corresponding worksheet and click **OK** to link.
7. Repeat to link all of your data sheets.

As long as you do not change the folders where the workbook and coding scheme are stored, this file path will continue to work.

Week	Date	Technical Meeting	General Meeting	Don	Joe	Sue
0	8/28/18					#1
1	9/3/18			#1		
	9/3/18		#1			
	9/3/18					#2
2	9/10/18				#1	
	9/10/18		#2			
	9/10/18					#3

Figure 2.16: Sample data table.

Selected Studies Using Sampling

Elliot, N., Kilduff, M. & Lynch, R. (1994). The assessment of technical writing: A case study. *Journal of Technical Writing and Communication, 24*(1), 19–36. https://doi.org/10.2190/53LM-VWV5-JFTV-B7H7 (best case sample).

Mackiewicz, J. (2010). Assertions of expertise in online product reviews. *Journal of Business and Technical Communication, 24*(1), 3–28. https://doi.org/10.1177/1050651909346929 (typical case sample).

McNamara, D. S., Crossley, S. A. & McCarthy, P. M. (2010). Linguistic features of writing quality. *Written Communication, 27*(1), 57–86. https://doi.org/10.1177/0741088309351547 (comprehensive sample).

Rude, C. D. (2009). Mapping the research questions in technical communication. *Journal of Business and Technical Communication, 23*(2), 174–215. https://doi.org/10.1177/1050651908329562 (criterion/stratified sample).

Schryer, C. F., Afros, E., Mian, M., Spafford, M. & Lingard, L. (2009). The trial of the expert witness: Negotiating credibility in child abuse correspondence. *Written Communication, 26*(3), 215–246. https://doi.org/10.1177/0741088308330767 (criterion sample).

For Further Reading

Alun Jones, R. (1994). The ethics of research in cyberspace. *Internet Research, 4*(3), 30–35. https://doi.org/10.1108/10662249410798894.

Bauer, M. & Aarts, B. (2000). Corpus construction: A principle for qualitative data collection. In M. Bauer & G. Gaskell (Eds.), *Qualitative researching with text, image and sound* (19–37). London: Sage.

Berger, P. L. & Luckmann, T. (1991). *The social construction of reality: A treatise in the sociology of knowledge*. London: Penguin.

Booth, W., Colomb, G. & Williams, J. (1995). *The craft of research (Chicago guides to writing, editing, and publishing)*. Chicago: Chicago University Press.

Creswell, J. W. (1994). *Research design: Qualitative and quantitative approaches*. Thousand Oaks, CA: Sage Publications

Department of Health and Human Services. (2010). The Belmont Report. Retrieved from https://www.hhs.gov/ohrp/regulations-and-policy/belmont-report/index.HTML.

Goetz, J. P. & LeCompte, M. D. (1984) *Ethnography and qualitative design in educational design* (pp. 63–92). Orlando, FL: Academic Press.

Hamel, J., with Dufour, S. & Fortin, D. (1993). *Case study methods* (pp. 40–44). Newbury Park, CA: Sage.

Markham, A. & Buchanan, E. (2012). Ethical decision-making and Internet research: Version 2.0—Recommendations from the AoIR Ethics Working Committee. Retrieved from https://aoir.org/reports/ethics2.PDF.

Miles, M. & Huberman, A. M. (1994). *Qualitative data analysis: An expanded sourcebook* (pp. 16–49). London: Sage.

Nissenbaum, H. (2004). Privacy as contextual integrity. *Washington Law Review*, *79*(1), 119.

Silverman, D. (2001). *Interpreting qualitative data: Methods for analyzing talk, text, and interaction* (pp. 54–56, 83–218). London: Sage.

Saldaña, J. (2009). *The coding manual for qualitative researchers*. Thousand Oaks, CA: Sage Publications Ltd.

Swales, J. (1990). *Genre analysis: English in academic and research settings*. Cambridge, UK: Cambridge University Press.

Chapter 3. Segmenting the Data

> In this chapter, you will segment the data streams you have selected for analysis into units appropriate to the phenomenon of interest. After learning about the units characterizing various kinds of verbal data, you will acquire and prepare your data, segment it, and then move and label it in preparation for coding.

Introduction to Segmenting

In verbal data analysis, a stream of language is first segmented and then, in a separate and independent step, each segment is selected and coded. The unit used for segmentation is explicitly defined and often linguistic in nature. As we will discuss later in this chapter, this unit may be the sentence, the clause, the t-unit, the topic, or any other unit appropriate to but distinct from the code that is eventually assigned to it. This approach to segmentation has two distinctive features that set it apart from other analytic techniques.

The Role of Rules in Segmenting

The first distinctive characteristic of segmentation in verbal data analysis: The decision about where to segment data is less a matter of judgment and more a matter of rules or structure. Where does the sentence end? Where does the topic change? Where is the end of the clause? While segmentation "errors" can occur—i.e., two people may segment the same string of language in two different ways—such lack of agreement should arise not out of differences in judgment, but out of fatigue or inattention, either of which be easily corrected.

By contrast, in content analysis, which can deal with a wider variety of data, analysts may use a unit of analysis that is not rule-based in nature. In her review of attempts to unitize in content analysis, for example, Neuendorf (2016) found researchers segmenting by topic change, by joke, by instance of violent behavior, and even by instance of cigarette smoking. Neuendorf cautioned that, "whenever researchers or coders are required to identify message units separately from the coding of those units, a unique layer of reliability assessment is in order." (2016, Kindle Locations 1707–1709). She is suggesting, that is, that an assessment of agreement between researchers should be carried out for segmentation—although she reports that few studies actually do so.

By keeping segmentation rule-based, verbal data analysis eliminates the need for an assessment of agreement at the segmentation stage. In many cases, what starts out as a segmenting choice fraught with the need for analytic judgment can be revised to function in a more rule-based manner. In the study by Morris (2009) cited by Neuendorf (2016), for example, the researcher started out by defining the joke as a set of comments organized around a cohesive target, a definition that required a great deal of analytic judgment. But Morris later switched to a more rule-based definition, defining jokes as comments that elicited audience laughter, one that required very little judgment on the analyst's part.

If we can identify instances of a phenomena using a set of unproblematic rules, then we can use it for segmentation as discussed in this chapter. If we find, however, that we cannot avoid analytic judgment, it may be more appropriate to treat segmentation as a coding issue as discussed in the next chapter. But even if we decide to go this route, we will still segment our data before coding for the reasons we discussed further below.

■ The Separation of Segmenting and Coding

The second distinctive characteristic of segmenting in verbal data analysis is the way it supports focused decision making by separating segmentation and coding into two independent steps. That is, the analyst first segments the entire data set using some well-defined unit of analysis, and only then goes back to code that data, segment by segment.

By contrast, in most qualitative approaches to coding, segmenting and coding are often combined into a single step: The analyst both selects and codes a single piece of data before going on to select/code the next piece of data. When the segmenting and coding decisions are linked in this way, the analyst must keep in mind both the question of where a topic begins and ends and the question of what the topic is. This is a heavy cognitive burden and can lead to a lot of variability between coders.

Thus the most obvious benefit of segmenting a stream of language independently of coding relates to the desirability of producing coding judgments that are systematic and replicable. By segmenting independently in advance of coding, analysts only face one decision at a time: Where does this segment begin and end? Is this segment an X? An agreement among coders on the second question is more simply defined as coming to the same decision about a given segment. Disagreements are consequently minimized.

A second benefit of segmenting data independently of coding relates to being able to measure the relative distribution of any given code. If a single similarly sized unit is used for segmentation, then we have a general sense of what it means to say that 20% of participants' discourse concerned fashion. If, on the other hand, segmenting is linked to the coding decision, then one excerpt coded as fashion may be a few sentences in length; another may be two pages in length. To say, then, that 20% of such variable excerpts concerned fashion does not convey as clearly how much of a participant's focus was actually on fashion.

A final benefit of segmenting data independently of coding is rhetorical. As rhetoricians, we believe that language does work as well as conveys meaning. For this reason, the linguistic unit we choose for analysis is significant. If, for example, we are interested in what domains of knowledge a participant is drawing on in his or her discourse, the appropriate linguistic segment may well be the noun phrase because it is with this unit that the work of naming is accomplished. If, on the other hand, we are interested in the nature of the moves a participant is making, the appropriate unit of segmentation may well be the main clause with all its subordinate clauses because it is at this level of language that the work of rhetorical moves takes place.

Avoiding Potential Pitfalls in Segmenting

Our goal in segmenting data in verbal data analysis is to choose the unit, usually linguistic, where our phenomenon "lives." Jokes, for example, usually take longer than a single sentence to tell, so if they are the phenomena in which we are interested, we would not choose the sentence or any of the even smaller units of language that we discuss later in this chapter. Instead, we would probably want to look at some of the longer units of language.

Pragmatically speaking, we want to choose a unit of segmentation that will allow us to divide the stream of language in a way that each segment will fit into one and only one category of our coding scheme. Making this choice can be tricky, however, since we often segment before we have our coding scheme worked out. In this case, then, we will need to rely on our intuitions about the phenomenon of interest.

To choose a unit of segmentation using our intuitions, we begin by identifying a salient difference across the contrast in our data. If, for instance, we are interested in kinds of negotiations that take place in email exchanges, we begin by looking through our data for instances of particularly successful negotiations, or failed negotiations, or protracted negotiations, and so on. The goal here is not yet to define what a negotiation is, but to observe the unit of language over which a negotiation occurs. When does the negotiation start? When is it over? Once we have two or three instances of negotiation, we can then review the units of analysis (described later in this chapter) to determine the one that seems to be where our phenomenon lives.

When we choose a unit of segmentation that matches our phenomenon, we will have a situation like that represented in Figure 3.1. Suppose we are interested, metaphorically speaking, in segmenting the "stream" of animals we see walking by on our daily walk. In Figure 3.1, we see this stream of pets divided into units by animal. When a coder looks at the second full unit in the stream and tries to code it—to determine, "Is it a cat?" or "Is it a dog?", the task is relatively easy, because the entire phenomena (the cat) is included in the unit.

Figure 3.1: Matching the unit of segmentation to the phenomenon of interest.

If, however, the unit we choose is too small for the phenomenon of interest, we will encounter coding situations like that represented in Figure 3.2. When the coder encounters the first unit, she may or may not code it as *cat* ("Could it be a dog?") because the information is ambiguous She will, however, probably code the next unit as a *cat* because the information there is more complete. In general, using a too-small unit of segmentation leads to more disagreement in coding decisions—some analysts will say *cat* while others say *dog*. It also fails to provide a good sense of how frequently our phenomenon occurs—do we have just one cat or two in Figure 3.2?

Figure 3.2: The unit of segmentation too small for the phenomenon of interest.

The final possibility of mismatching the unit of segmentation to the phenomenon of interest arises if the unit is too big. This situation is represented in Figure 3.3. In this case, the coder sees two different instances of the phenomenon of interest, both a cat and a dog, in the same unit. How should it be coded? In systems of qualitative analysis that allow more than one code to be applied to a unit, we might be tempted to code it both ways, but this would be problematic for verbal data analysis in ways we will discuss further in Chapter 4.

Figure 3.3: The unit of segmentation too big for the phenomenon of interest.

Another option, if we really want to make sure we see all of the cats in our analysis, would be to include a rule such as, "If you see a cat in the unit, code it as *cat* no matter what else you may see there." The result of using a rule like this is to underreport dogs and other pets in favor of identifying all of the cats. While this might be an acceptable outcome for some purposes, we usually try to avoid this situation by getting the best match of unit to phenomenon of interest that we can at the segmentation stage.

Of course, in verbal data analysis, we are not coding for non-verbal phenomena like cats and dogs. But these instances are intended to illustrate conceptually some of the potential problems that can later arise from inappropriate segmenting, so that you can try to avoid them at this early stage of analysis.

Basic Units of Language

In this section, we describe some of the basic units of language into which any stream of verbal data can be segmented. Then, in subsequent sections we discuss units characteristic of specific types of verbal data. Finally, we close the chapter by describing the process of segmentation and pointing to some of the issues you may encounter and ways to handle them.

T-Units

Syntactically, a stream of language is structured as a set of t-units, the smallest group of words which can make a move in language. By move, we mean the work that a piece of language does to advance communication. In traditional argument, rhetorical moves advance the reader or listener along the path the speaker or writer is constructing (Kaufer & Geisler, 1991). More generally, a rhetorical move can be understood as the work done by language to fulfill any communicative purpose (Biber & Kanoksilapatham, 2007, p. 23).

A t-unit consists of a principle clause and any subordinate clauses or non-clausal structures attached to or embedded in it. The following are all t-units:

> **I ran to the store because we needed flour for the cake for Martha's birthday.**
>
> **Jen is the mail carrier who replaced the one we liked.**
>
> **Walking is my favorite form of exercise, the one with the least impact.**

T-units are one of the most basic units of language. If the phenomenon in which you are interested is associated with the moves that a speaker or writer makes, the t-unit may be the most appropriate unit for your segmentation. You might, for example, look at each t-unit in the transcript of a meeting of an engineering design meeting for the kind of move it makes: descriptions, proposals, questions, evaluations, and so forth. You could also look only at t-units that make proposals. The length of t-units has also been used as a measure of syntactic maturity (Kellog, 1978).

To segment a stream of language into t-units, begin by finding the first inflected verb that has a subject. In the following sentence, the first inflected verbs with subject is I ran:

> ***I ran*** **to the store because we needed flour for the cake for Martha's birthday.**

Next, look for the next inflected verb with a subject. If it stands on its own, then segment the stream at the most logical place between them, as shown in the following:

> ***I ran*** **to the store.**
>
> ***We needed*** **flour for the cake for Martha's birthday.**

If the second inflected verb you does not stand alone, keep it together with the first one:

> ***I ran*** **to the store because** ***we needed*** **flour for the cake for Martha's birthday.**

In this example the two clauses with inflected verbs are linked with the subordinate conjunction *because*. As a result, the second clause cannot stand alone and would not be divided from its main clause:

> ***I ran*** **to the store because** ***we needed*** **flour for the cake for Martha's birthday.**

If you are working with language that is spoken or with informal written language, you may find that some subordinate clauses are made to stand alone and should be treated as its own t-unit:

> **David: I ran to the store this morning.**
>
> **Josh: Why'd you do that?**
>
> **David: Because we needed flour for the cake for Martha's birthday.**

Here David's answer is a subordinate clause but because it is spoken by a separate speaker, it would be segmented from the other speaker's question.

Keep in mind that many inflected verbs do not stand independently because they do not have their own subjects and should instead be kept with their main clauses:

Needing flour, I ran to the store.

I ran to the store and fell.

In the first of these t-units, the -ing form of need takes its subject from its main clause (*I*) and thus cannot stand alone from it. In the second, the inflected verb *fell* shares a subject with *ran* and thus stays in the same t-unit.

If you have trouble distinguishing between main and subordinate clauses, you may want to take a refresher course online. Here are a few you might consider:

- Clauses: the Essential Building-Blocks, Capital Community College Foundation, http://grammar.ccc.commnet.edu/grammar/clauses.htm
- Identifying Independent and Dependent Clauses, Purdue Online Writing Lab, https://owl.purdue.edu/owl/general_writing/punctuation/independent_and_dependent_clauses/index.HTML

Clauses

Clauses are the smallest units of language that make a claim—that predicate something—about an entity in the world. A clause is a group of words containing a subject—the entity—and a predicate—the claim being made about the subject. When clauses stand alone, they are said to be independent. When they make sense only in conjunction with an independent clause, they are said to be dependent. As we have already seen, an independent clause with all of its dependent clauses makes up the t-unit. The following are all independent clauses:

the committee requested the prior report from the president

once upon a time two children were lost in the woods

The underlined language in the following are all dependent clauses:

He refused when the committee requested the prior report from the president.

She told us that two children were lost in the woods.

If your phenomenon of interest is related to the claims that a speaker or writer makes about the world, the clause may be the right unit of analysis for you.

To segment a stream of language into clauses, begin as with t-units by finding the first inflected verb that has a subject. Then look for the next inflected verb with a subject. Segment the stream at the most logical place between them:

> **He refused**
>
> **when the committee requested the prior report from the president**

The resulting segmented stream will consist of a mix of independent clauses and dependent clauses. Any stream of language that has been segmented using t-units can easily be further subdivided into clauses.

■ Noun Phrases

Noun phrases are the units of language which pick out objects in the world, both concrete objects and those which are abstract. In clauses, noun phrases can serve as subjects, but they may take other roles as well, as the following examples suggest:

> **That cat is obnoxious.**
>
> **The day I was born was cold.**
>
> **June is a hot month in Kentucky.**

If your analysis is concerned with what is being spoken or written about, you may want to use the noun phrase as your unit of analysis. Noun phrases can help you identify the domains of knowledge from which speakers or writers draw, the worlds of discourse through which they move.

Choosing to analyze noun phrases is inherently selective--you make the decision not to look at the predicates that make up the clauses that, in their turn, make up the stream of verbal data. If you are going to look at noun phrases, you will probably want to choose some slightly larger unit (such as the clause) by which to segment the data, and then look at each noun phrase within that segment.

The easiest way to segment your discourse by noun phrase is to break the discourse up by clause, and then underline each noun phrase you find within each clause.

> Critical care patients have often suffered a "disturbance" to the normal operation of their physiological system;
>
> this disturbance could have been generated by surgery or some sort of trauma.

When you give coders data with this kind of selective segmentation, make sure that they understand that they are to code only the language that is underlined.

Verbals

Verbals are the unit of language which convey action, emotion, existence. Inflected verbals—those with tense—fill the predicate slot in clauses, both independent and dependent, as in the following:

> When you back up your hard drive regularly, you prevent data loss.

Other verbals come as reduced verb phrases:

> The purpose for backing up your hard drive should be obvious.

In this example, "backing up" is actually serving as part of a noun phrase, but it is clearly a reduced form of the verbal "back up" used in the previous example. Some verbals like "back up" are idiomatic combinations of verb forms with prepositions, back + up, where the meaning is quite different from the sum of the parts. In these cases, the verbal is the entire idiom.

If you are interested in the schema being invoked by your speakers or writers, you will want to select the verbal as your unit of analysis. The verbal, "back up your hard drive regularly," for example, invokes a schema related to computer use in the same way that "went on a date" invokes a courtship schema. Using verbals, you can track the way schemas shift through your data set.

Because of their relationship to schemata, verbals are often indicative of genre choices, or shifts within genres from one part to another. In news reports, for example, hot news is often presented using present perfect tense:

> The government has announced support for the compromise bill.

Details are then presented in simple past tense:

> The compromise was worked out in committee yesterday.

In a similar fashion, in narratives, main events tend to be in simple past tense:

> **She went to see him one day and she said, "Has anybody been to see you?"**

while really significant events may be presented in the historic present:

> **And he says, "No, but a right nice young lady came to see me."**

Background events tend to be in progressive form:

> **This friend of mine brought these photographs out, of the family through the years, and, passing them around, and he's looking at them, and he said, "Oh! That the young lady that came to see me when I was in bed."**

If you are interested in genre, you may want to consider the verbal as a unit of segmentation. A complete list of verb tenses with examples can be found at https://www.grammarly.com/blog/verb-tenses/ if you need to refresh your memory.

The easiest way to segment your discourse by verbal is to break the discourse up by clause, and then underline any verbal you find within each clause.

> **Critical care patients**
>
> **have often suffered a "disturbance" to the normal operation of their physiological system; this disturbance**
>
> **could have been generated by surgery or some sort of trauma. The critical care physician**
>
> **is to maintain certain patient state variables within an**
>
> **acceptable operating range.**
>
> **Often the physician**
>
> **will infuse several drugs into the patient**
>
> **to control these states close to the**
>
> **desired values.**

Notice that here in this scientific language, you find quite a few reduced verbals; that is, verbals that are reduced from full clauses. "Acceptable operation range," for example, is a reduction of the clause, "a range that is acceptable to operate within" and "desired values" is a reduction of the clause, "values that are desired." In identifying the verbals, underline any phrase that can be expanded to a full verb. And remember, when you give coders data with this kind of selective segmentation, make sure that they understand that they are to code only the language that is underlined.

Topical Chains

Topical chains in both spoken and written interactions are what allow participants to understand their discourse as being about something. To some extent, the topic of a discourse can be established by how it points to or indexes objects in the world; listeners and readers will understand language which points to the same object to be somewhat cohesive. But the true workhorses of cohesion are the topical chains that writers and speakers establish.

Topical chains are constructed out of continuous units—either the t-units (frequent in formal discourse) or clause (not uncommon in informal discourse); each continuous unit may either start a new topic or continue the same topic as the one before it. When a writer constructs a long topical chain, or when two interlocutors work together to extend one another's thoughts through a long topic chain, they develop the complexity of the topic.

Topical chains are often held together by the following kinds of referentials:

- personal pronouns: it, they, he, she, we, them, us, his, her, my, me
- demonstrative pronouns: this and that, these and those
- definite articles: the
- other expressions: such, one
- elipses and repetition

In oral discourse, the boundaries of topical chains are often marked (*OK*, *well*).

If you are interested in the conceptual complexity of discourse, the extent to which a topic is developed, the depth of interaction on a topic, you may want to use the topical chain as your unit of analysis. You may also want to use the topical chain as a unit of analysis if you wish to do a selective analysis of discussions that concern a specific topic. Next to the t-unit, the topical chain is one of the most useful units for segmenting language.

To segment a stream of language into topical chains, it's easiest to begin by segmenting the stream of language into t-units for formal language or clauses for informal language. Then begin to study the way the referential language works to introduce topics or refer to topics already introduced, looking for breaks in the topical chain.

In the conversation shown in Figure 3.4, for example, Speaker A introduces the topic of keywords in clause 2 with the indefinite phrase "keywords." In clause 3, he uses "several" to refer back to it. In clause 4, "one" also refers back to it; in clause 5, "they" again refers back to it; in clause 7, "keywords" is actually repeated for the first time since clause 2, but this time with the definite article ("the keywords") to let us know that it is continuing the same topic.

All of these referentials indicate the topical connection among clauses 1 through 7, and it is not until clause 8 that we fail to find a reference back to keywords and instead see the introduction of a potential new topic, "the papers"; clause 10 takes up the papers topic with "them." Clauses 10 and 11 briefly introduce a potentially new topic of abstracts but with just a few exceptions, the topic of papers is referred to over and over again through to the end of the excerpt, even across four speaker changes.

Speaker A:

1 The way I work with sources is

2 I go on the Web, to the Library Search and put in keywords [KEYWORDS] and

3 I use several [KEYWORDS]

4 so there's one [KEYWORD] for Chemistry

5 and there's one [KEYWORD] for Engineering

6 because they [KEYWORDS] don't all cover the same journals.

7 And you put in the keywords [KEYWORDS]

8 and you find the papers [PAPERS]

9 And you go get them. [PAPERS] [. . . .]

10 reading abstracts [ABSTRACTS]

11 so—I always read the abstract [ABSTRACT] first

12 and I see if they [PAPERS] are useful.

13 And then when I get the paper,—[PAPER]

14 read the abstract, [ABSTRACT] and

15 I read the conclusions

16 before I decide if I'm gonna read the rest of the paper. [PAPER]

17 And then I have—

18 let me open up my file cabinet

19 see that I have folders of by topic,

20 so I work with composites

21 so there will be some [PAPERS] on nanoparticles polymer [that] faculty or (which is thermocetics?) or, you know, categorize them [PAPERS]

Speaker B:

22 So you actually print them [PAPERS] out

23 after you have a look at the abstract [ABSTRACT] on the web

24 and then print it [PAPER] out

25 if you think it's [PAPER] interesting

26 and you file it [PAPER]?

Speaker A:

27 Right—

28 read it [PAPER] and

29 file it [PAPER]

Speaker B:

30 Read it [PAPER]

31 and file it [PAPER]

Speaker A:

32 And I often hand them [PAPERS] to my students

Figure 3.4: Following the topical chains in a conversation.

By using referentials to track and label the topics, as in Figure 3.4, we can clearly see where breaks in the topical chain occur. When you first begin to segment by topical chain, you may find it useful to track and label topics as we have done. With some practice, however, you will be able to sense the breaks without this kind of extensive annotation.

Units in Conversation

In addition to the basic units that characterize all verbal data described above, specific kinds of verbal data have additional regularities that can be exploited as units of segmentation. In this section, we look at regularities in conversation that suggest a variety of units of segmentation.

Conversational Turns

Conversations are made up of *turns*. For the most part, only one speaker talks at a time, although there is often some overlap at the edges. Much can be learned from looking at the turns in a conversation, particularly by speaker. How turns are allocated among possible speakers tells a great deal about relative power in a conversation: Who speaks most often? Whose turns are longest? Whose turns initiate new topics? If you are interested in phenomena of power, you may well want to look at the turn as a unit of segmentation.

To segment a stream of language into turns, simply segment at the borders between speakers.

Conversational Sequences

Conversation does not take place through the random accumulation of speaker's turns. Instead it is organized by its participants into *sequences*. A conversational sequence can be thought of as a joint project undertaken by two or more speakers, using language. It is made up of the following components.

1. Initiation: the first speaker proposes a "joint project"
2. Response: the speaker responds to the proposal

3. Follow-up: the speaker acknowledges the response

There exist a variety of kinds of joint projects, with routinized initiations that call for expected responses. A question, for example,

> **Speaker 1: What time is it?**

generally receives a reply that contains the information requested:

> **Speaker 2: Six-thirty**

and that is followed up by some acknowledgment:

> **Speaker 1: Thanks.**

Other routinized exchanges include greetings:

> **Kate: Hi.**
>
> **Ron: Hi.**

and invitations:

> **June: Can you come to my party Saturday night?**
>
> **Nance: Sure.**
>
> **June: Great!**

There are many more.

While initiations in conversational sequences call for a certain preferred response, interlocutors need not give the preferred response. In fact, interlocutors have four options when faced with a conversational proposal in the form of an initiation:

1. Compliance: Interlocutor takes up the proposed project
2. Alteration: Interlocutor proposes an alternative project
3. Declination: Interlocutor declines the proposed project
4. Withdrawal: Interlocutor withdraws from considering the proposed project

These four options are roughly ordered in terms of the first speaker's preferences. That is, first speakers hope their interlocutors will comply, but if not, perhaps propose an alternative:

> **Don: How 'bout dinner on Saturday?**
>
> **Jen: Sorry. Can't. But what about tonight?**

If no alternative is possible, the speaker hopes at least to get a declination that includes a reason for declining:

> **Don: How 'bout dinner on Saturday?**
>
> **Jen: Sorry. Can't. I am going out of town to see my mom this weekend.**

From the speaker's point of view, the worst response is a withdrawal:

> **Don: How 'bout dinner on Saturday?**
>
> **Jen: You've got to be joking.**

Lots of information can thus be gained by looking at the conversational sequence as a unit of segmentation. If interlocutors routinely give dispreferred responses rather than preferred responses, for example, it is a sign of a lack of cooperation.

The nature of conversational sequences can also shift significantly with context. With question-answer sequences for example, the speaker is not supposed to know the information being requested. In school, however, teachers routinely ask for information they already know and then use their follow-up turn to evaluate the student's answer:

> **Teacher: Who knows the capital of New York?**
>
> **Jean: New York City**
>
> **Teacher: Good guess, Jean, but not quite right. Johnny?**
>
> **Johnny: Albany?**
>
> **Teacher: Good!**

This IRE (Initiation-Response-Evaluation) sequence is so closely tied to the context of school that even adults long out of school will feel like they are in school if subjected to this sequence structure. Other contexts appear to have their own specific sequences as well. Thus, if you are interested in looking for variations in context, such as from teacher-directed discourse to peer-to-peer collaboration—the conversational sequence may be your best unit of segmentation.

To segment a conversation into sequences, begin by locating an initiation (questions, invitations, etc.). If several initiations are repeated within the same speaker's turn as rephrasings of each other, then treat them as a single initiation. Mark the segmenting boundary prior to the initiation either immediately before it, or, if the previous t-units were used by the same speaker to introduce the initiation, then right before these introductory t-units.

To locate the segmenting boundary following the initiation, examine the nature of the response:

1. No Response: If the initiation does not receive a response from a second speaker, divide after the initiation when silence is noted in the transcript.
2. Response Only: If a response is given by the second speaker and not commented on by any other speakers, then divide after the response. Responses can take more than one t-unit.
3. Response + Comment: If a response is given by a second speaker and then commented on either by the first speaker or by other speakers, then divide after these comments. In general, all comments by speakers on previous speakers' turns should be included in the sequence. A comment is related material, but has to be related to what comes immediately before it.

Interview Responses

Often implicitly, interviewers select the *response* as their unit of segmentation. That is, they look only at what is said in response to interview questions rather than at the interview as a whole. Such a move often helps to focus on the situation or person of interest, but it should never be done without considering the extent to which these responses have been shaped by conversational imperatives set up by the interviewer's questions.

Interviews are often structured according to an interview schedule—that is, with certain fixed questions that are asked of all those interviewed or are asked repeatedly of the same person over time. In such situations, it is possible to use the question as a unit of segmentation: to look at all responses to the same question. Since questions often direct respondents to particular topics, this unit of segmentation will help to focus on phenomenon related to topic.

No guarantee exists, however, that the same topic will not have come up elsewhere in an interview. Thus, if you are concerned to be comprehensive, you may want to begin with the answers to certain questions and then move outward to look for the same topics elsewhere in the interview transcript.

Units in Text

Written texts have a variety of characteristics, some associated with conventions of publication, others with conventions of typography, and still others associated with the rhetorical interactions with readers at a distance. All of the following can serve useful purposes as units of analysis for textual data.

The Text

Perhaps the most obvious unit for analyzing textual data is the text itself. Unlike the stream of conversational data which must often be bounded in some arbitrary fashion for the purposes of analysis, written texts often have well-established boundaries. In a classroom, for example, students generally write and bind (with staples or paperclips) individual texts separately: the boundaries of individual student "papers" are seldom hard to determine. In published formats, conventions exist for separating individual texts: the chapters of an edited volume, the articles in a magazine or journal, the stories in a newspaper.

From the writer's point of view, many phenomenon occur at the level of the text: the quality of the text, the genre of the text, the implied audience for the text. From the reader's point of view, texts also have a variety of characteristics that can be examined: their persuasiveness, their familiarity, their importance, and so on. If you are concerned with any of these or similar phenomena, from either the writers' or the readers' point of view, you may find the text itself a good unit with which to segment textual data.

Genre Elements

Most texts belong to families of texts we call genres. While genres are not rigid, texts in certain genres do tend to share common features and common structures. Genres represent a typified response to a typified rhetorical situation.

They thus exhibit many typified features: typified moves, typified relationships to audience, typified reading patterns, typified publication venues.

You can use specific information you have about a genre to select or analyze specific genre-related elements—the abstracts of research articles, the response of readers to scientific articles, and so on. You may even use marked sections as the unit of segmentation when you want to look at kinds of rhetorical moves that tend to happen in certain places. You might, for example, look at the opening section of research articles to examine citation patterns since these openings often contain reviews of the literature. Or, looking for the same phenomenon, you might examine all sections in which citations are made.

Opening sections are also good places for looking at phenomena related to the voice of a piece or the relationship defined between author, reader, and context. Other times, you will want to skip opening sections and choose text from middle sections. Letters, for example, tend to have routinized openings that precede getting to the real issues with which the letter deals.

To segment a written text using a genre element, use the distinguishing features of the element to locate its boundaries in your discourse. Salutations in letters, for example, appear on paper in just one or two places. Comments on online news articles always come after the news story itself. If you want to segment by section, use the headings and our spacing within the discourse as your boundaries.

Typographical Units

Texts are structured by their layout with a variety of characteristics, any of which can be used as a unit of segmentation. As units, they can serve useful purposes as ways of selecting data when the phenomenon of interest is assumed to be regularly distributed through the text and you simply need some way of selecting part of the data.

You might choose, for instance, every third sentence, every fifth paragraph, every other page, or the first ten lines of each section. Keep in mind that typographical units are relatively meaningless rhetorically. While paragraphs, for example, may be used for topical development by some writers, many writers simply break a paragraph based on relative length. If you want to use a rhetorically meaningful unit for segmentation, one in which the language does work of some kind, avoid using typographical units. But typographical units can be quite handy as a way of making a stratified or random selection of textual data.

To segment your data using a typographical unit, insert line breaks after each unit. Paragraphs, of course, may already have line breaks. To segment by sentence, you can use a search and replace function to replace periods (.) with a period followed by a carriage return.

Other Selective Units

Indexicals

Indexicals provide language with ways to anchor interactions to the specific context in which they occur. The essential indexicals are *I*, *here*, and *now*. With *I*, the speaker or writer points to him- or herself. With *here*, he or she anchors the discourse in place, and with *now*, he or she anchors it in time. Many other expressions depend upon our ability to identify the essential indexicals. For example, we cannot comply with the following sentence:

Bring the book tomorrow.

without identifying the implicit *I* (to surmise what book might be relevant), the *now* (to figure out what is tomorrow), and the *here* (to know where to bring it). The essential indexicals scope out the beginnings of a common ground that interlocutors share, a common ground that can be increasingly enriched by further interactions.

Speakers and writers use the demonstrative pronouns, *this* and *that*, *these* and *those*, to point to objects locating them physically or metaphorically with respect to the here of the discourse:

Not this one; that one.

These indexicals can also give you a handle on the extent to which interlocutors are coordinating with each other.

If your analysis is concerned with understanding the development and nature of the common ground that speakers or writers create with their interlocutors, you may want to use one or more of the indexicals as your unit of segmentation:

1. Pronouns: *I, he, she, it*
2. Demonstratives: *this* and *that*, *these* and *those*
3. Adverbs: *here, now, today, yesterday, tomorrow*
4. Adjectives: *my, his, her*

The easiest way to segment your discourse by indexical is to break the discourse up by clause, and then underline any indexical you find within each clause.

Personal Pronouns

Personal pronouns—*I, me, you, he, she, him, her, they*, and *them*—point to the world of interlocutors in which a speaker or writer takes as common ground. As we have already seen, pronouns are indexical. Focusing on the personal pronouns as a specific kinds of indexical can give you clues about the scope of the human world in which writers or speakers see themselves as acting. Looking specifically at first person pronouns (*I, me*) can help you to examine the agency of the speaker or writer. Personal pronouns can be looked at for themselves (how many time did the speaker use *I*?), for what they refer to (Where did the speaker talk about her family), or they can be used to select other phenomenon for analysis (what kind of verbals does the speaker attribute to herself).

To use personal pronouns to segment your discourse, underline each pronoun and then break the discourse right before each one. Or you may choose to segment your discourse first by some larger comprehensive unit such as the t-unit or clause, and then underline each personal pronoun within each of these larger units.

Modals

Modals provide language users with a way to indicate the attitude or stance of the writer or speaker toward the message he or she is conveying. The stance can range from bald assertion:

> Sally will leave tomorrow.

to assertions with less definite status

> Sally might leave tomorrow.
>
> Sally could leave tomorrow.
>
> Sally will probably leave tomorrow.
>
> Sally will certainly leave tomorrow.

In general, modality can communicate probability (she might go tomorrow) advisability (she ought not go tomorrow), or conditionality (she would have gone yesterday). Modality is often conveyed through the modal auxiliary verbs: *might*, *may*, and *must*, *can* and *could*, *will* and *would*, *shall* and *should*, *ought*. Modality can be conveyed in many other ways however as the following lists suggest:

1. Modal auxiliaries: *might, may* and *must, can* and *could, will* and *would, shall* and *should, ought*
2. Conditionals: *if, unless*
3. Idioms: *have to, need to, ought to, have got to, had better, need to*
4. Adverbials: *probably, certainly, most assuredly*
5. Verbs: *appear, assume, doubt, guess, looks like, suggest, think, insist, command, request, ask*

All modals convey information about the level of obligation or certainty that speakers or writers associate with the content of what they are saying. If you are interested in tracking the degree of certainty with which interlocutors assess their claims, you may want to use modals as a unit of segmentation.

The easiest way to segment your discourse by modality is to break the discourse up by clause, and then underline any modal you find within each clause.

Metadiscourse

Metadiscourse is the part of discourse that talks about the discourse: the metadiscourse. If you can imagine that a text has a primary channel in which information is conveyed, the metadiscourse forms a background channel through which the writer talks to the readers to tell them how to understand and interpret the text.

There are two primary kinds of metadiscourse. Textual metadiscourse directs the reader in understanding the text. Textual connectives such as *first, next,* and *however* help readers recognize how the text is organized. Illocution markers like *in summary, we suggest,* and *our point is* point to the kind of work the writer is trying to do. Narrators such as *according to, many people believe that,* and *so-and-so argues that* let readers know to whom to attribute a claim. Textual metadiscourse is directly related to the rhetorical awareness exhibited in the text, and can be used as a unit of segmentation when you are concerned with rhetorical sophistication.

A second kind of metadiscourse is interpersonal, and serves to develop a relationship between writer and reader. Validity markers such as hedges (*might, perhaps*), emphatics (*clearly, obviously*), and narrators (*according to*) give the reader guidance on how much face value to give to the claim with which they are associated. Other attitude markers like *surprisingly* and *unfortunately* communicate the writer's attitude toward the situation and invite the reader to share the same stance. Commentaries such as as *we'll see in the following section* and *readers are invited to peruse the appendix* are more extended directions to the reader.

Interpersonal metadiscourse is directly related the degree to which a text shows evidence of audience awareness. Interpersonal metadiscourse can vary by genre, by rhetorical sophistication, and by the degree of comfort an writer has with the audience addressed. If you are interested in phenomenon related to audience, you may well wish to look at interpersonal metadiscourse as a unit of segmentation.

The easiest way to segment your discourse by metadiscourse is to break the discourse up by t-unit, and then underline any metadiscourse you find within each t-unit.

Exercise 3.1: Test Your Understanding

Within each group below, match the unit in the first column with the kind of phenomenon it can be used to study in the second column. (You can download this exercise at https://wac.colostate.edu/books/practice/codingstreams/).

Group 1

1	the text in written interactions	a	the certainty or obligation of claims
2	t-units in language	b	the domains of knowledge a writer or speaker refers to
3	modals in language	c	rhetorical awareness in text
4	metadiscourse in written interactions	d	the moves a writer or speaker makes
5	noun phrases in language	e	quality of writing

Group 2

6	responses in interviews	f	frequency or distribution of textual phenomenon
7	sentences in written interactions	g	context of interaction
8	topical chains in language	h	the perceptions, feelings, beliefs of an interviewee
9	sequences in conversation	i	the complexity and depth of ideas
10	verbals in language	j	the schemata a writer or speaker uses

Group 3

11	turns in conversation	k	the claims a writer or speaker makes
12	genre elements in written interactions	l	relative power among speakers
13	personal pronouns in language	m	the common ground and/or coordination between participants
14	clauses in language	n	typified action in writing
15	indexicals in language	o	references to the human world

For Discussion: How can you see the phenomenon at work in each unit?

Memo 3.1: Unit of Segmentation

Find two to three sections of your data that show the kind of phenomenon that is of interest to you. Carefully note what you are seeing.

Next, look for several sections that show the absence or the opposite of this phenomenon. Also carefully describe what you are seeing.

Finally, consider the kind of unit over which this phenomenon occurs in your selection, reviewing the options for segmenting outlined earlier in this chapter.

Document your choice of unit of analysis, its relationship to the phenomenon that interests you, and your reasons for rejecting other units of analysis that might also have been appropriate.

Segmenting the Data

The goal of segmenting data to produce a file where each unit is separated from the next by a single paragraph break. Such data will be easy to move into an analysis program for further manipulation.

Segmenting Comprehensive Units

Segmenting by comprehensive units is perhaps the easiest task. Comprehensive units are those units which include the entire stream of language. That is, every word in the discourse is included in a segment to be further analyzed. All streams of language, for example, can be divided into t-units, clauses, or topical chains and every word in the stream will be part of some t-unit, clause, or topical chain. The following discourse has been segmented by t-unit (The paragraph symbol, ¶, is shown in order to clearly indicate the paragraph breaks).

> **Critical care patients have often suffered a "disturbance" to the normal operation of their physiological system;¶**
>
> **this disturbance could have been generated by surgery or some sort of trauma.¶**
>
> **The critical care physician is to maintain certain patient state variables within an acceptable operating range.¶**

> **Often the physician will infuse several drugs into the patient to control these states close to the desired values.¶**
>
> **For example, in the case of critical care patients with congestive heart failure, measured variables that are of primary importance include mean arterial pressure (MAP) and cardiac output (CO).¶**
>
> **Secondary variables which are monitored, but not regulated as tightly as the primary variables, include heart rate and pulmonary capillary wedge pressure.¶**
>
> **The physician uses her/his own senses for other variables that are not easily measured, such as depth of anesthesia, and often infers them from a number of measurements and patient responses to surgical procedures.**

See Procedure 3.1 for more information on segmenting using comprehensive units.

■ Segmenting Conversational data

Segmenting conversational data poses some special challenges. This data often takes the following form with the name of the speaker, a colon, and then the actual conversational snippet:

> **P: okay . . . ah . . . in terms of your overall plan . . . then . . . where do you move from here . . . after you finish extracting information . . .**
>
> **J: which is going to be a chore . . . considering . . .**
>
> **P: it's going to take a while right . . .**

If you are moving your data into Excel, you will want the speaker identification in one column and the actual conversation, divided into your chosen units, in an adjacent column. In the Excel example given in Figure 3.5, for example, the

Procedure 3.1: Segmenting Using Comprehensive Units

https://goo.gl/1jf8Up

1. Working with a single stream of language in a word processing program, place your cursor at the break between one segment and the next.
2. Hit enter.

Speakers names (P and J) are in the first column. In the second column, each clause appears, one line at a time.

See Procedure 3.2 for more information on segmenting conversational data.

P:	okay ... ah ... in terms of your overall plan ... then ... where do you move from here ...
	after you finish extracting information ...
J:	which is going to be a chore ... considering ...
P:	it's going to take a while right ...
	okay ... ah ... in terms of your overall plan ... then ... where do you move from here ... after you finish extracting information ...

Figure 3.5: Conversational data, segmented by clause and moved into Excel.

Procedure 3.2: Segmenting Conversational Data

https://goo.gl/1jf8Up

1. Working with your stream of conversation in a word processing program, turn off **Autocorrect** in your **Preferences** under the **Word** menu item.
2. Replace the colons after speaker names with colon + tab.
3. Place your cursor at the break between one segment and the next.
4. Hit enter to insert a carriage return and then add a tab before the second unit

The results should look like the following with -> represeting tabs:

P:->	okay . . . ah . . . in terms of your overall plan . . . then . . . where do you move from here . . .
->	after you finish extracting information . . .
J:->	which is going to be a chore . . . considering . . .
P:->	it's going to take a while right . . .

Segmenting for Selective Units

Unlike comprehensive units, such as t-units and clauses, selective units include just part of the stream of language. As we suggested earlier, in the first approach to segmenting for selective units, you simply underline each selective unit and then segment the discourse right before each one. Using our cats and dogs metaphor from earlier in this chapter, this method of segmentation is equivalent to dividing the stream right before each animal's nose, so that later you can code each wet nose as a dog and each dry nose as a cat.[3]

In a more relevant example of this approach to selective segmentation, this one taken from Rick Steves' online guide on Internet Security for Travelers (https://www.ricksteves.com/travel-tips/phones-tech/internet-security-for-travelers), we have underlined modals for further analysis and placed each one on its own line in Excel, ready to be coded in the adjacent column:

1	If you're taking your devices on the road, be aware that gadget theft is an issue in Europe. Not only	
2	should you take precautions to protect your devices from thieves, but you	
3	should also configure them for maximum security so that	
4	if they are stolen, your personal data	
5	will stay private.	

This way of segmenting for selective units not only clearly communicates to coders which text is supposed to be considered in coding (the underlined words), but also supplies them with the full context to support that coding.

As you can see from this example, however, the text shown on each line is rather arbitrary and meaningless. And we will often encounter discourse that has long passages without a selective unit, as in this passage further along in Steves' article:

[3] I now realize that this rule of thumb does not actually work for coding cats and dogs, but I was taught it when I was very young and it does illustrate the point nicely.

21	Many laptops have a file sharing option. Though this setting is	
22	likely turned off by default, it's a good idea to check that this option is not activated on your computer so that people sharing a Wi-Fi network with you	
23	can't access your files	
24	(if you're not sure how, do a search for your operating system's name and "turn off file sharing"). Newer versions of Windows have a "Public network" setting (choose this when you first join the network) that automatically configures your computer so that it's less susceptible to invasion. Once on the road, use only legitimate Wi-Fi hotspots. Ask the hotel or café for the specific name of their network, and make sure you log on to that exact one. Hackers sometimes create bogus hotspots with a similar or vague name (such as "Hotel Europa Free Wi-Fi") that shows up alongside a bunch of authentic networks. It's better	
25	if a network uses a password (especially a hard-to-guess one) rather than being open to the world.	
26	If you're not actively using a hotspot, turn off Wi-Fi so that your device is not visible to others.	

Not only is this first way of segmenting selective units unrelated to meaning, but it presents problems for understanding the frequency of your phenomenon. In this example, the length of the segments is arbitrary, ranging from four words in segment 23 to 106 words in segment 24. Thus to give a sense of the relative frequency of modals, we could not rely on the number of segments as a basis for our analysis; that is, there is no communicative value in saying that there was on average one modal per segment, since definitionally we have insured that there will be one modal per segment. To give a better sense of frequency, then, we will have to use some other base metric, saying, for example, that there were five modals in 185 words, or an average of 2.7 (5/185) modals per 100 words.

A second problem with this first kind of segmentation arises if you should wish to code your data in a second way, a not uncommon strategy as we'll see in the next chapter. Going back to our cats and dogs example, suppose we decide we want not only to code for cats and dogs that are in our stream, but also for the kinds of flowers we see. Since the natural segmentation unit for flowers is the plant, we could go back and resegment our stream in an entirely different way than by the nose in order to code for flowers, but this would be a tremendous amount of work.

As this metaphorical example suggests, a second and simpler approach to segmenting for selective units is often called for. This second approach involves picking a comprehensive unit to start with and then using underlining to identify the selective units. In our cats and dogs and plants example, this might mean segmenting our stream by property lot, and then coding each lot first for pets and second for plants in bloom. We might have to deal with the problem of a few lots that had both cats and dogs (perhaps by adding a category for *both*), but this approach to segmenting would allow us to look for relationships between pet ownership and the state of the lot's landscape.

Coming back to the Rick Steves example, this second approach to selective segmentation approach would involve segmenting the discourse first by clause, and then underlining each modal within the clause:

1	If you're taking your devices on the road,	
2	be aware	
3	that gadget theft is an issue in Europe.	
4	Not only should you take precautions to protect your devices from thieves,	
5	but you should also configure them for maximum security	
6	so that if they are stolen,	
7	your personal data will stay private.	

This kind of segmentation allows you to describe the frequency of modality with a statement such as, "71% (5 of 7) of clauses contained modals," which does give a more informative sense of their frequency. In the later section with fewer modals, segmenting first by clause and then underlining the modals would produce the following:

1	Many laptops have a file-sharing option.	
2	Though this setting is likely turned off by default,	
3	it's a good idea to check	
4	that this option is not activated on your computer	
5	so that people sharing a Wi-Fi network with you	
6	can't access your files	
7	(if you're not sure how,	
8	do a search for your operating system's name	
9	and "turn off file sharing").	
10	Newer versions of Windows have a "Public network" setting	
11	(choose this	
12	when you first join the network)	
13	that automatically configures your computer	
14	so that it's less susceptible to invasion.	
15	Once on the road, use only legitimate Wi-Fi hotspots.	
16	Ask the hotel or café for the specific name of their network,	
17	and make sure	
18	you log on to that exact one.	
19	Hackers sometimes create bogus hotspots with a similar or vague name (such as "Hotel Europa Free Wi-Fi")	
20	that shows up alongside a bunch of authentic networks.	
21	It's better	
22	if a network uses a password (especially a hard-to-guess one) rather than being open to the world.	
23	If you're not actively using a hotspot,	
24	turn off Wi-Fi	
25	so that your device is not visible to others.	

Now we can say that the same five modals occur over 25 clauses or at a rate of one every five clauses.

When you use this kind of combination of comprehensive and selective segmentation, you may find that more than one example of the selective unit occurs within the comprehensive unit. The following passage, for example, has been segmented by clause and then for noun phrases. Each of the clauses contains more than one noun phrase:

1	Critical care patients have often suffered a "disturbance" to the normal operation of their physiological system;	
2	this disturbance could have been generated by surgery or some sort of trauma.	

Our interest here is not, of course, whether the clauses have noun phrases, but what kind of noun phrases; perhaps we want to code each noun phrase for the use of everyday language or medical jargon. This would require us to pull out each noun phrase on a separate line for coding. Ideally, our data would look like that shown in Figure 3.6 once in Excel:

A	B	C	D	F
clause #	noun phrase #	Clause/Noun phrase	Code 1	Code 2
1		Critical care patients have often suffered a "disturbance" to the normal operation of their physiological system;		
	1a	Critical care patients		
	1b	a "disturbance" to the normal operation of their physiological system;		
2		this disturbance could have been generated by surgery or some sort of trauma		
	2a	this disturbance		
	2b	surgery		
	2c	some sort of trauma		

Figure 3.6: Data first segmented comprehensively by clause and then selectively by noun phrase.

This data is set up so that 1) the noun phrases are numbered in column B (1a, 1b, 2a, 2b, 2c) and can be coded using column D; and 2) the clauses are numbered in column A (1, 2) and can be coded in column F. The greyed-out cells in each column help to tell the coder what data not to code. We will describe the procedure for formatting this kind of data before moving it into Excel in the section on Moving the Segmented Data.

Creating a Segmenting Style

A file full of text segmented using paragraph breaks can be difficult to read:

> Critical care patients have often suffered a "disturbance" to the normal operation of their physiological system; this disturbance could have been generated by surgery or some sort of trauma.
> The critical care physician is to maintain certain patient state variables within an acceptable operating range.
> Often the physician will infuse several drugs into the patient to control these states close to the desired values.
> For example, in the case of critical care patients with congestive heart failure, measured variables that are of primary importance include mean arterial pressure (MAP) and cardiac output (CO).

This problem that can remedied by applying stylistic formatting to shape the text into a more readable form (see Procedure 3.3). For example, it is often helpful to increase the spacing after each segment in order to distinguish segmenting breaks from simple text wrapping:

> Critical care patients have often suffered a "disturbance" to the normal operation of their physiological system; this disturbance could have been generated by surgery or some sort of trauma.
>
> The critical care physician is to maintain certain patient state variables within an acceptable operating range.
>
> Often the physician will infuse several drugs into the patient to control these states close to the desired values.
>
> For example, in the case of critical care patients with congestive heart failure, measured variables that are of primary importance include mean arterial pressure (MAP) and cardiac output (CO).

Memo 3.2: Segmenting Procedure

Using the unit of analysis you selected in Memo 3.1, segment four to five pages of your data. Make sure to select typical data—data from the middle of a conversation or text, data from across your built-in contrast, and so on.

Annotate your segmentation, noting where you are uncertain of your segmentation. Consult with an online source or a colleague to help you resolve your uncertainties.

Document your segmenting decisions so that you can maintain consistency as you segment all of your data.

Procedure 3.3: Using a Style to Format your Data

https://goo.gl/1jf8Up

To create a new style in Microsoft Word:

1. Select a segment.
2. Format it in the way you want.

For example, you might increase the spacing after a segment to 6 points by placing the cursor in the segment, invoking the **Paragraph** command on the **Format** menu, and increasing the spacing after the paragraph to 6.

3. Click on the **Style Panes** icon to open the **Style Pane**.
4. Click on the **New Style** button.
5. Name your new style.

To apply this style to other segments:

6. Select the other segments to which you want to apply the new style.
7. Then choose the new style from the drop down **Style** menu.

To change a style:

8. Change the style the way you want in one segment.
9. Then in the **Style Pane**, hover over the style name until you see the drop down menu to the right.
10. From that drop down menu, choose **Update to Match Selection.**

Word will automatically apply the new style changes to every segment with that style in your file.

Moving the Segmented Data

Once the text has been segmented appropriately in your word processing application, you are ready to move the segmented data into your data analytic application. This procedure differs slightly depending on whether your data is segmented comprehensively or selectively. We start by describing the methods to use with comprehensively segmented data and then review those for data that has been selectively segmented.

Moving Comprehensively Segmented Data

If you have segmented your data using a comprehensive unit, you will now want to move it into your analytic application. Procedures for Excel (3.1 and 3.2) and MAXQDA (3.1 and 3.2) provide guidance on this process.

Excel Procedure 3.1: Moving and Numbering Comprehensively Segmented Data into Excel

https://goo.gl/1jf8Up

1. Select and copy the data to be moved from Word.
2. Paste it into a worksheet, starting with Column C, leaving Columns A and B free for the labels you will insert later.

Generally speaking, each data stream (interview, transcript, text) should be placed on its own worksheet. Make sure to label the worksheets as you go.

After segments are moved into Excel, you should label them:

3. In Column B, insert numbers starting with 1 and continuing for 3 or 4 segments.
4. Select these cells and drag down to fill the column.
5. In Column A, type a label next to the first segment.
6. Copy the label and select the rest of the cells next to the rest of the data and issue the paste command.

Numbering and labeling segments in this way will insure that each segment has a unique identity in analysis.

If you have conversational data, you will also want to insure that each segment is labeled for speaker.

Exercise 3.2: Try It Out

In word processing, segment the following text by t-unit, move it into Excel or MAXQDA. Make sure to number and label the segments if necessary. Compare your results with others in your class. (You can download this exercise at https://wac.colostate.edu/books/practice/codingstreams/).

> The language people speak or write becomes research data only when we transpose it from the activity in which it originally functioned to the activity in which we are analyzing it. This displacement depends on such processes as task-construction, interviewing, transcription, selection of materials, etc., in which the researcher's efforts shape the data. Because linguistic and cultural meaning, which is what we are ultimately trying to analyze, is always highly context-dependent, researcher-controlled selection, presentation, and recontextualisation of verbal data is a critical determinant of the information content of the data. Data is only analyzable to the extent that we have made it a part of our meaning-world, and to that extent it is therefore always also data about us. Selection of discourse samples is not governed by random sampling. Discourse events do not represent a homogeneous population of isolates which can be sampled in the statistical sense. Every discourse event is unique. Discourse events are aggregated by the researcher for particular purposes and by stated criteria. There are as many possible principles of aggregation as there are culturally meaningful dimensions of meaning for the kind of discourse being studied.

For Discussion: What issues did you have to resolve to do this segmenting?

MAXQDA Procedure 3.1: Importing Comprehensively Segmented Data

https://goo.gl/1jf8Up

Moving comprehensively coded data into MAXQDA is very easy.

1. In a new project in MAXQDA, from the **Documents** menu, select the segmented files you want to import.
2. Click **Open**.

Generally speaking, each data stream (interview, transcript, text) should be placed on its own document. Make sure to label the documents with identifying information as you go.

Each file will be imported and automatically numbered by segment. MAXQDA will also automatically keep track of the source of each segment. Thus, you do not need to do any additional numbering or labelling.

Moving Selectively Segmented Data

If you have segmented first with a comprehensive unit and then with a selective unit, you may want to number your segments *before* moving them. With the method described in Excel Procedure 3.2 and MAXQDA Procedure 3.2, you can automatically and separately number both the comprehensive units and the selective units as shown in Figure 3.7. The process is a bit complicated, but it sure beats doing it by hand.

	A	B	C	D
1	clause #	noun phrase #	Clause/Nount phrase	Code
2	1		1 Critical care patients have often suffered a "disturbance" to the normal operation of their physiological system;	
3	1	a	Critical care patients	
4	1	b	a "disturbance" to the normal operation of their physiological system;	
5	2		2 this disturbance could have been generated by surgery or some sort of trauma	
6	2	a	this disturbance	
7	2	b	surgery	
8	2	c	some sort of trauma	
9	3		3 this disturbance could have been generated by surgery or some sort of trauma	
10	3	a	this disturbance	
11	3	b	surgery	
12	3	c	some sort of trauma	

Figure 3.7: Selectively segmented data numbered in Excel.

Excel Procedure 3.2. Numbering and Moving Selective Segments in Excel

https://goo.gl/1jf8Up

1. Working with a stream of language in Microsft Word, underline the selective segments in your comprehensive unit:

   Critical care patients have often suffered a "disturbance" to the normal operation of their physiological system

2. Create a copy of the comprehensive segment below the comprehensive unit and edit it so that each selective unit is located on a separate line beneath the comprehensive unit:

Continued . . .

Excel Procedure 3.2: Numbering & Moving Selective Segments (continued)

https://goo.gl/1jf8Up

Critical care patients have often suffered a "disturbance" to the normal operation of their physiological system

Critical care patients

a "disturbance" to the normal operation of their physiological system

After you have edited all of your segments:

3. Select all of the segments you want to number, both comprehensive and selective.
4. Select **Outline Numbered** from the **Bullets and Numbering** option under the **Format** menu.
5. Select the third format option (1. 1.1. 1.1.1) and click **Customize.**
6. With Level 1 selected, add a second period to the number format so that it is a number followed by two periods (1..).
7. Select Level 2 and change the **Number Style** to a, b, c
8. Edit the number format so that it is a period followed by a number followed by a letter followed by a period (.1a.) and click **OK**.
9. To move the selective segments to level 2, select and indent them.
10. Check to make sure that the text looks appropriately numbered, with comprehensive segments numbered 1, 2, and so on followed by two periods, and selective segments numbered under their comprehensive segments as 1a 1b and so on with a period before and after the numbering.
11. Save your file as a text file (.txt).

To import your data:

12. From within Excel, put your cursor in cell B2 and invoke the **File** > **Import** command.
13. Select text file from the file types and click **Import**.
14. Select the file you want to import and click **Get Data**.
15. In Step 1 of the **Text Import Wizard**, select **Delimited** as your file type and click **Next**.
16. In Step 2 of the **Text Import Wizard**, uncheck all delimiters and type a period (.) in the box following **Other:**.
17. In Step 3 of the **Text Import Wizard**, click **Finish**.
18. In the **Import Data dialogue box**, make sure the data will go into an existing worksheet with =$B$2 as the destination and click **OK**.

Issues in Segmenting

As you segment verbal data, a few issues will arise that may require special handling. In closing this chapter, we call your attention to some of these.

Fragments

Particularly if you are working with oral or online conversations, you may need to deal with fragments of language that don't quite add up to the full unit you are using for segmentation. Not only do we encounter the *uhms* and *ohs* with which people fill their speech, but we also hear the fits and starts of unfinished ideas, a clause started and left hanging. You will need to decide how to handle these fragments and be consistent in your treatment.

MAXQDA Procedure 3.2: Importing Selectively Segmented Data

https://goo.gl/1jf8Up

1. In Word, underline the selective segments in your comprehensive unit:

   Critical care patients have often suffered a "disturbance" to the normal operation of their physiological system

2. Create a copy of the segment and place the selective units beneath the comprehensive unit:

   Critical care patients have often suffered a "disturbance" to the normal operation of their physiological system

   Critical care patients

   a "disturbance" to the normal operation of their physiological system

3. Select each of the selective units and change the font color:

   Critical care patients have often suffered a "disturbance" to the normal operation of their physiological system

   Critical care patients

   a "disturbance" to the normal operation of their physiological system;

When you import the data into MAXQDA, it will preserve the font colors, and you will be able to tell a coder to code just those segments in black (the comprehensive units).

You might, for example, treat the monosyllabic back channeling by a second speaker as separate turns as has been done in the following transcript (Li et al., 2010):

> **Dr.: I'll give a prescription for the codeine.**
>
> **Pt.: Uhm.**
>
> **Dr.: You're a pretty damn healthy guy so it shouldn't be a problem.**
>
> **Pt.: Uhm.**

Or you might routinely decide just to include them in the first speaker's turn in square brackets as has been done here:

> **Dr.: I'll give a prescription for the codeine [Uhm] You're a pretty damn healthy guy so it shouldn't be a problem [Uhm]**

If you are trying to capture the back and forth of the conversational dynamics, you should use the first method. But if you intend to code the segments for meaning, you might prefer to use the second method.

With incomplete thoughts, where a speaker has started one way and then started over to continue in a different way, it is probably best to treat them as separate segments:

> **I was just wondering if . . .**
>
> **I was just wondering when we are planning to leave?**

■ Center Embedding

Another issue that you may encounter involves center-embedded clauses. Most of the clauses in English come one right after another and can easily be segmented as in this earlier example from Rick Steves:

> 1 **Many laptops have a file-sharing option.**
>
> 2 **Though this setting is likely turned off by default,**
>
> 3 **it's a good idea to check**
>
> 4 **that this option is not activated on your computer**

Occasionally, however, one clause is embedded right in the center of another clause:

5 . . . people who share a Wi-Fi network with you
6 can't access your files

In this example (modified slightly from Steves original), the subordinate clause, *who share a Wi-Fi network with you*, is plopped right in the center of another clause, *people can't access your files*. The way we have done the segmentation separates the subject of the clause, *people*, from its verb, *can't access*. You might be tempted to draw the segmentation so that at least the embedded clause is correctly segmented:

5 so that people
6 who share a Wi-Fi network with you
7 can't access your files

But while this segmentation may be more technically correct, it does little to support our intended coding. For the most part, we have found it best to keep the embedded clause with the part of the surrounding clause that it modifies, leaving only the remainder of the clause for a separate segment. However you choose to handle center embedding, be consistent about it.

Pronouns

A final issue you may encounter in preparing data for coding involves pronouns. Pronouns pose more difficulties in interpretation than the noun phrases to which they refer. Many references are vague; others refer to persons or things outside of rather than in the text. And, of course, anytime you ask people to take the additional step of deciding what a pronoun refers to before they decide how to code it, there will be increased variation.

To manage this referential complexity, you can take one of two approaches as you segment the data. The first is simply to remove pronouns from coding if your unit of analysis would otherwise indicate that the should be coded. So, for example, if you are planning to code all nominals, you might decide not to code any nominal that was a pronoun. While such a decision might seem to eliminate a lot of data, if the elimination is spread proportionately through your coding categories, the overall patterns will be preserved.

Sometimes, however, you will not be able to eliminate the pronouns because they contain important information about the phenomenon of interest. If, for example, you are looking at references to human agents, you may not want to eliminate pronouns because they disproportionately contain a lot of information about agency in verbal data.

In this case, you may pre-process the verbal data to insert into the data the noun to which the pronoun should be understood to refer. So, for example, if the pronoun "he" is used to refer to Harry, we could insert it as follows:

> **He [Harry] was taking his dog for a walk.**

Resolving pronominal reference in this way in advance of coding will allow the data to be coded with greater consistency. But this technique is inherently tricky: if the referent is unclear or vague, you may need to read too much into the data to resolve it. Thus you may find it best to resolve only those references about which there is no ambiguity.

■ Memo 3.3: Data Set for Analysis

Complete the segmentation of your data set and move it into the data analytic application of your choice.

Document your data set. Create a table that shows how many segments you have for each text/transcript across your build in contrast. Include a verbal description of the table in your notes.

■ Selected Studies Using Segmentation

Graham, S. S., Kim, S-Y., DeVasto, D. M. & Keith, W. (2015). Statistical genre analysis: Toward big data methodologies in technical communication. *Technical Communication Quarterly*, 24(1), 70–104. (By paragraph.)

Imbrenda, J-P. (2016). The blackbird whistling or just after? Vygotsky's tool and sign as an analytic for writing. *Written Communication, 33*(1), 68–91. (By sentence.)
Kuhn, D., Hemberger, L. & Khait, V. (2015). Tracing the development of argumentative writing in a discourse-rich context. *Written Communication, 33*(1), 92–121. (By idea unit.)
Ngai, C. S. B. & Jin, Y. (2016).The effectiveness of crisis communication strategies on Sina Weibo in relation to Chinese publics' acceptance of these strategies. *Journal of Business and Technical Communication, 30*(4), 451–494. (By genre element, response).
Shin, W., Pang, A. & Kim, H-Y. (2015). Building relationships through integrated online media: Global organizations' use of brand web sites, Facebook, and Twitter. *Journal of Business and Technical Communication, 29*(2), 184–220. (By genre element—website, Facebook profile, wall post, Twitter profile, tweet).
Swarts, J. (2015). Help is in the helping: An evaluation of help documentation in a networked age. *Technical Communication Quarterly, 24*(2), 164–187. (By t-unit.)
Walker, K. C. (2016). Mapping the contours of translation: Visualized un/certainties in the ozone hole controversy. *Technical Communication Quarterly, 25*(2), 104–120. (By sentence.)

■ For Further Reading

Biber, D. & Kanoksilapatham, B. (2007). Introduction to move analysis. In D. Biber, U. Connor & T. A. Upton (Eds.), *Discourse on the move: Using corpus analysis to describe discourse structure*. Amsterdam: John Benjamins.
Clark, H. (1996). *Using Language*. Cambridge, UK: Cambridge University Press.
Heritage, J. (1984). *Garfinkel and Ethnomethodology*. Cambridge, UK: Polity Press.
Kaufer, D. S. & Geisler, C. (1991). A scheme for representing written argument. *The Journal of Advanced Composition, 11*(1), 107–122.
Kolln, M. & Funk, R. (1998). *Understanding English grammar*. Boston: Allyn and Bacon.
Krippendorff, K. (2013). *Content analysis: An introduction to its methodology* (3rd ed.). Los Angeles: Sage.
Li, H. Z., Cui, Y. & Wang, Z. (2010). Backchannel responses and enjoyment of the conversation: The more does not necessarily mean the better. *International Journal of Psychological Studies, 2*(1), 25–37.
McCarthy, M. (1996). *Discourse Analysis for Language Teachers*. Cambridge, UK: Cambridge University Press.

Mehan, H. (1979). *Learning lessons: Social organization in the classroom*. Cambridge, MA: Harvard University Press.

Morris, J. S. (2009). The Daily Show with Jon Stewart and audience attitude change during the 2004 party conventions. *Political Behavior*, *31*(1), 79–102.

Neuendorf, K. (2016). *The Content Analysis Guidebook* (2nd ed.). London: Sage Publications. Kindle Edition.

Saldaña, J. (2016). *The coding manual for qualitative researchers*. London: Sage Publications.

Chapter 4. Coding the Data

> In this chapter, you will code the data you segmented in the previous chapter. After you devise an initial start list of codes, you will use an iterative process to move back and forth between sample data and coding scheme to develop a procedural coding scheme that best tracks the phenomenon that interests you. You will also be introduced to automated coding and to using an enumerative coding scheme.

■ Concepts in Coding

Coding is the analytic task of assigning codes to non-numeric data. Coding language data is a technique used in a variety of research traditions. In traditional content analysis, coding falls under the heading of "human coding" and makes use of a codebook which, according to Neuendorf (2016) should be set up in advance of coding and should be "so complete and unambiguous as to almost eliminate the individual differences among coders" (Chapter 5, Section on Codebooks and Coding Forms, para. 1). In qualitative analysis, coding is treated as an activity that creates and assigns a word or phrase to symbolize, summarize, or otherwise capture some attribute of "a portion of language-based or visual data," often in interaction with that data (Saldaña, 2016, Chapter 1, Section on What is a Code?, para. 1). Finally, in text mining, especially that using supervised machine learning, language data is often coded in a first stage of work to create a corpus from which a machine can then "learn" (Geisler, 2016b; Omizo & Hart-Davidson, 2016a).

Coding Schemes

The way that the segments are assigned codes is governed by some kind of coding guide. In content analysis, guides to coding are gathered together into a *codebook*, which provides analysts with detailed directions for coding along all the dimensions defined for the data. A draft codebook is developed based on the literature and then further refined during coder training. It reaches its final form before final coding. Neuendorf (2016) provides an example of a codebook for female characters in James Bond films (Box 5.1) that provides directions for coding such simple dimensions as Name ("If the character's name is provided, list this name . . .") and more complex dimensions such as this one for Physical Appearance:[4]

> Indicate whether the female character is extremely attractive (professional model status), attractive (very pleasant looking, above average), average (pleasant looking, but average in looks), below average (not pleasant looking, below average looks), extremely unattractive (extremely unpleasant looking, considered homely). (Chapter 5, Box 5.2, para. 14).

In qualitative analysis, codes may be gathered together into a coding system (MAXQDA), a coding tree (Dedoose) or, more generically, a coding scheme (Silver & Lewins, 2017). These coding schemes may be developed in advance of the coding, but undergo substantial refinement throughout the coding process. Particularly during second cycle coding, groups of codes may be collected together, rearranged, subsumed one under another, and so on. One example of an emergent category cited by Saldaña (2016) from Maykut and Morehouse (1994) provides a rule for inclusion along with sample data:

> **Physical Health:** The participant shares matters related to physical health such as wellness, medication, pain, etc.: "I'm on 25 milligrams of amitriptyline each night"; "I've lost ten pounds on this new diet." (p. 11)

---

4 We might cringe at the subject, but this is one of only a few clear, accessible examples of a complex coding scheme.

For our purposes, a coding scheme should articulate clearly the procedures used to code your data. It serves two functions. In the next stage of analysis, it will serve as a set of directions to a second coder. Later on, when you publish your study, it will serve to let your reader know how you have defined your categories and how you have assigned data to them.

A sample coding scheme can be found in Figure 4.1. As you can see, it is written as a set of directions to a coder and includes the following:

- The name of the dimension being coded for. In Figure 4.1, the name of the dimension being coded for is the World of Discourse. The name of the dimension should be clearly identified at the top of the coding scheme.
- The names of the coding categories. In Figure 4.1, these include *Rhetorical Process*, *Domain Content*, and *Narrated Cases*, and are clearly labeled in bold type.
- The unit of analysis to which the codes are to be applied. In Figure 4.1, the unit mentioned as being coded is the t-unit.
- A definition for each coding category. In Figure 4.1, the definition for *Rhetorical Process*, for example, is given as "the worlds in which people make claims as authors."
- An enumeration of the kinds of cases that the coding category includes. In Figure 4.1, *Rhetorical Process* includes cases referring to texts as well as cases referring to authors.
- One or more examples of each case. Examples of authors in Figure 4.1 include "Childress," "I," and "you."

Coding the World of Discourse

The following figure shows an example of a procedural coding scheme.

> Code as **Rhetorical Process** any t-unit that refers to the worlds in which people make claims as authors. This includes referring to:
>
> - the texts, or parts of texts, in which claims are made: "the book," "the introduction";

- the authors of claims, including the students and teachers as makers of claims: "Childress," "I," "you";
- nominals that characterize actions taken by authors as claim makers: "question-begging";
- descriptions of the interactions among authors as claim makers: "discussions," "disagreements";
- the requirements or directions for the assignment: "a paper in two sections";
- general categories of claims that can be made by authors: "a definition," "a justification," "a reason," "a question"; and/or
- any consideration or product relevant to the generation of claims: "my notes."

Code as **Domain Content** any t-unit that refers to the world of truths about paternalism. These truths have an external flavor to them: They are said to be true independent of any claim. This will include t-units referring to:

- philosophical concepts related to paternalism: "paternalism," "respect for persons";
- terms for the standard components of paternalism taken in an abstract way: "agent," "actions," "features," "case";
- relationships between these concepts or components: "connection"; and/or
- characteristics, either positive or negative, of these concepts or components: "principle."

Code as **Narrated Case** any t-unit that refers to particular worlds in which (paternalistic) narratives take place that are taken to exist independently of domain concepts. These will include:

- specific people or actions that are taken to exist independently of the concepts in the domain but that may potentially be characterized with respect to these concepts;
- general categories of people or actions that are taken to exist independently of the concepts in the domain but that may potentially be characterized with respect to these concepts;

- characteristics of specific or general people or actions that are taken to exist independently of the concepts in the domain but that may potentially be characterized with respect to these concepts; and/or
- "you" or "I" when cast in a role involving an action that is taken to exist independently of the concepts in the domain but that may potentially be characterized with respect to these concepts.

Figure 4.1: Sample procedural coding scheme.

The ultimate goal of coding verbal data is to label segments of verbal data in a way that represents the phenomenon in which you are interested and to do so systematically and reliably. Keep in mind that due to the complexity of language, coders will always need to draw on their intuitions about what language does and means. No amount of effort in constructing a coding scheme will eliminate the need for a coder to use interpretive judgment in coding. It is impossible, in other words, for a coding scheme to be as "complete and unambiguous" as Neuendorf (2016) exhorts. Instead, the best coding schemes work with, massage, and otherwise direct a coder's intuitions into ways of interpretation intended by the researcher.

Mutual Exclusivity in Coding

Although there are variations that we discuss at the end of this chapter, in general, each segment should be assigned to one and only one code. That is, the codes should be mutually exclusive. Mutual exclusivity refers to the requirement that each piece of data should be assigned to one and only one code. It is often seen as one of the major dividing practices between qualitative and quantitative approaches to coding. In fact, some content analysts suggest that non-mutual exclusivity is a "fatal flaw" in qualitative approaches (Boettger & Palmer, 2010; Bourque, 2004; Stemler, 2001). Examined more closely, however, these two analytic traditions are often closer than we might expect. In fact, mutual exclusivity is best understood in terms of what we'll call the dimensionality of verbal data.

Language is inherently multidimensional. As a consequence, coding frequently has dimensions to it as well. In practical terms, this often means that an analyst considering how to code a piece of language often sees multiple ways to code it. This will be true whether one is approaching coding from the perspective of content analysis, in which the goal is to create mutually exclusive categories, or from the perspective of qualitative analysis, in which double coding is not uncommon.

Where content coding and qualitative coding do differ is in what they do in the face of this inclination to double code. Krippendorff (2013), one of the leading scholars of content analysis, suggests that the inclination to double code arises out of a conceptual confusion over what one is looking for (p 132). In this case, the best solution is to more clearly distinguish among the dimensions of the data. In this way, a scheme that looks like it is not mutually exclusive might be developed into a set of dimensions.

For example, in developing a coding scheme for a set of interviews with students from a writing class, an analyst might first be inclined to create a four-code system.[5]

> **Concept:** Code as Concept any explanation of a concept covered in class.
>
> **Process:** Code as Process all expressions of the student engaging in any process related to writing.
>
> **Value:** Code as Value any expression of beliefs or values about the concept or process.
>
> **Problem:** Code as Problem, any instance of expressing a problem with a process.

The analyst finds, however, that she is inclined to double code statements like the following:

> "I'm a real procrastinator, so I just start writing without an outline."

Here the analyst sees evidence of a problem (*procrastinator*), a process (*start writing*), and a concept (*outline*).

---

[5] We want to thank Barbara Bird, Dean of Faculty Development at Taylor University, for allowing us to share this example with readers.

Following Krippendorf, we find opportunities to untangle multiple dimensions in this scheme. Even the code definitions themselves seem to suggest one dimension related to writing topics (concepts or processes), and perhaps two other dimensions, one related to values and the other related to problems (although these two might be able to be combined). The Writing Topics dimension would have two mutually exclusive codes (concept or process). The statements in the Values and Problem dimensions might just be coded as present or absent, or might be further developed to reflect possible kinds of values (positive, negative . . .) or problems.

Overall then, a one-dimension scheme that originally contained four categories that were not mutually exclusive could be developed into a three-dimensional analysis where each dimension had its own mutually exclusive codes. Thus, as Neuendorf (2016) seems to suggest, mutual exclusivity can best be understood as the outcome of the work of developing a coding scheme rather than as a stipulated pre-condition.

In qualitative analysis, the value of mutual exclusivity is often rejected outright as rigid systematicity. But Saldaña (2016) acknowledges that the use of many such "simultaneous codes" can be a sign of researcher indecisiveness. He also suggests that while many first cycle approaches to coding allow for multiple codes to be applied to the same piece of data, many second cycle approaches try to do work similar to that described for content analysis. That is, they take a hodgepodge of coding categories created during the first cycle of coding and try to organize and condense them onto a small set of non-overlapping categories that capture underlying relationships.

The process of code development that we outline in this book works toward mutual exclusivity as the foundation for a systematic and reliable analysis. In the rest of this chapter, we walk you through the process of building a coding scheme.

Getting Ready to Code

Developing a coding scheme involves an iterative process of moving back and forth between the developing scheme and a sample of the data to be coded.

Selecting a Sample

Select parts of the stream of verbal data that can be easily coded in one sitting while at the same time giving you enough data to see all the relevant variations of your phenomenon. Your goal is to see enough of the data to develop a coding scheme that is comprehensive. Give some care to deciding how to select this initial sample. You will want to maximize the amount of variation in the phenomenon being investigated. In most situations, this means selecting a sizable amount of data from both sides of any contrasts you have built into your design.

From each side of the built-in contrast, try to select a part of the stream of verbal data that represents the best case for the phenomenon: From one side of the contrast, choose the part of the data in which the phenomenon is most obvious, or strongest. On the other side of the contrast, choose a part of the data in which you expect the phenomenon to be different. This initial comparison can be quite simple, for example choosing samples where the phenomenon might differ in terms of strength, sophistication, or focus. The aim of the comparison is to understand your built-in contrast a little better, especially in terms of how an emerging coding scheme might change along the lines of the contrast. Focusing on the differences between cases in your contrast will help you develop a coding scheme that highlights those differences.

How much data should you select? Select too little data and your coding scheme may not contain references to code categories that are relevant to the larger data set. Select too much data and you will code more than you need to establish the regularities you want to track. As a rule of thumb, you will want to select somewhere between 200 and 500 segments if they are shorter units (clauses, t-units, etc.) and significantly fewer if you are working with longer units (exchanges, topical units), maybe 50–100. Overall, you want to balance the amount to be read (10 pages seems about the most that someone can code initially), the number of segments to be coded, and the range of the phenomenon to be considered. Move each part of your contrasting sample into Excel or MAXQDA using the procedures described in Chapter 3.

In the Excel example to be used in this chapter, as shown in Figure 4.2, we begin with the data after it is segmented and moved to a spreadsheet. In this case, the data are taken from the email exchanges between users of a 3D imaging software package and are focused on the different ways that participants frame their discussion of the software. The data have been segmented using the clause as the unit of analysis. The data recorded for each segment of user action consist of the unit number (column A), the year posted to the list (column B), the writer (hidden in column C), and the clause itself (column D). Frame (column E) and Alignment (column f) represent the coding dimensions applied to this data set.

Unit	Year	Content	Frame	Alignment
1	2011	I'm a student of a Biomedical Engineering Master of Barcelona,		
2	2011	and I'm doing my Master Thesis about virtual endoscopy.		
3	2011	Specifically I'm trying the endoscopy module of the 3D slicer in the Abdominalatlas2011 data set.		
4	2011	First I'm testing the navigation mode,		
5	2011	I create a Fiduacil list and Fly through,		
6	2011	but I wanted to know if it possible to record		
7	2011	and make a video of the navigation.		
8	2011	From the other hand I also wanted to know if it is possible to		
9	2011	and how can I create a centerline to place the fiducials in it to navigate.		

Figure 4.2: Segmented data for coding.

Managing Coding

To manage the coding, always store your coding scheme in a way that is directly linked to the data that has been coded with that scheme. When you return to the data after days, months, or even years, this practice will alleviate the need to hunt for the scheme underlying an analysis. It will also enable you to keep track of which version of a coding scheme was used, with which set of coded data. Otherwise, proliferating coding schemes and multiple copies of data sets can make your life unbearable. See Excel Procedure 4.1 and MAXQDA Procedure 4.1.

Excel Procedure 4.1: Linking to Coding Scheme in Excel

https://goo.gl/5Q4Jgr

You can link coded data to its coding scheme in one of three ways:

1. Write your coding scheme in a separate document file.
2. Link to it with a hyperlink from your Excel workbook.

Or

3. Write your coding scheme in a separate worksheet in your Excel workbook.

Or

4. Insert the coding categories and definitions as a comment using **Insert** > **New Comment** as shown in Figure 4.3.

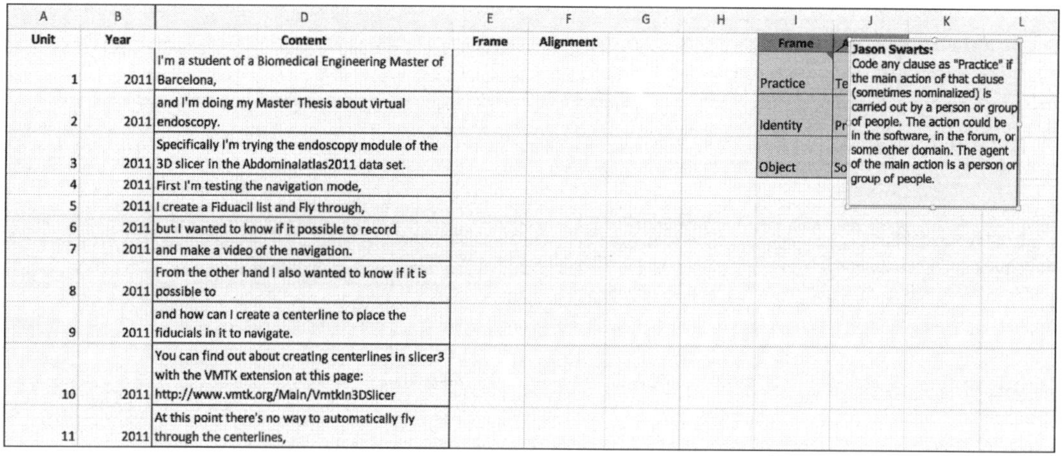

Figure 4.3 Inserting coding definitions as comments in Excel.

MAXQDA Procedure 4.1: Linking to Your Coding Scheme in MAXQDA

https://goo.gl/5Q4Jgr

In MAXQDA, your coding scheme is stored in the **Code System** window. Full definitions are stored as memos attached to each code name. To open the full coding scheme:

1. Double click on the **Memo** icon for each code in the order in which they are to be considered.

All of the relevant codes will apear in a tabbed **Memo** window as shown in Figure 4.4.

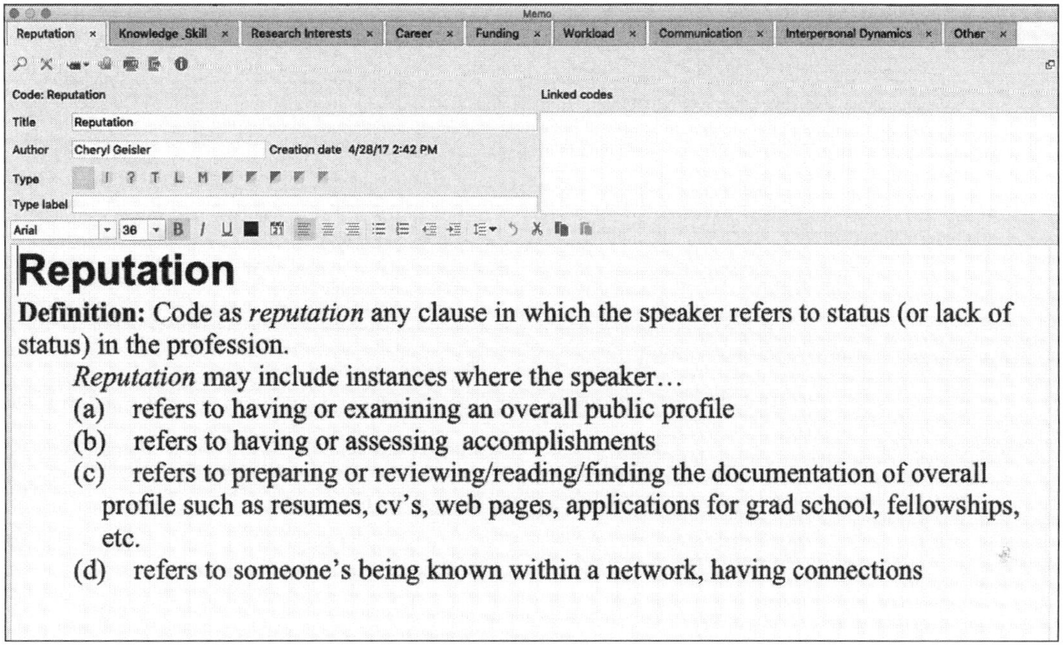

Figure 4.4 Opening the full coding scheme in MAXQDA.

Deciding on a Coding Framework

Two methods exist for generating a coding scheme. In the first, you begin with existing categories. Your review of the literature, while designing the analysis, might have suggested coding categories that characterize the phenomenon of interest. Or your work on the analytic design may have already suggested the ways in which the built-in contrasts in your data set should be different. And finally, especially if you have mucked around in a site, you may have strong intuitions about what to look for. All three of these sources—literature, built-in contrasts, and intuition—should be consulted to create a "start list" of possible categories that may be relevant to coding. You will, of course, need to extend and modify this start list as you go along, in order to mold your categories more appropriately to the data.

The second method for generating a coding scheme is to look at the initial data set and let it "speak to you." That is, you let each segment of the data suggest appropriate categories to describe what is happening with the phenomenon of interest. Such categories are more grounded in the data than those gleaned from external sources like the literature but cannot help but be influenced by the knowledge and experience you bring to the analysis.

Although in this second method of developing a coding scheme you are letting the data speak to you, the process of developing coding categories need not be without structure. Books on coding, discourse analysis, rhetorical theory, social theory, or others can provide useful interpretive frameworks for narrowing your investigation of the data based on what you suspect to be of interest in the phenomenon of study. For example, any of the following might be useful frameworks for investigating your data:

- Relationships Coding: the researcher pays attention to formal or informal connections between people or things, especially when the phenomenon of interest might be interpersonal or intrapersonal relationships (e.g., see Gee, 2005).
- Values Coding: the researchers pays attention to words and phrases that indicate values, attitudes, and beliefs expressed in the verbal data stream. This approach may be useful if the phenomenon of interest is

thought to be influenced by belief systems or cultural values (Saldaña, 2016, pp. 131–132).

- Practices Coding: the researcher pays attention to words and phrases that indicate the presence of an emerging practice. This approach might be useful for seeing if a group of people interact as a community (e.g., see Wenger, 1998).
- Genre Coding: the researcher pays attention to words and phrases that define a conventional and habitual form of written or spoken communication. This approach might be useful for seeing attention to recurring work that is supported with written or spoken discourse (e.g., see Bazerman, 1988)

Choosing codes for exploring the data can be a matter of intuition or it can be suggested by the design of your analysis. Often you will try to code the data using more than one coding pass, until deciding on one that will lead to a productive analysis. The process can be time consuming, but it is better to spend that time at this stage of the research than to discover later on, in the analysis, that your coding scheme is not capturing characteristics of the phenomenon that are most interesting to you.

Finally, a somewhat less structured approach to letting the data speak to you would be using the results of a keyword or collocation analysis that we suggested in Chapter 2. The data resulting from a study of keywords in AntConc can sometimes point to clusters of words that have some shared "aboutness" (Scott, 1997) that could suggest a code. For example, studying interactions between tutors and students in a writing center might reveal keywords such as "tell" or "read" or "explain" which could suggest a focus on coding tutor actions.

Using a Coding Scheme

The process of developing a coding scheme, no matter how you started it, involves the same process (see Excel Procedure 4.2 and MAXQDA Procedure 4.2). Take each segment in your initial data sample and try to assign it one of the codes in your scheme. As long as such an assignment can be made, coding continues. You should assign each segment of data to one and only one category in the coding scheme. As shown in Figure 4.5, for example, each segment of the sample data has been coded for *Frame*. Segments 13, 14, and 15 all fit under the category of *Object* since they are describing or naming a feature of the software under discussion.

	A	B	D	E	F	G	H
14	13	2011	Also, the info pasted below should help you get the slicer images in a format that can be used to make a movie of the fly through.	Object			
15	14	2011	It is possible to convert a centerline from the VMTKCenterline module to a FiducialList.	Object			
16	15	2011	There is a panel for that in the module.	Object			
17	16	2011	This fiducialList can be the input for the Endoscopy module.				
18	17	2011	I stand corrected				
19	18	2011	I guess you looked at the documentation of VMTKCenterlines (http://www.slicer.org/slicerWiki/index.php/Modules:VMTKCenterlines)				
20	19	2011	and did not find the feature there..				
21	20	2011	Somebody must have forgotten to document it.. ;)				
22	21	2011	Thank you very much,				
23	22	2011	that information was really useful.				
24	23	2011	Otherwise, I have some problems to save all the fiducials lists (seeds, targets) and centerline,				

Figure 4.5 Assigning a code in Excel.

Excel Procedure 4.2: Assigning a Code in Excel

https://goo.gl/5Q4Jgr

To assign a code to a unit of data in Excel:

1. Label the coding column with the name of the coding dimension.
2. Position your cursor in the coding column in the cell that is adjacent to the unit to be coded.
3. Type in the name of the code you want to assign.

Once you have assigned a code, using it again is relatively easy with Excel's auto-completion.

4. Position your cursor in the coding column next to the unit to be coded.
5. Start typing the code.

As soon as you type the first few letters of a code you have used previously, Excel will automatically suggest that completion.

6. To select it, hit enter.

To use auto-completion effectively, it is best to use codes that are distinct in their first few letters.

Revising a Coding Scheme

When you encounter a segment that is not covered in the coding scheme, you need to revise your scheme. The process of revising your coding scheme should accomplish two things. First, the revision process helps you to come up with a set of coding categories that best reveal the distinctions that you consider important in tracking the phenomenon of interest. Second, and almost as important, the revision process should help you to understand the phenomenon of interest better—what is it that you are coding for? In the next few sections we talk about further development of coding schemes to reflect this growing understanding.

Clarifying a Definition

If you encounter a unit that you feel sure belongs in a specific coding category, but which does not clearly fit your working definition, you may need to clarify the coding definition. Coding definitions may be clarified by revising the coding definition, by adding cases to indicate the kinds of phenomena to which a

MAXQDA Procedure 4.2: Assigning a Code in MAXQDA

https://goo.gl/5Q4Jgr

Many different ways exist to assign codes in MAXQDA; here we cover just a few of them. You may want to consult the online documentation for more possibilities.

1. Select the paragraph number next to the unit to be coded.
2. Drag the selected unit onto the desired code in the list of codes found in the **Code System** window.

You will notice that the last code chosen is visible in the code drop down list in the **Document Browser** toolbar as shown in Figure 4.6. If you want to choose this code again,

3. Click on the **Code symbol** to the right of the drop down list in the **Document Browser** toolbar.

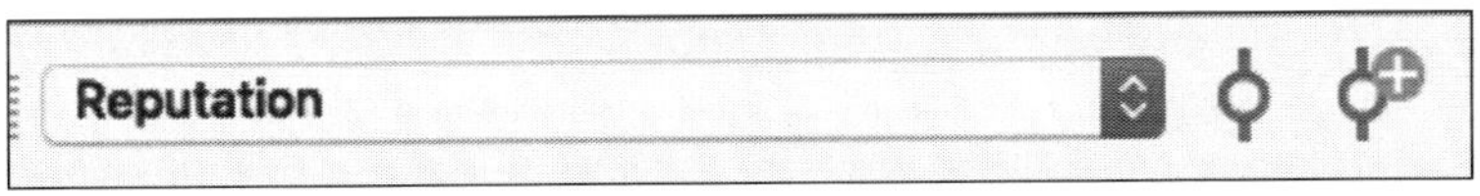

Figure 4.6: Assigning a code in MAXQDA.

code applies, by adding examples to illustrate those cases—or all of the above. In general, clarification is the easiest way to revise a coding scheme and is the one you should consider before more complex revisions.

Adding a Category

If you feel that a unit does not fit into any of your existing categories, you may want to add a new category (see Excel Procedure 4.3 and MAXQDA Procedure 4.3). For example, when the coder reached Segment 36 in our example, she realized that the statement "Anything else would require programming" was not really a reference to a practice, but innovation of the software. So she added a new code *Innovation* to cover the case. Applying codes and generating new codes as needed continues until the sample of data taken for initial coding has been coded.

Breaking a Category Apart

Breaking a category apart is required when you realize that you have been lumping together phenomena that need to be distinguished. For example, suppose the coder has reached Segment 36, in which the user stated that "Anything else would require programming," and instead of deciding that this clause was a different kind of frame (*Innovation* as opposed to *Practice*) she decided that innovation was really just a different kind of *Practice* in that it is a way of interacting with the software. In this case, the *Practice* code would need to be broken apart.

Once you decide to break apart an existing code into components, begin by editing your coding scheme to remove the current category and replace it with codes for the new categories (see Excel Procedure 4.3 and MAXQDA Procedure 4.3). Next, review all data coded thus far and recode with the new codes using the procedure described below. Thus, if our coder decided to split the *Practice* code into different kinds of practices, she would need to add codes for *Innovation* and other kinds of practice that are differentiated from *Innovation* (e.g., *Update*, *Use*, etc.). She would then revise the coding for all of the segments coded so far, accounting for the new coding scheme.

Excel Procedure 4.3: Creating a Code in Excel

https://goo.gl/5Q4Jgr

To create a new code in Excel, as shown in Figure 4.7:

1. Add a new code to your coding scheme.
2. After the code name include the unit of analysis to which it applies, and a definition of the coding category in the following form:

   Code as [code name] any [unit] that [definition].

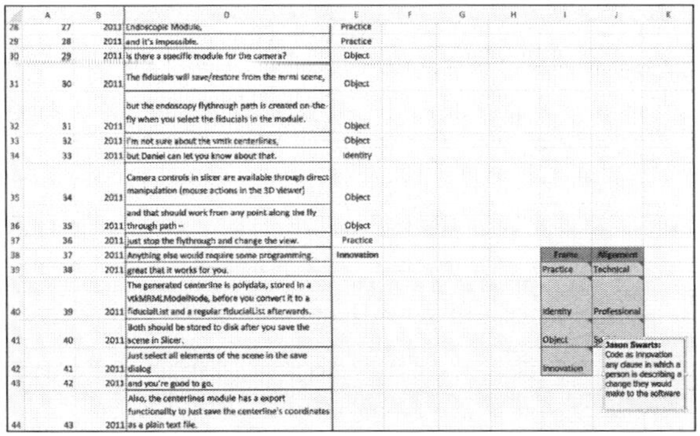

Figure 4.7 Creating a code within Excel.

You need not add cases and examples at this point, but you may want to as you encounter them.

MAXQDA Procedure 4.3: Creating a Code in MAXQDA

https://goo.gl/5Q4Jgr

To create a new code in MAXQDA:

1. Click on the code symbol with the plus sign in the **Document Browser** toolbar.
2. Type the name of the code into the resulting dialog window.
3. Use the **Memo** field to write a definition in the following form:

   Code as [code name] any [unit] that [definition].

Your new code will now be listed in the **Code System** window.

Be careful about how you split categories into sub-components. Make sure that the new distinctions that you are entering into your coding scheme are both relevant to your phenomenon of interest and at the same level as the remaining codes in your scheme. In other words, codes within a single dimension should have a parallelism to them. For example, once our coder splits the *Practice* code, she may begin to wonder whether the remaining codes in her coding scheme, also need further refinement. If there are multiple kinds of *Practice*, perhaps the same is true of *Object* and *Identity*. Deciding whether to take this course of action, however, requires you to consider the net benefit to analysis gained by making your coding scheme more complicated.

Collapsing Categories

At other times, you may find that working up to a coding scheme from early exploratory coding leaves you with too many coding categories, not all of which are distinct enough to stand alone. If you find that there are some segments of data that are not easily or definitively placed in a particular coding category, it may be worthwhile to collapse coding categories together.

Before taking this step, verify that two other kinds of corrections might not work better. First, consider whether there is some ambiguity in the wording of two code definitions that could be clarified in a way that makes coding of all segments clearer. Second, consider how often you encounter the segments that are unclear. If appropriate, you can make a decision about segments that are unclear and specify that they should be included in one coding category over the other. If neither of these fixes solves the problem, you may need to collapse codes together.

The advantage of combining codes is that the coding decisions become a little bit easier since the code category is larger and more inclusive. Less coder discrimination among segments is now required. The clear disadvantage is that in making coding decisions easier, the coder loses some ability to tease apart one code from another. This is only a problem if that distinction matters to the analysis. In some cases, it may not. If you do combine codes, the same reconstructive work required for breaking code categories apart also applies to collapsing categories. The coder must go back through the previously coded work and collapse together codes that were once separate.

Re-coding Data

When you decide to revise, add, or collapse codes in your coding scheme, you will need to recode the data you have coded thus far (see Excel Procedure 4.4, MAXQDA Procedure 4.4, and MAXQDA Procedure 4.5). Going through the data a second time with new coding categories in mind can help you to spot the consequences of your revisions. It is often the case that a new or revised code affects far more data than you originally expect.

Excel Procedure 4.4: Re-coding Data in Excel

https://goo.gl/5Q4Jgr

To try out a new coding scheme:

1. Add a new coding column as shown in Figure 4.8.
2. Use it to apply your new coding categories.

Which coding scheme better gets at what you are interested in?

It is not at all uncommon for a coder to decide that the first scheme is better than the more detailed scheme. If this is the case, then keeping rather than deleting the first coding will save a great deal of reconstructive work.

	A	B	D	E	F	G	H	I
1	Unit	Year	Content	Frame	Alignment	Frame		
29	28	2011	and it's impossible.	Practice	Technical			
30	29	2011	Is there a specific module for the camera?	Object	Technical			
31	30	2011	The fiducials will save/restore from the mrml scene,	Object	Technical			
32	31	2011	but the endoscopy flythrough path is created on-the-fly when you select the fiducials in the module.	Object	Technical			
33	32	2011	I'm not sure about the vmtk centerlines,	Object	Technical			
34	33	2011	but Daniel can let you know about that.	Identity	Social			
35	34	2011	Camera controls in slicer are available through direct manipulation (mouse actions in the 3D viewer)	Object	Technical			
36	35	2011	and that should work from any point along the fly through path –	Object	Technical			
37	36	2011	just stop the flythrough and change the view.	Practice	Technical	Use		
38	37	2011	Anything else would require some programming.	Practice	Professional	Innovation		
39	38	2011	great that it works for you.	Identity	Social			
40	39	2011	The generated centerline is polydata, stored in a vtkMRMLModelNode, before you convert it to a fiducialList and a regular fiducialList afterwards.	Object	Technical			
41	40	2011	Both should be stored to disk after you save the scene in Slicer.	Object	Technical			
42	41	2011	Just select all elements of the scene in the save dialog	Practice	Technical	Use		
43	42	2011	and you're good to go.	Identity	Social			
44	43	2011	Also, the centerlines module has a export functionality to just save the centerline's coordinates as a plain text file.	Object	Technical			
45	44	2011	This file can be also imported again using the centerlines module.	Practice	Technical	Use		
46	45	2011	I'm trying now to create a surface model from an abdominal TAC (800 DICOM images).	Identity	Professional	Use		
47	46	2011	I would like to know	Identity	Professional			
48	47	2011	which is the best module to create the labelmap of the colon.	Object	Technical			
49	48	2011	After creating the label, how can I create the surface model to navigate through it?	Practice	Technical			

Figure 4.8: Adding a trial coding column in Excel.

MAXQDA Procedure 4.4: Re-coding Data in MAXQDA

https://goo.gl/5Q4Jgr

In MAXQDA, changes in your coding scheme will require you to review and possibly recode the data.

1. Double click the **Memo** icon next to the code you want to revise.
2. Edit the definition to make changes.
3. Read through your already coded data using this newly revised definition.
4. To delete a code from a segment, right click on the code and select delete.
5. To add a code to a segment, click on the segment number and apply the new code.

MAXQDA Procedure 4.5: Collapsing Coding Categories in MAXQDA

https://goo.gl/5Q4Jgr

If you want to collapse two categories into a new code in your coding scheme, make them into subcodes of the new code:

1. Click on the **New Code** icon in the **Code System** window.
2. Name and define the new code.
3. Drag the desired subcodes on top of the new code in the **Code System** window.

As shown in Figure 4.9, the dragged code becomes a subcode of the main code.

Figure 4.9: Making a subcode in MAXQDA.

Adding Another Dimension

A related problem to collapsing coding categories is one where a coder finds the need to apply two different codes to the same segment. As we have already said, a scheme should be so devised that the codes are mutually exclusive. If the two codes that you want to apply are of the same type and do belong to the same dimension, consider collapsing the codes together (e.g., *Use* and *Innovation*) but if the codes are different kinds of observations, then it may indicate that you are dealing with two dimensions of the phenomenon that ought to be coded separately.

A dimension is a range of variation, presented through a coding scheme, representing an aspect of the data that can stand as conceptually independent of other features. Each coding scheme should be associated with only one dimension of data variation that, in turn, should correspond to only one feature of the phenomenon of interest. When you realize that you are dealing with two distinct dimensions of your data, you should separate them, develop a separate coding scheme for each one, and then apply each scheme to the data separately (see Excel Procedure 4.5 and MAXQDA Procedure 4.6).

Excel Procedure 4.5: Adding a Dimension in Excel

https://goo.gl/5Q4Jgr

To add a dimension in Excel:

1. Create a new second coding scheme.
2. Create a new coding column in your data worksheet.

The new coding scheme should have all of the elements of a good scheme: the name of the new dimension, its coding categories, the unit of analysis, and at least a definition of each category.

You will most likely be moving a coding definition into your new scheme from your original coding scheme. But you will probably add other categories as well.

Each of your coding schemes should be developed and applied to the data in a separate pass. It is too much to ask a coder to work with more than one dimension at a time.

For example, when our coder wondered why *Innovation* should have its own code while *Use* does not, she could have begun to think about separating her analysis into two distinct dimensions. She might have realized that the code *Practice* did not so much represent a different kind of frame as much as a distinct way of engaging the software. For this reason, rather than revising the coding scheme for frame, then, our coder could instead create a new dimension for coding called Engagement and develop a coding scheme to track it. In this example, our coder would code the entire sample of data for Frame first and then return to do a second pass through the data on this new dimension of Engagement.

MAXQDA Procedure 4.6: Adding a Dimension in MAXQDA

https://goo.gl/5Q4Jgr

The best way to add a dimension in MAXQDA is to reorganize your codes into separate Code Sets, each of which represents a separate dimension. To create a new Code Set, as shown in Figure 4.10:

1. Right click on **Sets** in the **Code System** window.

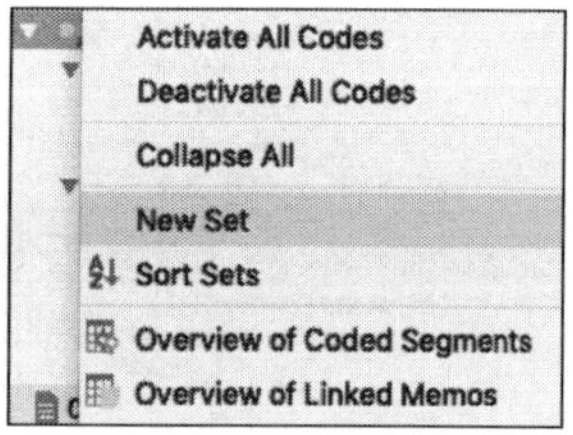

Figure 4.10: Creating a new code set in MAXQDA.

2. Choose the option to create a **New Set** and name it with the name of your first dimension.
3. Then drag and drop into the new set the appropriate codes from your **Code System** list.
4. To create your new second dimension, create a second **Code Set** in the same way.

To focus on a single dimension for coding:

5. Right click in the grey area of the coding column in the **Document Browser**. Choose the option **Only activated codes**.
6. Return to the **Code System** window and activate the current dimension's codes by clicking the small grey circles in front of the dimension's name.

Exercise 4.1 Test Your Understanding

Open any piece of writing from any source and segment that content into sentences. Use the coding scheme below to code that data. Pay attention to problems that arise in using this coding scheme, note those problems and discuss how to fix them.

- **Information:** Code as Information any sentence in which the author is reporting factual content.
- **Description:** Code as Description any sentence in which the author is relying on sensory information to create a mental picture for the reader.
- **Persuasion:** Code as Persuasion any sentence in which the author is using reasoning and evidence to advance a point.
- **Explanation:** Code as Explanation any sentence in which the author is making something clear by adding detail and motivation.
- **Humor:** Code as Humor any sentence in which the author is attempting to be funny.
- **Narration:** Code as Narration any sentence in which the author is telling a story.

For Discussion: What are the problems that you discovered when using this coding scheme? What are the different approaches for dealing with those problems?

Memo 4.1 Dimensions of Analysis

Reflect on your phenomenon of study and the qualities about it that interest you. Make a list of those qualities and begin sorting them into categories of like items. What are the potential dimensions of your analysis and what are the categories that belong to those dimensions?

Techniques for Inspecting Coding

As you develop a coding scheme during the iterative back and forth between data and scheme, you will often want to look at all of the data to which you have assigned a specific code. You can then check to see whether your coding decisions have been consistent (see Excel Procedure 4.6 and MAXQDA Procedure 4.7).

The most important technique for inspecting codes in Excel is Filtering. When you ask Excel to filter your data, you ask it to show you data that meets certain criteria and hide the rest. In Figure 4.11, for example, a Filter has been activated in Column B showing all data that has been coded as referring to units posted in 2011.

	A	B	D	E	F	G	H
1	Unit	Year	Content	Frame	Alignment		
29	28	2011	and it's impossible.	Practice	Technical		
30	29	2011	Is there a specific module for the camera?	Object	Technical		
31	30	2011	The fiducials will save/restore from the mrml scene,	Object	Technical		
32	31	2011	but the endoscopy flythrough path is created on-the-fly when you select the fiducials in the module.	Object	Technical		
33	32	2011	I'm not sure about the vmtk centerlines,	Object	Technical		
34	33	2011	but Daniel can let you know about that.	Identity	Social		
35	34	2011	Camera controls in slicer are available through direct manipulation (mouse actions in the 3D viewer)	Object	Technical		
36	35	2011	and that should work from any point along the fly through path –	Object	Technical		
37	36	2011	just stop the flythrough and change the view.	Practice	Technical		
38	37	2011	Anything else would require some programming.	Practice	Professional		
39	38	2011	great that it works for you.	Identity	Social		
40	39	2011	The generated centerline is polydata, stored in a vtkMRMLModelNode, before you convert it to a fiducialList and a regular fiducialList afterwards.	Object	Technical		
41	40	2011	Both should be stored to disk after you save the scene in Slicer.	Object	Technical		
42	41	2011	Just select all elements of the scene in the save dialog	Practice	Technical		
43	42	2011	and you're good to go.	Identity	Social		
44	43	2011	Also, the centerlines module has a export functionality to just save the centerline's coordinates as a plain text file.	Object	Technical		
45	44	2011	This file can be also imported again using the centerlines module.	Practice	Technical		
46	45	2011	I'm trying now to create a surface model from an abdominal TAC (800 DICOM images).	Identity	Professional		
47	46	2011	I would like to know	Identity	Professional		
48	47	2011	which is the best module to create the labelmap of the colon.	Object	Technical		

Figure 4.11: Using a filter to inspect coding in Excel.

Excel Procedure 4.6: Inspecting by Code in Excel

https://goo.gl/5Q4Jgr

To inspect by code in Excel:

1. Select the column containing the coding (Column B in this case).
2. Click **Data** > **Filter** from the toolbar.

Dropdown arrows will appear at the top of the column (Figure 4.11).

3. Click on the dropdown arrows and unselect the option **Select all**.
4. Then select the code that you would like to inspect (in this case 2011).
5. To turn the filter off, return to the **Filter** command under **Data** in the toolbar and deselect it.

MAXQDA Procedure 4.7: Inspecting by Code in MAXQDA

https://goo.gl/5Q4Jgr

Inspecting data by code is accomplished in MAXQDA in the **Retrieved Segments** window as shown in Figure 4.12.

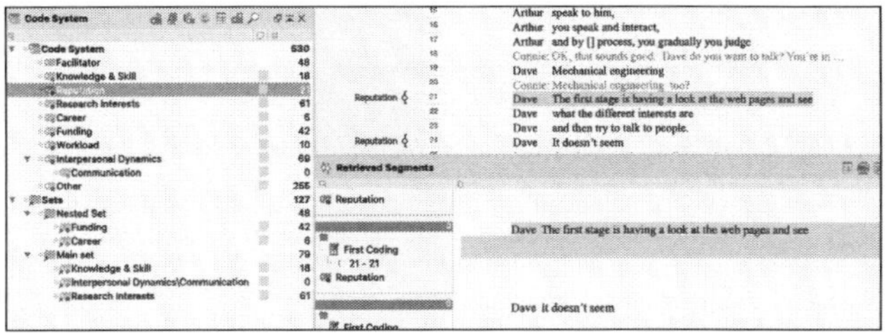

Figure 4.12: Retrieving data by the code Reputation in the Retrieved Segments window.

To retrieve data by code in MAXQDA:

1. Activate the document or documents you want to inspect in the **Document System** window.
2. Activate the code you want to inspect in the **Code System** window.
3. Scroll through the retrieved segments in the **Retrieved Segments** window.
4. To examine the segment in full context, click on the source information to its left in the **Retrieved Segments** window and the full context will appear in the **Document Browser** window.

Techniques for Automated Coding

Up to this point, we have largely been talking about using manual coding techniques for exploring your data. Working from a coding scheme, you apply a code category to each segment of data and then investigate the patterns. What you have likely noticed, both in developing and applying your code scheme, is that sometimes key terms or phrases seem to accompany your codes. If you are coding for hypothetical statements, for example, you might notice the presence of terms like "may" and "might" or phrases like "perhaps we can" or "maybe if" and recognizing these patterns can be the key to unlocking the potential of automated coding techniques to supplement the manual coding we have been discussing in this chapter so far. What follows is a brief overview of different ways to inspect your data for keywords in AntConc that might yield insights that lend themselves to automated coding.

Identifying Keywords in AntConc

The way that AntConc generates a list of keywords is by analyzing words and their frequencies in a study corpus by comparing it to a reference corpus. Often, a researcher will study keywords by choosing a reference corpus that offered some useful contrast with the study corpus. For example, one studying corporate apology letters might collect a sample of apology letters as a study corpus and then download an existing corpus of common business English to use as a reference corpus. Comparing the study corpus to the reference corpus would reveal words used in the apologies that are different from "normal" business English because of their unusual frequency. In our example, a comparison of corporate apologies against common business English might reveal the unusual frequency of words like "ensure" and "promise" and the way to interpret this result is that terms like "ensure" and "promise" are unique to the corporate apologies. They are key to understanding what apologies are about and how they differ from the "normal" business English to which they are compared. A simple keyword analysis can reveal a number of words that have keyness value, but not all matter for your analysis.

Although there are some free corpora for download (e.g., Supreme Court Decisions, Wikipedia) one need not go to such lengths to find a suitable reference corpus—you already have one in your built-in contrast. The data from your built-in contrast ought to be a sample of discourse that is akin to the discourse that you want to study but is different in that the phenomenon you want to study appears differently. This quality makes the contrast data a suitable reference corpus because it will highlight in the study corpus words that may be directly associated with the phenomenon that you want to study.

Load in your reference corpus and study corpus to AntConc following the instructions laid out in Chapter 2. To find keywords in the study corpus, begin by uploading a stopword list (see Procedure 4.1), which you can generate from a list of common stop words that is easily found on the internet. Just be careful because some stop lists will include common function words that may be important to your analysis (e.g., conditionals, modals, indexicals).

Procedure 4.1: Adding a Stop List in AntConc

https://goo.gl/5Q4Jgr

1. Click **Settings** > **Tool Preferences** and then click the **Word List** tool (Figure 4.13).
2. Add words in the **Add Word** field or upload a .txt file with a list of stop words using the **Add Words From File** field.

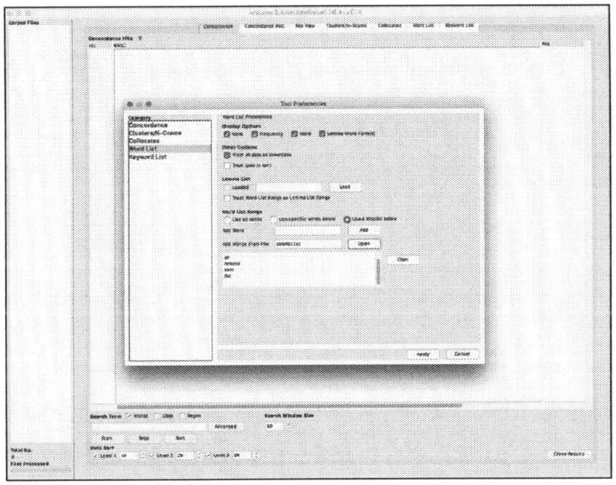

Figure 4.13 Adding a stop word list in AntConc.

Now you are ready to review your study corpus for a list of keywords.

Keyness is a measure of how unusually frequent the term is in your study corpus. Generally, a word with a keyness rating (Log-Likelihood, which is the default measure) higher than 3.84 is considered significant enough for further inspection (https://www.lancaster.ac.uk/fss/courses/ling/corpus/blue/l08_4.htm).

With this list of keywords to examine, your job is to investigate words that have some affinity to them and that match to a coding category in your coding scheme. For example, if we had a coding scheme for analyzing corporate apologies that used a dimension for classifying types of statements, a keyword list generated from a corpus of apology letters might reveal words like "ensure," "promise," and "unwavering" which seem to point to statements of commitment. It might also be the case that there are more collective references like "we," "us," and "team" which seem to indicate statements of shared responsibility. If these words have high keyness ratings then this inspection will show that those statements are important to understanding the "aboutness" of those apologies. In effect, the keyness analysis is a check on the meaningfulness of the codes you have incorporated into your scheme (see Procedure 4.2).

■ Examining Keyword Clusters in AntConc

We can also inspect the meaningfulness of our codes by looking at keywords in context. Sometimes seeing the words that the keywords are associated with can give a richer understanding of the "aboutness" of those terms, how they are used in the stream of language that you are studying. This further step can help you decide if those keywords are pointing to the phenomenon that you are most interested in studying.

The clusters that are returned in a search will give you a better indication of ways that your keywords are used in context and will help you verify if the keywords in a text are both aligning with your code categories and with the phenomenon of interest in the data (see Procedures 4.3, 4.4, and 4.5).

In the end, your inspection of keywords one at a time in the Concordance and Cluster tools will reveal to you which terms coincide best with the coding categories you have developed and will show you which terms and code categories offer you the most traction in analyzing your data set. Create lists of associated key terms for use in automated coding, which we cover in the next section.

Procedure 4.2: Generating Keywords in AntConc

https://goo.gl/5Q4Jgr

1. From the main AntConc screen, click the **Word List** tab and then **Start** to generate a list of words in your study corpus.
2. The list generated will show all words, minus stop words, grouped and ordered by frequency (Figure 4.14).
3. Click on the **Keyword List** tab and then **Start** for a list of keywords sorted by keyness. (Figure 4.15)

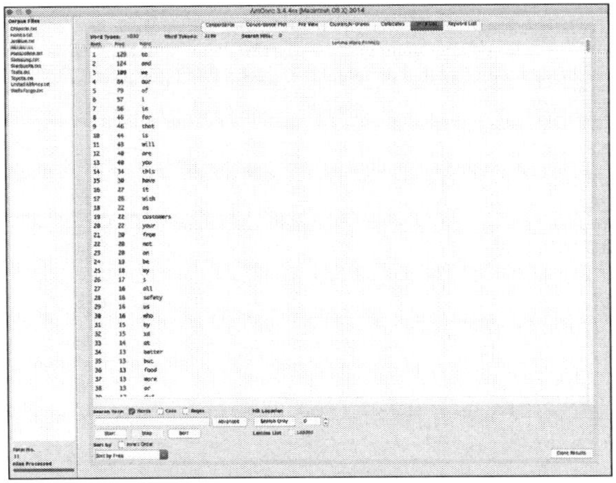

Figure 4.14: Word list function in AntConc.

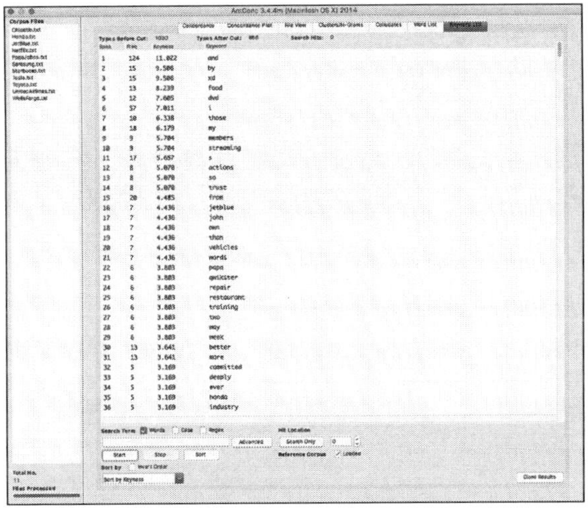

Figure 4.15 Keywords found in the study corpus.

Procedure 4.3: Examining Keywords in Context

https://goo.gl/5Q4Jgr

1. From the keyword list on the **Keyword** tab, click on any word that is of interest.

AntConc will redirect you to the **Concordance** tab, which will show a list of references to those key terms in context (Figure 4.16). You will see the word, the sentence that it appears in, and the file in which that sentence occurs.

2. Inspect the keyword in context.

Inspecting in this way can help you see how prevalent each keyword might be across the cases in the study corpus. The view will also let you see how frequently the term occurs and the contextual information will allow you to determine if the word is both a good indicator of a particular code category and if the code category points to something meaningful about Keyness in our verbal data phenomenon.

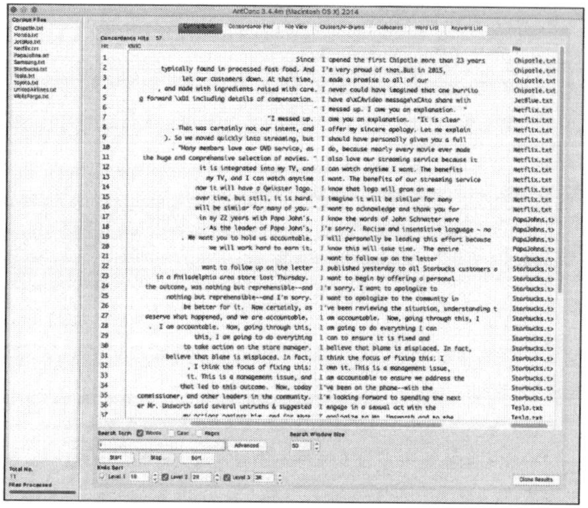

Figure 4.16 Seeing keywords in context in AntConc.

Procedure 4.4: Examining a List of Keywords in Context

https://goo.gl/5Q4Jgr

If you want to see an entire list of keywords in context, it is also possible to do that.

1. On the **Keyword** tab, type in one of your keywords in the search field and then click **Advanced**.
2. On the **Advanced** screen check the option for **Use search term(s)** from list below and enter the remaining keywords, each on its own line.
3. Click **Apply** and return to the **Cluster** tool.
4. Click **Start**.

The list returned will show the phrases for all of your keywords.

Procedure 4.5: Examining Keyword Custers

https://goo.gl/5Q4Jgr

You can further refine the code categories by looking at the word clusters that keywords appear in (Figure 4.17).

1. Click on the **Cluster/N-gram** tool.
2. Check the option **Search Term: Word**.

The **Cluster** tool will return phrases in which your searched keyword appears.

3. Set the parameters of the search by changing the **cluster size**, to designate how many words to the left and right to include in the cluster around your key term.
4. Set the minimum frequency (**Min.Freq.**) and minimum range (**Min. Range**) for your results.

Minimum frequency sets a lower threshold for how many times a cluster needs to appear in the study corpus before it is returned as a hit. Set this number fairly low to start.

The **minimum range** sets the lower threshold for the number of files or samples that the cluster must appear in to be returned in the results. You should also set this number fairly low to start.

5. Type in a search term (i.e. one of your keywords) and see what clusters are returned.

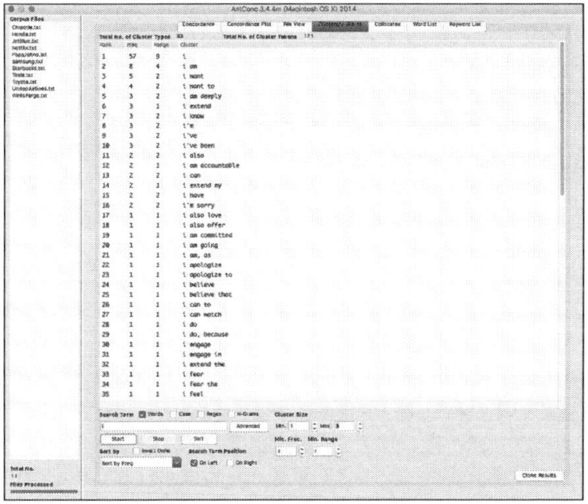

Figure 4.17 Analysis of a study corpus with clusters.

Memo 4.2: Emerging Patterns

Reflect on keywords that might be emerging from the data as you examine the results in AntConc. Consider what keywords might be worth deeper investigation. Consider also what these emerging keywords might mean in terms of your research questions.

Using Automated Coding

With manual coding the researcher is able to pay closer attention to details in the language and perhaps apply codes that require more interpretation. When using automated techniques, the researcher can more easily code greater quantities of data, even approaching the ability to code some corpora of data at scale (see Procedure 4.6, Excel Procedure 4.7, and MAXQDA Procedure 4.8). For example, imagine attempting to code a data set of interactions from student team meetings. If we are talking about data from a single semester, across a handful of classes, that is a manageable data set for manual coding. But imagine a larger data set that includes all student teams across all sections of a class across multiple years. Imagine now including student teams from different schools. The data set quickly gets out of hand as a project for the manual coder and heightens the appeal of tools that can be used for automating the coding, at least as a first pass in the analysis. In Figure 4.19, for example, we have an example where the clauses shown in Column D have been automatically coded for the presence or absence of various modals such as may, might, can, could, will, and would.

Correcting Autocoding

Procedures for automated coding will often overcode. That is, they will assign code to segments to which the code should not properly be applied. For this reason, most autocoding procedures require some kind of correction process. The easiest, though not quickest, way to correct autocoding is to inspect the coded data one segment at a time and remove any inappropriately applied codes. Often, the judicious use of wildcards or spaces in the search string can eliminate inappropriate matches. In any case, when setting up a new automated coding procedure, make sure to inspect the results of a small selection of data to insure you are getting what you intend.

Procedure 4.6: Automated Coding in Word

https://goo.gl/5Q4Jgr

1. Select the **Find** command under the **Edit** menu bar.
2. Select the the **Replace . . .** option.

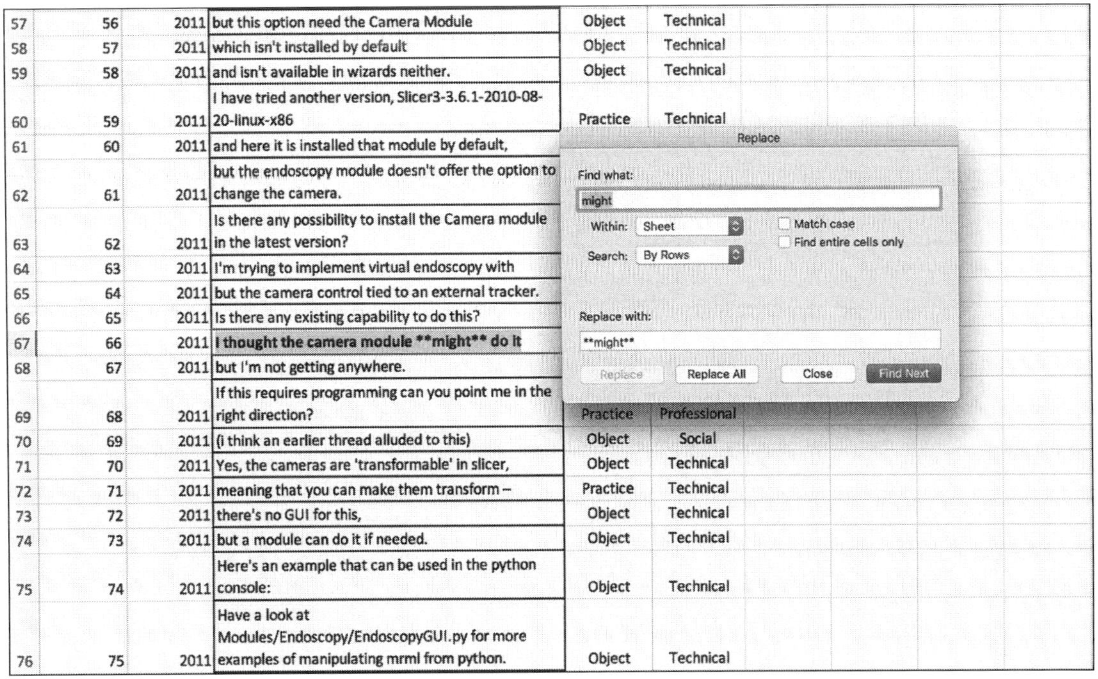

57	56	2011	but this option need the Camera Module	Object	Technical
58	57	2011	which isn't installed by default	Object	Technical
59	58	2011	and isn't available in wizards neither.	Object	Technical
60	59	2011	I have tried another version, Slicer3-3.6.1-2010-08-20-linux-x86	Practice	Technical
61	60	2011	and here it is installed that module by default,		
62	61	2011	but the endoscopy module doesn't offer the option to change the camera.		
63	62	2011	Is there any possibility to install the Camera module in the latest version?		
64	63	2011	I'm trying to implement virtual endoscopy with		
65	64	2011	but the camera control tied to an external tracker.		
66	65	2011	Is there any existing capability to do this?		
67	66	2011	**I thought the camera module **might** do it**		
68	67	2011	but I'm not getting anywhere.		
69	68	2011	If this requires programming can you point me in the right direction?	Practice	Professional
70	69	2011	(i think an earlier thread alluded to this)	Object	Social
71	70	2011	Yes, the cameras are 'transformable' in slicer,	Object	Technical
72	71	2011	meaning that you can make them transform –	Practice	Technical
73	72	2011	there's no GUI for this,	Object	Technical
74	73	2011	but a module can do it if needed.	Object	Technical
75	74	2011	Here's an example that can be used in the python console:	Object	Technical
76	75	2011	Have a look at Modules/Endoscopy/EndoscopyGUI.py for more examples of manipulating mrml from python.	Object	Technical

Figure 4.18: Using find and replace to highlight key words.

3. As shown in Figure 4.18, type the specific word or phrase to be automatically coded (such as might) into the **Find** field and something easier to find (such as **might**) in the **Replace** field.
4. Click **Replace All**.

Not only will Word make all the replacements, but it will also report to you how many such replacements it made.

Excel Procedure 4.7: Automated Coding in Excel

https://goo.gl/5Q4Jgr

Automated pattern matching in Excel is accomplished as follows:

1. Into Row 1, type the keyword or phrase you want to code for.
2. Into the first data cell of your coding column, type the following formula:

   =IF(ISERR(SEARCH(PATTERN,SEGMENT)),0,PATTERN)

3. Edit the formula as follows:
   - Replace PATTERN with the name of the coding column followed by $1.
   - Replace SEGMENT with the name of the cell in which the first data segment is found preceded by a $.
4. Drag the formula down to fill the rest of the column until the last line of data.

	A	B	D	E	F	G	H	I	J	K	L	M
1	Unit	Year	Content	Frame	Alignment	may	might	can	could	will	would	
2	1	2011	I'm a student of a Biomedical Engineering Master of Barcelona,	Identity	Professional	0	0	0	0	0	0	
3	2	2011	and I'm doing my Master Thesis about virtual endoscopy.	Identity	Professional	0	0	0	0	0	0	
4	3	2011	Specifically I'm trying the endoscopy module of the 3D slicer in the Abdominalatlas2011 data set.	Practice	Technical	0	0	0	0	0	0	
5	4	2011	First I'm testing the navigation mode,	Practice	Technical	0	0	0	0	0	0	
6	5	2011	I create a Fiduacil list and Fly through,	Practice	Technical	0	0	0	0	0	0	
7	6	2011	but I wanted to know if it possible to record	Practice	Technical	0	0	0	0	0	0	
8	7	2011	and make a video of the navigation.	Practice	Technical	0	0	0	0	0	0	
9	8	2011	From the other hand I also wanted to know if it is possible to	Identity	Technical	0	0	0	0	0	0	
10	9	2011	and how can I create a centerline to place the fiducials in it to navigate.	Practice	Technical	0	0	can	0	0	0	
11	10	2011	You can find out about creating centerlines in slicer3 with the VMTK extension at this page: http://www.vmtk.org/Main/Vmtkln3DSlicer	Practice	Technical	0	0	can	0	0	0	
12	11	2011	At this point there's no way to automatically fly through the centerlines,	Object	Technical	0	0	0	0	0	0	
13	12	2011	so you would need to add fiducials at key points along the centerline you want to follow.	Practice	Technical	0	0	0	0	0	would	
14	13	2011	Also, the info pasted below should help you get the slicer images in a format that can be used to make a movie of the fly through.	Object	Social	0	0	can	0	0	0	
15	14	2011	it is possible to convert a centerline from the VMTKCenterline module to a FiducialList.	Object	Technical	0	0	0	0	0	0	
16	15	2011	There is a panel for that in the module.	Object	Technical	0	0	0	0	0	0	
17	16	2011	This fiducialList can be the input for the Endoscopy module.	Object	Technical	0	0	can	0	0	0	
18	17	2011	I stand corrected	Identity	Social	0	0	0	0	0	0	
19	18	2011	I guess you looked at the documentation of VMTKCenterlines (http://www.slicer.org/slicerWiki/index.php/Module s:VMTKCenterlines)	Practice	Social	0	0	0	0	0	0	

Figure 4.19: Automated coding in Excel.

Note that, in Figure 4.19, we have an example where the clauses shown in Column D have been automatically coded for the presence or absence of various modals such as may, might, can, could, will, and would.

MAXQDA Procedure 4.8: Automated Coding in MAXQDA

https://goo.gl/5Q4Jgr

MAXQDA has a variety of procedures for automated coding which can be accessed under **Lexical Search** on the **Analysis** menu. To autocode in MAXQDA as shown in Figure 4.20:

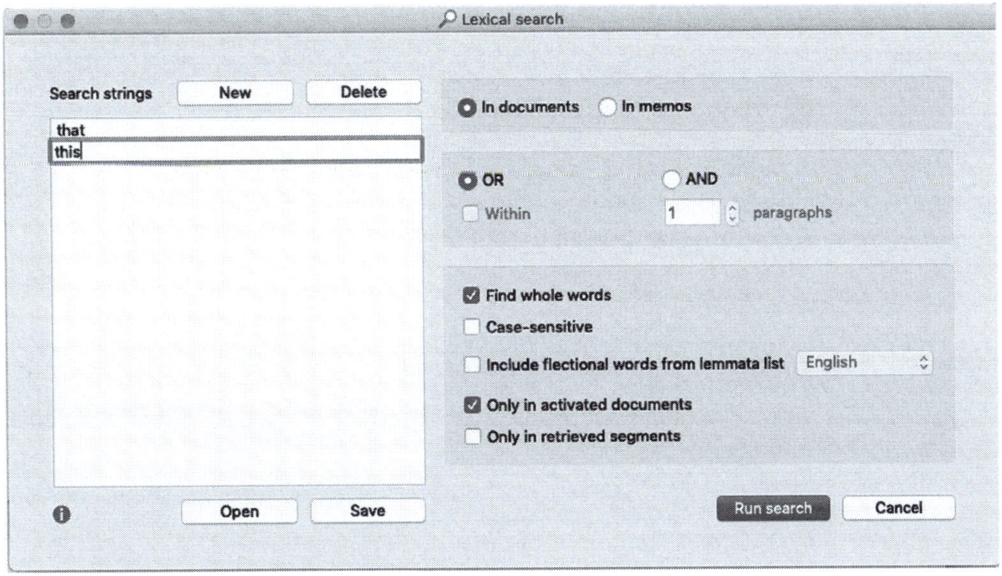

Figure 4.20: Autocoding with lexical search in MAXQDA.

1. Select **Lexical Search** from the **Analysis** menu.
2. Add keywords by clicking **New** and typing in one or more keywords for which you want to search.
3. Choose to search in documents and find whole words.
4. Click **Run Search**.
5. In the **Search Results** window, click on the **Autocode search results** icon and then chose the code with which you want to autocode.
6. Chose **paragraph** as the unit for autocoding and click **autocode**.
7. Inspect autocoded segments by clicking on the segment in the **Search Results** window.

The segment will appear in the **Document Browser** window.

Exercise 4.2 Try It Out

In one of your data files, use automated coding for the word "we" in either Excel or MAXQDA. Inspect and describe the results. Which of these are appropriate? Which of these are plainly wrong. Devise one or two methods to reduce the errors.

For Discussion: Under what circumstances could you imagine using automatic coding with your data? What is it good for? In what ways is it limited?

■ Nested Coding

A complex coding situation can arise when you want to nest one coding scheme within another. Suppose you code the conversational turns of a tutor in a writing center using a coding scheme that includes *responds to text*, *discusses assignment*, and *talks about other things*. You then want to go on to look more closely at those turns that *responds to text*, to decide whether they were facilitative or directive. You would then be using nested coding schemes in which the second dimension (*facilitative* vs. *directive*) was applied selectively only to data that had been placed in a specific category as a result of the first coding scheme.

Nested coding can also be used following automated coding (see Excel Procedure 4.8 and MAXQDA Procedure 4.9). The automated coding produces a selection of segments that the second or nested coding can further analyze. Such a nesting procedure not only allows you to focus on the results of the automated coding but also allows you to correct for any overcoding that may have occurred.

■ Enumerative Coding Schemes

The kind of coding schemes we have been talking about so far in this chapter can be thought of as procedural. They provide decision rules that will allow us to place each segment into the category intended by the researcher.

A second kind of coding scheme exists that is enumerative rather than procedural. Instead of providing cases and examples of those cases, a complete

Excel Procedure 4.8: Nested Coding in Excel

https://goo.gl/5Q4Jgr

In Excel, to prepare for nested coding of data once the first coding is complete,

1. Grey out the cells for which no further coding is needed as shown in Figure 4.21.

Here, we are preparing to further code just those segments that were coded as "Indexed" using the first coding scheme in Column D.

2. Use the next column for your second nested coding as shown in Column E.

The dark shading in cells in Column E tells us that those particular segments are not to be coded, but by keeping them in the worksheet while we code, we have access to the full context of the surrounding segments.

	A	B	C	D	E	F	G	H
27	25	Cheryl	You did print it out?	Not indexed				
28	26	John	Ed printed it out.	Not Indexed				
29	27	Ed	I printed it out.	Not Indexed				
30	28	John	We all got a copy, and then I . . .	Not Indexed				
31	29	Cheryl	Oh, then I might have it here.	Indexed				
32	30	Ed	You might have it here,.	Indexed				
33	31	John	Folded it up	Not Indexed				
34	32	Cheryl	Oh, here it is.	Indexed				
35	33	John	Exactly, that's exactly it.	Indexed				
36	34	John	She's got it.	Not Indexed				
37	35	Cheryl	Oh, well I didn't take it out.	Not Indexed				
38	36	John	Okay	Not Indexed				
39	37	Cheryl	Well, I'll just put it in the folder here.	Indexed				
40	38	Cheryl	Well it's : okay.	Indexed				
41	39	John	Do you want	Not indexed				
42	40	John	me to read it to you?	Not Indexed				
43	41	Ed	We've eliminated side desks with private workstations.	Not Indexed				
44	42	John	Yes	Not Indexed				
45	43	Cheryl	Of course, I can't ...	Not Indexed				
46	44	John	Yes, we've eliminated	Not Indexed				
47	45	Cheryl	Wait a minute. I can't type here and be looking over there.	Indexed				
48	46	John	Yeah. I know	Not Indexed				
49	47	John	what you are saying.	Not Indexed				
50	48	John	We've eliminated side desks with private work stations.	Not Indexed				
51	49	John	We've preserved central table with built-in public screens.	Not Indexed				
52	50	John	We introduced a personal communications device which includes sketch pad, video capture, keyboard, mouse (or trackball) and the ability to display from remote machines.	Indexed				
53	51	John	We've added video and audio capture and video link for remote conferencing.	Not Indexed				
54	52	John	We're using	Not Indexed				
55	53	John	private computers remotely located or portables as the private workstations.	Indexed				
56	54	John	The private machines should be whatever platform	Indexed				
57	55	John	the user likes.	Indexed				
58	56	John	We are now thinking of this as a piece of furniture and not a room.	Indexed				
59	57	Cheryl	That's it.	Indexed				
60	Chart Area 8	John	Okay. Well, we're reviewing that for today,	Indexed				
61	59	John	I guess to see whether	Not Indexed				
62	60	John	we want to add anything.	Not Indexed				
63	61	Cheryl	Did we want to put anything about the number of :	Indexed				
64	62	John	there's some things in here.	Indexed				
65	63	John	Oh, the number of people.	Indexed				
66	64	Cheryl	Yeah, that it's variable;	Not Indexed				

Figure 4.21: Preparing for nested coding in Excel.

MAXQDA Procedure 4.9: Nested Coding in MAXQDA

https://goo.gl/5Q4Jgr

In MAXQDA, you can create nested coding using separate code sets for the main and nested coding as shown in Figure 4.22.

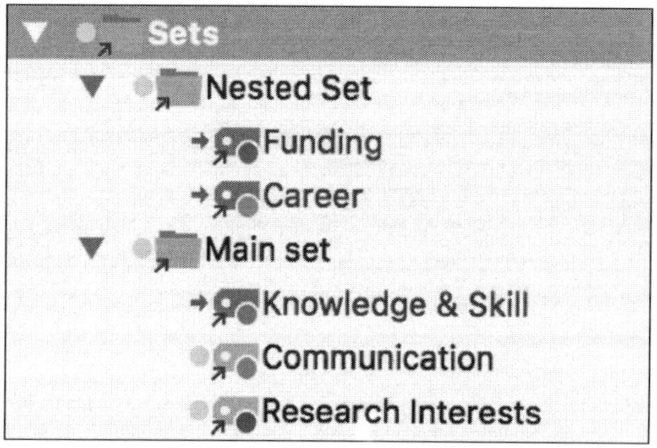

Figure 4.22: Main and nested coding sets in MAXQDA.

1. In the **Code System** window, right click on **Sets** and choose the **New Set** command.
2. Type in the name of your main dimension.
3. Drag and drop into the main coding set appropriate codes from your **Code System** list.
4. Right click in the grey area of the coding column in the **Document Browser** and choose the option **Only activated codes**.
5. Activate the main coding set.
6. Code your data with the main coding set.
7. To create your nested dimension, create a nested coding set by right clicking on **Sets** and choosing the **New Set** command.
8. Drag and drop into the nested coding set appropriate codes from your **Code System** list.
9. To code with the nested coding scheme only those segments that were coded with a specific code in the main dimension, activate just this specific code in the main coding set.
10. Use the codes in the nested code set to code the segments with visible codes (from the main coding set) in the **Document Browser**.

enumeration is provided. In Figure 4.23, for example, a complete enumeration is provided of the text codes used in a study of desktop activity. Each distinct text that was accessed during the desktop session is listed here and assigned its own number. In the data itself then, these numeric codes have been used to code the data for the dimension of Text.

	A	B	C	D	E	F
1	#	Structure	Header	Text		
2						
3	1	calendar	Daily Calendar [Feb 5]			
4	2	Out box	Out			
5	3	In box	In			
6	4	email	Activity Theory Refs	see email "activity theory refs" in research folder		
7	5	email	have you heard of this	I've been searching on sources for enculturation in professional writing and have come across a german journal more than a few times. It is called Die Unterrichtspraxis. Have you heard of this journal?		
8	6	email	have you heard of this	I'm afraid I haven't.		
9	7	email	Fabric.com: A "We Love You" Sale	Good Friday Morning. I hope this note finds you well and ready to enjoy a pleasant and relaxing weekend.		

Figure 4.23: Enumerative coding.

Generally, a procedural coding scheme is to be preferred to an enumerative scheme because neither your second coders nor your readers can hold in their minds and make meaning of long lists. A few important exceptions exist. First, if the dimension shows relatively small variation along recognizable categories, an enumerative list can suffice. Second, if the concept underlying the dimension is hard to grasp, perhaps because the distinction is part of the culture being studied but not part of the culture of your second coder or your readers, an enumeration may be the best way to communicate the fuzzy set.

Memo 4.3: Coding Scheme Rationale

Examine the coding scheme you have developed. Explain the choices behind it:

- What kind of coding scheme is it?
- How is it related to prior research?
- How does it address your research question?

Selected Studies Using Procedural Coding

Angeli, E. L. (2015). Three types of memory in emergency medical services communication. *Written Communication, 32*(1), 3–38.

Breuch, L. K., Bakke, A., Thomas-Pollei, K., Mackey, L. E. & Weinert, C. (2016). Toward audience involvement: Extending audiences of written physician notes in a hospital setting. *Written Communication, 33*(4), 418–451. https://doi.org/10.1177/0741088316668517.

Geisler, C., Rogers, E. H. & Haller, C. R. (1998). Disciplining discourse: Discourse practice in the affiliated professions of software engineering design. *Written Communication, 15*(1), 3–24. https://doi.org/10.1177/0741088398015001001.

Jones, J. (2008). Patterns of revision in online writing: A study of Wikipedia's featured articles. *Written Communication, 25*(2), 262–289.

Lancaster, Z. (2014). Exploring valued patterns of stance in upper-level student writing in the disciplines. *Written Communication, 31*(1), 27–57. https://doi.org/10.1177/0741088313515170.

Perl, S. (1979). The composing processes of unskilled college writers. *Research in the Teaching of English, 13*(4), 317–336.

Selected Studies Using Automated Coding

Abbasi, A. (2007). Affect intensity analysis of Dark Web forums. *IEEE Intelligence and Security Informatics* (pp. 282–288). https://doi.org/10.1109/ISI.2007.379486.

Steinfeld, N. & Lev-On, A. (2014). "Well-done, Mr. Mayor!": Linguistic analysis of municipal Facebook pages. *Proceedings of the 15th Annual International Conference on Digital Government Research*, USA, 273–279. https://doi.org/10.1145/2612733.2612763.

For Further Reading

Bazerman, C. (1988). *Shaping written knowledge. The genre and activity of the experimental article in science.* Madison, WI: University of Wisconsin Press.

Boettger, R. K. & Palmer, L. A. (2010). Quantitative content analysis: Its use in technical communication. *IEEE Transactions on Professional Communication, 53(4),* 346–357. https://doi.org/10.1109/TPC.2010.2077450.

Bourque, L. B. (2004). Coding. In M. S. Lewis-Beck, A. Bryman & T. Futing Liao (Eds.), *The Sage encyclopedia of social science research methods* (132–136). Thousand Oaks, CA: Sage.

Coffey, A. & Atkinson, P. (1996). Concepts and coding. In A. Coffey & B. Atkinson (Eds.), *Making sense of qualitative data: Complementary research strategies* (pp. 26–53). Thousand Oaks, CA: Sage.

Gee, J. P. (2005). *An introduction to discourse analysis: Theory and method.* New York: Routledge.

Kelle, U. (2000). Computer-assisted analysis: Coding and indexing. In M. W. Bauer & G. Gaskell (Eds.), *Qualitative researching with text, image, and sound* (pp. 282–298). Thousand Oaks, CA: Sage.

Krippendorff, K. (2013). *Content analysis: An introduction to its methodology* (3rd ed.). Los Angeles: Sage.

Kronberger, N. & Wagner, W. (2000). Keywords in context: Statistical analysis of text features. In M. W. Bauer & G. Gaskell (Eds.), *Qualitative researching with text, image, and sound* (pp. 299–317). Thousand Oaks, CA: Sage.

Miles, M. B. & Huberman, A. M. (1994). Codes and coding. In M. B. Miles, A. M. Huberman & J. Saldaña (Eds.), *Qualitative data analysis: An expanded sourcebook* (pp. 55–65). Thousand Oaks, CA: Sage.

Neuendorf, K. (2016). *The content analysis guidebook.* London: Sage Publications.

Saldaña, J. (2016). *The coding manual for qualitative researchers* (3rd ed.). Los Angeles: Sage.

Scott, M. (1997). PC analysis of key words—and key key words. *System,* 25(2), 233–245.

Stemler, S. (2001). An overview of content analysis. *Practical Assessment, Research & Evaluation,* 7(17). Retrieved from http://pareonline.net/getvn.asp?v=7&n=17.

Wenger, E. (1998). *Communities of practice: Learning, meaning, and identity.* Cambridge, UK: Cambridge University Press.

Chapter 5. Achieving Reliability

> In this chapter, you will work with a second coder to check intercoder agreement and use the results to revise your coding scheme. After you get a second coding on your data set, you will calculate the agreement between coders, using formulas for both simple and corrected agreement. You will then inspect the disagreements between coders and refine your analytic procedures to reduce them. This process should be repeated until an adequate level of agreement has been reached.

■ Introduction to Reliability

Reliability refers to the degree of consistency with which coding segments are assigned to the same categories. To say a coding scheme is reliable is to say that it can be used consistently, over and over again, to produce the same results, from day to day or coder to coder. That is, your coding scheme yields results that are replicable. When you achieve a reliable coding scheme, you assure yourself that the meaning of the coding scheme is clear to you and to those to whom you will be reporting your research.

The key tool in achieving a reliable coding scheme is intercoder agreement. Intercoder agreement is a measure of the extent to which coders assign the same codes to the same set of data. When two coders agree perfectly on their assignment of coders, they have an intercoder agreement of 100% or 1.0. When they totally disagree, they have an intercoder agreement of 0% or 0.0.

Perspectives on Intercoder Agreement

Perhaps no issue is more contentious in the coding of verbal data than reliability. Neuendorf (2016) argues that quantitative content analysis conducted in the positivist tradition should produce a "scientific" analysis that is reliable. That is, the phenomenon is expected to be stable and the analytic procedures so explicit than any reasonably qualified person would get the same results. In this view, the measuring instrument is the coding scheme, and that instrument is expected to work consistently.

In the qualitative tradition, positions on reliability are more varied. Those who favor a more subjective interpretation see the researcher herself as the measuring instrument, one honed by immersion in the context of the language production, producing interpretations that cannot be replicated by those outside that context. From this perspective, measuring reliability makes little sense as there is neither the need nor the possibility of achieving intercoder agreement.

Many qualitative researchers take a less radical approach to subjectivity and see interpretation as embedded in social life and thus able to be shared with others. Coding, then, need not be totally individualistic, but may be taken on by a team who work together to establish agreement among coders. Taking a grounded theory perspective, for example, Charmaz (2014) describes how team coding can contribute to a developing analysis:

> In team research, several individuals may code data separately and then compare and combine their codes to evaluate their fit and usefulness. Might one team member come up with different codes than other members? Yes, our perspectives, social locations, and personal and professional experiences affect how we code. Thus, team researchers can scrutinize how differences among team members may generate new insights, rather than dismiss a colleague's codes that differ.

Saldaña (2016) too refers to the role that checking intercoder agreement can play in a team coding environment, describing it as a kind of "crowd-sourcing reality check" (p. 36). For many qualitative researchers, then, intercoder agreement is valued as a tool for developing an analysis rather than a means for validating it.

■ The Role of Context in Limiting Intercoder Agreement

From our perspective, the extent to which two people looking at the same verbal phenomena will make the same interpretation depends upon the extent to which the context of interpretation overlaps with the context of production.

The conditions for overlap are not fixed, however. As the diagram in Figure 5.1 suggests, some phenomena are more transparent than others. With relatively transparent phenomenon, the limits of interpretation extend far from the context of production, nearly reaching to the boundaries of the context in which your analysis is to be interpreted. With opaque phenomenon, on the other hand, the limits of interpretation are wrapped tightly around the context of production and few if any outside of that context can expect to be able to interpret what's going on.

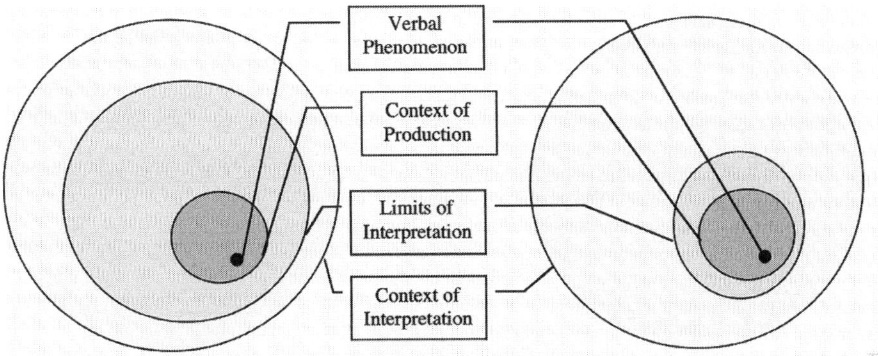

Figure 5.1: Transparent and opaque phenomenon.

For example, if we are coding for the phenomenon of author mentions—how often and when an interviewee mentions the names of the authors she is reading (Geisler, 1994)—we might expect the phenomenon to be relatively transparent. That is, in the context in which such an analysis might be expected to be interpreted, what is and is not an author mention would not seem to be problematic:

> P: at what point did you stop on . . . Friday I guess it was . . . yeah Friday

> V: can't even remember . . . [] seemed like years ago . . . I should write down like . . .
>
> P: well it's not important that I get precisely . . . what you were doing . . .
>
> V: I don't remember what I was doing . . .
>
> P: but just tell me about what you were doing . . .
>
> V: I think I was reading this . . . um . . . I was reading over Gerald Dworkin . . . [flipping pages]

In this example, even if we are not familiar with the context, most of us can recognize that the phrase "Gerald Dworkin" refers to the author of a text the interviewee was reading.

With other verbal phenomena, interpretation is far more difficult for those outside of the context of production. If, for example, we were coding indexicals for what they refer to, most of us would be hard pressed to interpret the this's, here's, and now's in the following conversational turn:

> J: But I think th-at it would be good for us to really imagine what this could be because there are a number of issues th-at come up down here: to the new goal: where am I? Oh, I'm here. I just went off the screen. I think I had: this is deriving from the last: you know, was the revised goal of the DCR the same as the first one. And this is the one here: network support. See, I'm not sure. What about the dominance? What about the dominance in the computer right now.

In this example, interpretation is complicated by the usual opacity of topical information ("it would be good for us to really imagine what this could be") and the temporal positioning of the conversation ("What about the dominance in the computer right now."). Interpretation is further complicated by the fact that J is looking at a computer screen ("where am I? Oh, I'm here. I just went off the screen.") and looking at a file containing text from which he may or may not be reading ("this is deriving from the last: you know, was the revised goal of the DCR the same as the first one. And this is the one here: network support.").

When phenomena are relatively transparent, when the context of production overlaps with the context of interpretation, we can expect achieving reliability to be relatively straightforward. That is, from one time to the next, from one coder to the next, judgments will remain relatively constant with respect to the phenomenon of interest (is this an author mention?). When phenomena are more opaque, when the context of production overlaps little with the context of interpretation, we can expect reliability to be harder, if not impossible, to achieve. In some cases, only the participant herself may be in a position to make a judgment (is this speaker deliberately lying?). Verbal phenomena, then, may range along a continuum of interpretation, with some phenomena being relatively opaque and some being relatively transparent, and a great many lying somewhere in between.

Uses of Intercoder agreement

In this chapter, we will describe methods aimed at achieving as reliable an analysis of verbal data as possible. Our position here is that reliability is important not because we expect verbal phenomenon to be wholly interpretable outside of its context of production (we do not) but because reliability is our key tool for insuring that we have been clear in the definition of our analytic constructs and that we have been explicit in our analytic procedures. As you will see, working with a second coder is an excellent way to understand the extent to which specific phenomenon are context bound and one of best ways to develop methods for communicating an interpretation of that phenomenon outside of the context of production.

Fundamentally, we believe that analysis is a rhetorical act of persuasion: We must persuade our intended readers that the pattern of phenomenon is as we claim. If a phenomenon is wholly opaque outside of its context of production, this rhetorical effort is hopeless. We can never expect to communicate an interpretation of what is going on to those who were not there. Happily, intended readers are usually more resilient in their powers of interpretation than that. Working to achieve reliability will help you to develop the means to help you and your readers to understand what you mean.

Measures of Intercoder Agreement

Simple Agreement

Intercoder agreement is a measure of the extent to which coders assign the same codes to the same set of data. In the first half of this chapter, we review the various measure associated with measuring intercoder agreement, some of which are complex. In the second half of the chapter, we introduce the less complex procedures you can use for your actual calculations.

The simplest measure of intercoder agreement is simple agreement, which is defined as the percentage of decisions that are agreements. If two coders agree entirely on how to code a data set, they will have an intercoder agreement of 100%. Simple agreement is calculated as

# of agreements / # of coding decisions

An example showing the calculation of simple agreement is shown in Figure 5.2. Column A contains the first coding; Column B the second coding; and Column C the agreement where 1 is used for agreement and 0 for disagreement. At the bottom of the column, we find the total number of agreements (14), the total number of coding decisions (16) and simple agreement (14/16 or .88).

Coder 1	Coder 2	
business	business	1
user	user	1
business	business	1
system	team	0
system	system	1
system	team	0
team	team	1
system	system	1
business	business	1
user	user	1
system	system	1
user	user	1
user	user	1
user	user	1
user	user	1
system	system	1
		14
		16
		0.88

Figure 5.2: Reliability data comparing the coding done by two coders.

Simple agreement is the most intuitive way to communicate the rate of intercoder agreement on a set of data. Your coding team will readily understand what it means when you say, "we agreed 88% of the time," and this easy-to-calculate measure is also useful for tracking improvements in intercoder reliability as a coding scheme is developed: "We agreed 88% of the time today, compared to just 73% of the time last week."

Corrected Agreement

Although simple agreement is an intuitive measure of reliability, using it alone doesn't take into account the fact that two coders could have agreed simply by chance.

To understand the impact of chance on levels of agreement, imagine that I give you a coding scheme that has only two categories. The chances that we would pick the same category in any given coding decision are rather high, one out of two. If, on the other hand, we are using a coding scheme that has 10 categories, the chance of accidental agreement is a lot lower, 1 out of 10. Thus achieving an agreement level of 90% with a two-category scheme is a lot easier than achieving that same level of agreement with a 10-category scheme. Methods of calculating corrected agreement are a way of taking that fact into consideration.

The traditional measure for correcting for agreement by chance is known as Cohen's kappa (κ), named for Jacob Cohen who proposed it in 1960. Cohen's kappa works by subtracting from the percentage for simple reliability a correction for chance agreement. So, for example, we would expect with Cohen's kappa that the .88 simple reliability calculated for the data in Figure 5.2 to be corrected downward.

More recently, some researchers are calling for the use of a different statistic, Krippendorff's alpha (α), championed by Klaus Krippendorff for use in content analysis (1970, 2016). Krippendorff's alpha corrects for the raters' bias as we'll discuss later. Krippendorff's alpha works by dividing the observed disagreement among coders by the disagreements one would expect if the coding was simply by chance.

Both of these measures of intercoder agreement can be calculated using a variety of on-line calculators, which we describe later in this chapter. But because we believe you should understand the underlying choices behind the statistics you choose to use and report, we spend some time in the rest of this section describing how Cohen's kappa and Krippendorff's alpha work and what the differences are between them. If you simply want to calculate your reliabilities, you can skip to the next major section.

Understanding Cohen's Kappa (κ)

Correcting agreement using Cohen's kappa begins with a table of agreements & disagreements like that shown in Figure 5.3. Down the side, we list the categories assigned by the first coder in lowercase. Across the top, we list the categories assigned by the second coder in uppercase. In the table itself, we list the number of times each combination occurred. For example, the table in Figure 5.3 shows that the number of times that the first coder assigned *Business* while the second coder assigned *user* was 0. The last column shows the row totals; the last row shows the column totals. Together, these two rows are often called the marginals. The lower right-hand corner contains the grand total, shown in blue (16). Values on the diagonal, shown in yellow, represent the number of times the two coders agreed.

	Business	User	System	Team	
business	3	0	0	0	3
user	0	6	0	0	6
system	0	0	4	0	4
team	0	0	2	1	3
	3	6	6	1	16

Figure 5.3: Table of agreements & disagreements for Cohen's kappa.

If the two coders had been in perfect agreement, all of the values would be on the diagonal, and the rest of the values in the table would be 0. Here, agreement was not perfect because of those 2 coding decisions where the first coder recorded *System* while the second coder recorded *team*.

Using this table, simple reliability can be calculated as the sum of the diagonals:

$$3+6+4+1=14$$

divided by the grand total of 16, or the value of .88 we calculated earlier.

Corrected agreement using Cohen's kappa is calculated using the expected level of agreement for each coding category if the decisions were made simply by chance. The expected level of agreement on a category involves calculating what is known as the joint probability of that category.

To calculate joint probability of agreement for a specific cell, we take the probability that the first coder chose a particular value—what's called its simple probability—and multiple it by the simple probability the second coder chose that same value. In our example, what is the joint probability of an agreement on *business* with *Business* just by chance? The first coder chose *business* 3 times out of 16 decisions so its simple probability is:

P(business) = 3 in 16 or .19

The second coder chose *Business* 3 times out of 16 decisions as well, so its simple probability is also

P(Business) = 3 in 16 or .19

The joint probability of *business* with *Business* is the two simple probabilities multiplied together:

P(business with Business) = P(business) * P(Business)

or

P(business with Business) = .19 * .19 = .035

To use the joint probability to calculate the expected frequency of a category, you multiply it by the total number of decisions made:

business with Business expected = P(business with Business) * Grand Total

or

business with Business expected = .035 * 16 = .56

The expected frequency for the other agreement combinations (*user* with *User*, *system* with *System*, *team* with *Team*) are calculated in the same way and then all of them are added up to give a total value for the expected level of agreement by chance, known as q.

P(business with Business)	0.56
P(user with User)	2.25
P(system with System)	1.5
P(team with Team)	.19
q (total)	4.5

Using q, we can then calculate Cohen's kappa as

Kappa = (d-q)/(N-q)

where

d = # of actual agreements

q = sum of agreement by chance

N = number of decisions

For the data in Figure 5.3, then,

kappa = (14 – 4.5) / (16 – 4.5)

or

kappa = 9.5 / 11.5 = .83

If we were to report the reliability for this coding scheme then, we could report, "Agreement between coders was .88 or .83 corrected using Cohen's kappa."

Understanding Krippendorff's Alpha (α)

Correcting agreement using Krippendorff's alpha begins with the recording of coincidences as shown in Figure 5.4. In this table, each pair of decisions from the reliability data in Figure 5.2 yields two coincidences, once for Coder 1 with Coder 2 and once for Coder 2 with Coder 1. Thus, the number of coincidences for two coders will always be twice the number of decisions. For example, the three agreements on *Business* shown in Figure 5.4 yield the six coincidences shown in light orange.

	Coding		Coincidences	
	Coder 1	Coder 2	Coder 1 with Coder 2	Coder 2 with Coder 1
1	business	Business	business w/ Business	Business w/ business
2	user	User	user w/ User	User w/ user
3	business	Business	business w/ Business	Business w/ business
4	system	Team	system w/ Team	Team w/ system
5	system	System	system w/ System	System w/ system
6	system	Team	system w/ Team	Team w/ system
7	team	Team	team w/ Team	Team w/ team
8	system	System	system w/ System	System w/ system
9	business	Business	business w/ Business	Business w/ business
10	user	User	user w/ User	User w/ user
11	system	System	system w/ System	System w/ system
12	user	User	user w/ User	User w/ user
13	user	User	user w/ User	User w/ user
14	user	User	user w/ User	User w/ user
15	user	User	user w/ User	User w/ user
16	system	System	system w/ System	System w/ system

Figure 5.4: Coincidence data for Krippendorff's alpha for intercoder agreement data given in Figure 5.2.

All of the coincidences are counted and entered into a coincidence matrix like that shown in Figure 5.5. Here we see that the six coincidences concerning the Business code show up in the Business/business cell, again shown in light orange. The rest of the coincidental agreements are shown in yellow and the total number of coincidences in blue. Notice how the Coincidence Table used for Krippendorff's has exactly twice the number of coincidences as there were decisions in the table of agreements and disagreements used with Cohen's kappa. This is because each decision, shown in the first two columns in Figure 5.4, yields two coincidences, as shown in the last two columns.

	Business	User	System	Team	
business	6				6
user		12			12
system			8	2	10
team			2	2	4
	6	12	10	4	32

Figure 5.5: Coincidence matrix for Krippendorff's alpha.

The formula for hand calculating Krippendorff's alpha from the coincidence table is complex (Krippendorf, 2013b), but we walk through it for those interested:

$$\frac{(n-1)\sum_c o_{cc} - \sum_c n_c(n_c-1)}{n(n-1) - \sum_c n_c(n_c-1)}$$

We begin with the numerator (top) of this formula. On its left-hand side, it multiplies together:

- the number of expected coincidences that are free to vary (n-1 or 32-1) and
- the sum of the total number of actual coincidences ($\sum_c o_{cc}$ or 6+12+8+2).

For our reliability data this equals (31*(6+12+ 8+2)) or 868.

Next, on its right-hand side, the formula subtracts the sum of the expected coincidences for Coder 1 using the formula $\sum_c n_c\ (n_c-1))$, which is calculated like this:

Coder 1 Marginals	Formula	Calculated Value
6	6*(6-1)	30
12	12*(12-1)	132
10	10*(10-1)	90
4	4*(4-1)	12
	sum	264

Subtracting this sum (264) from our first number (868) yields a value of 604 (868 – 264) for the numerator in the formula for Krippendorff's alpha.

On its left-hand side, the denominator (bottom) of this formula multiplies together:

- the total number of coincidences (n or 32) and
- the number of expected coincidences that are free to vary[6] (n-1 or 32-1).

For our reliability data this yields 992.

On its right-hand side, the formula then subtracts a measure of the expected coincidences for Coder 2 ($\Sigma_c n_c(n_c-1)$) which is exactly the same as for Coder 1 above. Subtracting this sum (264) from our first number (992) yields a value of 728 (992 – 104) for the denominator in the formula for Krippendorff's alpha.

The final value for Krippendorff's alpha then is the numerator calculated earlier (604) divided by this denominator (728) which yields .83.

Choosing a Measure of Corrected Agreement

As you may have noticed from the values just calculated, the values for Cohen's kappa and Krippendorff's alpha are often not far apart. For the data in Figure 5.2, Cohen's kappa yields a value of .83, the same as Krippendorff's alpha. As we shall see, when bias enters into your intercoder agreement data—bias toward favoring one code over another, making it so that there is a higher probability of agreement on that code—the two measures can become quite different. In this situation, Krippendorff's alpha will give you a more accurate estimate of the reliability of your coding scheme.

As Krippendorff's 2004 analysis shows, Cohen's kappa becomes an inaccurate measure of intercoder agreement when there is bias in the distribution of disagreements. In the agreements and disagreements for our sample

6 The term "free to vary" refers to the fact that if the sum of a given set of values is known (264 in our example), and the total number of expected coincidences is known (32 in our example),then the first 31 of these expected coincidences can take on all possible values (in other words "are free to vary"), but the last value, the 32nd value, is not free to vary because it along with the other 31 coincidences, has to add up to the known sum (268). So it is not free to vary.

data as shown in Figure 5.3, there is very little bias in the disagreements because there were very few disagreements: The first coder disagreed with the second coder just two times. Another way to tell that there is little bias in our data is that the marginals for the two coders are very close: 3, 6, 6, 1 for the first coder and 3, 6, 4, 3 for the second coder. To be fair, our sample data does suggest a slight bias towards using team on the second coder's part, but the fact that Cohen's kappa and Krippendorff's alpha are almost equal suggests that the bias is very small.

Such is not always the case. In particular, the data Krippendorff (2004) used, shown in Figure 5.6, well illustrates the impact of bias on calculations of Cohen's kappa. In both tables, there are 46 agreements and 54 disagreements. In both tables, the agreements are distributed the same way: Aa =12; Bb = 14, and Cc = 20. The disagreements, however, are not distributed the same way. In the table on the top, the 54 disagreements are distributed absolutely without bias: 9 in each cell off the diagonal of agreements. In the contingency table on the bottom, however, the 54 disagreements show substantial bias. All of the disagreements are now distributed in the upper right-hand corner, shown in pink. And the marginals confirm the bias: 48, 32, and 20 are quite different from 12, 32, and 56.

	A	B	C	
a	12	9	9	30
b	9	14	9	32
c	9	9	20	38
	30	32	38	100

	A	B	C	
a	12	18	18	48
b	0	14	18	32
c	0	0	20	20
	12	32	56	100

Figure 5.6: Contingency tables where disagreements are without bias (at the top) and with maximum bias (at the bottom). Data taken from Krippendorff (2004).

No one would argue that the amount of intercoder agreement in the table on the bottom is greater than that for the table on the top. But, because of the way it is calculated, Cohen's kappa for the biased data on the top is actually higher than for the unbiased data on the bottom: .26 versus .19. This is a situation where using Cohen's kappa can be misleading.

To illustrate the magnitude of possible distortion, look at Figure 5.7, which illustrates the way that Cohen's kappa increases as the bias among disagreements increases. When the bias is 0, that is when the disagreements are all equal to 9 as shown in the top table of Figure 5.6, the kappa is .19 as we just mentioned. If 1/9 of the values below the diagonal migrate above the diagonal—i.e., all values below the diagonal become 8 and all values above the diagonal become 10—the kappa becomes a little higher. When all of the values below the diagonal migrate, leaving all 0s below the diagonal and 18s above the diagonal, we have a situation of strong bias and the kappa is .26. With Krippendorff's alpha, by contrast, strong bias does not have distorting effects. It yields an intercoder agreement measure of .19 for both the biased and unbiased data, and thus is a more accurate estimate of reliability.

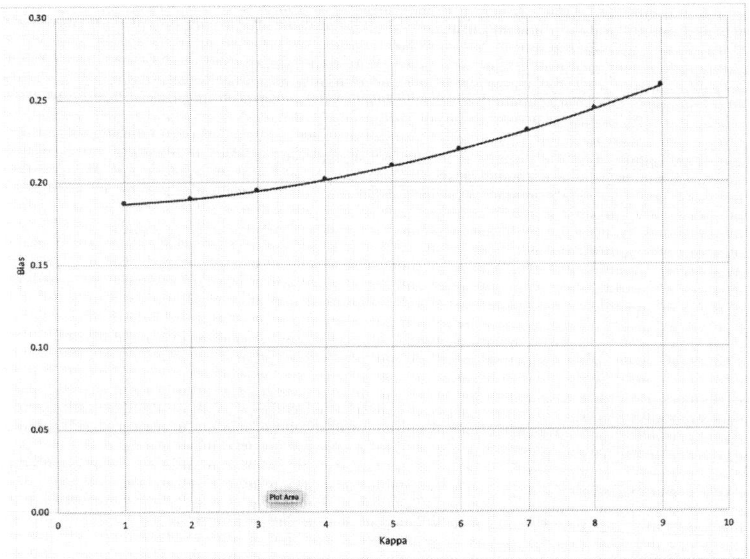

Figure 5.7: The increase of Cohen's kappa with increase in bias.

Bias is more common in coded data than you might expect. If you have a Miscellaneous or None category, one of your coders may default to it in cases where she is not sure. Or when two codes are hard to differentiate, one coder may prefer the first code while the second coder prefers the second code. Cohen's kappa is the more common measure of intercoder agreement, but the important take away for researchers seeking a measure of corrected intercoder agreement is not to rely on Cohen's kappa alone. Check the marginals for your data to see if one of your coders shows bias toward some codes over others. If so, calculate both Cohen's kappa and Krippendorff's alpha and report Krippendorff's alpha as the best measure of reliability when there is a discrepancy between the two.

Exercise 5.1 Test Your Understanding

You can download this exercise at https://wac.colostate.edu/books/practice/codingstreams/.

The data shown in Figure 5.8 below and in the "unbiased" sheet of the Excel worksheet at the link above shows a low level of agreement, but no bias. That is, the marginals in the table of agreements and disagreements are identical. Simple agreement equals just .50, and if we used one of the online calculators described later in this chapter we would find that Cohen's kappa is .34 and Krippendorff's alpha is also .34.

	Coding			Coincidences	
	Coder 1	Coder 2	Agreement	Coder 1 with Coder 2	Coder 2 with Coder 1
1	business	Business	1	business w/ Business	Business w/ business
2	team	User	0	team w/User	User w/ team
3	business	Business	1	business w/ Business	Business w/ business
4	system	Team	0	system w/ Team	Team w/ system
5	system	System	1	system w/ System	System w/ system
6	system	Team	0	system w/ Team	Team w/ system
7	team	Team	1	team w/ Team	Team w/ team
8	system	System	1	system w/ System	System w/ system

9	business	Business	1	business w/ Business	Business w/ business
10	user	System	0	user w/ System	System w/ user
11	system	System	1	system w/ System	System w/ system
12	user	System	0	user w/ System	System w/ user
13	team	User	0	team w/User	User w/ team
14	user	Team	0	user w/ Team	Team w/ user
15	team	User	0	team w/User	User w/ team
16	system	System	1	system w/ System	System w/ system

Figure 5.8: Worksheet for Exercise 5.1.

In the worksheet labeled "exercise," change the data to increase the bias of Coder 2 toward the Business code. Keep the level of agreement the same. [Hint: The easiest way to do this is to change Coder 2's codes for every line where there is 0 agreement; these cells are marked in orange in the worksheet.] The table of agreements below the data in the worksheet will automatically be updated.

What do you predict will happen if we recalculate the reliability measures? Will simple reliability go up or down or remain unchanged? Will kappa go up or down or remain unchanged?

For Discussion: Looking at the marginals of your table of agreements and disagreements. Under what conditions might you expect this kind of bias to arise?

Standards for Intercoder Agreement

All measures of reliability vary between 0 and 1.0, and, as you work with a second coder to develop a reliable coding scheme, you should see your measure of intercoder agreement move closer to 1.0. But you may well be wondering how far you need to go to reach an acceptable level of agreement. As Neuendorf (2016) has pointed out, there are no uniform standards for intercoder agreement. Rules of thumb have been proposed for good agreement using Cohen's kappa of .75 (Banerjee et al. 1999), .80 (Popping, 1988) and .81 (Landis & Kocj, 1977). Krippendorff (2013) has set .80 as the standard for reliability for Krippendorff's alpha. We ourselves have used .80 as our goal for an acceptable level of corrected agreement, though with particularly difficult coding schemes a .75 may be acceptable as the best that can be achieved.

Selecting Data for Second Coding

We agree with Neuendorf's (2016) endorsement of Lombard et al.'s (2002) three-part recommendation for achieving reliability:

- use at least two coders,
- calculate a measure of intercoder agreement for each coding scheme you use, and
- report the size of the sample you used to establish that agreement as well as your rationale for selecting it.

Keep in mind that the process of establishing intercoder agreement may require several cycles of second coding. As you will see, once you have coded a set of data and calculated your agreement with a second coder, you will inevitably refine your coding scheme and then try it out again. Each cycle will require a separate subset of the data; if you were to use the same subset over and over again with the same coders, they would gradually memorize the "correct" coding rather than follow the revised coding scheme. In order to avoid this effect, you will need to use a fresh sample of data for each cycle of second coding.

Generally speaking, researchers use at least 10% of the data for the final second coding to establish intercoder agreement; for smaller sets, the sample may get closer to 25%. In cycles of second coding leading up to this final cycle, you may use less than 10%, but make sure it is a well-chosen sample (more on this below). In any case, it is not unusual to go through two to four cycles of second coding in developing a coding scheme, so you need to start with a sample that is large enough to support the repeated subsampling for code development as well as the 10% you need for the final reliability check.

You need to be careful about how you choose a sample for second coding. Your goal is to develop a coding scheme that is sensitive to the range of variation in your data. To do that, you need to get this range of variation into the sample of data you use for second coding. If the design of your analysis includes major differences across data sets, you should include some data across each of these differences. If, for example, you are studying writing across the curriculum in the sciences and in the humanities, you would want to develop and test your coding scheme with some data from the sciences and some from the humanities. If you are looking for gender differences in contributions to online forums, you might want to select data from the range of forums you have looked at as well as selections of those forums in which women were active, men were active, and perhaps when both are active.

The selection of coders is equally important. Even if you plan to code the full data set yourself, you will need to work with at least two other people in second coding. For the purposes of developing your coding scheme, you will first want to choose someone who is willing to work with you over several cycles of second coding, perhaps extending over several weeks. A member of your own research team is ideal since the process of discussing coding decisions can enrich your team's analysis, a benefit of particular interest to those taking a qualitative perspective. If you are working on your own, you may want to partner for second coding with another researcher who also needs a second coder. This kind of reciprocal arrangement can enrich both projects.

Once you have reached an acceptable level of intercoder agreement with your first second coder, you will want to do a final coding with a different coder using the final data sample of 10% and the final coding scheme. This final second coder should not be someone from your team who has participated in the coding scheme development, but rather someone who comes to the final coding with fresh eyes. The measures of intercoder agreement that you calculate for this final second coding will be the ones that you report for your study.

Memo 5.1: Sampling for Second Coding

Compile a sample of your data to use to check the reliability of your coding. Make sure to pull together data that shows the full range of variation in your design. Include enough data to support several rounds of preliminary coding as well as 10% of the data for final coding.

Document the rationale behind your choices.

Managing the Second Coding

Coding is intense work. In early coding sessions, plan to give a second coder no more data than can be coded in a sitting of one to one and one-half hours. For the final coding, get as close as possible to 10% of the data. Coders are usually trying to do their best, so it makes sense to give them the most comfortable and least distracting circumstances possible.

Preparing the Data for Second Coding

To prepare data for a second coding, organize the data in such a way to give the second coder no hints about how the segments have been coded previously (see Excel Procedure 5.1 and MAXQDA Procedure 5.1)

Handling the Session

Begin the coding session with about 15 minutes familiarizing the coder with the coding scheme, the data, and the coding task. Concerning the data, make sure they understand how the data have been segmented and where they are to record their coding decisions. Concerning the coding scheme, make sure they know what the categories mean and how to apply them. One of the best ways to do this is to prepare a very small data set, formatted in the same way as the data to be coded, and ask them to try to apply the scheme. As they do so, you can then work through any questions they have about procedure.

Avoid using this training period to give the coder information about coding that is not included in the coding scheme itself. Of course, you never let them know what kinds of patterns you expect to see in the data (i.e., that you expect turns by one speaker to have more X than by another speaker). But even further, be sure not to communicate to them any additional information about how to decide how to apply the codes. After all, you are trying to find out how well your coding scheme can communicate—both to coders and to your eventual readers—the nature and variation in the data.

Excel Procedure 5.1: Preparing Excel Data for Second Coding

https://goo.gl/GDW4CW

Prepare your data for second coding in Excel as follows:

1. Hide the results of your first coding by selecting the column and using the **Column/Hide** command under the **Format** menu as shown in Figure 5.9.

The coder ought to be able to see the column headers on the data sheet at all times. This can be accomplished by splitting the window as follows:

2. Use the **Split** command under the **Window** menu to split the window in two. Then drag the tiny bar at the top of the scroll bar to arrange the top pane so that the column header is the only thing visible as shown in Figure 5.10.
3. Choose the **Freeze Panes** command under the same **Window** menu.

Your second coder will also need to be able to consult the full coding scheme at all times. To insure this:

4. Print out the coding scheme.
5. Make sure it is formatted for ease of use, with names of codes in bold, cases indented and bulleted (See Figure 4.1 in Chapter 4 for an example).

Ideally a coding scheme is 1 page long; it should never exceed 2 pages.

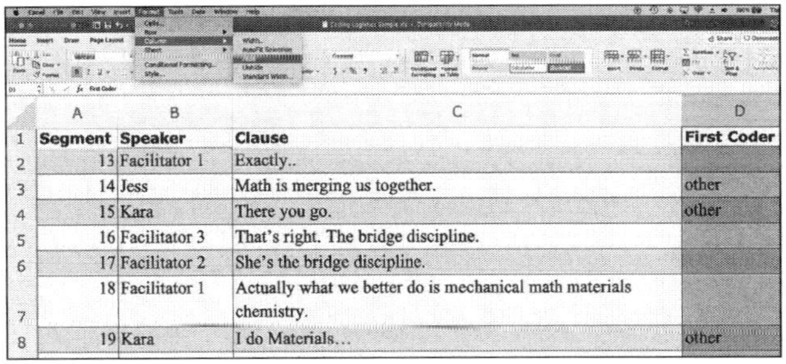

Figure 5.9: Hiding columns to prepare for a second coder in Excel.

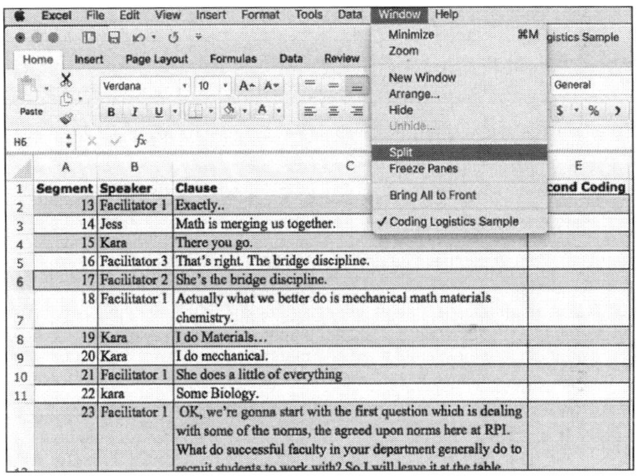

Figure 5.10: Splitting the window using Split command in Excel.

MAXQDA Procedure 5.1: Preparing MAXQDA Data for Second Coding

https://goo.gl/GDW4CW

Prepare your data for second coding in MAXQDA as follows:

1. Duplicate the project with the first coding using the **Duplicate Project** command under **Project** in the menu bar.
2. Export your coding system from the duplicate project using the **Export Code System** command under **Codes** in the menu bar. Use the MAXQDA format.
3. Delete all the codes in the duplicate project by right clicking on each code in the **Code System** window and then selecting **Delete**. This will remove your first coding.
4. Import the code system back into the duplicate project using the **Import Code System** command under **Codes** in the menu bar.

The duplicate project will now be ready for second coding.

5. In the **Code System** window, in turn, click on each memo containing the code definition attached to a code.

As shown in Figure 5.11, the definitions will then open in a tabbed memo window with one tab for each code definition. Your second coder can click through them to consult the full coding scheme. Give some thought to the order in which they are placed, with preferred codes coming before less preferred codes.

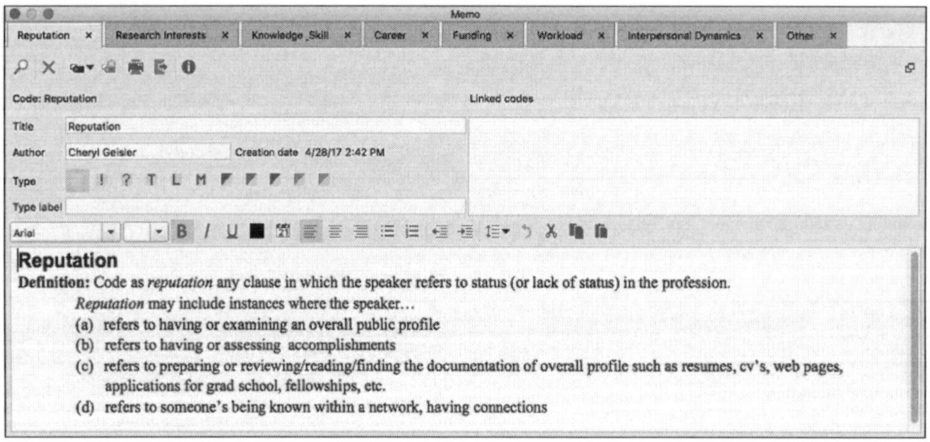

Figure 5.11: Making the full coding scheme available in MAXQDA used a tabbed code window.

Memo 5.2: Second Coding

Identify an appropriate second coder for your data. Prepare the data and coding scheme and schedule a time for a training session. Make sure to give your second coder only as much data as can be managed in a reasonable session of one to one and a half hours.

Document your round of coding. Make sure to link the coding results to the correct version of the coding scheme that you used.

Calculating Item-by-Item Agreement

Once a second coder has completed coding the sample data set, you need to put the two codings side by side and then calculate the level of agreement between the two codings (see Excel Procedures 5.2 and 5.3 and MAXQDA Procedures 5.2 and 5.3). As discussed earlier, intercoder agreement should be calculated both as simple agreement, which is a straightforward measure of agreement, and as corrected agreement using either Cohen's kappa or Krippendorff's alpha or both.

Excel Procedure 5.2: Putting the Two Codings Side by Side

https://goo.gl/GDW4CW

When you get the worksheet with the second coding in Excel back from your second coder:

1. Select the columns on either side of the hidden column.
2. Choose the **Column Unhide** command under the **Format** menu.

This will place the two codings side by side in Excel.

Excel Procedure 5.3: Checking Item-by-Item Agreement

https://goo.gl/GDW4CW

Once your data is side-by-side in Excel:

1. Next to the first line of codes and in the third column, type =IF
2. Click on the first code in the first column and then type =
3. Click on the first code in the second column and then type ,1,0)
4. Hit enter.
5. Select the cell containing the new formula and drag it down next to each pair of codes.

In this formula, we tell Excel to check whether the code assigned by the first coder is the same as the code assigned by the second coder. If this is true, we tell Excel to record a 1 for 1 agreement. If there is no match, we tell Excel to record a 0 for no agreement. If you have no coding for some segments (as we do for the segments that have darkened cells in Figure 5.12), make sure to delete the formula from the Agreement column. Otherwise, those rows will count as agreements and artificially raise your agreement numbers.

	C	D	E	F	G
1	Speaker	Clause	First Coder	Second Coder	Agreement
2	Facilitator 1	So we'll begin. Do you have the questions handy?			
3	Facilitator 2	Maybe we should just go around the room and make sure everyone knows every one else. I'm Debbie Kaminski from Mechanical			
4	Annie	Antoinette Maniatty from Mechanical Engineering	other	Other	1
5	Lakshmi	Linda Schadler from Material Science and Engineering	other	Other	1
6	Kara	Kristin Bennett from Math	other	Other	1
7	Jess	I'm Julie Stenckman in Chemistry	other	Other	1
8	Savannah	Susan Sanderson from Management	other	Other	1
9	Polly	I'm Pat Search from Language, Literature and Communication	other	Other	1
10	Facilitator 3	Cheryl Geisler Language Literature and Communication.You can see that we're kind of a really wide ranging group.			
11	Unknown	If you count all the engineers among us… [laughter]	other	Other	1
12	Unknown	that's because we don't have men in the room. ..	other	Other	1
13	unknown	they would do it some other way	other	Other	1
14	Facilitator 1	Exactly..			
15	Jess	Math is merging us together.	other	Other	1
16	Kara	There you go.	other	Other	1

Figure 5.12: Checking item-by-item agreement in Excel.

MAXQDA Procedure 5.2: Putting the Two Codings Side by Side

https://goo.gl/GDW4CW

1. Merge the two codings into the same project using the **Merge Projects** command under **Projects** in the menu bar.

The two codings appear as different documents shown in Figure 5.13.

Figure 5.13: The two codings in parallel documents after merging projects in MAXQDA.

2. Run an intercoder analysis using the **Intercoder Agreement** command under **Analysis** in the menu bar. Choose **Segment Agreement** as your type of agreement and set the level to **100%** as shown in Figure 5.14.
3. Click on the **Excel** symbol in the upper right of the window containing the intercoder agreement results as shown in Figure 5.15.

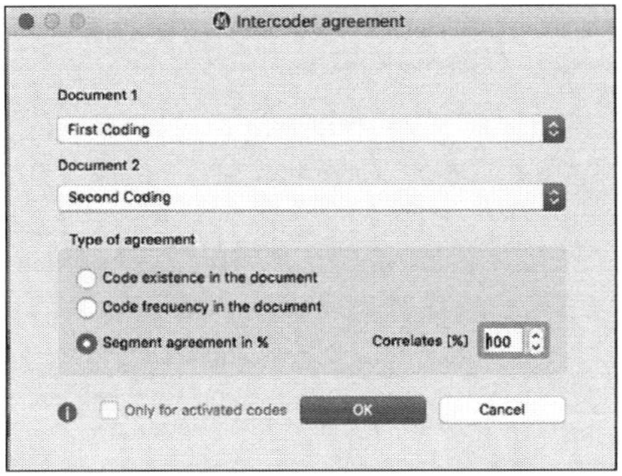

Figure 5.14: Running intercoder agreement analysis by segments at 100%.

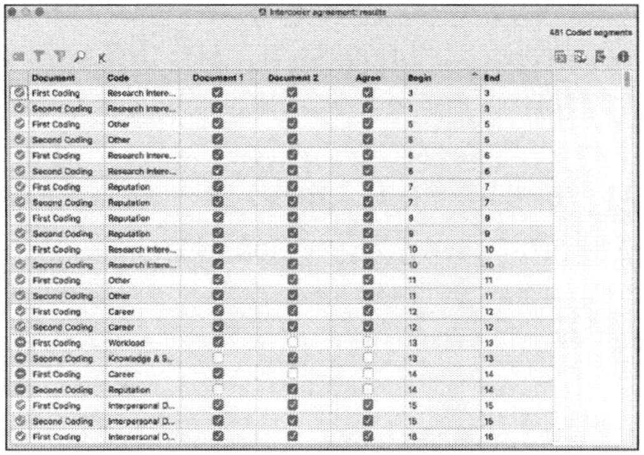

Figure 5.15: Intercoder agreement results.

This will open the data in Excel. To manipulate the data to put the two codings side by side:

4. Insert a second coding column next to the first one as shown in Figure 5.16. Change its format from **Text** to **General** using the **Number** tab of the **Cells** command under **Format** on the menu bar.

Continued . . .

MAXQDA Procedure 5.2: Putting the Two Codings Side by Side (continued)

https://goo.gl/GDW4CW

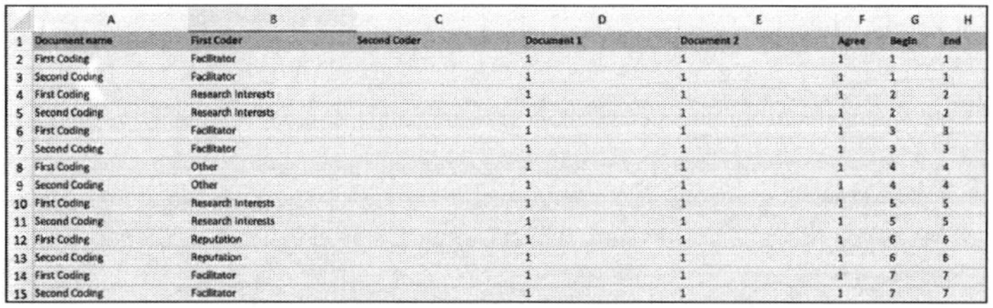

Figure 5.16: Inserting a column for the secondcoder next to first coder column after opening MAXQDA data in Excel.

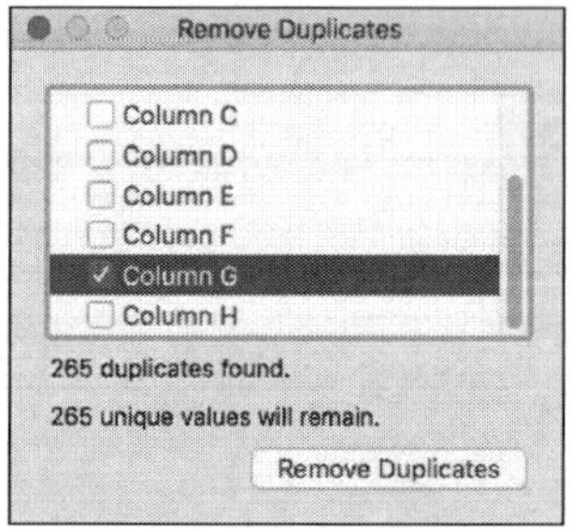

Figure 5.17: The Remove Duplicates dialog box in Excel.

5. Select these two cells and drag down to the end of the the data in the second column.
6. To fix these values in the second column, select the second column, copy it, and then, without moving your insertion point, use the **Paste Special Values** command.

Now the second column will contain fixed values for second coder codes rather than formulas.

7. Select all the data and use the **Remove Duplicates** command under the **Data** tab.
8. In the dialogue box, shown in Figure 5.17, choose the column with Begin as its header (Column G in our example). Click **Remove Duplicates**.
9. Filter the First Coder column for any dummy codes you may have used, and delete them in both the first and second coder columns.

In our data, this meant removing the Facilitator codes. The results should look like those shown in Figure 5.18.

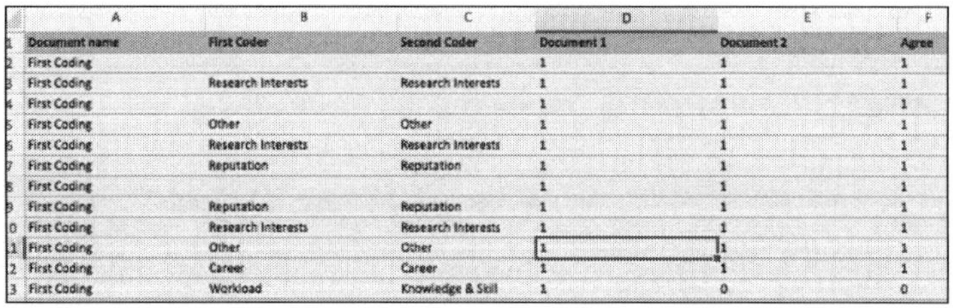

Figure 5.18: MAXQDA intercoder agreement data manipulated in Excel to place first and second codings side by side in columns B and C.

MAXQDA Procedure 5.3: Checking Item-by-Item Agreement for MAXQDA Data

https://goo.gl/GDW4CW

There is no easy way to check intercoder agreement for segmented verbal data in MAXQDA. You can calculate the Brennan-Prediger kappa (Brennan & Prediger, 1981) in MAXQDA by clicking on the kappa symbol in the upper left of the intercoder agreement results window in Figure 5.15. We do not recommended this method, but you can read the rationale of the developers of MAXQDA at https://www.maxqda.com/help-max12/intercoder-agreement/the-agreement-testing-concept-in-maxqda to decide for yourself.

Otherwise, once you have put your coding data side by side in Excel:

1. Type

   =IF

2. Click on the first code in the first column and then type

   =

3. Click on the first code in the second column and then type

   ,1,0)

4. Hit enter.
5. Select the cell containing the new formula and drag it down next to each set of codes.

Calculating Simple Agreement Only

If you only want to calculate the rate of simple agreement between two coders, you can easily do this. Keep in mind, however, that using simple agreement only does not adjust for the degree of agreement that might occur just by chance. Especially if you have just a few categories, you will not want to rely just on a measure of simple agreement. Nevertheless, you may want to use the procedures shown in Excel Procedures 5.4 and MAXQDA Procedures 5.4 to quickly calculate simple agreement just to see how you're doing as you develop your coding scheme.

Excel Procedure 5.4: Calculating Simple Agreement in Excel

https://goo.gl/GDW4CW

1. To calculate the sum of agreements, in the first cell below the data in your agreement column, type

   =SUM(

2. Then click and drag the cells above it (the 1s and 0s).
3. Type)
4. Then hit enter.
5. In the second cell down calculate the number of decisions by typing

   =COUNT(

6. Then click and drag the cells you want to count.
7. Type)
8. Then hit enter.
9. In the third cell down, calculate simple agreement by typing

   =

10. Click on the cell holding the sum.
11. Type /
12. Then click on the cell holding the count and hit enter.

Calculating Cohen's kappa only

You can rely on Cohen's kappa for an estimate of the reliability of your intercoder agreement if your marginals are pretty evenly distributed, showing little bias in the off-diagonal disagreements. Begin by making and formatting a table of agreements & disagreements (see Excel Procedures 5.5 and 5.6 and MAXQDA procedures 5.5 and 5.6) and then using that as input to GraphPad, an online calculator (see Excel Procedure 5.7 and MAXQDA Procedure 5.7).

The results of GraphPad's calculations are shown in Figure 5.24. The simple agreement is reported in the first line under the table as 65.58%. When this is corrected for agreement by chance using Cohen's kappa, the reliability is 56.2%. Note that GraphPad has a more generous understanding of what good intercoder reliability than the standards we described earlier.

MAXQDA Procedure 5.4: Calculating Simple Agreement for MAXQDA Data

https://goo.gl/GDW4CW

1. To calculate the sum of agreements, in the first cell below the data in your agreement column, type

   =SUM(

2. Then click and drag the cells above it (the 1s and 0s).
3. Type)
4. Then hit enter.
5. In the second cell down calculate the number of decisions by typing

   =COUNT(

6. Then click and drag the cells you want to count.
7. Type)
8. Then hit enter.
9. In the third cell down, calculate simple agreement by typing

   =

10. Click on the cell holding the sum.
11. Type /
12. Then then click on the cell holding the count and hit enter.

Excel Procedure 5.5: Making a Table of Agreements & Disagreements for Excel Data

https://goo.gl/GDW4CW

1. Make sure that there is nothing in the three columns of intercoder agreement data except the coding decisions and the agreement calculations.
2. Select the three columns of intercoder agreement data (First Coder, Second Coder, Agreement).
3. Use the **Summarize with Pivot Table** command under **Data** on the menu bar to create a pivot table.
4. Use the defaults for the data range and where to place the pivot table (a new worksheet) and click **OK**.

As shown in Figure 5.19:

5. Drag First Coder to the **Columns** field.
6. Drag Second Coder to the **Rows** field.
7. Drag Agreement to the **Values** field.
8. Finally, in the **Values** field, change Sum to Count by clicking on the **i** symbol to the right of **Agreement** in the **Values** field and as shown in Figure 5.20.

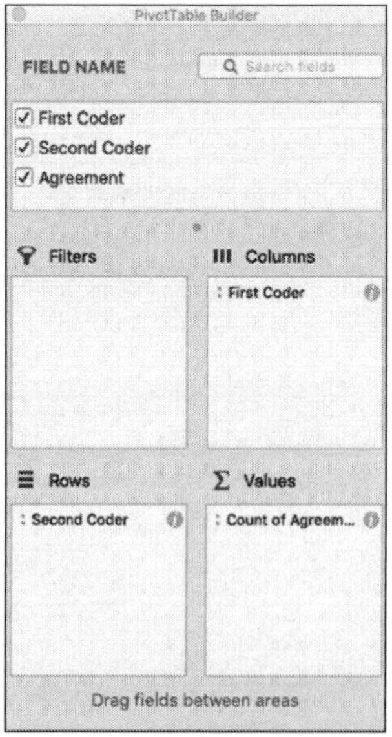

Figure 5.19: Selecting the parameters for the pivot table.

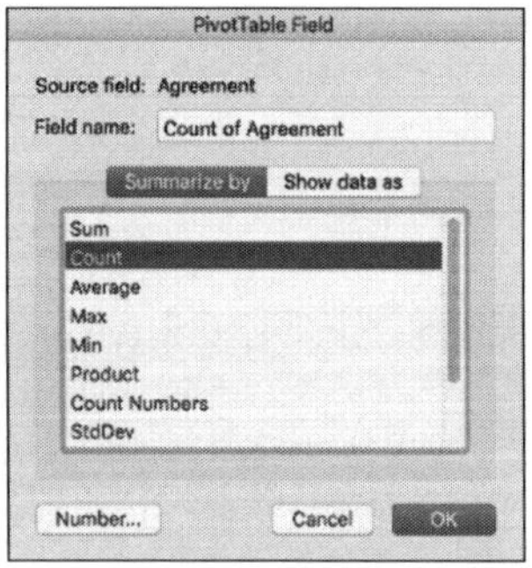

Figure 5.20: Changing Sum to Count in the PivotTable Field for Values.

Excel Procedure 5.6: Formatting a Table of Agreements & Disagreements for Excel Data

https://goo.gl/GDW4CW

1. Select just the body of the pivot table beginning with Row Labels and Ending with the Grand Total as shown in the Figure 5.21.

Row Labels	career	funding	interpersonal	Knowledge	other	reputation	Research	Grand Total
Career	17	0	13	0	10	11	2	53
Funding	0	11	0	0	1	0	0	12
Interpersonal	1	0	1	0	3	0	0	5
Knowledge	0	0	1	0	0	0	0	1
Other	1	0	1	0	46	0	0	48
Reputation	2	0	3	0	0	16	0	21
Research	1	0	2	0	1	0	10	14
Grand Total	**22**	**11**	**21**	**0**	**61**	**27**	**12**	**154**

Figure 5.21: A table of agreements & disagreements created from the data using a pivot table.

2. Copy the selected portion and then paste it below the original pivot table.
3. Compare the codes listed across with those listed down. If one or more codes are missing, add a column or row for each missing code.

In Figure 5.19, we added a column for Knowledge, which was missing from the pivot table because Coder 1 did not use it.

4. Delete any columns or rows labeled blank or with dummy codes.
5. Add gridlines with the **Borders** menu on the **Home** ribbon.
6. Fill every other row with color.
7. Fill values on the diagonal with yellow to highlight the agreements.

MAXQDA Procedure 5.5: Making a Table of Agreements & Disagreements for MAXQDA Data

https://goo.gl/GDW4CW

Once your MAXQDA data is in Excel with Item-by-Item agreement calculated, you can make a table of agreements & disagreements:

1. Select the three columns of intercoder agreement data (First Coder, Second Coder, Agreement).
2. Use the **Summarize with Pivot Table** command under **Data** on the menu bar to create a pivot table.
3. Use the defaults for the data range and where to place the pivot table (a new worksheet) and click **OK**.

As shown in Figure 5.19:

4. Drag First Coder to the **Columns** field.
5. Drag Second Coder to the **Rows** field.
6. Drag Agreement to the **Values** field.
7. Finally, in the **Values** field, change Sum to Count by clicking on the **i** symbol to the right of **Agreement** in the **Values** field and as shown in Figure 5.19.

MAXQDA Procedure 5.6: Formatting a Table of Agreements & Disagreements for MAXQDA Data

https://goo.gl/GDW4CW

1. Make a copy of the pivot table beginning with row labels and ending with the grand total below the original pivot table.
2. Compare the codes listed across with those listed down. If one or more codes are missing, add a column or row for each of the missing codes.

In Figure 5.21, we added a column for Knowledge, which was missing from the pivot table because Coder 1 did not use it.

3. Delete any columns or rows labeled blank or with dummy codes (such as Facilitator).
4. Add gridlines with the **Borders** icon.
5. Fill every other row with color.
6. Fill values on the diagonal with yellow to highlight the agreements.

Exercise 5.2 Try It Out

You can download this exercise at https://wac.colostate.edu/books/practice/codingstreams/).

Create a table of agreements & disagreements for the data found in the linked worksheet using a pivot table. Format it to highlight the agreements.

For Discussion: Are you satisfied with this level of agreement?

Excel Procedure 5.7: Using GraphPad's Online Calculator for Cohen's Kappa for Excel Data

https://goo.gl/GDW4CW

Make sure you have Table of Agreements & Disagreements as input.

1. Access the input screen for GraphPad's Online Calculator for Cohen's Kappa, shown in Figure 5.22, at https://graphpad.com/quickcalcs/kappa2/
2. Select the number of categories in your pivot table.
3. Type the data into the browser window as shown in Figure 5.23.
4. Click **Calculate Now**.

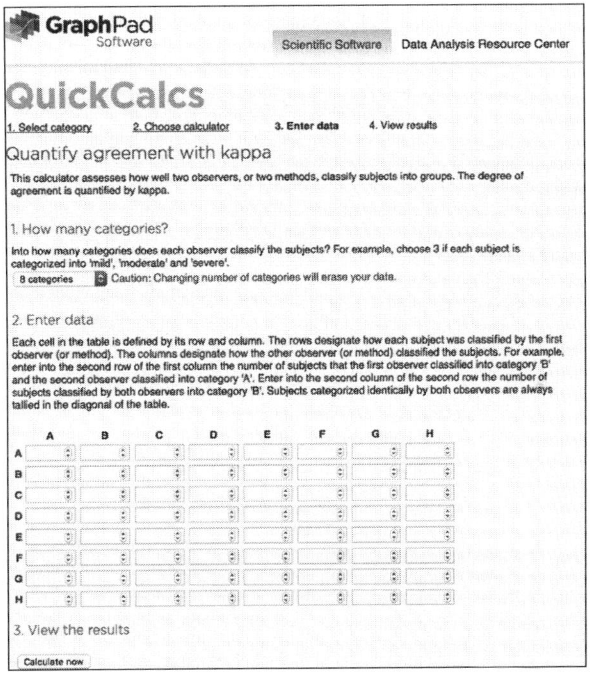

Figure 5.22: GraphPad's online calculator for Cohen's kappa.

MAXQDA Procedure 5.7: Using GraphPad's Online Calculator for Cohen's Kappa for MAXQDA Data

https://goo.gl/GDW4CW

Make sure you have Table of Agreements & Disagreements as input.

1. Access the input screen for GraphPad's Online Calculator for Cohen's Kappa, shown in Figure 5.22, at https://graphpad.com/quickcalcs/kappa2/.
2. Select the number of categories in your pivot table.
3. Type the data into the browser window as shown in Figure 5.23.
4. Click **Calculate Now**.

A	B	C	D	E	F	
	0	13	0	10	11	2
	11	0	0	1	0	0
	0	1	0	3	0	0
	0	1	0	0	0	0
	0	1	0	46	0	0
	0	3	0	0	16	0
	0	2	0	1	0	10›

Figure 5.23: Entering data from a pivot table into GraphPad's calculator for Cohen's kappa.

	A	B	C	D	E	F	G	Total
A	17	0	13	0	10	11	2	53
B	0	11	0	0	1	0	0	12
C	1	0	1	0	3	0	0	5
D	0	0	1	0	0	0	0	1
E	1	0	1	0	46	0	0	48
F	2	0	3	0	0	16	0	21
G	1	0	2	0	1	0	10	14
Total	22	11	21	0	61	27	12	154

Number of observed agreements: 101 (65.58% of the observations)
Number of agreements expected by chance: 32.9 (21.36% of the observations)

Kappa= 0.562
SE of kappa = 0.046
95% confidence interval: From 0.473 to 0.652
The strength of agreement is considered to be 'moderate'.

Figure 5.24: GraphPad results for Cohen's kappa.

Calculating Both Krippendorff's alpha and Cohen's kappa

As we mentioned in the first half of this chapter, using Cohen's kappa alone can run the risk of over-stating your level of agreement if your marginals show bias. To get both Cohen's kappa and Krippendorff's alpha, you can use the ReCal2 online calculator as described below. To use this calculator, you must first put the agreement data in numeric form and then save it in the CSV format. See Excel Procedures 5.8 and 5.9, Procedure 5.1, and MAXQDA Procedures 5.8 and 5.9.

Excel Procedure 5.8: Converting Codes to Numeric Values for Excel Data

https://goo.gl/GDW4CW

To convert verbal codes into numeric codes:

1. Make a copy of your worksheet showing the intercoder agreement data.
2. In the duplicate worksheet, insert 2 new columns next to your original two coding columns.
3. Copy the contents of the original columns into the 2 new columns.
4. Temporarily make a list of your codes and assign each one a number, beginning with 1.
5. Select the two newly copied columns.
6. Select the **Replace** command under the **Find** option of the **Edit** menu.
7. Enter your first non-numeric code and the numeric value you want to replace it with.
8. Click **Replace All**.
9. Continue in this manner until you have replaced all of your non-numeric codes.
10. After you have replaced all of your verbal codes with numeric codes, delete any uncoded data as well as all columns to the left of the numeric codes.

The result should be a file with just two columns of numeric codes.

Excel Procedure 5.9: Saving to Alternative File Formats for Excel Data.

https://goo.gl/GDW4CW

The online calculator for Cohen's kappa and Krippendorff's alpha only accepts files in CSV format.

1. Use the **Save As** command under **File** on the menu bar.
2. Select **Comma Separated Values** (.CSV) from the drop down menu under **File Format**.
3. Click **Save**.

Procedure 5.1: Using the ReCal2 Calculator for Cohen's Kappa & Krippendorff's Alpha

https://goo.gl/GDW4CW

1. Go to the ReCal2 online calculator at http://dfreelon.org/utils/recalfront/recal2/
2. Click **Choose File** and select the CSV file containing your numerically coded data.
3. Click **Calculate Reliability**.

The results of Recal2's calculations are shown in Figure 5.25. Here we see the same results for simple reliability (65.6%) and Cohen's kappa (56.2%) as well as similar results (55.5%) for Krippendorff's alpha.

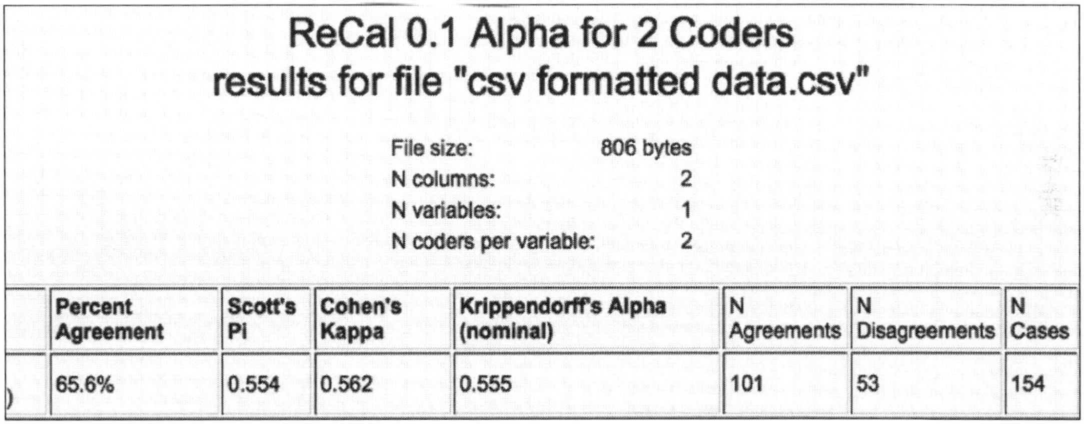

ReCal 0.1 Alpha for 2 Coders
results for file "csv formatted data.csv"

File size: 806 bytes
N columns: 2
N variables: 1
N coders per variable: 2

	Percent Agreement	Scott's Pi	Cohen's Kappa	Krippendorff's Alpha (nominal)	N Agreements	N Disagreements	N Cases
)	65.6%	0.554	0.562	0.555	101	53	154

Figure 5.25: Results from ReCal2.

MAXQDA Procedure 5.8: Converting Codes to Numeric Values for MAXQDA Data

https://goo.gl/GDW4CW

To convert verbal codes into numeric codes for MAXQDA data in Excel:

1. Make a copy of your worksheet showing the intercoder agreement data.
2. In the duplicate worksheet, create 2 new columns next to your original two coding columns.
3. Make a list of your codes and assign each one a number, beginning with 1.
4. Select the two newly copied columns.
5. Select the **Replace** command under the **Find** option of the **Edit** menu.
6. Enter your first non-numeric code and the numeric value you want to replace it with.
7. Click **Replace All**.
8. Continue in this manner until you have replaced all of your non-numeric codes. After you have replaced all of your verbal codes with numeric codes, delete any uncoded data as well as all columns to the left of the numeric codes.

MAXQDA Procedure 5.9: Saving to Alternative File Formats for MAXQDA Data

https://goo.gl/GDW4CW

The online calculator for Cohen's kappa and Krippendorff's alpha only accepts files in CSV format.

1. Use the **Save As** command under **File** on the menu bar.
2. Select **Comma Separated Values** (.CSV) from the drop down menu under **File Format**.
3. Click **Save**.

Exercise 5.3 Test Your Understanding

You can download this exercise at https://wac.colostate.edu/books/practice/codingstreams/.

A set of 20 data segments were coded using two different coding schemes. One had 10 categories (A-J) and the other had five categories (A-E). When the researcher went to check the reliability of each scheme using second coders, the simple agreement using in both cases was pretty poor—the second coders agreed with her only 50% of the time.

Look at the table of agreements and disagreements and the corrected reliability for these two schemes given in Figure 5.26 and in the worksheet at the link above. Are both schemes equivalent in terms of their reliability; or is one more reliable than the other?

	a	b	c	d	e	f	g	h	i	j	
A	1										1
B		1				1			1		3
C					1						1
D											0
E					3	1					4
F								1	1		2
G							1				1
H		2					1	1			4
I								1	1		2
J										2	2
	1	3	0	0	4	2	2	3	3	2	20

Simple Agreement: .50
Kappa: 0.422

	a	b	c	d	e	
A	1		1	1		3
B	1	2		1		4
C		2	1		1	4
D		1	1	1		3
E	1				5	6
	3	5	3	3	6	20

Simple Agreement: .50
Kappa: 0.36

Figure 5.26: Sample table of agreements and disagreements for Exercise 5.3.

For Discussion: Be prepared to explain your answer to your classmates.

Memo 5.3: Intercoder Agreement

Calculate measures of intercoder agreement between your two coders. Calculate simple reliability in Excel and corrected reliability using an online calculator for either Cohen's kappa, Krippendorff's alpha, or both.

Document the results of your calculations, making sure to clearly identify the coders, the data sample, and the version of the coding scheme that you used.

Revising Your Analytic Procedures

Increasing the reliability of a coding scheme involves inspecting the disagreements between coders for each category, identifying probable causes, and then revising your analytic procedures to eliminate them.

Inspecting Your Disagreements

Begin by looking at your table of agreements & disagreements to identify combinations in which there are disagreements. They often cluster in just a few areas. For example, the table of agreements & disagreements shown in Figure 5.27 suggests that the second coder is using the code *Career* far more often than Coder 1.

	Career	Funding	Interpersonal	Knowle	Other	Reputation	Research	
Career	17	0	13	0	10	11	2	53
Funding	0	11	0	0	1	0	0	12
Interpersonal	1	0	1	0	3	0	0	5
Knowledge	0	0	1	0	0	0	0	1
Other	1	0	1	0	46	0	0	48
Reputation	2	0	3	0	0	16	0	21
Research	1	0	2	0	1	0	10	14
	22	11	21	0	61	27	12	154

Figure 5.27: Table of agreements & disagreements.

Next return to your coding sheet and use Autofilter to look at one combination at a time. Returning to our data sheet, as shown in Figure 5.28, we filter Column E to show all data that was coded with *Career* by the second coder. We could further filter Column D a code at a time to look at the choices made by the first coder. Looking at the data and the coding scheme, we try to understand the nature and cause of the disagreements.

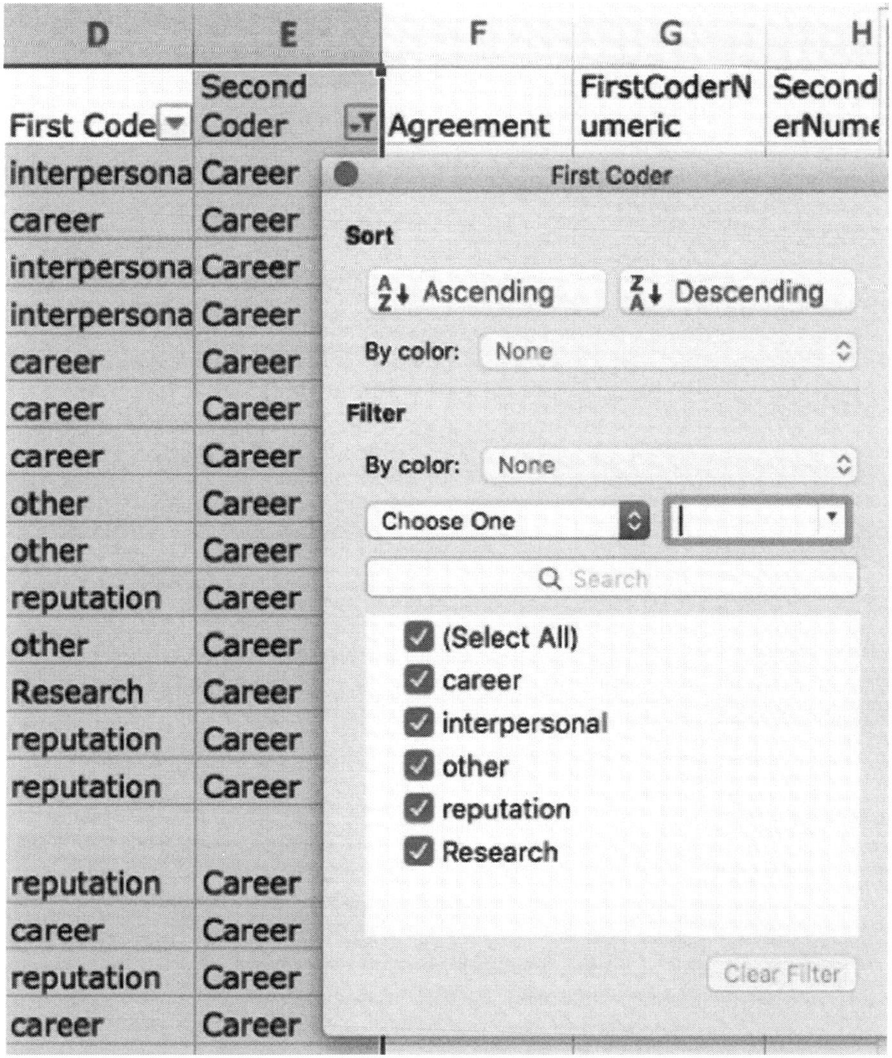

Figure 5.28: Filtering on disagreements over the use of the code Career.

Exercise 5.4 Try It Out

You can download this exercise at https://wac.colostate.edu/books/practice/codingstreams/.

Roger created a 4-category coding scheme and applied it to a 99-segement sample of data. When he checked the level of agreement with a second coder, he was happy to find that his simple reliability was high: 80%. But when he looked at the corrected agreement using Cohen's kappa, he was concerned. It was only .42. His table of agreements and disagreements looked like the one shown in Figure 5.29.

	N	P	R	O	SUM
N	5	4	0	0	9
P	3	71	0	0	74
R	2	2	1	0	5
O	1	8	0	2	11
SUM	11	85	1	2	99

Figure 5.29: Table of agreements and disagreements for Exercise 5.4.

He is considering three different strategies to improve this reliability:

- Revise the definition of category *N* to eliminate the second coder's confusion with category *P*.
- Revise the category *O* to eliminate the coder's confusion with categories *N*, and *P*.
- Eliminate the category *O* altogether, including it in *R*.

Modify his coding data (available at the link above) in one of these three ways; then recalculate his simple and corrected reliability.

For Discussion: Based on the results of you and your classmates, which of the three strategies do you recommend that Roger adopt? What generalization might you make about the best strategies for improving reliability using the Table of Agreements & Disagreements as a guide?

Revising the Coding Scheme

In the simplest cases, disagreements between coders arise from lack of clarity in the coding scheme. By adding cases and examples of those cases, we can often better indicate to a coder that certain kinds of verbal data should go in one category rather than another. In the coding scheme found in Chapter 4, Figure 4.1, for example, coders were initially inconsistent in how they categorized t-units which contained phrases such as "definition" and "justification." After reflection it became clear that such words signal attention to the discourse functions of a text and therefore should be coded as *Rhetorical Process*. The following case with examples under *Rhetorical Process* clarified this decision and eliminated this kind of confusion:

> **"general categories of claims that can be made by authors: "a definition," "a justification," "a reason," "a question";**

Occasionally, you will find that some verbal phenomena consistently confuse your coders and need to be addressed explicitly. In the example coding scheme on Worlds of Discourse, for example, t-units with "you" in them always confused coders. Sometimes they were coded as Rhetorical Process, and sometimes as *Narrated Cases*. Looking at these disagreements, I realized a need to explicitly address the use of "you" that should be included in Narrated Cases, which I did with this addition to the coding scheme under Narrated Case:

> **"you" or "I" when cast in a role involving an action that is taken to exist independently of the concepts in the domain but that may potentially be characterized with respect to these concepts.**

Finally, coding schemes can be revised to add categories or refocus definitions of categories so that analytic constructs are better understood. It was this kind of move that prompted me to add the category of Narrated Cases to my original scheme which had only included Rhetorical Process and Domain Content on its start list.

Changing the Unit of Analysis

More complex revisions to analytic processes can be made by changing the unit of analysis. As described in Chapter 3, if the unit of analysis is inappropriate to the phenomenon of interest, coders will have great difficulty using a coding scheme. If the unit is too large, more than one category may apply. If the unit is too small, coders may not recognize the phenomenon as it is broken across segments. To remedy these problems, return to the original data in Word, resegment, recode, and then compare the results of a second coding.

■ Adding Another Dimension

As described in Chapter 4, we often find ourselves placing too much into a single coding scheme, trying to ask a coder to look for things that are, in essence, quite different. It is as if we were to ask a coder to tell us, "is it a yellow chick or a brown goat?" and then finding they do not know what to do with brown chicks. We could revise our coding scheme to direct the coder to put any brown chick into the Yellow Chick category, but this might violate coders' intuitions and lead to inconsistent coding. A better approach might be to realize that our scheme had conflated two different dimensions, color and animal type.

If you realize that you have conflated dimensions of a phenomenon into a single coding scheme, you will need to break your scheme into two different schemes and code with each one separately. We would, for example, ask our coders to first decide whether the animal was a chick or a goat and only later ask whether it was yellow or brown.

■ Moving to Nested Coding

Another option in dealing with what looks like distinct dimensions of a phenomenon is to move to a nested coding scheme as described in Chapter 4. Suppose, for example, that we do not care much about goats in the previous example, but only want to look at the chicks. In this case, rather than code all the data for color, we might code in two stages. In the first stage, we would ask our coders to decide if it was a chick or not. Only if the answer were yes, would we go on to ask whether the chick were yellow or brown.

Acknowledging the Limits of Interpretation

Finally, in inspecting disagreements, you may realize that your judgments are relying on knowledge so contextualized that you could not expect a second coder to duplicate your judgments. In this case, you have two alternatives.

One choice is to move to an enumerative coding scheme where you list all of the cases which you, with your deep knowledge of the context, judge to be in a given category. Such an enumerative scheme can go a long way in communicating to your readers the substance of an analytic construct.

A second option is to admit the limits of interpretation on the analytic construct, attempt to describe and illustrate it as best you can in your report, but abandon the attempt to get a high level of agreement with a second coder. This step should be viewed as a last resort, of course, because what we often start out thinking cannot be made explicit can be done with more thought. Nevertheless, it is important not to narrow one's vision of verbal data in a way that unduly favors the relatively transparent (and perhaps less important) over that which is relatively opaque (and perhaps more important).

Occasionally, you will find that you have not reached anywhere near satisfactory levels of reliability even after several rounds of second coding. In such cases, you will want to step back from the analysis and think through the analytic constructs with which you are working. They may be unclear. Or the data may simply not be describable in their terms. Quite frankly, you may be looking for the rabbit in the wrong hole. While no one likes to abandon an analysis, sometimes that is the best course. Often, you can return to it at a later time when a fresh perspective and further insight may give you better guidance.

Memo 5.4: Revisions for Reliability

Review your table of agreements and disagreements to identify the areas that are causing the greatest disagreement. Examine each combination in the data and then develop a strategy for improvement. Make appropriate revisions to the coding scheme, to the segmenting procedure, or to the dimensions of the analysis.

Document your revisions and plan your next step to achieving an appropriate level of reliability.

Finalizing Reliability

Once you have revised your analytic procedures, you should repeat the process of working with a second coder until an adequate level of reliability is reached. Generally, you would like to see simple agreements of .80 or better, corrected agreement of 70% or better. This can usually be reached after two or three rounds of second coding.

Once you have reached this level of agreement, you need to take a new and as yet uncoded section of data, and give it to a new second coder, someone who has not yet worked with you. The level of agreement you achieve with this fresh data and fresh coder, along with the stabilized coding scheme that produced it, is what you include in your report of the analysis.

Generally speaking, you need not have this final second coder code your entire data set, unless the set is small enough that the task can be completed in a reasonable time. Since verbal data sets tend to be quite large, a more selective approach to final second coding is required. As mentioned earlier, at least 10% of the data ought to receive a second coding, with each kind of data represented. Your overall goal is to verify the reliability of your coding scheme on the full breadth and depth of the data even when it cannot all be coded twice.

After data has received a final second coding, you will still find disagreements between coders. To prepare the data for further analyses as we describe in the next few chapters, you will need to reconcile those disagreements. Inspect each one carefully and decided which coding decision to adopt.

Make sure to retain records of each round of your coding attempts, which version of the scheme was used, what level of agreement was received, how each segment of data was coded by each coder. For this reason, it is probably best to create a separate coding workbook for each round of coding and to label it with the date of the second coding. Then, if ever necessary, you can go back and recover your steps.

Memo 5.5: Final Reliability

Once you have reached an acceptable level of reliability, document the final coding scheme, the data used to achieve this level of reliability, and its reliability statistics.

Selected Studies Reporting Reliability

Campbell, K. S. & Naidoo, J. S. (2017). Rhetorical move structure in high-tech marketing white papers. *Journal of Business and Technical Communication, 31*(1), 94–118.

De Groot, E., Nickerson, C., Korzilius, H. & Gerritsen, M. (2016). Picture this: Developing a model for the analysis of visual metadiscourse. *Journal of Business and Technical Communication, 30*(2), 165–201.

Felton, M., Crowell, A. & Liu, T. (2015). Arguing to agree: Mitigating my-side bias through consensus-seeking dialogue. *Written Communication, 32*(3), 317–331.

Graham, S. S., Kim, S-Y., DeVasto, D. M. & Keith, W. (2015). Statistical genre analysis: Toward big data methodologies in technical communication. *Technical Communication Quarterly, 24* (1), 70–104.

Hyland, K. & Jiang, F. (K.). (2016). Change of attitude? A diachronic study of stance. *Written Communication, 33*(3), 251–274.

Shin, W., Pang, A. & Kim, H. J. (2015). Building relationships through integrated online media: Global organizations' use of brand web sites, Facebook, and Twitter. *Journal of Business and Technical Communication, 29*(2), 184–220.

For Further Reading

Banerjee, M., Capozzoli, M., McSweeney, L. & Sinha, D. (1999). Beyond kappa: A review of interrater agreement measures. *Canadian Journal of Statistics, 27*(1), 3–23.

Brennan, R. & Prediger, D. J. (1981). Coefficient kappa: Some uses, misuses, and alternatives. *Educational and Psychological Measurement, 41*(3), 687–99.

Cohen, J. (1960). A coefficient of agreement for nominal scales. *Educational and Psychological Measurement, 20*(1), 37–46. https://doi.org/10.1177/001316446000200104.

Gaskell, G. & Bauer, M. W. (2000). Towards public accountability: Beyond sampling reliability, and validity. In M. W. Bauer & G. Gaskell (Eds.), *Qualitative Researching with Text, Image, and Sound* (pp. 336–350). Thousand Oaks, CA: Sage.

Geisler, C. (1994). *Academic literacy and the nature of expertise: Reading, writing, and knowing in academic philosophy*. Hillsdale, NJ: Lawrence Erlbaum Associates.

Goetz, J. P. & LeCompte, M. D. (1984). *Ethnography and qualitative design in educational research* (pp. 211–220). Orlando, FL: Academic Press.

Krippendorff, K. (2004). Reliability in content analysis: Some common misconceptions and recommendations. *Human Communication Research, 30*(3), 411–433.

Krippendorff, K. (2013a). *Computing Krippendorff's alpha-reliability*. Retrieved from https://repository.upenn.edu/asc_papers/43/.

Krippendorff, K. (2013b). *Content Analysis: An Introduction to its methodology* (3rd ed.). Los Angeles: Sage.

Landis, J. R. & Koch, G. G. (1977). The measurement of observer agreement for categorical data. *Biometrics, 33*(1), 159–174.

Lombard, M., Snyder-Duch, J. & Bracken, C. C. (2002). Content analysis in mass communication: Assessment and reporting of intercoder reliability. *Human Communication Research, 28*(4), 587–604.

Miles, M. B. & Huberman, A. M. (1994). *Qualitative data analysis: An expanded sourcebook* (pp. 277–280). Thousand Oaks, CA: Sage.

Neuendorf, K. (2016). *The content analysis guidebook*. London: Sage Publications.

Popping, R. (1988). On agreement indices for nominal data. In W. E. Saris & I. N. Gallhofer (Eds.), *Sociometric research: Volume 1, data collection and scaling* (pp. 90–105). New York: St. Martin's.

Saldaña, J. (2016). *The coding manual for qualitative researchers*. London: Sage.

Chapter 6. Seeing Patterns of Distribution

> In this chapter, you will look for patterns in how your verbal data are distributed across the categories of your coding scheme. Using a frequency table, you will create and interpret distribution graphs of their patterns. Techniques for graphing are introduced.

Introduction to Patterns of Distribution

In this chapter we take the first step in seeing patterns in the data you have just coded. In particular, we ask, "How did the way I assigned data to my coding categories vary with my built-in contrasts?" The answer to this question is called its distribution and visual representations of this pattern are called distribution graphs.

A Note on Counting

Before we go into to the details of how to create and understand patterns of distribution like those shown in Figure 6.1, we need to address the issue of counting. Behind every pattern visualized in a distribution graph is an act of counting. Judgments about the frequency with which something occurs—judgments of *more* or *less*, *similar* or *different*, are based on counting. In the case of distribution, we are basing our judgments on counting the number of segments that have been assigned to the coding categories in a coding scheme.

Counting has often been identified as the dividing line between qualitative and quantitative approaches to analysis. Simplistically, quantitative researchers use numbers; qualitative researchers don't. But, as Maxwell (2010) has pointed out, many prominent qualitative researchers, including literacy researchers Shirley Brice Health and Brian Street (2008), do use numbers.

Making meaning of patterns is more than a matter of counting. Saldaña (2016) repeatedly warns us that, "Frequency of occurrence is not necessarily an indicator of significance." But as Miles, Huberman, and Saldaña (2014) acknowledge, numbers are often important to meaning making. In particular, these researchers identify three reasons for counting: First, they help us see overarching patterns in our data that we might otherwise not notice when focused on individual pieces of data. Second, they can help to verify (or question) a hypothesis that we bring to the data. Finally, they can serve as a check on our intuitions, a test for our biases.

Our focus in this and the following chapters is on using numbers to identify patterns, using what Sandelowski, Voils, and Knafl (2009) have called "quantitizing" (p. 210), the direct counting of qualitative data. Their discussion of quantitizing is useful because it describes the judgment underlying two important moves we make in coding verbal data: identifying clear and non-overlapping boundaries, the essential move we made in segmentation as described in Chapter 3, and sorting into categories, the essential move we made in coding as described in Chapter 4.

Maxwell (2010) notes the importance of the use of numbers to support the "internal generalizability" (p. 478) of a researcher's claims. We have already seen the power of numbers at work in Chapter 5 on reliability. There, counting the number of agreements and disagreements helped us to refine our intuitions and identify our biases as we worked to achieve reliability. In this chapter, we see another example of the power of numbers at work, this time helping us to provide evidence that the claims we want to make are actually characteristic of the data set as a whole, not just the result of selective and biased focus.

Basics of Distribution

Distribution refers to the way that your data is spread among the categories in your coding scheme. It is the topology of the data. The patterns shown in Figure 6.1, for example, are distribution graphs of speaker data across the categories of Ed, John, and Cheryl for Meetings 1 and 2.

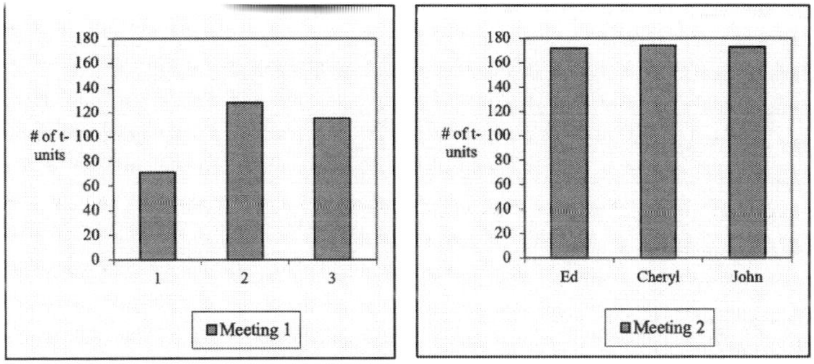

Figure 6.1: Distribution of speaker frequency in two meetings.

The most obvious use for distribution graphs comes when you want to know whether the distribution of the data varies according to the built-in contrasts that you created in your original analytic design. With that design, you articulated a plan for selecting data that you expected to show contrasting coding patterns in the phenomenon of interest. With these distribution graphs, you can begin to see whether your expectations were met: Does the distribution of your data over the categories in your coding scheme vary by the source of the data?

If, for example, we had chosen to look at data from Meeting 1 and Meeting 2 because we expected a built-in contrast, we could use the distribution shown in Figure 6.1 to see how these two meetings differed along the dimension of speaker participation. When the frequencies are looked at visually, we see two things immediately: that Meeting 2 was a lot more talkative and that Meeting 2 was a lot more equitable.

Absolute versus Relative Frequency

While the graphs in Figure 6.1 showed us distribution in terms of absolute frequency, those in Figure 6.2 show it in terms of relative frequency. That is, we have graphed the percentages of time that each category occurred. This data does not show us how talkative one meeting was compared to the other. For that we would have to go back to the graphs in Figure 6.1. But these graphs tell us what proportion of the talk was contributed by each speaker and how those proportions varied between the two meetings.

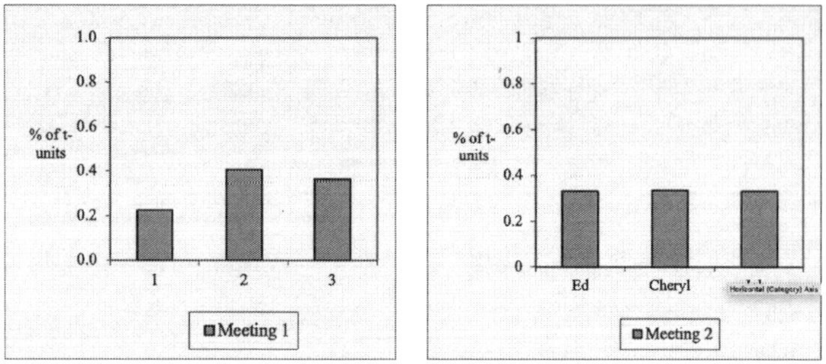

Figure 6.2: Relative frequencies of speaker distributions in two meetings.

If the total number of segments in one set of data is quite different from the total number in a comparison set, then comparing the absolute frequencies can be quite deceptive. In Figure 6.1, for example, we see that the frequencies for John are 115 in Meeting 1 and 173 in Meeting 2, two figures that seem quite different. But when we look at them as relative frequencies, as in Figure 6.2, we see that in Meeting 1, John spoke 37% of the time while in Meeting 2, he spoke 33% of the time, two figures that seem more similar. The difference here lies in the differences in the total number of segments in the two meetings. In Meeting 1 there were a total of 314 segments; in Meeting 2, there were 519 segments, two-thirds again as much. So while John spoke more often in absolute terms in Meeting 2, in relative terms, he spoke about as often.

Which of these two ways of looking at distribution is better, using the absolute frequency as we have done in Figure 6.1 or using relative frequency as we have done in Figure 6.2? The answer is both. Relative frequencies like those shown in Figure 6.2 allow us to compare across data sets. But if we looked at relative frequencies alone we might overlook important differences among the data sets in terms of overall size like the difference in meeting length shown in Figure 6.1.

It is also possible that a given category occurs with the same absolute frequency across data sets, rather than in terms of relative frequency. If we looked, for example, at the frequency of greetings in speeches, we would see about the same absolute number of greetings across speeches, even though the speeches themselves might vary widely in length. That is, no matter how long the speech, speakers may tend to give the same number of greetings in their opening remarks.

This pattern of absolute size would not show up if we just looked only at relative frequency. The point is that both measures of frequency tell us important information about the way our data is distributed over the categories making up our coding scheme. As a consequence, you should always examine both.

Exercise 6.1 Test Your Understanding

The two graphs in Figure 6.3 show the absolute and relative frequency of men and women 13 or more years past dissertation who have been promoted to the rank of full professor in the five colleges at a university. What do the absolute frequencies tell you? What do the relative frequencies tell you? What are the differences between them?

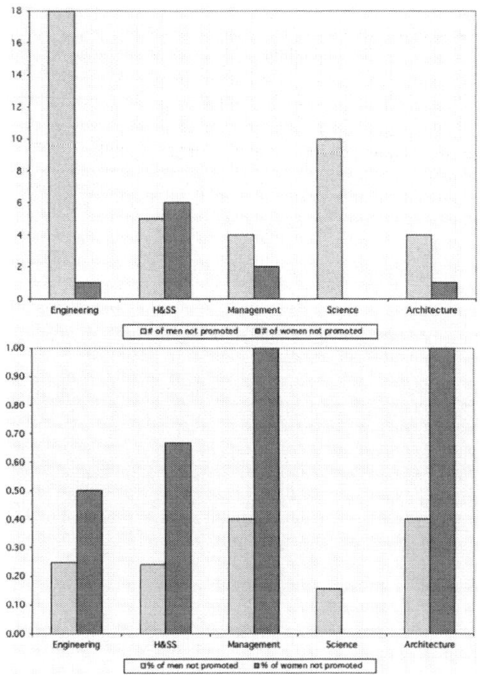

Figure 6.3: The absolute and relative frequency of promotion to the rank of full professor.

For Discussion: Which graph would you use to call attention to the problem of promotion among women faculty? Why?

Building a Frequency Table

Graphs like those shown in Figure 6.1 and 6.2 are based on frequency tables that summarize the data from a data worksheet. A frequency table shows the number of times data segments were coded in each of the categories of a coding scheme (see Excel Procedures 6.1 and 6.2 and MAXQDA Procedure 6.1). Along the side are the names of the coding categories, along the top are the names of the data samples. In Figure 6.4, for example, we have set up a frequency table for the speaker data for Meeting 1. On the top, we have labeled the source of the data (Meeting 1). Along the side, we have listed the categories (Ed, Cheryl, and John).

	Meeting 1
Ed	71
Chery	128
John	115

Figure 6.4: A frequency table.

Memo 6.1: Building Frequency Tables

Build a frequency table for each of your data sets, making sure to add marginals.

What are your thoughts about how they compare?

Excel Procedure 6.1: Naming Data in Excel

https://goo.gl/LUK52D

In Excel, we begin building a frequency table by naming the appropriate data range in the data worksheet.

1. In your data worksheet, select the column for the dimension you want to analyze for frequency.
2. Select the **Define Name** command under the **Insert** menu.
3. In the dialogue box as shown in Figure 6.5, give the data range a name that combines the data source and the dimension name.

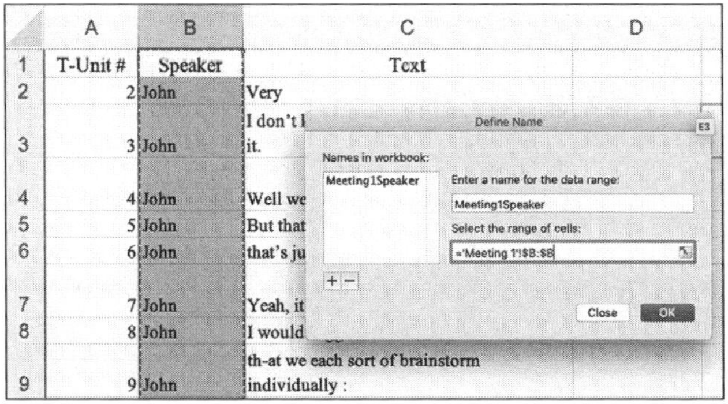

Figure 6.5: Naming a Data Range.

For example, we could name a data sheet Meeting1Speaker.

4. Click **OK** to complete the naming process.

Excel Procedure 6.2: Making a Frequency Table in Excel

https://goo.gl/LUK52D

1. Create a frequency table with data source at the top and coding categories down the side.
2. Click in the first blank cell of your table.
3. Type in the following formula:
   =countifs(
4. Choose your first data range by clicking **Insert** > **Name** > **Paste** as shown in Figure 6.6.

Continued . . .

Excel Procedure 6.2: Making a Frequency Table in Excel (continued)

https://goo.gl/LUK52D

Figure 6.6: Filling a Frequency Table with a countifs formula in Excel.

5. Click **OK**.
6. Type a comma and then click on the cell corresponding to first coding category.

Note that the spelling and case must be an exact match.

7. Type) to close the formula and hit enter.

The number of times the first coding category was used in your first data set now appears in the cell.

To use this formula to fill the rest of the frequency table, edit and drag the formula using the following procedure:

8. Click into the cell with the countifs formula.

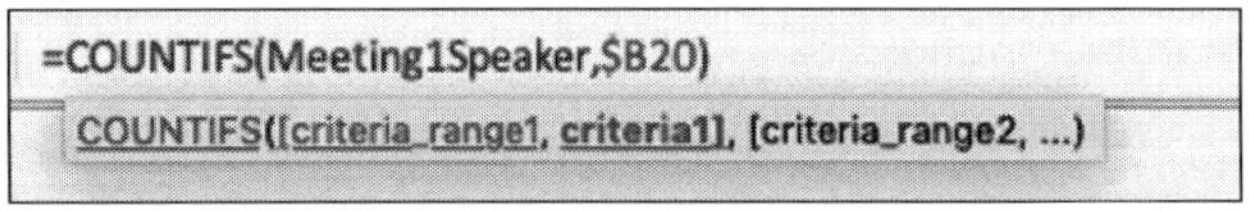

Figure 6.7: Editing the column name in the countifs formula in Excel.

9. Edit the countifs formula by placing a $ before the column name category as shown in Figure 6.7.
10. Select and drag this edited formula down the column.

MAXQDA Procedure 6.1: Making a Frequency Table in MAXQDA

https://goo.gl/LUK52D

1. In the **Document System** window, activate the document for which you want to build a frequency table.
2. In the **Code System** window, activate the codes for your chosen dimension.
3. Select the **Overview of Codes** command from the **Codes** menu.
4. Click on the **Statistic** icon at the top of the **Overview of Codes** window.
5. In the **Statistic of Document Variables** window, select **Coded segments of activated documents** in the drop-down menu at the top.

MAXQDA will display a frequency table like that shown in Figure 6.8.

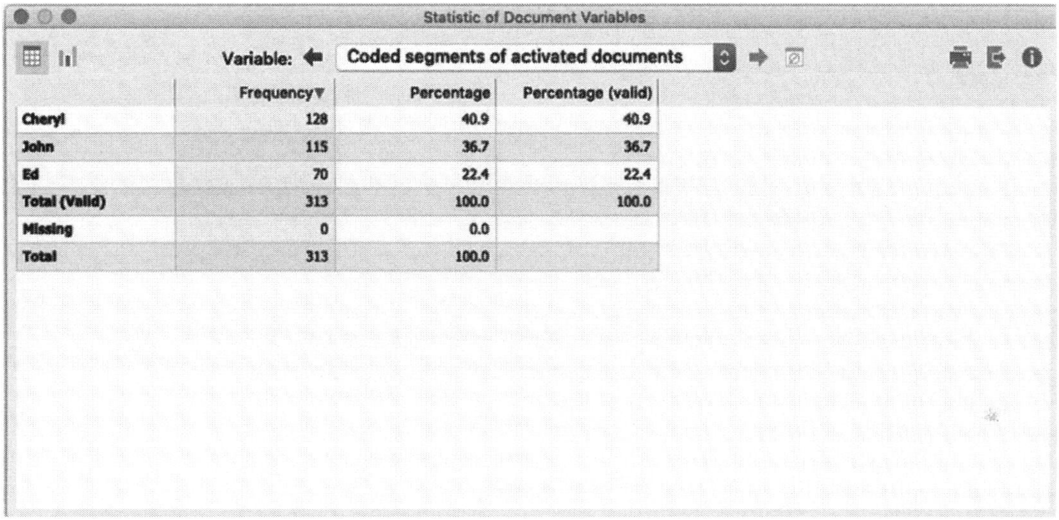

	Frequency▼	Percentage	Percentage (valid)
Cheryl	128	40.9	40.9
John	115	36.7	36.7
Ed	70	22.4	22.4
Total (Valid)	313	100.0	100.0
Missing	0	0.0	
Total	313	100.0	

Figure 6.8: Frequency table displayed in the Code Matrix Browser in MAXQDA.

■ Graphing Distribution

One of the best ways to see patterns in verbal data is through graphs—the spatial array of data points on a two- and sometimes three-dimensional coordinate system. Almost all of us are better able to see and interpret patterns through the spatial arrays shown in Figures 6.1 than the numeric frequency tables like the one in Figure 6.4. It is relatively easy to move from frequency table to distribution graph (see Excel Procedure 6.3 and MAXQDA Procedures 6.2 and 6.3).

Exercise 6.2 Try It Out

In the exercise available at https://wac.colostate.edu/books/practice/coding streams/, create a graph of the distribution of speaker for Meeting 2 in the same style as the graph for Meeting 1. Do this by creating a style template for the Meeting 1 graph and then applying it to the Meeting 2 graph.

■ Memo 6.2: Distribution Graphs

Create a distribution graph for each of your data sets. Make sure they have a common scale on the vertical axis.

What patterns do you now see with these visual representation?

Excel Procedure 6.3: Creating a Distribution Graph for Excel Data

https://goo.gl/LUK52D

1. As shown in Figure 6.9, select the cells of the frequency table representing your code totals and code names. Do not select column totals.

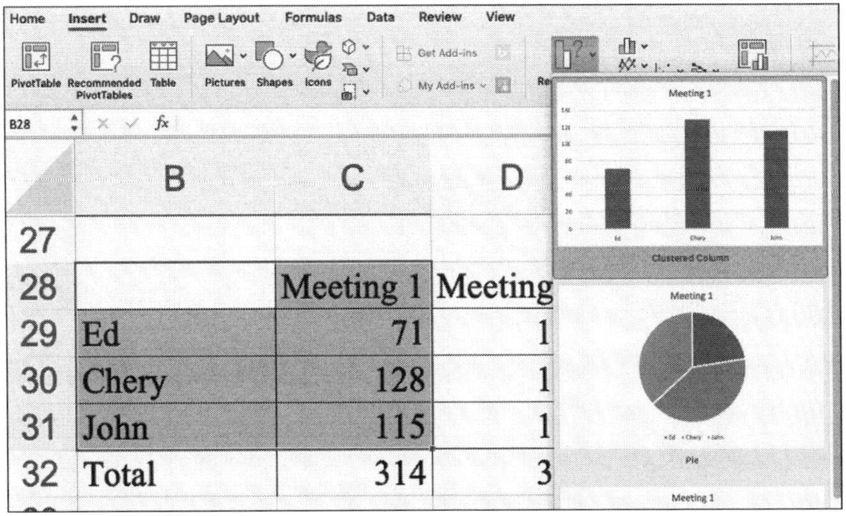

Figure 6.9: Inserting a clustered column chart in Excel.

2. On the **Insert** menu, select **Column** from the **Chart** options.
3. Add a label to your primary vertical axis by choosing **Vertical Axis** under **Axis Titles** using the **Add a Chart Element** command on the **Chart Design** tab.

Excel will now display a distribution graph.

To insure that distribution graphs are on the same scale:

4. Double click on the vertical axis.
5. In the **Format Axis** pane, under **Axis Options**, set the **Minimum and Maximum** bounds as desired.

To transfer these features to other distribution graphs:

6. Click on the chart with the desired features.
7. On the **Chart Design** tab, under **Change Chart Type**, select the **Save as Template** command.

MAXQDA Procedure 6.2: Creating a Distribution Graph in MAXQDA

https://goo.gl/LUK52D

1. Select the **Overview of Codes** command from the **Codes** menu.
2. Click on the **Statistic** icon at the top of the **Overview of Codes** window.
3. In the **Statistic of Document Variables** window, select **Coded segments of activated documents** in the drop-down menu at the top.
4. Click on the **Chart View** icon at the top of the window.

MAXQDA will now display a distribution graph for the activated document.

MAXQDA Procedure 6.3: Creating Distribution Graphs with a Common Scale for MAXQDA Data

https://goo.gl/LUK52D

MAXQDA does not allow you to adjust the scale of the axis in its charts. If you want to use a common scale for a set of distribution charts, you may want to export the frequency table to Excel and then produce your distribution graphs as follows:

1. Select the **Overview of Codes** command from the **Codes** menu.
2. Click on the **Statistic** icon at the top of the **Overview of Codes** window.
3. In the **Statistic of Document Variables** window, select **Coded Segments** of activated documents in the drop-down menu at the top.
4. Click on the **Export** icon to save the frequency table to Excel.
5. As shown in Figure 6.9, select the cells of your frequency table representing your code totals and code names. Do not select the column totals.
6. On the **Insert** menu, select **Column** from the **Chart** options.
7. Add a label to your primary vertical axis by choosing **Vertical Axis** under **Axis Titles** using the A**dd a Chart Element comman**d on the **Chart Design** tab.
8. Excel will now display a labeled distribution graph.

Continued . . .

Interpreting Patterns of Distribution

Once you have constructed distribution graphs of the absolute and relative frequencies of your coding categories for each sample of your data, you are in a position to begin the process of interpreting the patterns they show. In other words, with the distribution graphs you have just created, you can begin to explore the nature of your built-in contrasts. To aid you in this endeavor, we review in the following sections the more common distribution patterns as well as ways you can look for patterns across streams of data and across categories.

Direct and Inverse proportions

When is the distribution of coding categories across one sample of your data similar to another sample? The simple cases are distributions where the frequencies of each coding category are identical. In the case of Meeting 1 and Meeting 2, for example, we would certainly say that the distributions are the similar if Cheryl, Ed, and John talked for exactly the same amount of time in each the two meetings.

MAXQDA Procedure 6.3: Creating Distribution Graphs with a Common Scale for MAXQDA Data (continued)

https://goo.gl/LUK52D

To insure that both distribution graphs are on the same scale:

9. Double click on the vertical axis.
10. In the **Format Axis** pane, under **Axis Options**, set the **Minimum and Maximum bounds** as desired.

To transfer these features to other distribution graphs:

11. Click on the chart with the desired features.
12. On the **Chart Design** tab, under **Change Chart Type**, select the **Save as Template** command.
13. Give the chart an appropriate name such as Frequency and click **OK**.
14. To use the frequency template, select it from the templates among the **Chart** options under the **Insert** menu.

Our understanding of similarity goes beyond identical frequencies, however. Suppose that Meeting 2 was twice as long as Meeting 1, but that the relative frequencies with which Cheryl, Ed, and John talked were the same. In this case, we usually say that the distributions are similar—that Cheryl, Ed, and John talked about the same amount across the two meetings—despite the overall difference in the length of the meetings.

The underlying pattern for this larger sense of similarity is called direct proportionality: With direct proportionality, as the absolute frequency of one category changes, the absolute frequency of other categories changes proportionately and in the same direction; if one goes up, the others go up. If one goes down, the others go down.

The two graphs in the top half of Figure 6.10 show distributions that are directly proportional to one another. Despite the fact that Meeting 1 is a lot longer than Meeting 2 (275 t-units versus 134 t-units), the relative frequencies of the coding categories are nearly identical between them: 64% for Ed, 24% for Cheryl, and 12% for John in Meeting 1, and 64% for Ed, 23% for Cheryl, and 13% for John in Meeting 2. Sometimes frequency distributions are inversely rather than directly proportional. In inverse proportion, as the absolute frequency of one category changes, the absolute frequencies of other categories change proportionately but in the opposite direction. If one goes up; the others go down. If one goes down, the others go up. This is the case for the pair of distribution graphs shown in the bottom half of Figure 6.10. In Meeting 1, Cheryl talked for 34% of the time and John for 66%; in Meeting 2, the relative frequencies are reversed with Cheryl talking for 66% of the time and John for 34%. This is a clear case of inverse proportion.

Direct and inverse proportions are relatively common in verbal data. For example, suppose you have two conversations with the same person. In the first conversation, she is rather quiet; in the second conversation, she is more loquacious. If we were to look at the distribution of talk between speakers in these two conversations, we would probably find they were directly proportional. That is, as your interlocutor spoke more (or less), you probably also spoke more (or less) in return. As a result, the speaker distributions in the two conversations, which vary in overall length, are nevertheless similar.

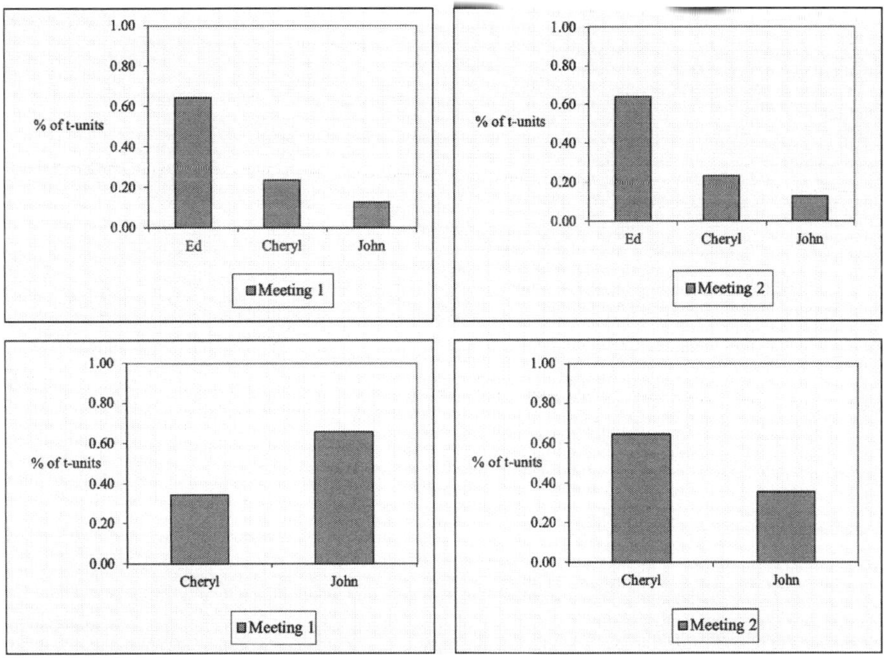

Figure 6.10: Patterns of direct (left) and inverse (right) proportion.

Suppose, however, that your conversations with your interlocutor occur within a formal one-hour meeting. Now, when she speaks more, she leaves less time for you to speak. As a result, the speaker distributions become inversely proportional. On days she speaks more, you speak less; one days she speaks less, you speak more. As this example suggests, inverse proportion is fairly common in cases of fixed resources—such as the total time available for a meeting.

Constants, Absolute and Proportional

Direct and inverse proportionality are patterns that reflect systematic differences between distributions. By contrast, some relationships between distributions can be characterized more by what they have in common than by how they differ. In the top of Figure 6.11, for example, the two distributions show a common value for Cheryl's contribution: Cheryl spoke 94 t-units in both

Meeting 1 and Meeting 2 even though Ed and John's contributions differed across the two meetings.

When one category has the same absolute frequency in two or more samples, we see in them a pattern involving an absolute constant. In our example, the absolute frequency of Cheryl's contributions—94 t-units—is an absolute constant across the two meetings.

A related pattern, shown in the bottom of Figure 6.11 involves a proportional constant. Here, the relative rather than absolute frequency remains constant across samples. In both meetings graphed in the bottom graphs in Figure 6.11, for example, Cheryl speaks about 33% of the time in both meetings.

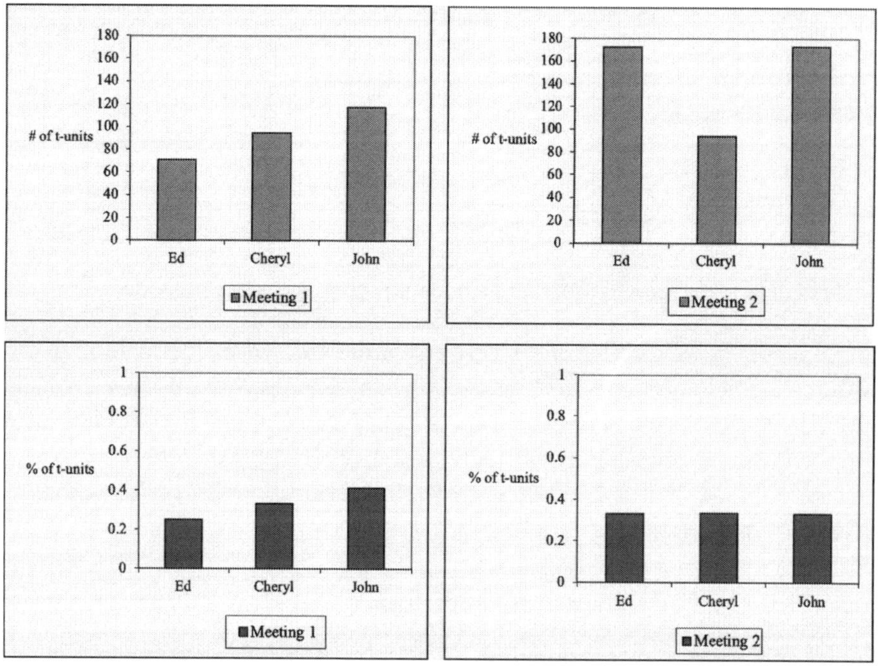

Figure 6.11: Patterns of absolute (top) and proportional (bottom) constants.

Absolute and proportional constants are not unusual in verbal data. Suppose, for example, a weekly meeting is always opened with a five-minute recap of last week's meeting. All verbal phenomenon associated with that recap will tend to be fixed in quantity regardless of how long the rest of the meeting takes. In this case, meetings from two different weeks will tend to exhibit a pattern of absolute constant.

Proportional constants are even more common. Suppose, for example, that the number of questions asked by the prosecution and defense in a trial was a fixed percentage of the trial proceedings. Then the contribution of attorneys' questions will be a proportional constant, increasing as the length of the trial increases, but remaining more or less at a constant proportion of the proceedings. Witness contributions, on the other hand, may be quite variable, with some witnesses responding extensively while others have relatively little to say. In this case, in contrast to attorneys' contributions, the length of witness contributions might have no relationship to the length of the trial.

Equity and Dominance

The distribution patterns shown in Figure 6.12 are last but not least in the analysis of verbal data. Here, in Meeting 1, we see a situation in which one category, speaker John, dominates. In Meeting 2, by contrast, speaker contribution is equitably distributed across speaker categories.

Patterns of equity and dominance are significant in the analysis of verbal data. In most classroom conversations, for example, the teacher's contributions tend to dominate regardless of other participation. Equitable distributions like those shown to the right in Figure 6.12 are relatively rare.

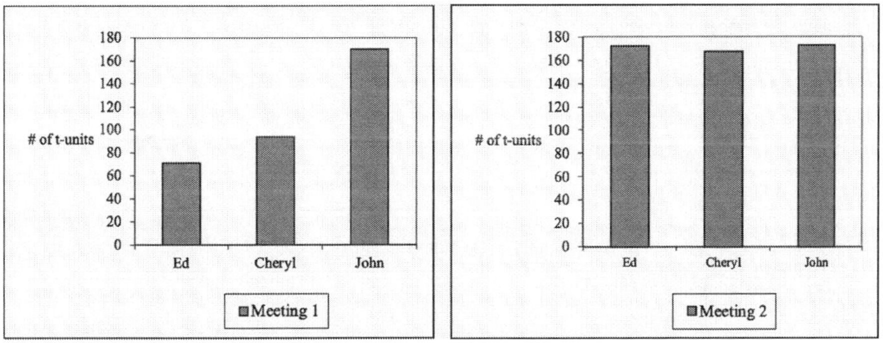

Figure 6.12: Patterns of equity and dominance.

■ Lack of Pattern

Finally, the last, and certainly not least important pattern to be on the lookout for in the analysis of distributions is the pattern of "no pattern." All verbal data is characterized by natural variations due to innumerable factors. Sometimes these variations add up to variation across distributions that cannot be described as falling into any particular pattern. In Figure 6.13, for example, no discernible pattern exists linking Meeting 1 and Meeting 2. Cheryl's contributions go way down; John's stay about the same; Ed's go up. While we can develop narrative descriptions of these relationships, there does not appear to be an overall pattern as was in the cases described in the previous sections.

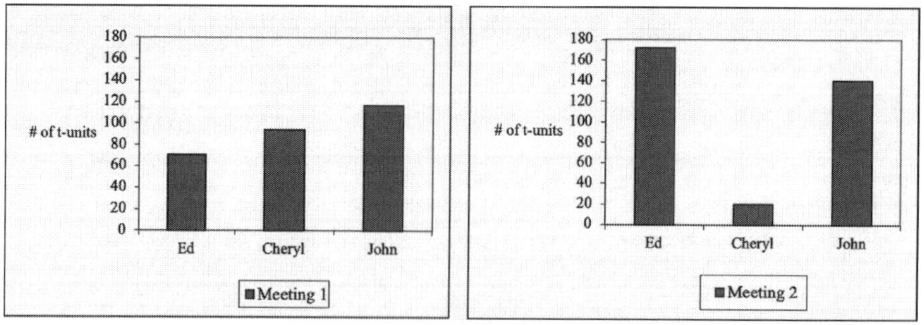

Figure 6.13: Distributions without pattern.

If, given the literature or general beliefs, you expected differences between data samples, the lack of pattern can be quite interesting. If, on the other hand, you are looking for ways to characterize the relationship between two data samples, the lack of pattern for the dimension analyzed should be a message to send you looking at other dimensions or to other phenomena altogether.

The patterns just reviewed are only some of those that you may encounter as you compare the distributions across the built-in contrasts of your design. They are tools to help you to notice and characterize the contours of your data samples. If they indicate that something is "going on" in your data, you may want to refine your analysis to produce a better characterization of the phenomenon. In the remainder of this chapter, we deal with two such refinements—collapsing streams and combining categories—as well as some of the interactions that can made such refinements overly simple and thus problematic.

Exercise 6.3 Try It Out

The graphs in Figure 6.14 show the absolute frequency and relative frequency with which texts that were private (intended for oneself as reader) and texts that were public (intended for other readers) were used during a working session that involved five different applications: desktop software for a personal digital assist (PDA), email, web browser, word processing, and spreadsheet. How would you describe the differences between the applications in terms of these distributions?

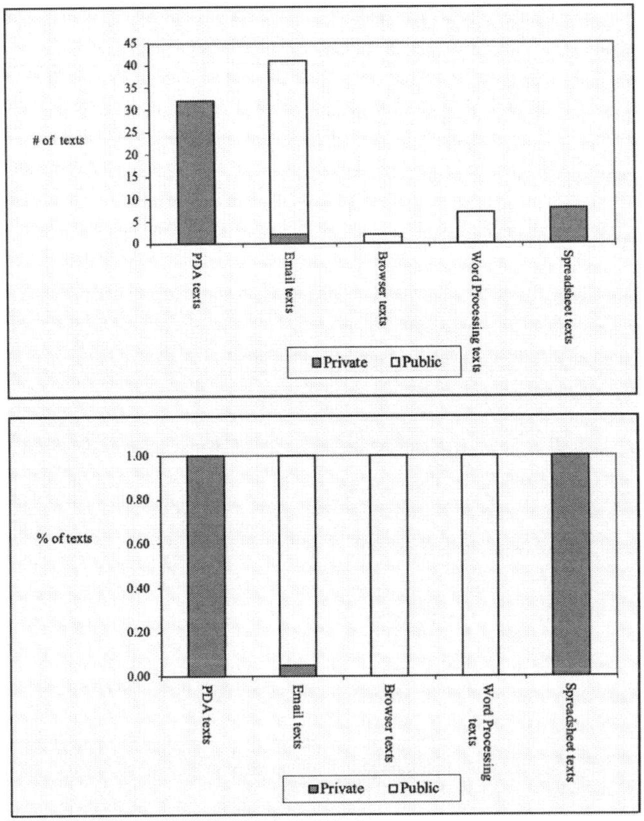

Figure 6.14: Distribution of public and private texts.

For Discussion: Compare your descriptions with those of your classmates.

Memo 6.3: Patterns

Review your distribution graphs across your built-in contrast. Do the distributions on one side of your contrast have more in common than they do with the distributions on the other side?

How would you best compare them?

Refining Patterns across the Built-In Contrast

Collapsing Streams

Thus far, we have described the distributions you may want to analyze as if they consist of just one stream of language on each side of your built-in contrast. Yet good analytic designs include multiple streams across a built-in contrast as we described in Chapter 2. Suppose, for example, we had designed our analysis to contrast two kinds of meetings—design meetings and managerial meetings—and we had transcripts from two meetings of each kind—four meetings in total.

Our analysis would begin, of course, with the distributions of each of the four streams as shown in Figure 6.15. In this case, we find that there is a proportional similarity between Meetings 1 and 2, the two design meetings, in which Ed and John talk with about the same relative frequency and Cheryl talks less frequently. The two managerial meetings, Meetings 3 and 4, are likewise similar to each other, though different from the design meetings. Here, Ed talks most frequently followed by Cheryl and with John left far behind.

When data streams have more in common with each other than they do with the streams across a built-in contrast, we may want to collapse data within the contrast in order to explore the pattern (see Excel Procedure 6.4 and MAXQDA Procedure 6.4). In Figure 6.16, for example, we have collapsed the data from the two design meetings and the two managerial meetings to give a portrait of how, overall, the design meetings and managerial meetings differ.

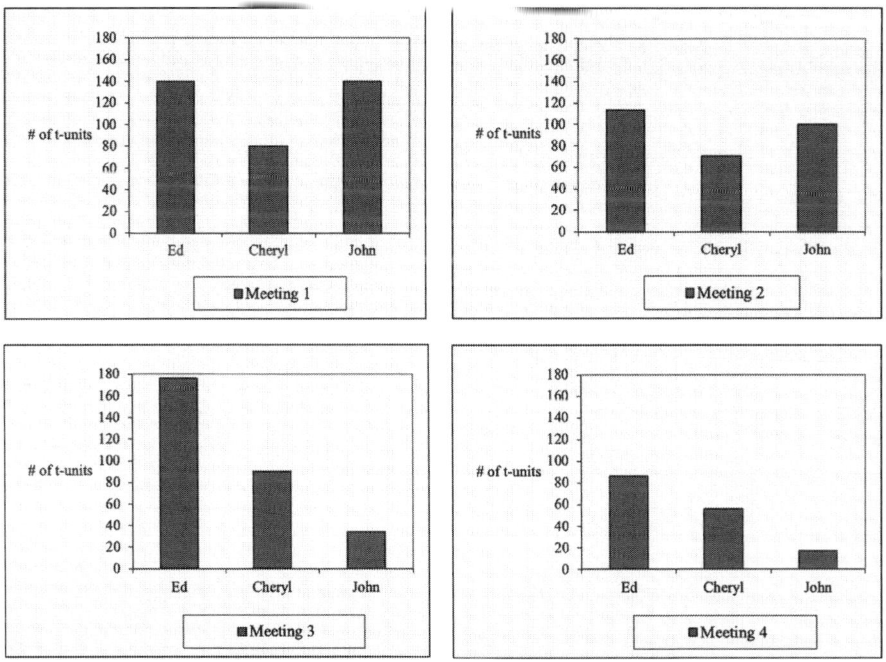

Figure 6.15: Distributions of multiple streams.

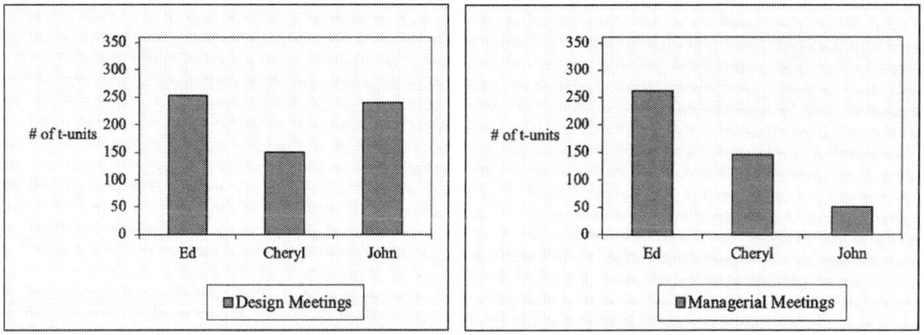

Figure 6.16: Collapsing streams.

Excel Procedure 6.4: Collapsing across Streams in Excel

https://goo.gl/LUK52D

To collapse data streams, add together the frequencies from the data sets on one side of the contrast as follows:

1. Create an empty summary frequency table like the one shown in the bottom of Figure 6.17. Label it to reflect one side of your built-in contrast.
2. Click in the first empty cell of this table and begin typing the formula with

   =

3. Click in the corresponding cell of the frequency table for the first data stream on one side of your contrast.
4. Type

   +

5. Click in the corresponding cell of the frequency table for the next data stream on the same side of your contrast.
6. Type

)

7. Hit enter to add the values together.

	Meeting 1
Ed	140
Cheryl	80
John	140
	Meeting 2
Ed	113
Cheryl	70
John	100
	Design Meetings
Ed	=C6+C11
Cheryl	
John	

Figure 6.17: Adding frequencies to collapse streams.

As shown in Figure 6.17, this procedure will enter the following formula in the first cell of your summary table:

=B6+B12

To add additional data streams to your summary, repeat steps 4 and 5, adding to your formula a + followed by the corresponding cell for each additional frequency table.

Fill the rest of the summary table by dragging the formulas down the column.

MAXQDA Procedure 6.4: Collapsing across Streams in MAXQDA

https://goo.gl/LUK52D

To collapse across data streams in MAXQDA, you create a document variable and use it to classify each of your documents according to your built-in contrast; then you collapse across documents.

1. From the Variables menu, select the **List of Document Variables** command.
2. In the pop-up **Document Variables** window, click on the **New Variable** icon.
3. Type in a name for the contrasting variable as shown in Figure 6.18 and click **OK**.

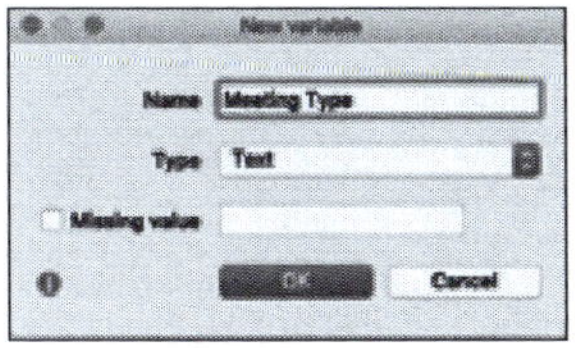

Figure 6.18: Adding a document variable in MAXQDA.

4. From the **Variables** menu, select the **Data Editor** command.
6. In the **Document** window, click in the first row under the new variable and type in the name for one side of your contrast as shown in Figure 6.19 and hit enter.

	Document g...	Document n...	Creation date	Number of c...	Number of ...	Author	Meeting Type
		Meeting 4	.../18 4:25 AM	159	0	Cheryl Geisler	Management
		Meeting 3	.../18 4:25 AM	301	0	Cheryl Geisler	Management
		Meeting 1	.../18 12:38 PM	313	0	Cheryl Geisler	Design
		Meeting 2	.../18 12:37 PM	314	0	Cheryl Geisler	Design

Figure 6.19: Classifying documents by variable in MAXQDA.

Continued...

MAXQDA Procedure 6.4: Collapsing across Streams in MAXQDA (continued)

https://goo.gl/LUK52D

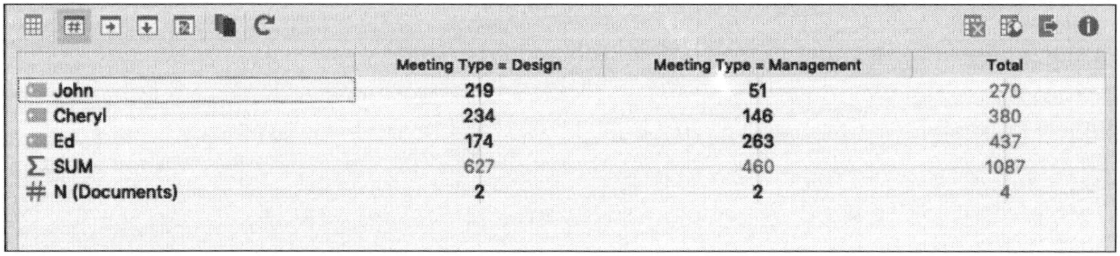

	Meeting Type = Design	Meeting Type = Management	Total
John	219	51	270
Cheryl	234	146	380
Ed	174	263	437
Σ SUM	627	460	1087
# N (Documents)	2	2	4

Figure 6.20: Frequency table for collapsed streams in MAXQDA.

7. In the next row, classify the next document, either by typing in the name or selecting from the drop-down menu and hit enter.
8. Repeat step 7 to complete the classification for all your documents.
9. From the **Mixed Methods** menu, select the **Crosstab** command.
10. In the **Crosstab** window, select your variable of contrast and click on the right arrow to move it into the second column.
11. In the third column, make sure that the = option is selected and use the drop-down menu to choose a value for your built-in contrast.
12. Repeat for the remaining variables of contrast.
13. Deselect the options for **Only activated documents** and **Only activated codes**, and then click **OK**.

A frequency table across your contrast will appear in the crosstab window as shown in Figure 6.20.

Calculating Averages

The data graphed in Figure 6.16 represent the total frequency of speaker categories in two design meetings and two managerial meetings. Another, perhaps more meaningful statistic for this data is the average frequency of speaker contribution per meeting. Averages can tell you the average frequency of a given code on one side of your built-in contrast. Ed, for example, contributed an average of 126.5 t-units per meeting in design meetings and 131.0 t-units per meeting in managerial meeting. Such averages give a better sense of the average magnitude of a phenomenon (like Ed's speaking) and are thus sometimes more useful in communicating with your readers. To learn more, see Excel Procedure 6.5 and MAXQDA Procedure 6.5.

Excel Procedure 6.5: Calculating Averages in Excel

https://goo.gl/LUK52D

1. Click in the cell where you want the average to appear.
2. Type

   =average(

3. Select the range of values you want to average together.
4. Type

)

5. Hit enter to complete the formula.

Excel will place a formula like the following in the cell:

=AVERAGE(C6:C7)

MAXQDA Procedure 6.5: Calculating Averages in MAXQDA

https://goo.gl/LUK52D

1. Right click on a code in the **Code System** window as shown in Figure 6.21 and select **Transform into a Document Variable**.
2. Close the **Document Variables** window that pops up.
3. Repeat steps 1–2 for each of your codes.
4. From the **Mixed Methods** menu, select the **Typology Table** command.
5. If necessary, select the names of your codes and click **Continue**.
6. In the **Typology Table** pop-up window, select your variable of contrast and click on the right arrow to move it into the second column.
7. In the third column, make sure that the = option is selected and use the drop-down menu to choose a value for your built-in contrast.
8. Repeat for the other value(s) of your built-in contrast.
9. Deselect the options for **Only Activated Documents** and then click **OK**.

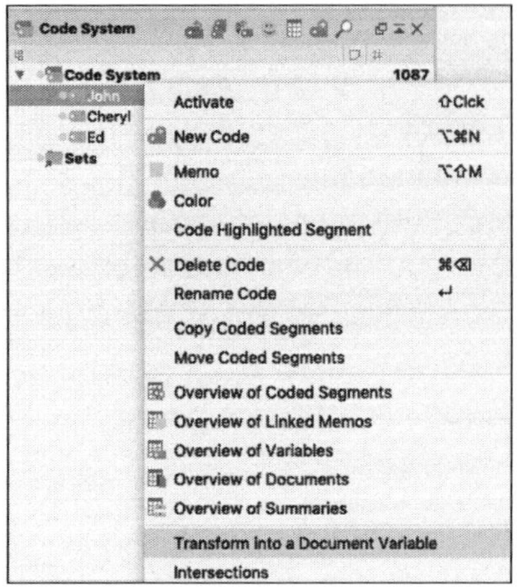

Figure 6.21: Transforming a code into a document variable in MAXQDA.

A typology table across your contrast will appear in the **Typology Table** window as shown in Figure 6.22. It shows the average (or mean) number of segments assigned to each code across your built-in contrast.

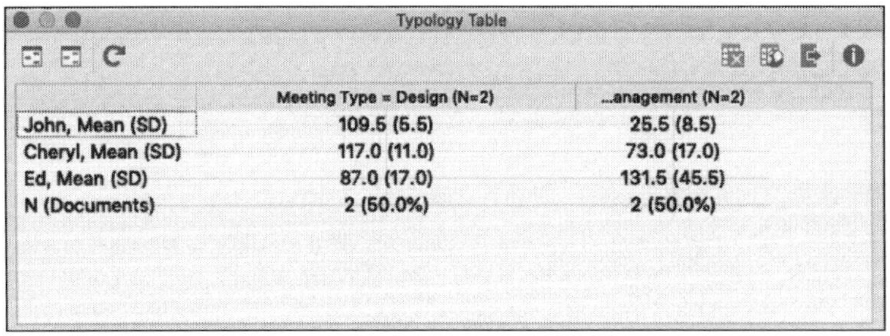
Typology Table

	Meeting Type = Design (N=2)	...anagement (N=2)
John, Mean (SD)	109.5 (5.5)	25.5 (8.5)
Cheryl, Mean (SD)	117.0 (11.0)	73.0 (17.0)
Ed, Mean (SD)	87.0 (17.0)	131.5 (45.5)
N (Documents)	2 (50.0%)	2 (50.0%)

Figure 6.22: A typology table showing the averages (means) for each code across a built-in contrast in MAXQDA.

Checking for Interactions

Whenever you collapse data streams, you make the implicit claim that the streams so collapsed follow the same basic pattern. Such need not be the case. Look at the data in Figure 6.23. As the frequency tables at the bottom of the figure suggest, the collapsed frequency for design and managerial meetings is the same here as it was in the data presented in Figure 6.16. In this case, however, this collapse presents a very misleading portrait of the individual streams.

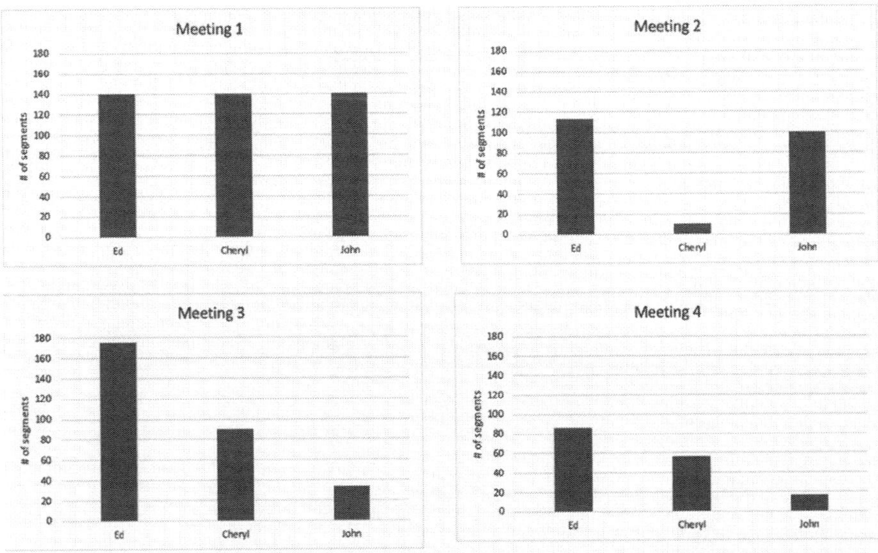

	Meeting 1
Ed	140
Cheryl	140
John	140

	Meeting 2
Ed	113
Cheryl	10
John	100

	Design Meetings
Ed	253
Cheryl	150
John	240

	Meeting 3
Ed	176
Cheryl	90
John	34

	Meeting 4
Ed	86
Cheryl	56
John	17

	Management Meetings
Ed	262
Cheryl	146
John	51

Figure 6.23: Interaction within streams.

To see how this is, compare the kinds of descriptions we might generate with the collapsed data with descriptions based on the individual streams. If we were to say, for instance, that Cheryl contributed, on average 75 t-units per meeting in the design meetings, this characterization would hardly be a good description of her contribution in Meeting 1 (where she spoke for 140 t-units) or her contribution in Meeting 2 (where she spoke for 10 t-units).

Nor are comparisons between her total contribution and the total contributions of Ed and John valid. In the collapsed data as shown in Figure 6.24, Cheryl looks as if she speaks less than either Ed or John. But the data for the individual streams in Figure 6.25 makes clear that in Meeting 1 she spoke with about the same frequency as Ed and John, but in Meeting 2, she spoke far less.

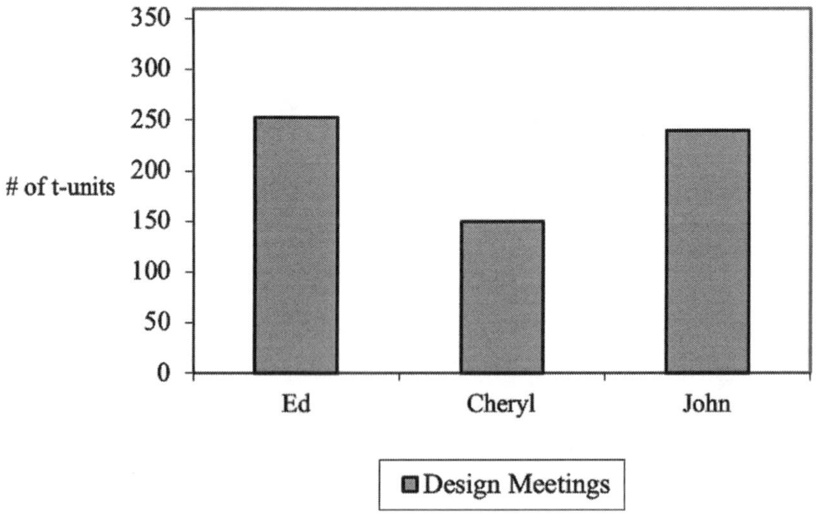

Figure 6.24: Misleading collapsed streams.

The situation we have been describing—in which the collapsing of streams provides a misleading portrait of the individual streams—is called an interaction. In an interaction, collapsing data across streams obscures major variations within the streams that makes the pooled statistics—either the collapsed frequencies or the averages—poor descriptions of the streams themselves. These are called interactions because the choice of stream interacts with pattern of distribution.

So, for example, if we want to answer the question, "how did the distribution of speaker contribution differ between the design meetings and the managerial meetings?" for the data presented in Figure 6.23, we would have to answer, "It depends. . . ." The first design meeting, Meeting 1, looks a lot more equitable than the managerial meetings, Meetings 3 and 4. But the second design meeting, Meeting 2, does not look at all equitable. In this data set, as in all interactions, there simply is no way to generate a general characterization that fits all the individual streams. Seeing these interactions may be telling you that the coding scheme you've chosen does not allow you to get at what makes the contrasts contrastive.

The overall lesson to be learned here is that while collapsing streams can be a very useful technique for exploring patterns, it can also be misleading if it obscures real variation within streams. Thus, it is important to always look at the distribution of each stream individually before taking the step of collapsing them together across your built-in contrasts.

Memo 6.4: Collapses across Contrast

Collapse your streams across contrast and create distributions graphs to show the sides of your built-in contrast with this collapsed data. Does the collapsed data match your intuitions that you developed earlier using single stream distribution graphs? Is the collapsed data a fair representation of the individual streams or do you have significant interactions?

Write one to two sentences describing each of your individual stream graphs as well as the collapsed graphs.

Refining Patterns Across Codes

A second technique for refining distribution patterns involves combining codes within your coding scheme (see Excel procedure 6.6 and MAXQDA Procedure 6.6). In Figure 6.25, for example, we show meetings with four speakers combined into two categories, managers and subordinates. This 100% stacked column graph neatly suggests that in both meetings managers spoke about twice as often as subordinates, a very suggestive finding.

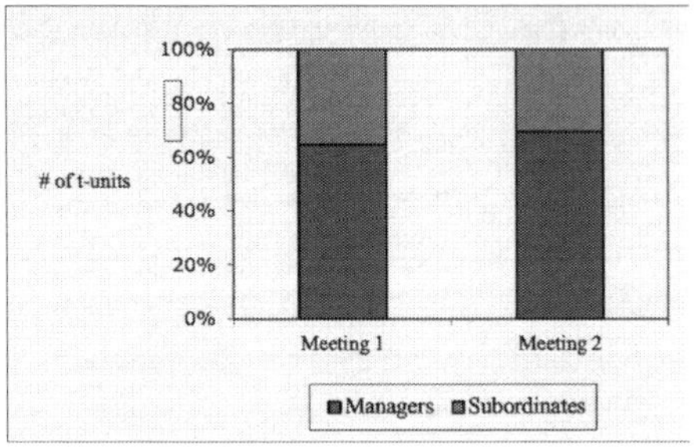

Figure 6.25: Combining categories.

Excel Procedure 6.6: Combining Codes in Excel

https://goo.gl/LUK52D

To add together the frequencies for two codes you want to combine:

1. Create an empty summary frequency table with cells for the frequencies of the new combined code.
2. Click in the first empty cell for the new combined code and begin typing the formula with =
3. Click in the cell with the frequency of the first code you want to combine.
4. Type +
5. Click in the cell with the frequency of the second code you want to combine.
6. Type) and hit enter to add the values together.
7. Fill in the remaining frequencies in the same way for the combined codes.

MAXQDA Procedure 6.6: Combining Codes in MAXQDA

https://goo.gl/LUK52D

1. Create a new higher-level code representing the combination.
2. Move the original codes under the new code to become its subcodes.
3. To create a frequency table for the higher-level codes:
4. From the **Codes** menu, select the **Overview of Codes** command.
5. In the **Overview of Codes** pop-up window, click on the icon for **Aggregate on 1st level**.

MAXQDA will now display the frequencies for just the top-level codes.

Limitations on Combining Codes

Two limitations need to be placed on the use of combing codes as a way of refining distribution patterns. To begin with, codes can only be combined in ways that made sense with respect to the phenomena. Combine apples with apples, not with oranges (unless you are interested in fruit!).

Second, you must always check the distributions of the individual codes in advance of combining them to make sure that no interactions exist. Look at the distributions in Figure 6.26, for example. These represent the individual streams combined to produce the patterns shown in Figure 6.25. Ed and Roger are the managers; Cheryl and John are the subordinates. Combing the speaker codes as we have done makes the implicit claim that Ed and Roger have more in common with each other than they do with Cheryl and John. But the individual streams in Figure 6.26 give lie to this claim. Here we see that Roger, although a manager, looks more like Cheryl and John in his participation than he does like Ed. Combing his data with Ed's data to produce an overall picture of managers' contribution is, therefore misleading. There is an interaction: how managers act depends upon which manager: Ed or Roger. In such cases as this one, you should avoid combining categories.

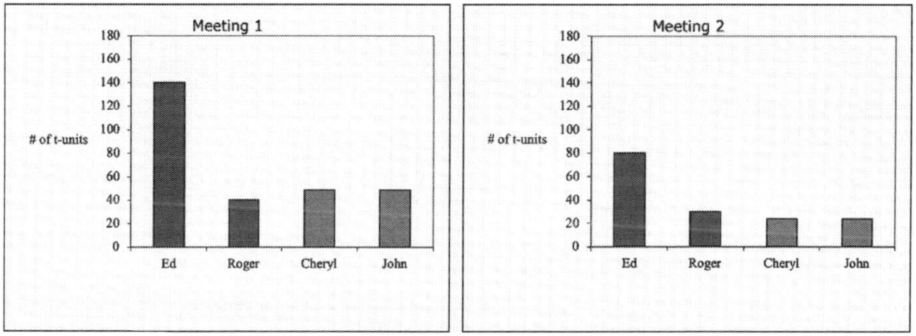

Figure 6.26: Interactions within categories.

Memo 6.5: Combined Codes

Are there codes that you might consider combining to better show the overall patterns in your data? Try to combine them and look again at the distribution of the combined codes.

Does the combined data fairly represent the individual codes?

Selected Studies Using Frequency Distributions

Campbell, K. S. & Naidoo, J. S. (2017). Rhetorical move structure in high-tech marketing white papers. *Journal of Business and Technical Communication*, *31*, 94–118.

For Further Reading

Heath, S. B. & Street, B. V. (2008). *Ethnography: Approaches to language and literacy research*. New York: Teachers College Press.

Maxwell, J. A. (2010). Using numbers in qualitative research. *Qualitative Inquiry* *16*(6), 475–482.

Miles, M. B., Huberman, A. M. & Saldaña, J. (2014). *Qualitative data analysis: A methods sourcebook*. Thousand Oaks, CA: Sage.

Saldaña, J. (2016). *The coding manual for qualitative researchers*. London: Sage.

Sandelowski, M., Voils, C. I. & Knafl, G. (2009). On quantitizing. *Journal of Mixed Method Research* 3(3), 208–222.

Chapter 7. Exploring Patterns Across Dimensions

> In this chapter, you will look at patterns that indicate how one dimension of your data is associated with another dimension. You will build contingency tables showing the relationship across the categories of two dimensions and block charts to examine their patterns. A process for the stepwise comparison of dimensional patterns across your built-in contrast and across multiple streams is introduced.

Dimensions

In the last chapter, we looked at the distribution of your data—the ups and downs created by the categories of your coding scheme. In this chapter, we add another dimension by looking at how these distributions are related to the distribution patterns of a second coding scheme. This kind of analysis will help you understand how the distribution of your data in one dimension is associated with its distribution in a second dimension. The nature of the association between the dimensions of your data can yield useful analytic insights. For example, seeing that two codes in different dimensions go up and down together can suggest a relationship worth investigating.

Adding a second dimension to an analysis involves coding your already-coded set of data with a second coding scheme. The goal is often to develop a greater understanding of the differences across your built-in contrasts. If, for example, you have discovered that design and management meetings are different along the dimension of speaker, you might then begin to wonder how these types of meetings varied along a second dimension—indexicality, for instance. Figure 7.1 shows a sample of data that has been coded in this way both for the dimension of speaker (in column B) and the dimension of indexicality (in column D).

	A	B	C	D
1	T-Unit#	Speaker	Text	Indexicality
2				
3	1	Cheryl	I mean ...	Not Indexed
4	2	Ed	Jesus.	Not Indexed
5	3	Cheryl	See I:	Not Indexed
6	4	Cheryl	see where	Not Indexed
7	5	Cheryl	this little thing is?	Indexed

Figure 7.1: Data coded along two dimensions: speaker and indexicality.

■ Questions of Distribution

By looking at your data across more than one dimension, you can ask two new kinds of questions. To begin with, you can ask how the distribution of data over the categories of the second coding dimension varies across your built-in contrast. This question is a question of distribution and it parallels the question you asked concerning your first dimension. For example, with the two dimensions shown in Figure 7.1, we can ask not only a question about distribution of speaker contribution: *Do design meetings differ from management meetings in the relative contributions made by speaker?* We can also ask a question about the distribution of indexicality: *Are design meetings more or less indexical than management meetings?*

While the distribution of codes from a single dimension can tell us something about the difference between design meetings and management meetings the perspective provided is . . . one dimensional. The qualities that make verbal phenomena significant and analytically interesting are often more complex than can be captured in a single dimension of coding. To get at this complexity, we must ask questions of association.

Questions of Association

If we stopped our analysis with answers to questions of distribution, our understanding of the data will be less than complete. We would fail to explore the associations between the two dimensions—how they are interrelated. For this we have to ask questions of association.

Generally, questions of association ask how variations along one dimension are associated with variations along the second dimension. In the case of the data in Figure 7.1, for example, we can ask a question about the association between speaker contribution and indexicality: Do some speakers employ more indexical language than other speakers? Furthermore, we can ask how that association plays out across our built-in contrasts: Does the rate of indexicality of a speaker vary by the kind of meeting they are attending? The procedures outlined in the rest of this chapter are designed to help you answer questions of association.

Memo 7.1: Second Dimension

Reflect on possibilities for a second dimension of coding that would help illuminate an aspect of your data. Consider dimensions of coding that help you understand distributions that you have already discovered. What questions of distribution and association could you ask with that second dimension and which seem the most likely to further your analysis?

Exercise 7.1 Test Your Understanding

Decide whether each of the following questions is a question of distribution or a question of association. Then label the dimension being used in each question.

- During what decade did Elvis record his most popular songs?
- How is the productivity of rock stars related to age and gender?
- Are men more likely than women to act aggressively in on-line interactions?
- Are certain topics associated with greater aggression among men than among women?

For Discussion: Discuss with your classmates the kind of data sheets that would allow you to answer each question.

Contingency Tables

Seeing associations across dimensions involves the use of contingency tables like the one shown in Figure 7.2. Simply put, a contingency table is a tabular array showing the frequency distributions of two different coding dimensions. The categories of one coding scheme are arrayed across the top of the table (*Indexed* and *Not Indexed*). Down the side are arrayed the categories of the second coding scheme (*Cheryl, Ed, John*). In the cells are listed the frequencies with which the two dimensions intersect. In appearance and effect, a contingency table is a matrix that shows the interrelationship between two coding dimensions. Instead of tracking the distribution of codes within a single dimension (e.g., indexed, not indexed) you are simultaneously tracking the distribution of codes from the first dimension across the second dimension. As seen in Figure 7.2, a portion of the segments that are coded as *Indexed* will be spoken by *Cheryl*, another by *Ed*, and another by *John*. Together, the sum of the indexed segments spoken by *Cheryl*, *Ed*, and *John* equals the total number of segments coded as indexed. For example, the upper left-hand cell represents the intersection of *Cheryl* with *Indexed*, and the cell itself tells us that 69 of Cheryl's t-units were coded as *Indexed*.

Contingency tables are useful, functional displays of data that can support a range of analyses. They are relatively easy to construct in Excel (see Excel Procedures 7.1, 7.2, and 7.3 and MAXQDA Procedures 7.1 and 7.2).

	Indexed	Not Indexed	**Total**
Cheryl	69	73	142
Ed	40	32	72
John	1	2	3
Total	110	107	217

Figure 7.2: A contingency table for data coded in two dimensions: speaker and indexicality.

Adding a Second Dimension

To add a second dimension to your analysis, return to the original data sheets and construct a second coding scheme whereby each segment of data is assigned to one of the categories associated with a second dimension. Refer to the procedures detailed in Chapters 4 and 5 for developing a coding scheme and confirming its reliability. The result will be data that has been coded along two dimensions.

Creating Core Contingency Tables

Begin by creating your core contingency tables, one table for each of your data streams. For example, if you have data from four meetings—two design meetings and two management meetings—you must build core contingency tables for all four of these meetings. The results should look similar to Figure 7.3.

Design 1	Indexed	Not Indexed	Total
Cheryl	49	71	120
Ed	46	55	101
John	51	72	123
Total	146	198	344

Management 1	Indexed	Not Indexed	Total
Cheryl	69	73	142
Ed	40	32	72
John	1	2	3
Total	110	107	401

Design 2	Indexed	Not Indexed	Total
Cheryl	59	125	184
Ed	12	39	51
John	39	127	166
Total	110	291	401

Management 2	Indexed	Not Indexed	Total
Cheryl	36	30	66
Ed	10	19	29
John	71	44	115
Total	117	93	210

Figure 7.3: Core contingency tables for all streams.

Exercise 7.2 Try It Out

Download a copy of the Design and Management meeting data from the book website and build core contingency tables of your own, following the examples described above and shown in the video.

Excel Procedure 7.1: Naming the Data Ranges for Each Dimension

https://goo.gl/tWgjbL

1. Go to the tab for the first data stream (e.g., Design 1) and click on the column header to select the first dimension (e.g., Speaker).
2. Click **Insert** > **Name** > **Define Name** as shown in Figure 7.4.
3. Label the data range with a name that combines the data stream name and the dimension name (e.g., Design1Speaker) and click **OK** as shown in Figure 7.5.
4. In the same tab, click on the column header to select the second dimension (e.g., Indexicality).
5. Click **Insert** > **Name** > **Define Name** and label the data range (e.g., Design1-Indexicality) Then click **OK**.
6. Repeat these steps for the data streams on the other tabs until you have all data ranges named and saved.

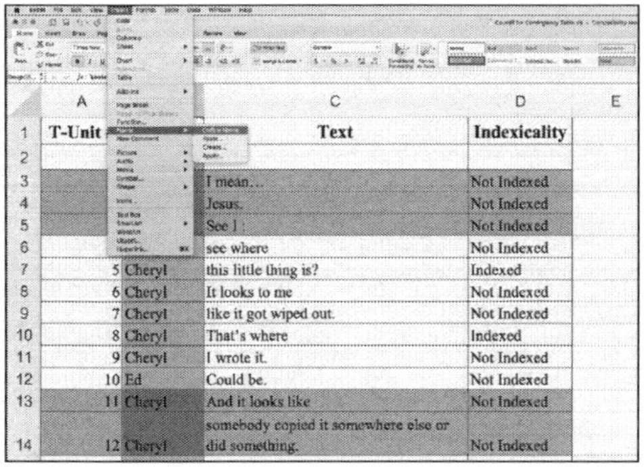

Figure 7.4: Insert a name for the data range.

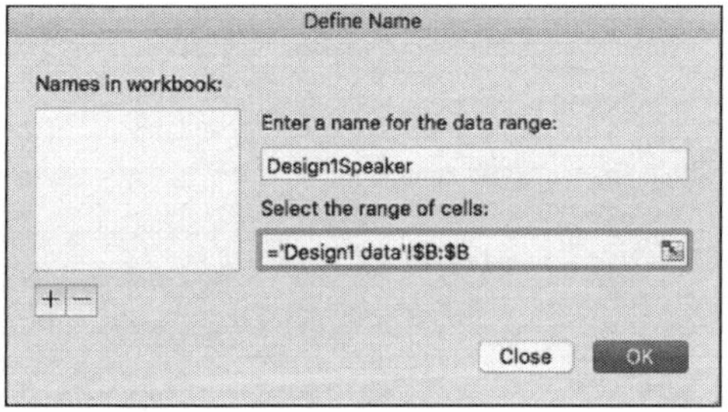

Figure 7.5: Choose a name for the data range.

Excel Procedure 7.2: Setting Up a Core Contingency Table

https://goo.gl/tWgjbL

You can use the named data ranges to set up and fill the core contingency tables.

1. Insert a worksheet to hold your contingency tables and label it as analysis.
2. Set up a table for your first data stream, with the categories of the first dimension down the side and the categories of the second dimension across the columns.
3. Make sure to include a label for the data stream as show in Figure 7.3

Excel Procedure 7.3: Filling Core Contingency Tables

https://goo.gl/tWgjbL

Each cell of the core contingency table is filled with a formula with the following structure:

```
=countifs(
 Dimension1DataRange,
 Dimension1Value,
 Dimension2DataRange,
 Dimension2Value)
```

To enter this formula into your table:

1. Click in the cell corresponding to the first intersection between your two coding dimensions.

For example: In Figure 7.6 B3 corresponds to the intersection between speaker and indexicality in which Cheryl uses an indexical.

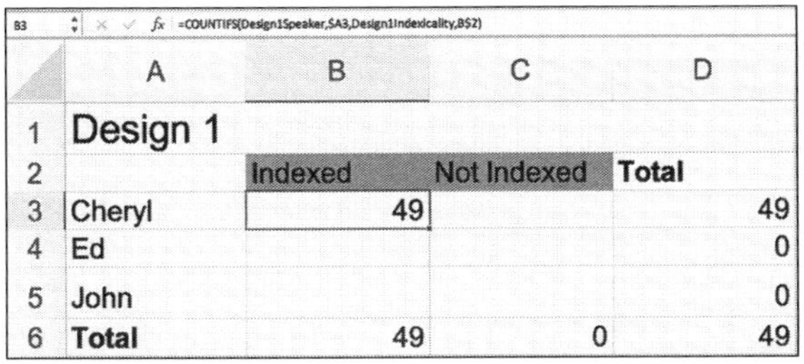

Figure 7.6: Add formula to the intersection of Dimension 1 and 2.

2. In the formula bar type

   =countifs(

3. Then click **Insert** > **Name** > **Paste** and choose the data range for the first dimension (e.g., "DesignSpeaker").
4. Type a comma.
5. Then click on the cell holding the name of the first coding category for the first dimension. This is the criteria for counting in the first data range.

Continued . . .

Excel Procedure 7.3: Filling Core Contingency Tables (continued)

https://goo.gl/tWgjbL

For example (see Figure 7.10), we click on A3 "Cheryl" meaning that we have supplied the first argument to look in the data range we named "Design1Speaker" and find every instance of "Cheryl."

6. Type another comma.
7. Then click **Insert** > **Name** > **Past** and choose the data range for the second dimension (e.g., "Design1Indexicality").
8. Type another comma.
9. Then click on the cell holding the name of the first coding category in the second dimension (e.g., Indexed).
10. Type) and hit enter.
11. Next, edit the formula to put a $ in front of the column for the first dimension and in front of the row for the second dimension. This "fixes" or keeps their values constant.

In our example, the forumula will now say:

> =countifs(Design1Speaker,$A3,
> Design1Indexicality,B$2)

This forumla looks in the data range Design1Speaker for the word Cheryl and then it looks in the data range Design1Indexicality to find the word indexed. It counts the number of times both criteria are met in the data ranges specified.

12. Drag this formula across the columns and then down the rows to fill your table.
13. Continue the same process for each of your data streams.

MAXQDA Procedure 7.1: Creating a Contingency Table with Two Dimensions

https://goo.gl/tWqjbL

The following procedure can be used to create contingency tables with two dimensions, like those shown in Figures 7.2 and 7.27. This can be used to produce charts such as those in Figures 7.11, 7.28, and 7.29.

1. Activate the document holding your first data stream.
2. Activate the codes for your first dimension.
3. Select **Visual Tools> Code Relations Browser**.
4. As shown in Figure 7.7, select **Activated codes** for rows.
5. Select **Choose top level codes** for columns.
6. Choose **Co-occurrence of codes** for type of analysis.
7. Make sure that **Only for activated documents** is checked.
8. Click **OK**.
9. In the next input window, select the categories for your second dimension as shown in Figure 7.8.

The pop-up window will now show a core contingency table with colored squares in the cells.

10. Click on the **Display nodes as values** icon to change squares to values.
11. Click on the **Sum** icon to add marginal sums.
12. Click on the **Open as Excel table** icon to open the table in Excel.
13. Repeat these steps for the rest of your documents/ data streams.

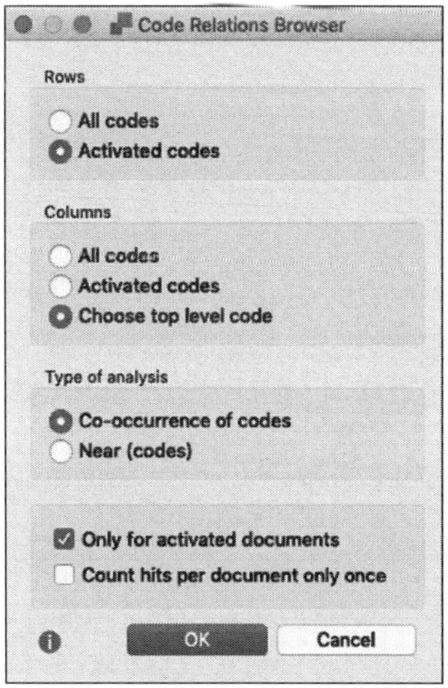

Figure 7.7: Input for a core contingency table in the Code Relations Browser in MAXQDA.

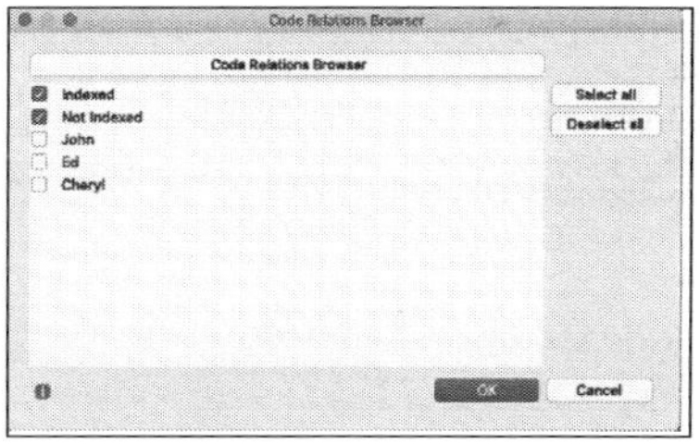

Figure 7.8: Selecting the codes for the second dimension for a core contingency table in the Code Relations Browser in MAXQDA.

MAXQDA Procedure 7.2: Creating a Contingency Table with One Dimension

https://goo.gl/tWgjbL

The following procedure can be used to create contingency tables with one dimension, like those shown in Figure 7.20 and on the top of Figure 7.23. These tables can be used to produce charts such as the two top graphs in Figures 7.25.

1. Activate the required documents/data streams.
2. Activate the codes of one dimension.
3. Select **Codes** > **Overview of Codes** to create a table like that shown in Figure 7.9.

All

3 (5) Codes

	Parent code	Code	Coded segments of all d...	Coded segment...	Author	Creation date	Code alias	% Coded segme...	% Coded segme...	Documents
●		Ed	257	101	Cheryl Geisler	.../18 9:56 AM		21.80	23.65	4
●		John	409	118	Cheryl Geisler	.../18 10:07 AM		34.69	27.63	4
●		Cheryl	513	208	Cheryl Geisler	.../18 9:55 AM		43.51	48.71	4

Figure 7.9: Unedited version of a contingency table with one dimension.

4. Click on the **Only activate codes** icon to see just one dimension.
5. Click on the **Open as Excel table** icon to open the table in Excel.
6. In Excel, label the table appropriately.
7. Delete from the table all columns except for the column with the codes and the column labeled **Coded segments of activated documents** as shown in Figure 7.10.

Management x Speaker	Coded segments of activated documents
Ed	101
John	118
Cheryl	208

Figure 7.10: Contingency table with one dimension made using Overview of Codes.

Graphing Dimensions

The rest of this chapter outlines a stepwise process for analyzing graphs constructed from the core contingency tables described in the last section. Before you go on to this analysis, however, we introduce the general procedure for constructing these graphs (see Excel Procedure 7.4 and MAXQDA Procedure 7.3).

Just as your analysis adds a dimension with the addition of a second coding scheme, so too do your graphing techniques. The basic graph used to explore data coded along two dimensions is called a block chart. As you can see from the example in Figure 7.11, a block chart is a three-dimensional graph. Along the x-axis are arrayed the coding categories of the first coding scheme. Along the z-axis are arrayed the coding categories of the second coding scheme. The third or y-axis shows the number of segments. The graph itself shows the distribution of the segments across the two coding dimensions.

In Figure 7.11, for example, we see that in the Management1 meeting, Cheryl was the most frequent speaker, Ed the second most frequent, and John hardly spoke at all. We also see that this pattern holds true both for contributions that were indexed (shown in blue) and those that were not indexed (shown in orange).

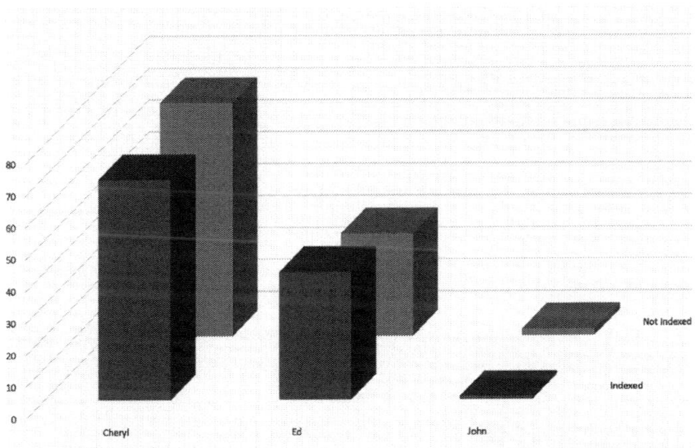

Figure 7.11: A block chart showing two-dimensional data for the Management1 Stream: speaker and indexicality.

Excel Procedure 7.4: Creating a Block Chart

https://goo.gl/tWgjbL

Creating a block chart for data coded along two dimensions involves the same basic process as creating a frequency chart.

1. Select the data in the contingency table, including both column and row headers, but excluding the marginals, as shown to the left of Figure 7.12.

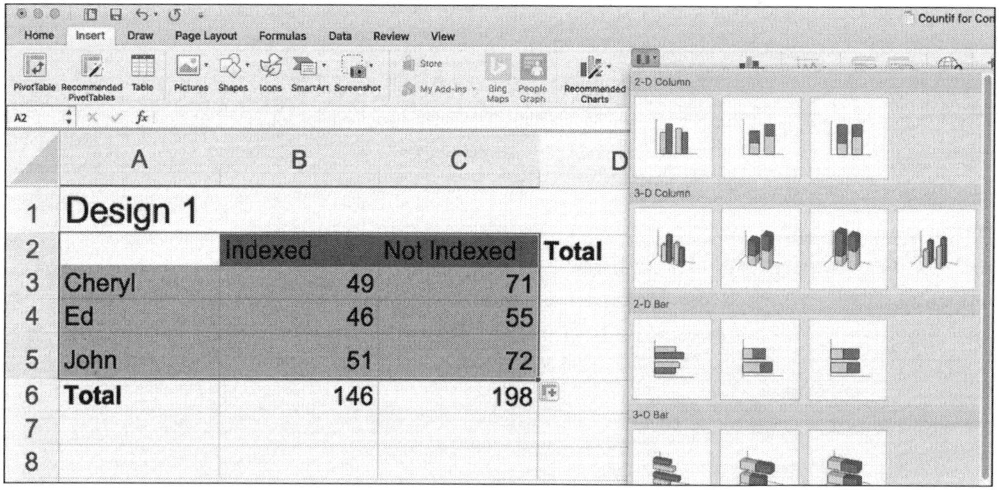

Figure 7.12: Selecting the data and the 3-D column graph to create a block chart.

2. Highlight the cells that include the data you want to graph.
3. Choose the **Insert** tab and choose 3-D column from under the column chart dropdown menu.

Block charts offer the same set of options that you have available for frequency graphs. The chart shown in Figure 7.11, for example, has the following:

- For the chart **Title**, we used the names of the two dimensions as well as the name of the stream (i.e., Speaker x Indexicality x Management1); this helps us to keep track of what we have graphed.
- For **Gridlines**, we have removed the default gridlines.
- For the **Legend**, we have deselected the **Show legend** box since it provides redundant information.

Create a chart style for your preferred options in a block graph to save considerable time.

MAXQDA Procedure 7.3: Making a Block Chart from MAXQDA Data

https://goo.gl/tWgjbL

Once MAXQDA data has been moved into Excel using MAXQDA procedure 7.1 or 7.2, you can use Excel to create a block chart as follows:

1. Select the data in the contingency table, including both column and row headers, but excluding the marginals, as shown to the left of Figure 7.12.
2. Highlight the cells that include the data you want to graph.
3. Choose the **Insert** tab and choose **3-D column** from under the column chart dropdown menu.

Block charts offer the same set of options that you have available for other graphs. The chart shown in Figure 7.11, for example, has the following:

- For the chart **Title**, we used the names of the dimensions as well as the name of the stream (i.e., Speaker x Indexicality x Management1).
- For **Gridlines**, we have removed the default gridlines.
- For the **Legend**, we have deselected the **Show legend** box since it provides redundant information.

■ Rotating the Chart

Although block charts have the value of showing distribution data in two dimensions, they have the flaw of being difficult to read and interpret. The forward plane of the graph often obscures the data on the planes behind it. Furthermore, the dimensionality of the graph often makes it difficult to compare magnitudes across planes.

To deal with difficulties in viewing patterns in a block chart, you will find it useful to rotate the chart (see Excel Procedure 7.5 and MAXQDA Procedure 7.4.

Rotating charts can help to refine your understanding of the patterns in three-dimensional block charts. In Figure 7.13, for example, while it was easy to see the contours across the dimension of speaker contribution, it was harder to compare across the dimension of indexicality. Are there more, less, or about the same numbers of indexed units as non-indexed? The view in Figure 7.13 made it hard to tell. Once the graph is rotated to the view shown in Figure 7.14, however, the answer is more easy to come by: The levels are more or less the same.

When you want to compare block charts, it is important that they have the same degree of rotation.

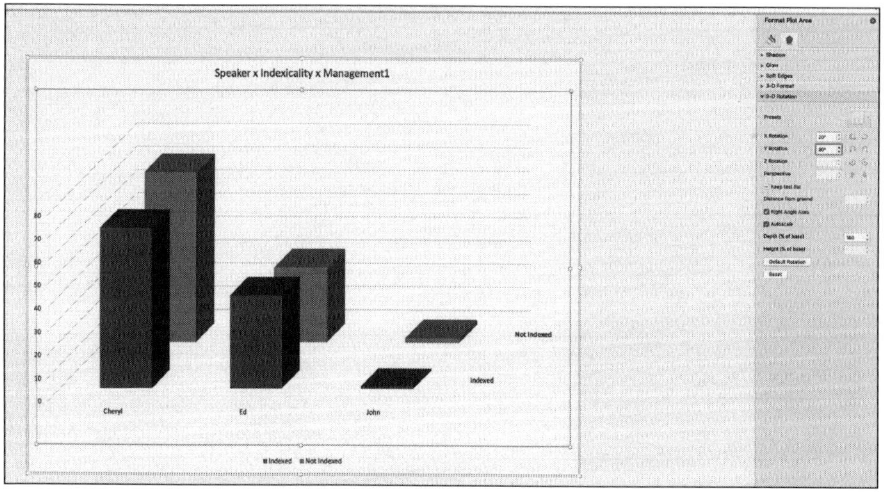

Figure 7.13: Rotating a block chart.

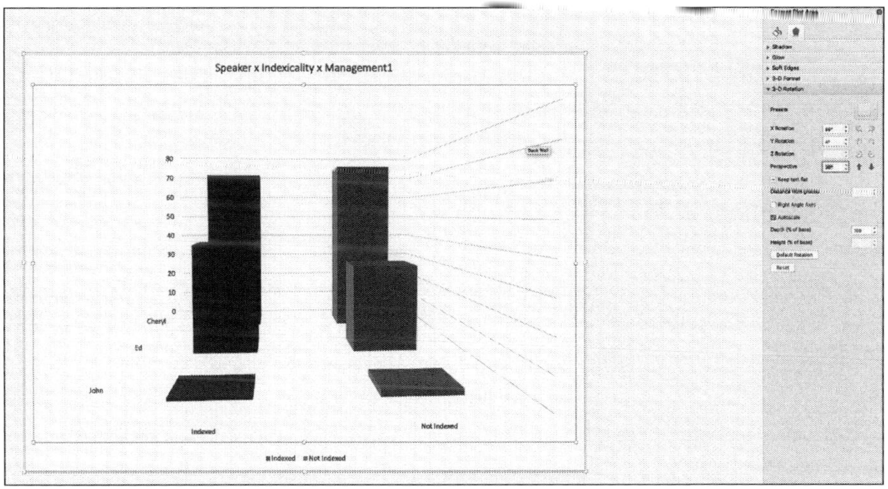

Figure 7.14: A rotated view of the same data shown in Figure 7.13.

Excel Procedure 7.5: Rotating a Block Chart in Excel

https://goo.gl/tWgjbL

1. Click on the block chart to select it, then right-click (control+click on Mac) to access the context menu.
2. Choose **3-D Rotation** from the **context** menu.
3. Adjust the values for X rotation and Y rotation until you can see the data that had been hidden (See Figure 7.13).

MAXQDA Procedure 7.4: Rotating a Block Chart for MAXQDA Data

https://goo.gl/tWgjbL

1. Click on the block chart to select it, then right-click to access the context menu.
2. Choose **3-D Rotation** from the **context** menu.

Adjust the values for X rotation and Y rotation until you can see the data that had been hidden (See Figure 7.13).

Refining Patterns

As you create block charts, you may find that the distribution patterns of certain categories are similar to one another and quite different from patterns for other categories. In Figure 7.15, for example, there appear to be three different patterns. First, we can see business, technology, and special interest publications as sharing the same pattern of dominance through the years. Another group of publications seems to have started from relatively modest numbers in 1996 and to have been increasing. And finally, a third group of publications wasn't on the horizon in 1996, but seems to have become a regular, if still small, publication venue by 2000.

When you see possible clusters in the distribution patterns of your data, you can reorder the categories in your data sheet to create block charts that better represent these clusters (see Excel Procedure 7.6 and MAXQDA Procedure 7.5). An example of a clustered block chart is shown in Figure 7.16. Here, we have placed the categories with the strongest incidence toward the left of the chart, the "medium" categories in the middle, and the relatively late-occurring categories toward the right. This kind of clustered display has greater ability to convey that the publication patterns for the articles.

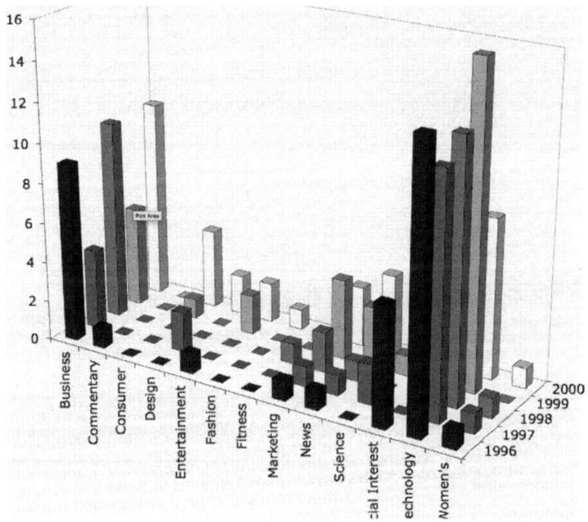

Figure 7.15: A block chart showing how the distribution of articles across publication type varies by year.

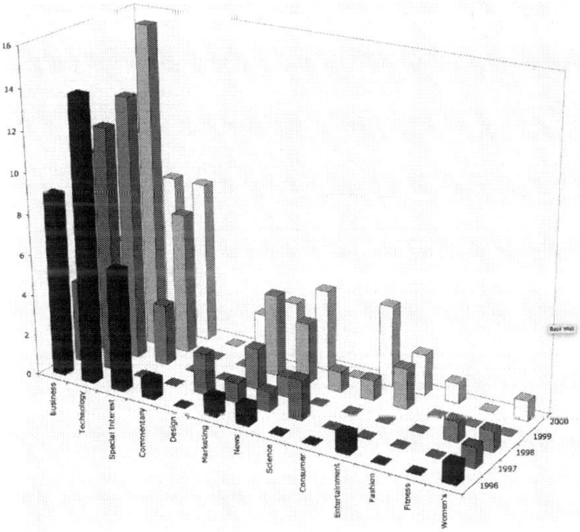

Figure 7.16: Clustering categories to reveal common patterns of distribution.

■ Memo 7.2 Core Contingency Tables

Build a set of core contingency tables for the dimensions of your data that you want to compare. From those tables, build a set of block charts and reflect on the patterns that are revealed. What meaningful relationships are emerging from the data? How can the data be clustered to clarify the visual representation of those relationships?

Exercise 7.3 Try It Out

For a study of PDA users (Personal Digital Assistants), we classified participants into three groups based upon the balance between work and life items in their PDAs: Strong Life, Strong Work, and Integrated. We were interested to understand the relationship between this Work-Life Balance classification and their home situation. The data are shown in the table in Figure 7.18 and available at https://wac.colostate.edu/books/practice/codingstreams/.

Use the techniques in this chapter to cluster together those participants with children, with partner but no children, and without family responsibilities.

	Single, living alone	Single, living with partner	Single, living with friends	Single, with children	Married, no children
STRONG LIFE	4	0	0	0	3
INTEGRATED	3	1	0	0	3
STRONG WORK	1	0	0	0	2
Total	8	1	0	0	8

	Married with children at home	Married, children grown	Divorced, with children	Other	Total
STRONG LIFE	2	0	1	0	10
INTEGRATED	9	3	2	0	21
STRONG WORK	6	2	0	0	11
Total	17	5	3	0	42

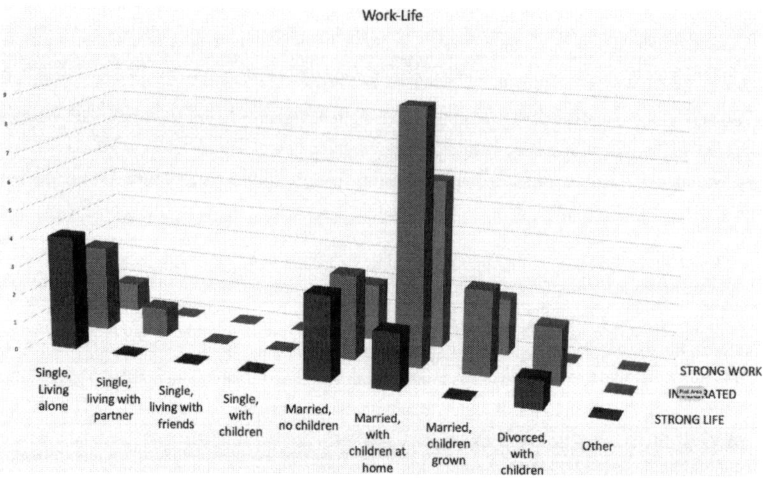

Figure 7.17: Relationship between work-life balance and home situation.

For Discussion: What relationship, if any, do you see between work-life balance and home situation?

Excel Procedure 7.6: Creating Clustered Categories in a Block Chart

https://goo.gl/tWgjbL

1. Return to your contingency table and insert a cluster value to group the data categories of interest.

For example, insert a column to the left to group data categories across the rows or a row across the top to group data categories across the columns (see Figure 7.18).

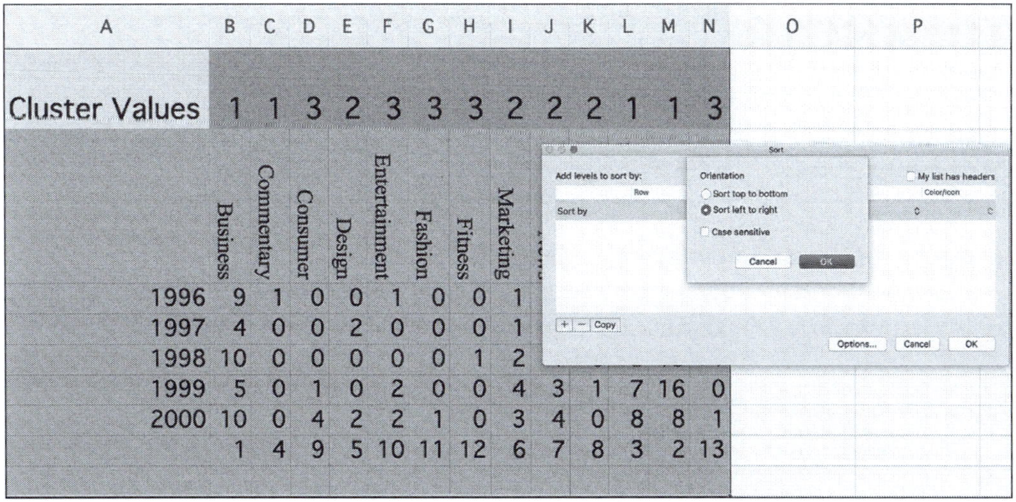

Figure 7.18: Assigning a cluster value to categories of data in the totals worksheet.

2. Assign a common cluster value to data points that you want to appear close together in the chart.

Assign low cluster values to data points that you want to appear on the left of the chart and high cluster values to data points you want to appear on the right (see Figure 7.18).

3. Select the entire table (including the cluster values) then click **Data** > **Sort.**
4. In the dialogue box that appears, choose the column holding your cluster values, and then click the **Option button** to choose the direction of the sort.
   - Sort top to bottom to sort by cluster values in a column.
   - Sort left to right to sort by cluster values in a row.

The result will be a clustered set of categories in your contingency table that will automatically update your associated block graphs to look like the one in Figure 7.17.

MAXQDA Procedure 7.5: Creating Clustered Categories in a Block Chart

https://goo.gl/tWgjbL

1. Return to your contingency table and insert a cluster value to group the data categories of interest.

For example, insert a column to the left to group data categories across the rows or a row across the top to group data categories across the columns (see Figure 7.18).

2. Assign a common cluster value to data points that you want to appear close together in the chart.

Assign low cluster values to data points that you want to appear on the left of the chart and high cluster values to data points you want to appear on the right (see Figure 7.18).

3. Select the entire table (including the cluster values) then click **Data** > **Sort**.
4. In the dialogue box that appears click the **Option button** to choose the direction of the sort:
   - Sort top to bottom to sort by cluster values in a column.
   - Sort left to right to sort by cluster values in a row.

The result will be a clustered set of categories in your contingency table that will automatically update your associated block graphs to look like the one in Figure 7.17.

Characterizing Dimensions

The analysis of verbal data across dimensions is a complex comparative process that builds up analyses from a basic understanding of how your codes are distributed across all of your data streams. One way to understand it is through the schematic given in Figure 7.19. The base of your analysis starts with characterizing the overall distribution patterns of each dimension (Dimension). From there, we split your data across both sides of the built-in contrast to see if the distribution holds (Dimension × Contrast). If the distribution pattern differs across the contrast, then the contrast may be analytically meaningful. Next, we examine the associations between dimensions and check them across the contrasts (Dimension × Dimension × Contrast). Finally, you take whatever patterns you find across dimensions and contrasts and see whether they hold true across cases (Dimension × Contrast × Stream).

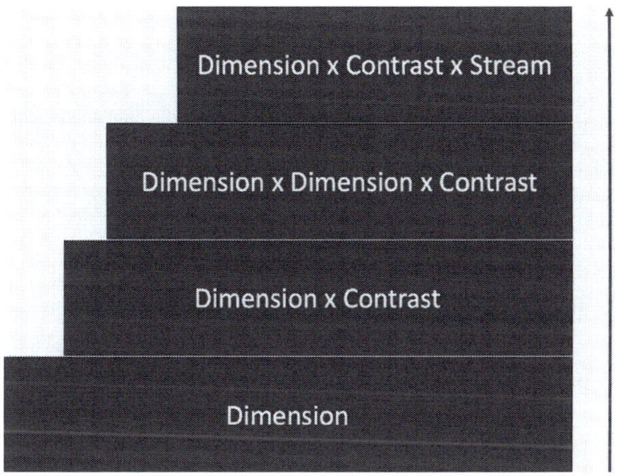

Figure 7.19: Schematic of the complex comparative process of analyzing data across dimensions.

As this schematic indicates, then, the distribution of codes within each dimension is the baseline of our analysis. While many factors arise that can complicate, if not compromise, the adequacy of these baseline characterizations, you will only be able to understand these complications if you begin with overall characterizations. Each successive layer of complexity in the analysis then becomes meaningful only by comparison to the baseline understanding upon which it is built.

A characterization of the overall pattern for a dimension is a description of the general contours of the data as it is distributed in the categories of your coding scheme—without regard to specific streams and without regard to the built-in contrast. If you have a coding scheme with three categories, for example, you ask yourself how, overall, the data have been placed in those categories: You can think about these distributions in terms of frequencies (e.g., 33 of 100 segments) or proportions (e.g., 33%).

Figure 7.20, for instance, shows the frequency and relative frequency of the coding categories for the categories of speaker (Cheryl, Ed, and John) and for the categories of indexicality (Indexed and Not Indexed). Notice that the totals for each table are identical because exactly the same set of segments has been classified according to both schemes.

■ Calculating Overall Frequencies

To calculate overall frequencies for each dimension and fill tables like those shown in Figure 7.20, sum the appropriate frequencies from the core contingency tables for each case (see Excel Procedure 7.7 and MAXQDA Procedure 7.6). If, for example, we have the same four meetings (two management, two design) described earlier, the overall frequency for Cheryl would be equal to the totals for Cheryl in Management1, in Management2, in Design1, and in Design2. The values we need to sum are, therefore, in all four core contingency tables, and we need to bring them together in one formula.

■ Establishing Overall Patterns

Because you will be comparing the overall patterns for each dimension to the patterns across built-in contrasts, the relative frequencies give you the best understanding of the overall patterns for each dimension. We can see from Figure 7.20, for example, that overall, 41% of the segments were indexed and 59% not indexed, a pattern in which, in general, the language is slightly less indexed than not indexed. Once we know this, we can then go on to see whether this overall pattern of indexicality holds across our built-in contrasts.

Speaker		
	Frequency	Relative Frequency
Cheryl	512	0.43
Ed	269	0.23
John	407	0.34
Total	1188	1

Indexicality		
	Frequency	Relative Frequency
Indexed	483	0.41
Not Indexed	705	0.59
Total	1188	1

Figure 7.20: Overall patterns for the dimension of speaker contribution and indexicality.

Memo 7.3: Emerging Patterns

Create contingency tables that sum across the data streams in your study. What are the patterns that begin to emerge? Are these patterns what you expected? What might these patterns be telling you about the phenomenon?

Graphing Overall Patterns

Sometimes you will want to create a graphic representation of the overall patterns for a dimension to compare with patterns across contrast. With a two-category coding scheme like indexicality, this is not particularly necessary because the overall pattern of 41% versus 59% is not hard to understand. But for dimensions with more numerous categories, graphing can be helpful.

Although you are working with one-dimension data, you will find it easier to use three-dimensional block charts to facilitate comparison with later block charts. Figure 7.21 shows block charts for the overall relative frequencies for both dimensions of the data seen earlier in Figure 7.20. You

Excel Procedure 7.7: Summing Overall Frequencies

https://goo.gl/tWgjbL

1. Build a table to hold the frequency values you wish to track.
2. Begin a sum formula (i.e.,=) and then **control+click (command click** on Mac) the values to be summed from each contingency table.

For example, Figure 7.20 shows the result of summing Cheryl's contributions from four contingency tables (Design 1, Design 2, Management 1, and Management 2) = D28+J28+D36+J36.

MAXQDA Procedure 7.6: Summing Overall Frequencies

https://goo.gl/tWgjbL

1. Activate the documents you wish to sum across.
2. Activate the codes you want to include.
3. Use the **Codes** > **Overview of Codes** command to create the table.

The sums will be found in the column labeled Coded segments of activated documents.

4. For a table with two dimensions, use the **Visual Tools** > **Code Relations Browser** to create the table as described in MAXQDA Procedure 7.1.

may notice that they are slightly different from one another. The dimension of speaker contribution is distributed along the x-axis; that for indexicality along the z-axis. This change facilitates comparison with the block charts we will create in general.

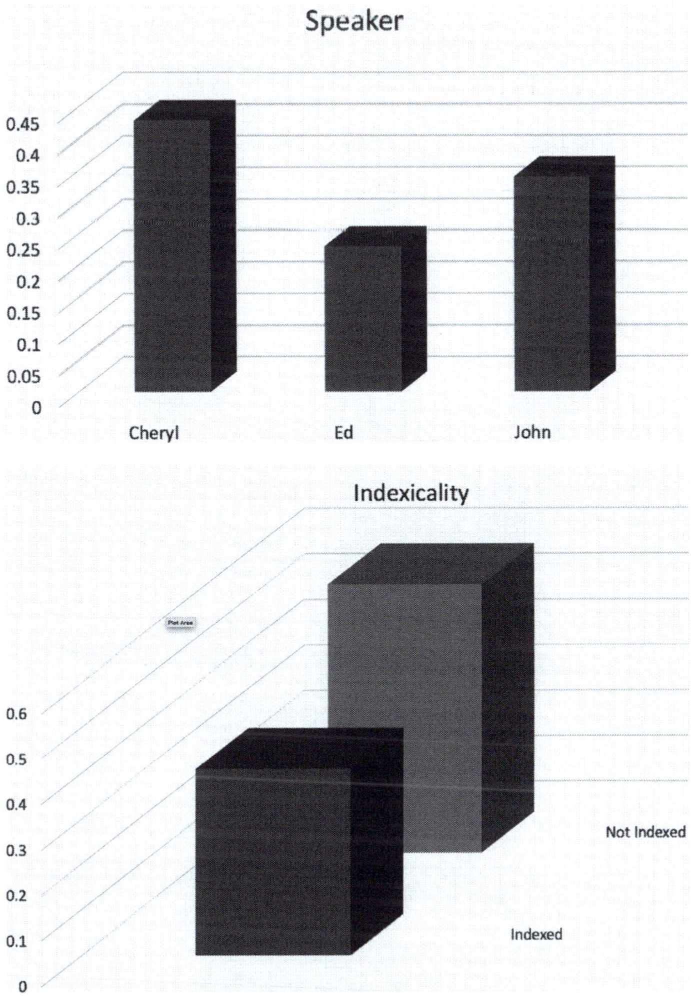

Figure 7.21: Block charts of the overall patterns for speaker contribution and indexicality.

When you create a three-dimensional graph using two-dimensional data, Excel will array that data along the x-axis by default. This will work well for your first dimension, but is not as easy to work with for your second dimension. To move a second dimension from the x-axis to the z-axis, select your graph and choose "switch row/column" from the Insert tab as seen in Figure 7.22.

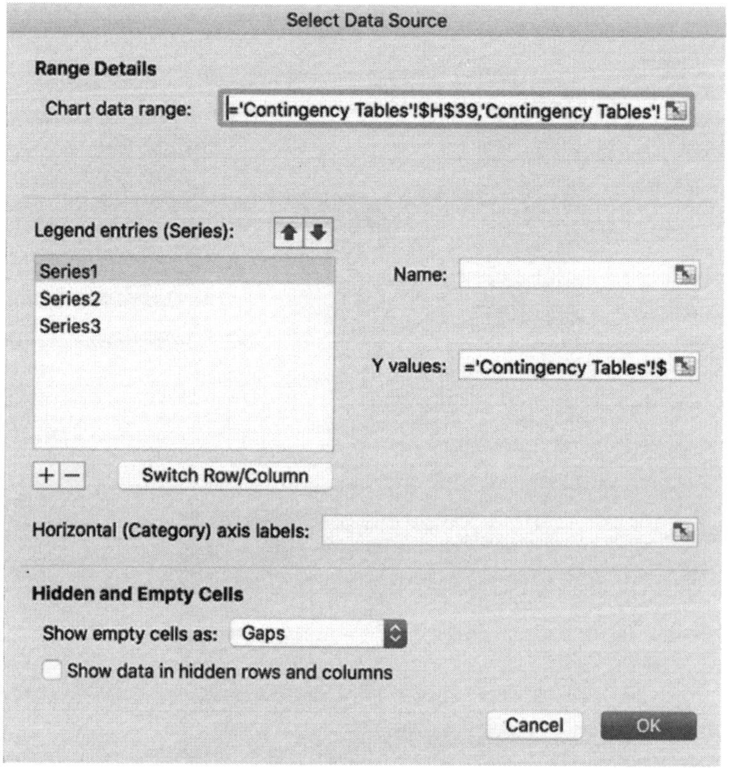

Figure 7.22: Button to switch graph perspective between data on rows and columns.

One final note about producing these block charts. With data laid out as shown in Figure 7.20, you cannot simply drag to select the data to produce block charts like those shown in Figure 7.21. As you can see, the data for relative frequency are not adjacent to the category names on the spreadsheet. While you could copy and rearrange the data in a more appropriate manner, a way does exist to select non-adjacent data (see Excel Procedure 7.8).

Checking Patterns across Contrast

Once you understand the overall patterns for each dimension of the data, you can explore how these patterns change across your built-in contrast. Examine each dimension separately.

Establishing the Contrast

Begin by constructing a set of contingency tables for each dimension that show the data on either side of your contrast. In Figure 7.23, for example, you can see two sets of contingency tables, one for the dimension of speaker contribution and one for the dimension of indexicality. These have been created by summing the relevant data from our core contingency tables.

Excel Procedure 7.8: Selecting Non-Adjacent Data for Graphing

https://goo.gl/tWgjbL

1. From the **Insert** tab, choose a blank 3-d column chart.
2. Right click in the blank chart and select **Series Data**.
3. Click on the graph icon in the field **Chart Data Range** and then select the two non-adjacent data series that you would like to graph.

For example, first choose the data series for the category names (e.g., H37:H39) and then choose the data series for the relative frequencies (e.g., H45:H46).

4. Separate those two data series by a comma and press enter to build your chart with the appropriate labels.

    =ContingencyTables!$H$37:$H$39,
    Contingency Tables!$H$45:$H$46

Assign a common cluster value to data points that you want to appear close together in the chart.

Speaker x Management		Speaker x Design		Speaker	
Cheryl	208	Cheryl	304	Cheryl	512
Ed	101	Ed	168	Ed	269
John	118	John	289	John	407
Total	427	Total	761	Total	1188

Indexicality x Management			Indexicality x Design			Indexicality		
Indexed	Not Indexed	Total	Indexed	Not Indexed	Total	Indexed	Not Indexed	Total
227	200	427	256	505	761	483	705	1188

Figure 7.23: Contingency tables across a built-in contrast.

Making the Comparison

Using these contingency tables, we then construct a set of block charts for each dimension and make comparisons with the baseline pattern for that dimension. Two outcomes are possible for these comparisons. On the one hand, the patterns on either side of the contrast may mirror the overall pattern for that dimension. In this case, we have evidence that the contrast may be irrelevant to the dimension. If, on the other hand, the patterns on either side of the built-in contrast shift as we move from one side of the contrast to another, we have evidence that the dimension may be relevant to the contrast. In other words, the dimension may highlight something significant about the contrast that bears further analysis.

For example, Figure 7.24 shows a comparison between the overall pattern for the dimension of speaker contribution and the patterns across the built-in contrast of management versus design. In Graph (A) we see a distribution of the relative frequencies for the dimension of speaker. In Graph (B) we see a distribution of the relative frequencies for the dimension of speaker in design meetings. In Graph C is the distribution for the dimension of speaker in management meetings. We can compare the distributions in B and C to the distribution shown in A so long as the scale of the axes are the same (see Excel Procedure 7.9).

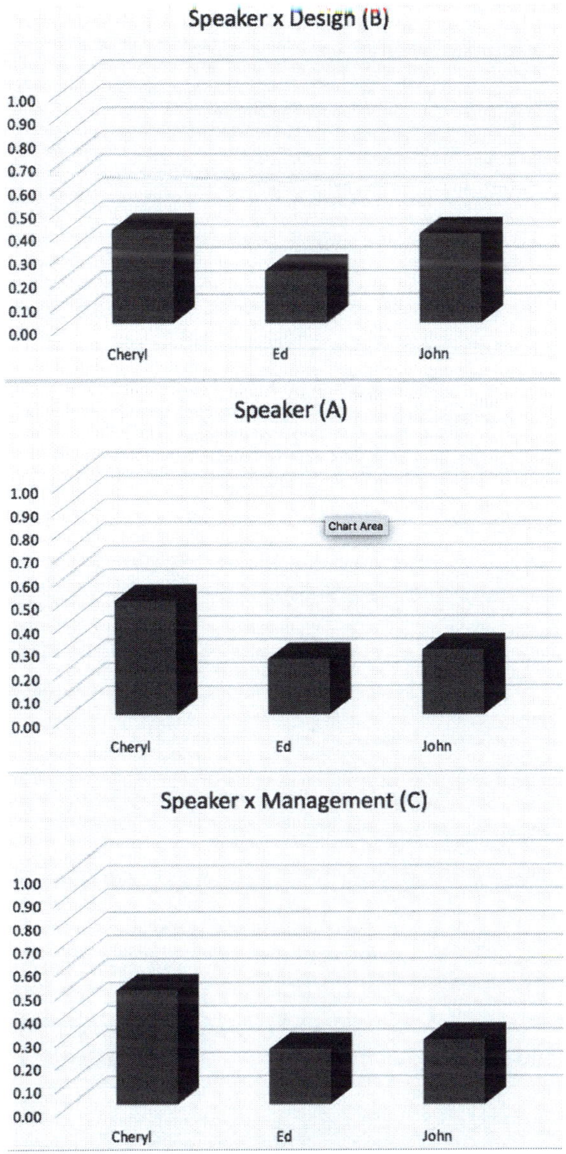

Figure 7.24: Checking the dimension of speaker across contrast of management versus design meetings.

After adjusting the axes, we can see that the contour of the distribution for talk by Cheryl, Ed, and John in the management meetings (B) pretty much mirrors the overall contour (A). The same is true for the design meetings (C) shown at the top.

The general order of speakers—Cheryl, John, Ed—and the general magnitude of the difference between them—Cheryl in the 40%'s, John in the 20%'s and Ed in the 30%'s—seem to suggest that the dimension of speaker contribution is not providing any meaningful insight into the differences between design and management meetings in the data set. As we shall see later on, this evidence is complicated by patterns revealed by later stages of our analysis, but at this stage, it is important to understand the preliminary evidence.

The sample comparisons across the contrast suggests a different story when we look at the second dimension of indexicality. Figure 7.25 shows this comparison. Here, unlike for speaker contribution, we do see substantial differences between the patterns on either side of the contrast and the baseline patterns. As you can see, indexicality appears to be lower, across the board, in design meetings than in management meetings. A look at the relative frequencies confirms this association:

	Overall	**Management**	**Design**
Indexed	0.41	0.53	0.34
Not Indexed	0.59	0.47	0.66

In the management meetings, the majority of the units are indexed; the opposite is the case in the design meetings, where the majority of units are not indexed.

In a situation where the baseline patterns are not borne out by the patterns across the built-in contrast, you find evidence that the contrast is associated with the dimension. What this means is that the overall pattern for a dimension (A)—41% indexed, for example—is not an adequate characterization of the data on either side of your built-on contrast—in this case, of neither the management data (C) (where the ratio was 53% vs. 47%) nor of the design data (B) (where the ratio was 34% vs. 66%). Such a pattern suggests, then, that your built-in contrast makes a difference—is associated—with this dimension.

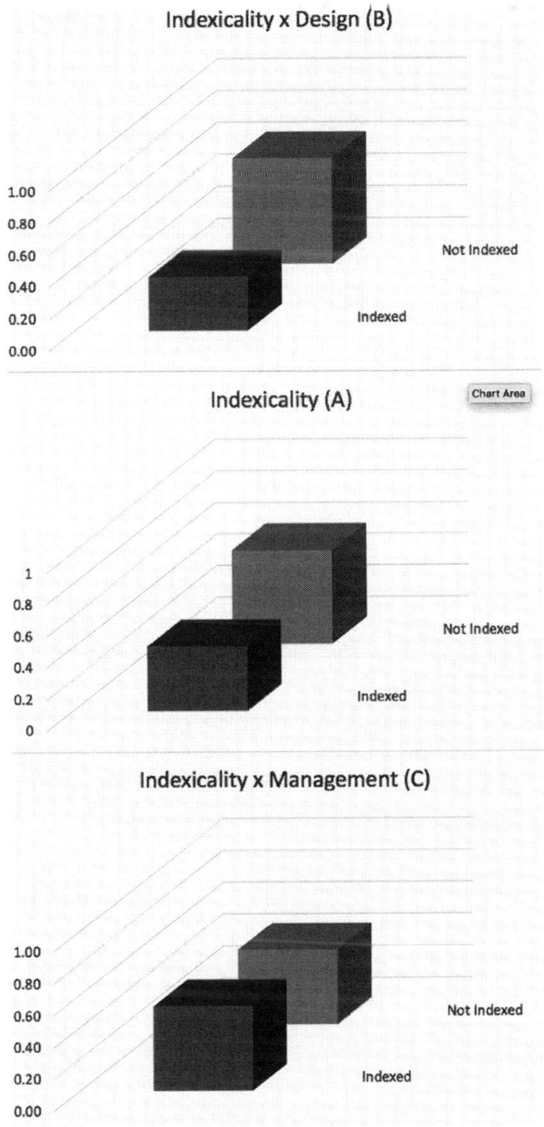

Figure 7.25: Checking the dimension of indexicality across contrast of management versus design meetings.

Checking Patterns across Dimensions

Once you have compared the overall pattern within each dimension with the patterns by contrast, the next step is to compare the patterns across dimensions. Looked at in isolation, dimensions of data may appear to be unassociated when a deeper look shows an association. Association might mean that a coding category from one dimension might *always* apply to the same data segments as a coding category from another dimension. Or it could mean that a coding category from one dimension is *never* applied to the same data segments as a coding category from another dimension. Or other patterns might become visible, which would complicate the analysis further. It might mean, in other words, that the categories within the dimensions are associated with each other.

Establishing the Associations

The foundation for checking patterns across dimensions is an understanding of the baseline associations across dimensions. The reason for making this kind of check is similar to the reason for checking the baseline distribution for each separate dimension. A baseline distribution showing how multiple dimensions intersect will allow you to determine whether the intersection of those dimensions is meaningful for understanding the built-in contrast. For example, if we know how often Cheryl, Ed, and John use indexed language across both the Management and Design meetings, we can compare that pattern to the ones for Management and Design meetings separately. Any variation from the baseline would indicate that the contrast is meaningfully influential on patterns of indexed speech. A contingency table that shows variations in the two dimensions of your analysis, such as that shown at the top of Figure 7.27, will help you to answer this question.

Developing a contingency table of the baseline associations requires summing data from the core contingency tables both across data streams and across contrasts (see Excel Procedure 7.7 and MAXQDA Procedure 7.6). For example, if we began with four core contingency tables, one for each of the two design meetings and one for each of the two management meetings, the contingency table of baseline associations will sum across those four contingency tables to produce one contingency table, the one shown to the right in Figure 7.27. A block chart of these baseline associations is shown in Figure 7.28.

Design 1

	Indexed	Not Indexed	Total
Cheryl	49	71	120
Ed	46	55	101
John	51	72	123
Total	146	198	344

Design 2

	Indexed	Not Indexed	Total
Cheryl	59	125	184
Ed	12	39	51
John	39	127	166
Total	110	291	401

Management 1

	Indexed	Not Indexed	Total
Cheryl	69	73	142
Ed	40	32	72
John	1	2	3
Total	110	107	217

Management 2

	Indexed	Not Indexed	Total
Cheryl	36	30	66
Ed	10	19	29
John	71	44	115
Total	117	93	210

Design Meetings

	Indexed	Not Indexed	Total
Cheryl	108	196	304
Ed	58	94	152
John	90	199	289
Total	256	489	745

Management Meetings

	Indexed	Not Indexed	Total
Cheryl	105	103	208
Ed	50	51	101
John	72	46	118
Total	227	200	427

Figure 7.27: Basic associations across dimensions.

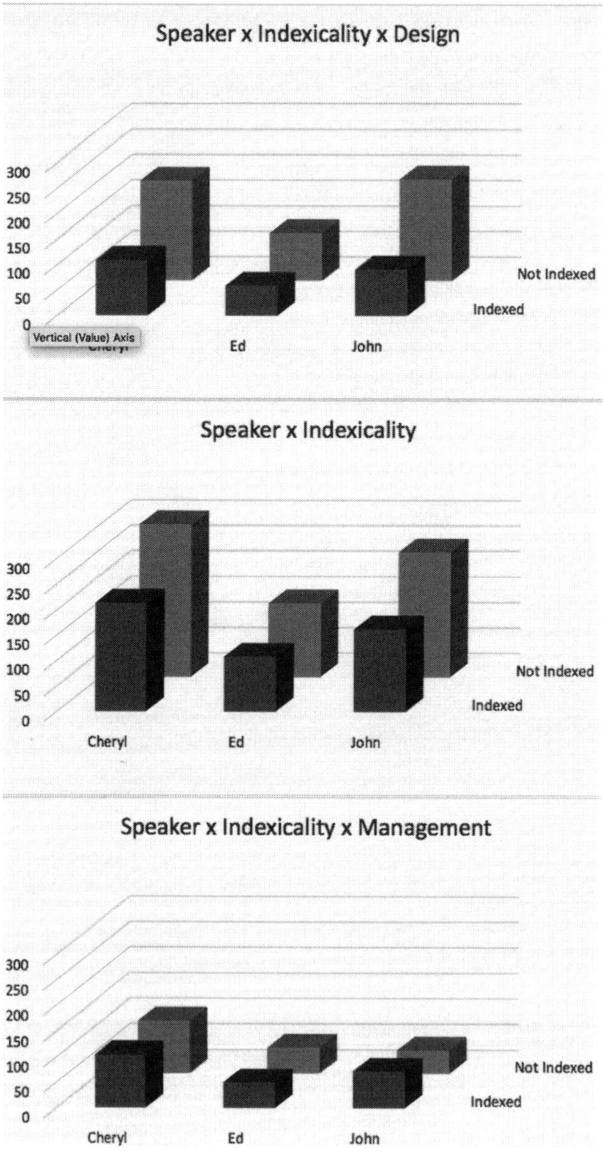

Figure 7.28: Comparing the basic associations across dimensions with the associations across contrasts.

Excel Procedure 7.9: Formatting a Graph Axis

https://goo.gl/tWgjbL

1. On your graph, click once on the Y axis (vertical) to select it.
2. Right click on the selected axis and choose **Format Axis** (Figure 7.26).
3. Adjust the bounds to go from a minimum of 0.0 to a maximum of 1.0 (for relative frequencies).

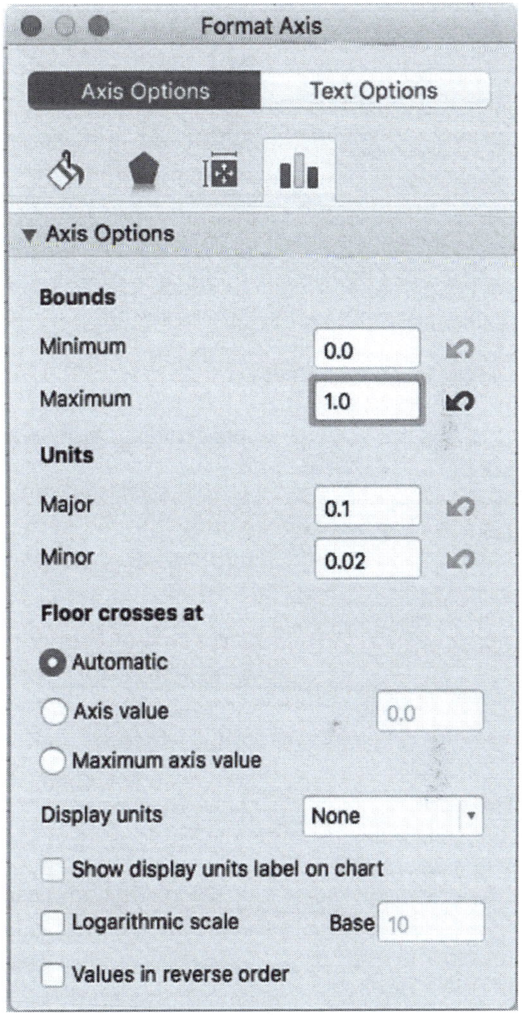

Figure 7.26: Formatting the horizontal (Y) axis.

Checking the Patterns

After establishing this baseline association across dimensions, your next step is to look at the two-dimensional patterns formed on either side of your built-in contrast. In Figure 7.27, we see an example of contingency tables that represent the intersections of the first and second dimensions (Speaker and Indexicality) with the built-in contrast (Management versus Design).

To construct these contingency tables, return to your core contingency tables and sum across data streams, but not across the contrast. In the case of our sample data, then, the original four contingency tables (two design meetings and two management meetings) are collapsed to produce two: one for design and one for management.

Block charts are then constructed from these contingencies like those shown in Figure 7.28. Make sure to adjust their scale to be equivalent if necessary.

Interpreting Comparisons

To make comparisons between the baseline two-dimensional contours and the contours found in the data across the built-in contrast, trace the baseline contour and then see whether that same contour is found in the data by contrast.

For example, as shown in Figure 7.28, we see that the baseline contour for speaker contribution in the indexed data (in the front plane of the chart) goes from a high with Cheryl, moves to a low for Ed, and then rises to an intermediate value for John. Next, we look to see whether this same contour is repeated in the management data. Here we find the same contour, albeit at a lower rate: starting from a high with Cheryl, moving to a low for Ed, rising to an intermediate value for John. In terms of the indexed data, then, the management data looks a lot like the data overall.

Next, we compare the contours for the non-indexed data. In the baseline associations, we see, as we have noted earlier, that across all speakers, contributions are less likely to be indexed than not indexed. In the management data, however, this is not the case; there, the data appear to be about equally indexed and not indexed. That is, the orange columns in the back plane are not that much higher than the blue columns in the front plane. Thus this contour looks quite unlike the unlike the baseline patterns of falling and rising that held true for the overall pattern.

Furthermore, John's contributions do not appear to mirror the general pattern. Indeed, in the non-indexed data, they appear to be no higher than Ed's. That is, the contour here is relatively flat as we move from Ed's column to John's column. Again, this is quite different from either the overall pattern or the pattern for indexed data where John's contributions were higher than Ed's.

Having seen two ways in which the management data do not parallel the two-dimensional contours of the baseline data, we next look to see what is going on in the design data. Here we see what looks like a more expected picture. That is, we see a contour that goes from a high with Cheryl, moves to a low for Ed, and then rises to an intermediate value for John in both data that is indexed and data that is not indexed.

Clearly then, something appears to be going on in the management meetings along both dimensions. In the management meetings, talk is relatively more indexed than usual and John's talk stands out as particularly highly indexed. You can see how this comparison focuses attention on John and the management meetings as potentially interesting from an analytic standpoint. These unusual patterns suggest that the two dimensions, speaker contribution and indexicality, have some association in this data set.

Checking Patterns across Data Streams

The last stage in an analysis across dimensions is to look at the patterns by comparing the data streams. That is, for any pattern that has emerged in the earlier stages of analysis, we need to know whether that pattern holds true for all streams in our data.

Two outcomes are possible. In the first situation, we may find that the patterns suggested in earlier stages of analysis hold true in specific data streams. In this situation, we can report the more general patterns as good characterizations of our data set. In the second situation, we may find that the generalizations suggested in earlier stages do not hold true of specific data streams. In this situation, we must acknowledge that the more general patterns do not provide an adequate characterization of our data set, that there are differences across the streams.

Block graphs of individual data streams can be constructed from the core contingency tables with which we started this chapter. For our sample data, this yields four block graphs, two for design meetings and two for management meetings. We can then compare these to the contours for the graphs established in the last section. That is, we can ask, if the patterns of association that seem to hold overall—between the dimensions of speaker contribution and indexicality and across the contrast of management and design—hold for the individual data streams.

In the design data, the pattern we want to confirm is that the general contours shown in the middle (A) of Figure 7.29 parallel the contours in the two stream-specific graphs above (B) and below it (C). This means that

- the contributions should, in general, be less indexed than indexed and
- that Cheryl should make the greatest number of contributions, followed by John, followed by Ed.

A preliminary comparison suggests that these two patterns do hold in the specific design meetings. That is, the contours of the block chart for Design1 and Design2 suggest both that the language is both less indexed than indexed and that the speaker contributions are ordered and of the same magnitude as in the general pattern.

As we noted earlier, the patterns in the management meetings were more complex than those in the design meetings. In particular, we found preliminary evidence that

- talk is relatively more indexed than usual, and
- that John's talk was particularly highly indexed.

At this final stage in our analysis, we need to understand how these complex patterns play out in the two management streams. Block graphs for the management data are shown in Figure 7.30.

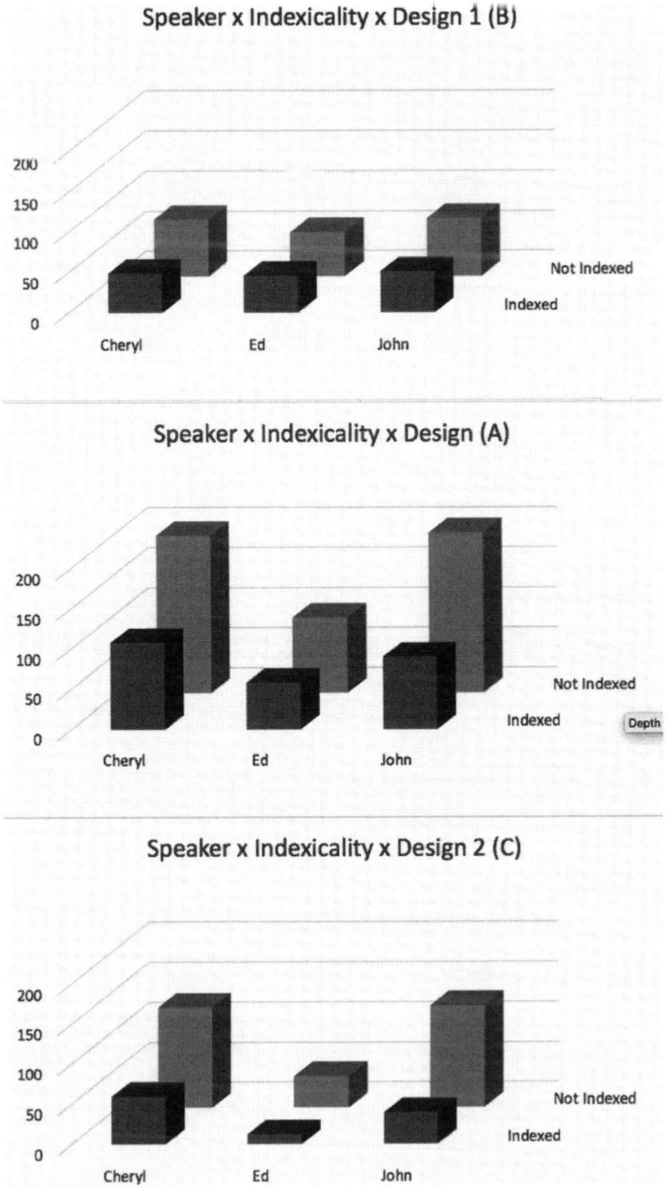

Figure 7.29: Checking patterns across streams in the design data.

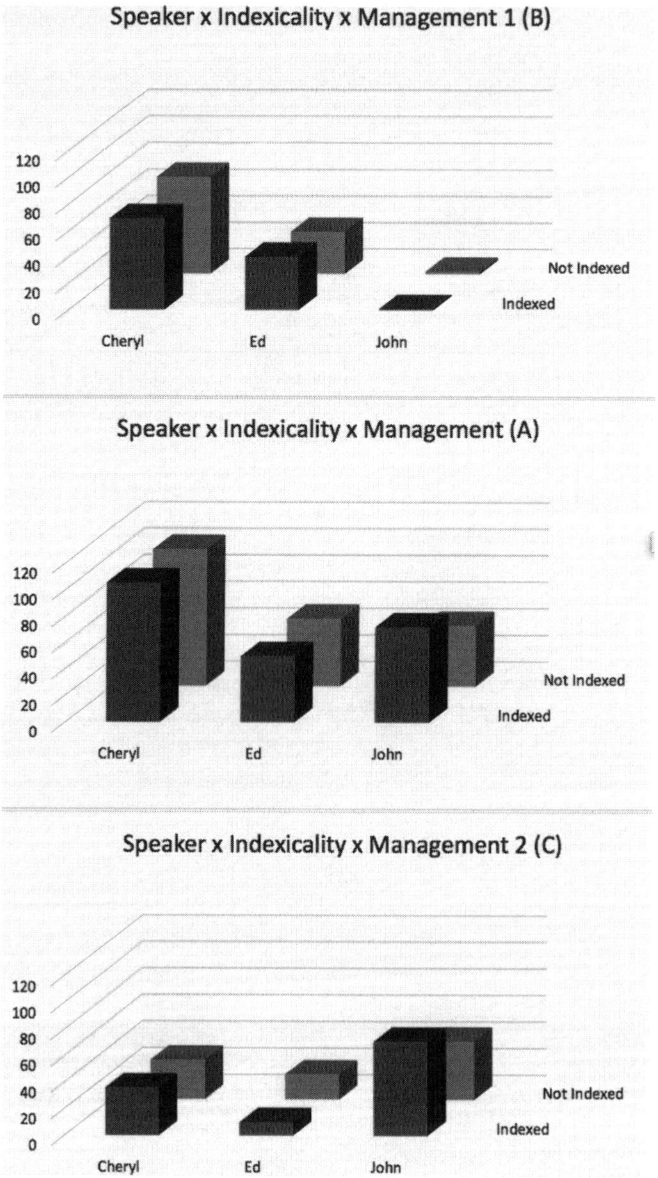

Figure 7.30: Checking patterns across streams in the management data.

Here, unlike in the design data, we find that the general patterns for the management data do not hold for the individual streams. That is, as we see in Figure 7.30, neither Management1 (B) nor Management2 (C) look like each other nor like the general pattern (A) already discussed. The patterns for Cheryl and Ed look relatively as expected, but John's talk is very different across the two management meetings. He talks more than anyone else in Management2 and almost not at all in Management1. In Management2, furthermore, his talk is relatively more indexed than not indexed.

What this finding might suggest is that any analysis that looks at the difference between design and management meetings will need to keep in mind that the management meetings differ from each other, particularly on the contributions that John makes. Since our ultimate aim is a descriptive analysis of the data, we are not troubled by the lack of consistency between management meetings, it is just another complexity to account for in the analysis.

Memo 7.4: Comparisons of Data Streams with Baseline Data

Compare your baseline data to your data streams and reflect on whether your streams are consistent with the patterns you have established. If the streams are similar in contour to the baseline, describe those similarities. If the streams are different, describe how they are different.

Putting It All Together

The process presented in this chapter, the process of analyzing across dimensions, involves so many comparisons and distinctions that it is not unusual, when you are done, to lose sight of the big picture. Keeping track of what you find at each stage of analysis can be complex and figuring out the relationships among the stages can be a real challenge.

You will find that the best technique for putting it all together is to write it out. That is, for each level of the analysis, write out any characterizations true at that level. Then, move to the next level of analysis and see whether those characterizations remain true or must be qualified or withdrawn entirely.

With our sample data, then, we begin with the dimensional analysis. Is there anything we can say about the dimension of speaker contribution that seems to hold overall? Originally it looked liked speakers were ordered in terms of relative contribution: Cheryl, John, Ed. This pattern held true, more or less, for the design meetings, but not for management meetings. In Management2, John dominated; whereas in Management1, he hardly talked.

What, then, might we say about the dimension of speaker contribution in this data set? The answer would be that while speaker contribution was relatively stable in design meetings, and relatively stable for Cheryl and Ed in management meetings, John's contribution in management meetings was highly variable.

Next we ask about the second dimension. Is there anything we can say about the dimension of indexicality that seems to hold overall? Originally, it looked like the language was generally less indexed than indexed. This pattern held true for the data in both design meetings. It was, however, reversed in the management data, except in Ed's talk in Management2. In terms of indexicality, then, we see some consistency across our built-in contrast, with talk in the management meetings being more indexed than in the design meetings, with the exception of Ed in Management2, whose language was not as highly indexed.

Characterizations like these, characterizations built on systematic analysis across dimensions, reflect both possible general statements about a given data set—

> Talk in the management meetings was more indexed than in the design meetings.

—and qualifications specific to particular data streams:

> The language of Ed in Management2 meeting was not as highly indexed.

Such characterizations help you to know what is going on in a given data set. They form a rock-solid foundation for the analyses described in the remaining chapters of this book:

- They become the source of questions that you pursue through the temporal analysis described in Chapter 8.
- They form the patterns whose significance you can test in Chapter 9.
- And they become the substratum of the detailed analysis you carry out in Chapter 10.

Take a moment to appreciate what you now know!

Memo 7.5: Generalizations

As you complete each level of analysis described in this chapter, write out some generalizations and ponder what kinds of conclusions you might reach? Which of these generalizations seem to be most strongly supported by the data and which are the most analytically interesting to you.

Selected Studies Exploring Patterns across Dimensions

Karatsolis, A. (2016). Rhetorical patterns in citations across disciplines and levels of participation. *Journal of Writing Research, 7*(3), 425–452. https://doi.org/10.17239/jowr-2016.07.03.06.

Swarts, J. (2018). Open-source software in the sciences: The challenge of user support. *Journal of Business and Technical Communication, 33*(1) , 60–90. https://doi.org/10.1177/1050651918780202.

Chapter 8. Following Patterns over Time

> In this chapter, you will look at patterns in streams of verbal data that indicate how aspects of your data vary over time. Looking for patterns in time helps to define the temporal shape of your coded data. We will consider simple temporal indexes and then go on to look at aggregate patterns.

Time

Verbal data is inherently temporal. That is, we expect language to be ever changing—minute by minute in oral interactions, line by line in written interactions, and minute by minute as well as line by line in electronic interactions. We all recognize that topics shift in conversation, that texts change as they structure the reader's experience, that what we say in an interview this week will be different from what we say a week from now. Surprisingly, however, relatively few researchers try to describe the patterns in language that occur over time—what Geisler has elsewhere called "temporal shape" (Geisler & Munger, 2001).

The neglect of time as an analytic construct in the analysis of verbal data may arise from the belief that the temporal shape of verbal data is unpredictable. The exact temporal shape of language might be thought too indirect and messy to be worth examining. Verbal interactions are, however, often more regular than might first appear. Conversations don't bounce from topic to topic without rhyme or reason, but often progress with some kind of rationale. Texts likewise don't shape the reader's experience without pattern.

Indeed, genre conventions exist to provide a kind of routinized shape that can structure the reading experience and help us make sense of what we're reading. For instance, despite what many students think, first person pronouns (I or we) are not absent in scientific texts; but neither are they distributed evenly throughout a text. Instead, they are more normally encountered in the introduction when authors announce the contribution they will make or in the conclusion when they summarize the contribution they have made. Looking at a text without a sense of how it evolves temporally may leave you unaware of such patterns. The techniques described in this chapter will help you to discover underlying temporal patterns in your streams of verbal data and thereby better understand how the stream of language shapes human experience over time.

Indexing in Time

The simplest temporal patterns involve indexing the distribution of your coding categories across any unit by which you have segmented the data. These can range from the obvious units of time itself (minutes, seconds, etc.) to segments of continuous discourse (words, lines, t-units, paragraphs, etc.). We might, for example, index how speakers change by t-unit within a meeting.

As you saw in Chapter 7, the overall distribution of speaker contribution can be examined by using distribution graphs like those in Figure 7.1 that show us, relatively speaking, how often speakers speak. When we index this data in time, we take this question one step further and ask how the speakers' contributions shift segment by segment during the course of the meeting: Did all speakers speak consistently throughout the meeting or were there clusters of interaction between one or more of the participants at some times and not at others?

The Temporal Index

A temporal index can help us to answer questions about temporal distribution. In Figure 8.1, for example, we see movement across the four speakers, Cheryl, John, Ed, and Lee, as we move across the first 180 t-units of a meeting. This temporal index suggests that although interaction between John and Cheryl was fairly even throughout this time, contributions by Lee and Ed were more sporadic. Lee came in just twice and said very little; Ed came in five times, three for relatively short contributions, but once for an extended interaction with Cheryl and a second time for a conversation primarily with John. Simple temporal indices like this, then, can tell us a great deal more about how a phenomenon of interest, like speaker contribution, plays itself out over time.

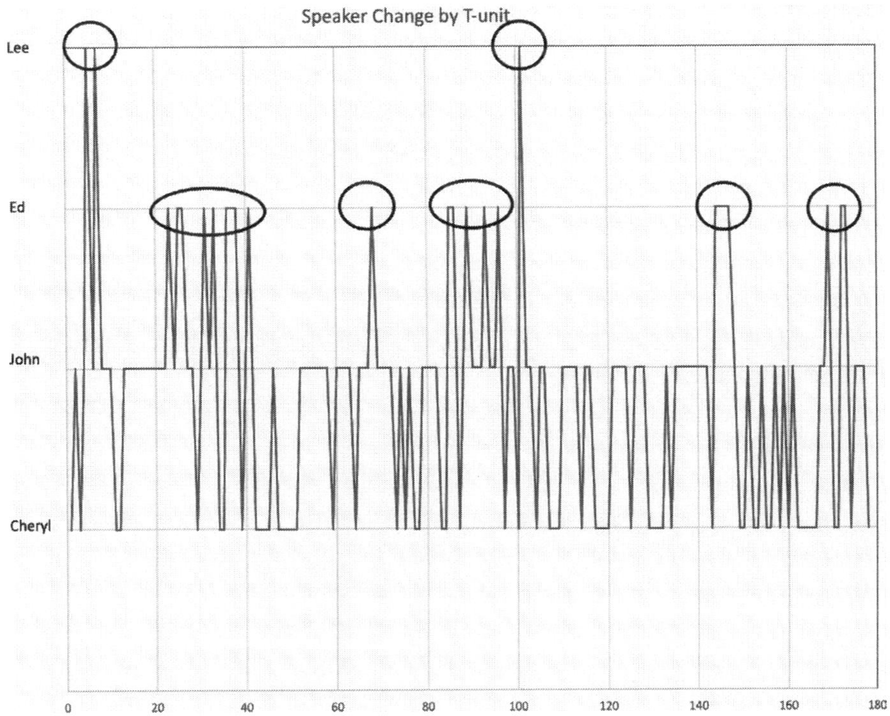

Figure 8.1: A temporal index in Excel showing speaker change by t-unit.

As shown in Figure 8.1, temporal indices map two variables against each other. One variable is temporal, the unit of segmentation such as the t-unit we have used in Figure 8.1. The second variable is the categorical dimension of the data you wish to index over time. In Figure 8.1, this dimension is speaker contribution. Conventionally, time goes on the x-axis; the categorical dimensional data on the y-axis. To read a temporal index, then, you move from left to right through time and up and down across the categories of your data.

Exercise 8.1 Test Your Understanding

In Figure 8.2 and Table 8.1 (available at https://wac.colostate.edu/books/practice/codingstreams/) you will find a temporal index of the agents that a student talked about during an interview about a writing project on paternalism. Use this temporal index to match the phenomenon listed on the left below with one or more portions of the index listed on the right.

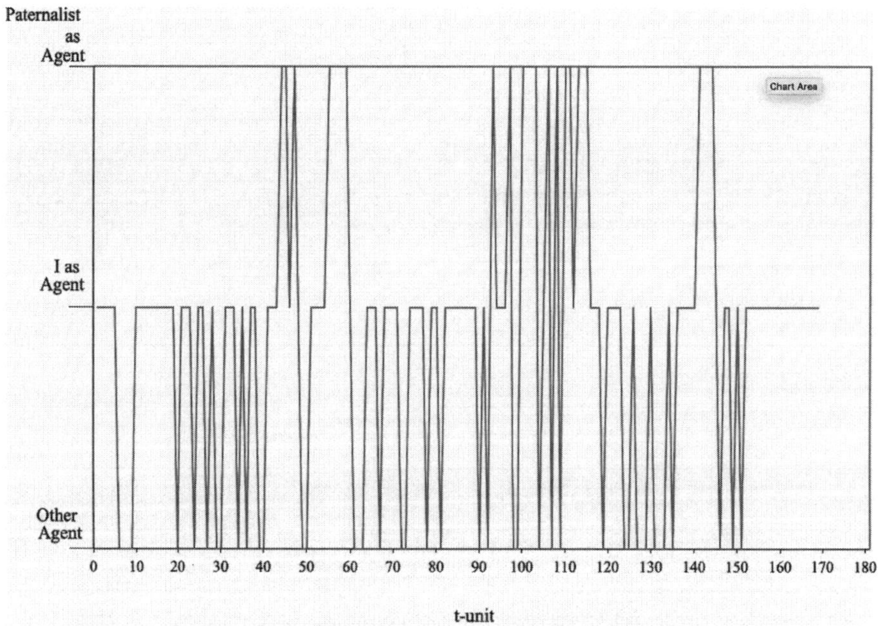

Figure 8.2: A temporal index of agency over the t-units of an interview.

Table 8.1: A temporal index of agency over the t-units of an interview.

1. The first time during the interview when the student talked a lot about the paternalist as agent. 2. The second time during the interview when the student talked a lot about the paternalist as agent. 3. The last time during the interview when the student talked a lot about the paternalist as agent. 4. A time when the student talked almost exclusively about herself as agent. 5. A time when the student talked not at all about herself as agent. 6. A period in which the student talked a great deal about agents other than herself or a paternalist.	a. 12–24 b. 27–48 c. 52–55 d. 52–67 e. 64–67 f. 70–109 g. 78–89 h. 106–128 i. 111–125 j. 128–141 k. 153–155 l. 164–181

For Discussion: Which of the following seems to happen more often: Mixing *I as agent* with *others as agent* or mixing *I as agent* with *paternalist as agent*?

Making a Temporal Index

Before you make a temporal index for your data, it is useful to consider the order in which you want the codes to be layered (see Excel Procedures 8.1 and 8.2 and MAXQDA Procedures 8.1 and 8.2). In Figure 8.1, for example, we have placed Cheryl at the bottom of the index, John second, Ed third, and Lee at the top. In general, it is often best to place the most frequently-occurring categories so that they will be plotted in the lower region of the index. For example, by placing the two most frequent speakers, Cheryl and John, in the lower ranges of the index in Figure 8.1, we have created a base against which we can more easily see the more intermittent participation of Ed and Lee.

Excel Procedure 8.1: Giving a Numeric Value to Codes for a Temporal Index in Excel

https://goo.gl/Bk9wHv

1. Assign each of the codes a numeric value, beginning with 1 for the code you want to be in the lowest position on the index.
2. In a copy of your worksheet, insert a new column for the numeric codes next to the coding column you want to track in the temporal index.
3. Copy the contents of the alphanumeric column into the new column.
4. Select the newly created column.
5. Select **Edit** > **Find** > **Replace** and then type the alphanumeric name of your first code under **Find what:** and the chosen numeric value under **Replace with**.
6. Click **Replace All** and then **OK**.
7. Repeats steps 5–6 until you have replaced all of your verbal codes with their chosen numeric values.

The newly created column should now be filled with the numeric values you have assigned to your codes as shown in Figure 8.3.

	A	B	C	D
1	**T-Unit #**	**Speaker #**	**Speaker**	**Text**
2	1	1	Cheryl:	We need a little hole in the middle of this table.
3	2	2	John:	Oh, Jesus! We could just go get a drill right now.
4	3	1	Cheryl:	We need one of these don't we?
5	4	2	John:	Or a big hammer.
6	5	4	Lee	It wouldn't actually have to be in the middle
7	6	2	John:	I mean

Figure 8.3: Assigning numeric values to categories of speaker in Excel.

Excel Procedure 8.2: Making & Formatting a Temporal Index in Excel

https://goo.gl/Bk9wHv

1. Select the column holding the unit numbering and the column holding your numeric coding.
2. From the **Insert** ribbon, insert chart as an **X-Y (Scatter) with Lines** as shown in Figure 8.4.
3. Using the **Move Chart** command on the **Chart** ribbon, move the chart to a new sheet, naming it appropriately.
4. If necessary, double click on the x-axis and change the **Maximum Bounds** to your last data point (180 in Figure 8.1)
5. Double click the y-axis and, under **Axis Options** in the **Format Axis** pane, change the **Major Unit** to 1 and the **Maximum Bounds** to the number of categories you have (4 for Figure 8.1).
6. Under **Labels** in the **Format Axis** pane, select **None** for the **Label Position**.
7. Select the graph and then grab the bottom right hand selection point. Move it right to make room for your code labels.
8. On the **Insert** ribbon, insert a text box on the graph using the **Text** drop-down menu as shown in Figure 8.5.
9. To label with code names, insert and arrange text boxes with code names next to the y-axis like those shown in Figure 8.1.

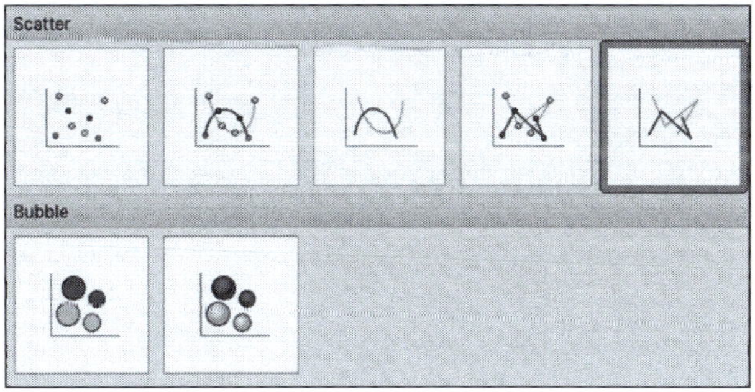

Figure 8.4: Choosing a scatterplot with the insert ribbon in Excel.

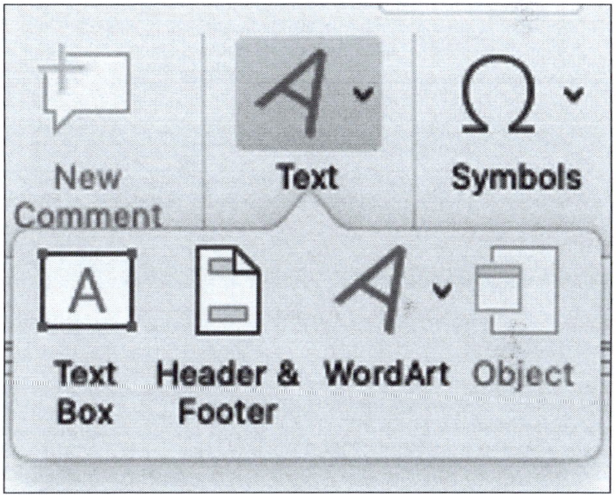

Figure 8.5: Inserting a text box to label lines from the chart with code names in Excel.

MAXQDA Procedure 8.1: Ordering Codes for a Temporal Index in MAXQDA

https://goo.gl/Bk9wHv

1. In the **Code System** window, select the code you want to be in the lowest position of your index.
2. Drag it to the end of the code list.

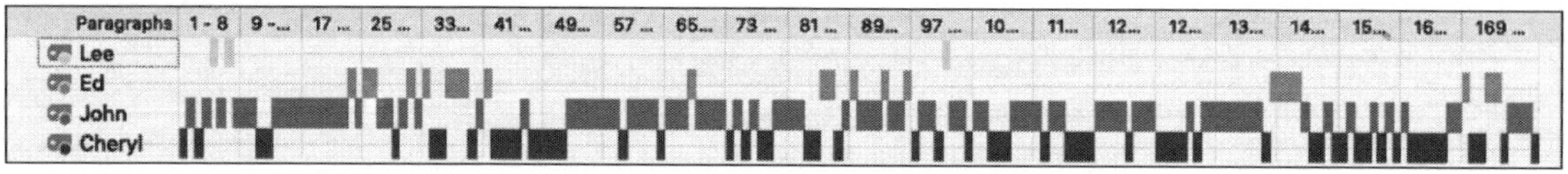

Figure 8.6: A temporal index in MAXQDA.

For the temporal index in Figure 8.6, we have dragged Cheryl to the end of the code list shown in Figure 8.7 in order to place it in the lowest position.

3. Drag the remaining codes to the positions you have chosen above this lowest code.

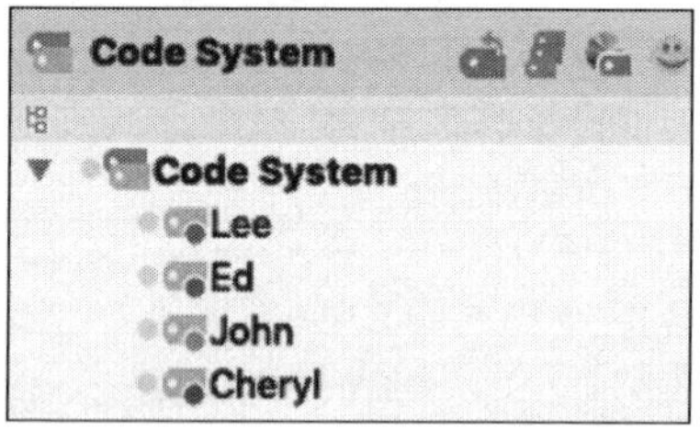

Figure 8.7: Ordering the codes in MAXQDA .

MAXQDA Procedure 8.2: Creating a Temporal Index in MAXQDA

https://goo.gl/Bk9wHv

1. Activate the codes and document you want to place on the temporal index.
2. Chose **Visual Tools** > **Codeline** and check the option for **Only for activated codes** command under the **Visual Tools** menu.

You can use the scroll bar along the bottom to move through the temporal index. The slider at the top can be adjusted to make the columns wider or narrower.

3. To adjust column size, grab its right-hand boundary, and drag as desired.
4. To make the index fit the window, click on the **Fit to window width** icon.
5. To refresh the index after making changes in the code order, click on the **Refresh** icon.
6. To open the index in Excel, click on the **Excel** icon.
7. To save the index as a image, click on the **Export** icon and choose an image format in the pop up window.

Exploring with Temporal Indices

Temporal indices function as indices into your data, helping you first to see patterns over time and then to explore the underlying language. Hovering over any point in a temporal index in Excel will show you the x- and y-coordinates of the temporal point. If, for example, we hover over the point with coordinates (68,3), this represents the 68th segment, which has been coded as speaker #3, *Ed*.

Temporal indices like those shown in Figures 8.1 and 8.6 can help us to pinpoint places that involve high periods of interactivity that involve all three main speakers and then return to the data to examine the nature of those interactive periods. From T-Unit 23 through T-Unit 41, for example, we see a period in which Cheryl speaks three times, John five times, and Ed six times, a level of interaction that occurs nowhere else in the meeting. An examination of the actual language used shows that the three participants are coming to an agreement about a set of design features, something that would require the participation of all three. The temporal index has given us a quick way of interrogating the sequence and then delving back into the verbal data to better understand them.

Temporal indices can also be compared, one index to the next, to identify differences in the temporal shape of two or more streams of verbal data. Geisler and Munger (2001), for example, compared the temporal shape of emergency runs with routine and critical care patients as shown in Figure 8.8. Any stream of language expected to have generic shape will exhibit a particular temporal shape, whether it be a written text or a routine class meeting. Constructing and comparing temporal indices across instances of these genres can help you to uncover interesting variations (see Excel Procedure 8.3 and MAXQDA Procedure 8.3).

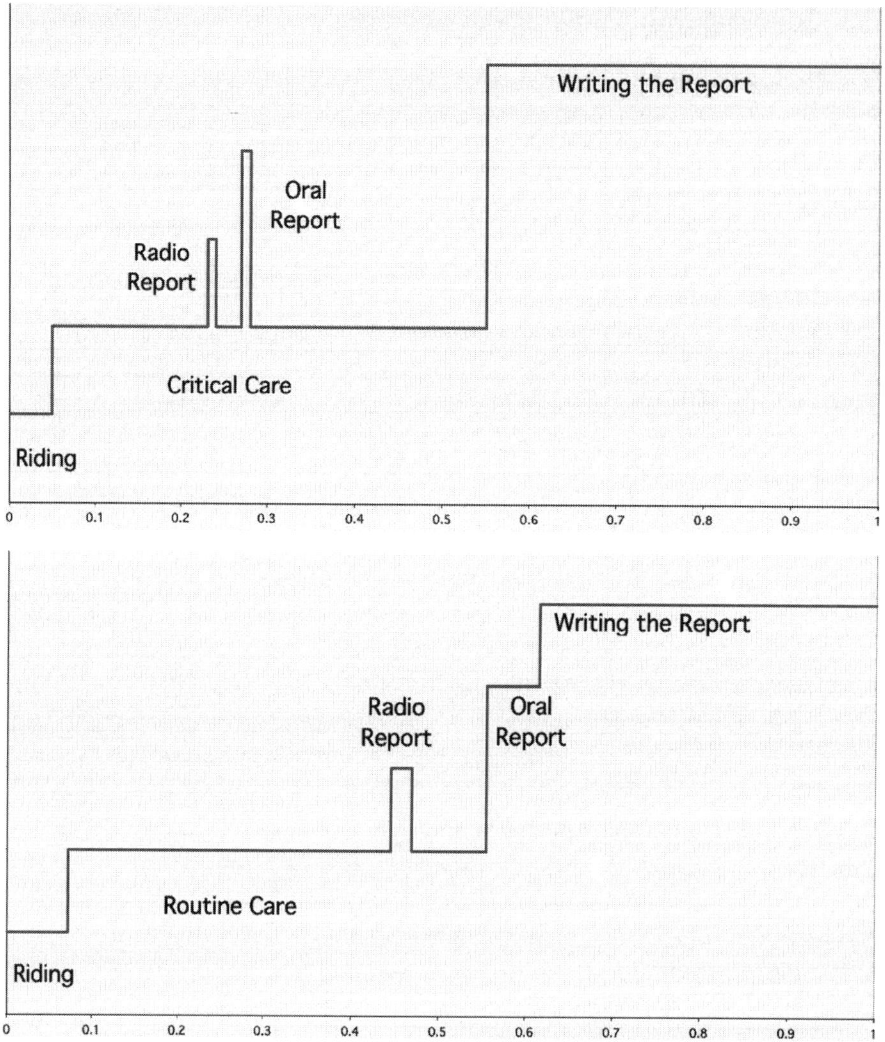

Figure 8.8: Comparing the temporal shape of two ambulance runs (from Geisler & Munger, 2001).

Exercise 8.2 Try It Out

Using the temporal index in Figure 8.1 or in 8.6, identify the sequence of interaction that seems to follow the interesting sequence pinpointed in Figures 8.9 or 8.11 (T-Units 23–41). How does this sequence appear to be different from the one that came before it?

For Discussion: If you were to retrieve the data associated with this second sequence, what questions would you want to try to answer using the verbal data itself?

Memo 8.1: Temporal Index

Construct a temporal index for each piece of your data across your built-in contrast.

Note overall differences in temporal shape among them. What differences do you see in how they unfold over time?

Are there specific sequences that you find interesting? Explore them further by using the temporal indices to look at the verbal data itself.

What might you conclude from looking at your temporal indices?

Excel Procedure 8.3: Exploring Verbal Data with a Temporal Index in Excel

https://goo.gl/Bk9wHv

1. Using a temporal index, pinpoint a interesting sequence for further exploration.
2. Hover over the beginning and end points to retrieve their x- and y-coordinates.

In Figure 8.9, for example, we have hovered over the beginning point of our interesting sequence and retrieved the coordinates (23,2).

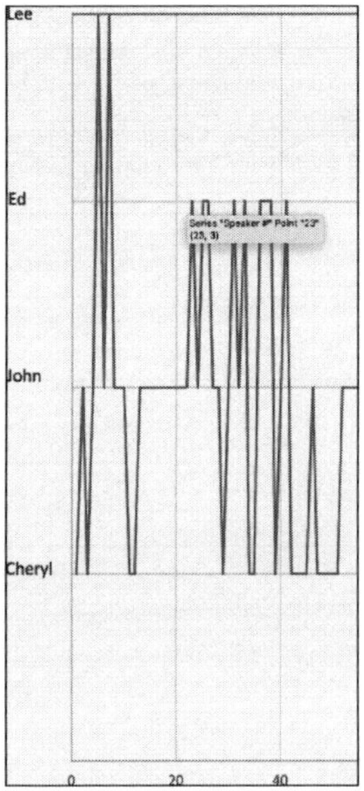

Figure 8.9: An interesting sequence pinpointed using a temporal index in Excel.

23	3	Ed:	I think
24	2	John:	Well, I like the one about the ports.
25	3	Ed:	I think
26	3	Ed:	it's achievable
27	2	John:	Yeah I think : so we :
28	2	John:	so that would be a piece of furniture.
29	1	Cheryl:	uh-hmm
30	2	John:	It would have all of the interactive.
31	3	Ed:	Well, what's the piece of furniture like? Does it :
32	2	John:	It's like the center part of this table
33	3	Ed:	***voice subsumed*** center part
34	1	Cheryl:	Yeah
35	1	Cheryl:	we need to work on this
36	3	Ed:	***voice subsumed*** so we're satisfied with this,
37	3	Ed:	I think th-at
38	3	Ed:	what we want to do is project these screens … ***voice subsumed***
39	1	Cheryl:	Because we are still sharing public monitors, right.
40	2	John:	Right
41	3	Ed:	… flat screens and I would like to ***voice subsumed*** positioning

Figure 8.10: Marking an interesting sequence with highlighting in Excel.

3. In the spreadsheet holding the verbal data, go to the segment numbered with the first coordinate (23 in our example).
4. To facilitate further analysis, highlight the data from this beginning point down to the segment with the first coordinate of the ending point (41 in our example).

Figure 8.10 shows an interesting sequence highlighted to facilitate further analysis.

MAXQDA Procedure 8.3: Exploring Verbal Data Associated with a Temporal Index in MAXQDA

https://goo.gl/Bk9wHv

1. Use the scroll bar at the bottom of the **Codeline** window to scroll through the temporal index to pinpoint an interesting sequence for further exploration, as shown in Figure 8.11.

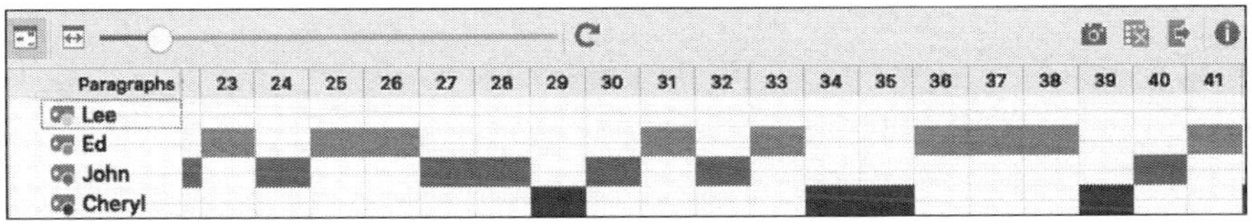

Figure 8.11: An interesting sequence pinpointed with a temporal index in MAXQDA.

2. Double click on the beginning cell of the interesting sequence.
3. The associated verbal segment will appear highlighted in the **Document Browser** window.
4. Select the text from this segment down to the ending point of the interesting sequence.
5. Click on on the icon for **Highlight Coding** to mark the sequence for further examination.

Figure 8.12 shows an interesting sequence marked with **Highlight Coding**.

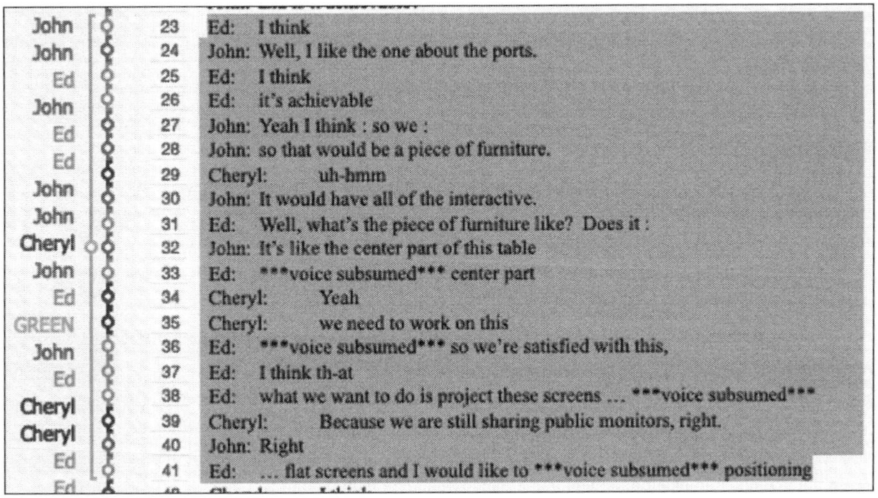

Figure 8.12: Marking an interesting sequence with highlight coding in MAXQDA.

Aggregating in Time

Temporal indices track segment-by-segment change across coding categories and often provide too much detail to be useful—a real case of not being able to see the forest for the trees. If you find that your temporal index obscures the differences that your distribution analysis suggests are there, you should consider aggregating your data into larger units of analysis. To see more of the forest, that is, you might aggregate:

- turns into conversational sequences,
- t-units into topical chains,
- seconds into minutes, and so on.

You could also aggregate your stream of language using what you take to be significant turning points in a conversation or text. In the transcript of classroom interactions, you might aggregate by curricular unit. In the printed text, you might aggregate by section.

Once your data is aggregated, you can construct an aggregate temporal graph like the one shown in Figure 8.13. In this graph, the number of t-units each speaker spoke in an aggregate are stacked one on top of the other for each conversational sequence. The total height of the stack shows you how much talk any individual aggregate exhibited. We can tell from Figure 8.13, for example, that interaction in Conversational Sequence 19 was quite lively compared to the interaction in Conversational Sequence 32.

Memo 8.2: Aggregate Unit

Examine your temporal index and your data overall. Are there larger temporal patterns that could be better captured by aggregating with a larger segmenting unit? If you have looked at a text by t-unit, what if you looked at it section by section? If you have examined a semester's worth of classroom sequences, what if you looked at it by curricular units? Chose an aggregate unit and document the rationale for your choice.

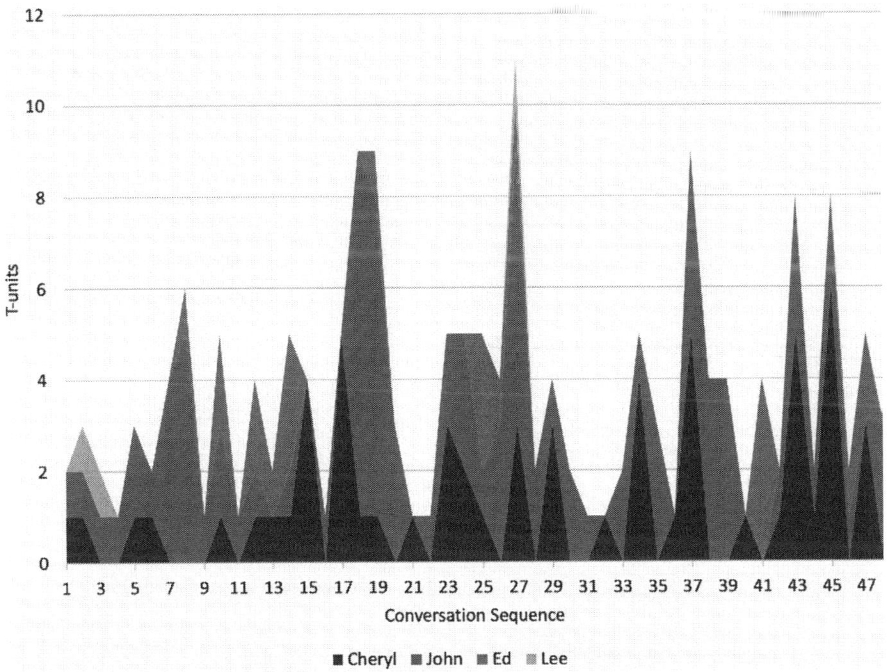

Figure 8.13: An aggregate temporal graph.

Making an Aggregate Temporal Graph

Creating an aggregate temporal graph takes several steps. Begin by choosing an appropriate aggregate unit and then marking its borders in your data. If you have been working in Excel, you will then number these new aggregates, get subtotals for them, and then use these subtotals to create an aggregate temporal graph. If you are working in MAXQDA, you will need to use both MAXQDA and Excel to create an aggregate temporal graph. Specifically, you will create a codeline in MAXQDA and then move it into Excel to use subtotals to create an aggregate temporal graph. Procedures for both are outlined in Excel Procedures 8.4 through 8.7 and MAXQDA Procedures 8.4 through 8.10.

Exercise 8.3 Try It Out

The data in Table 8.2 (available at https://wac.colostate.edu/books/practice/codingstreams/) has been segmented by the second. For example, 002.36 equals 2 minutes and 36 seconds. Aggregate the data by the minute. That is, demarcate the boundaries and number the minutes from 1 to 6.

Table 8.2: Data Segmented by the Second

Sequence	Time in Minutes	Time in Seconds	Text	Tool
1		000.00		PDA
2		000.10	Make second Palm Movie (Mar 21)	PDA
3		000.13	Send Teri Pilot proposal (Mar 21)	PDA
4		000.18		PDA
5		000.45	Take in leave request (Mar 26)	PDA
6		000.58		PDA
7		001.01		PDA
8		001.13	email programmer (Mar 26)	PDA
9		001.26		PDA
10		001.28		PDA
11		001.36		spreadsheet
12		001.39		spreadsheet
13		001.47		PDA
14		001.49	call about hotel bill [Mar23, Maint]	PDA
15		002.08		PDA
16		002.17		PDA
17		002.18		PDA
18		002.19	email programmer (Mar 26)	PDA
19		002.24		PDA
20		002.25	Take in leave request (Mar 26)	PDA
21		002.32		PDA
22		002.34	hotel bill	Off-line
23		005.27		PDA
24		005.27	call about hotel bill [Mar23, Maint]	PDA
25		005.34		spreadsheet
26		005.38		PDA

Sequence	Time in Minutes	Time in Seconds	Text	Tool
27		005.41		spreadsheet
28		006.33	Book Prospectus	spreadsheet
29		006.49	Discipline	spreadsheet
30		006.53	Book Prospectus	spreadsheet

Excel Procedure 8.4: Marking the Aggregate Borders in Excel

https://goo.gl/Bk9wHv

1. Make a copy of your original data sheet.
2. Insert a new column to the left of the original segmenting unit.
3. Locate the beginning of each aggregate unit and place a zero (0) next to it in the new column.

In Figure 8.14, for example, we placed a zero at the beginning of each aggregate. These zeroes function as placeholders that will be relaced by numbers in the next step.

	A	B	C	D	E
1	Interchange	T-Unit #	Speaker #	Speaker	Text
2	0	1	1	Cheryl:	We need a little hole in the middle of this table.
3		2	2	John:	Oh, Jesus! We could just go get a drill right now.
4	0	3	1	Cheryl:	We need one of these don't we?
5		4	2	John:	Or a big hammer.
6		5	4	Lee:	It wouldn't actually have to be in the middle
7	0	6	2	John:	I mean
8		7	4	Lee:	You could put it like right here off to the side.
9	0	8	2	John:	Yeah
10	0	9	2	John:	We could probably put one in every thing,
11		10	2	John:	and then when we're not using it; stick flowers in it or
12		11	1	Cheryl:	Yeah, right.

Figure 8.14: Delimiting the aggregate units with zeroes in Excel.

Excel Procedure 8.5: Numbering the Aggregate Units in Excel

https://goo.gl/Bk9wHv

1. Filter the column so only the zeroes are visible.
2. In the first data cell of the new column, replace the zero with the following formula:

   =MAX($A$1:AX)+1

   where AX is the the name of the cell above the current cell.

	A	B	C	D	E
1	Interchange	T-Unit #	Speaker #	Speaker	Text
2	1	1	1	Cheryl:	We need a little hole in the middle of this table.
3	1	2	2	John:	Oh, Jesus! We could just go get a drill right now.
4	2	3	1	Cheryl:	We need one of these don't we?
5		4	2	John:	Or a big hammer.
6		5	4	Lee:	It wouldn't actually have to be in the middle
7	3	6	2	John:	I mean
8		7	4	Lee:	You could put it like right here off to the side.

Figure 8.15: Filling each aggregate unit with the new numbering in Excel.

In the worksheet shown in Figure 8.15, for example, the formula in cell A2 would be

=MAX($A$1:A1)+1

3. Drag the formula down to fill the column.
4. Remove the filter.
5. Select the column and **Paste Special** in place for **Values only**.
6. Within each aggregate unit, drag the unit number down.

The result is that each of the larger aggregate units are progressvely numbered as has been done for sequence 1 in Figure 8.15.

Excel Procedure 8.6: Subtotaling by Aggregate Unit

https://goo.gl/Bk9wHv

Excel gives us the ability to create subtotals for the data in each of our aggregate units.

1. Place your cursor anywhere in the data for which you want subtotals.
2. Click on the **Subtotal** icon on the **Data** ribbon.
3. As shown in Figure 8.16, In the field **At Each change in:** choose the column with your aggregate unit numbering.
4. In the field **Use function:** choose **Sum**.
5. Under **Add subtotal to:** check off the columns for which you want subtotals.
6. Click **OK**.

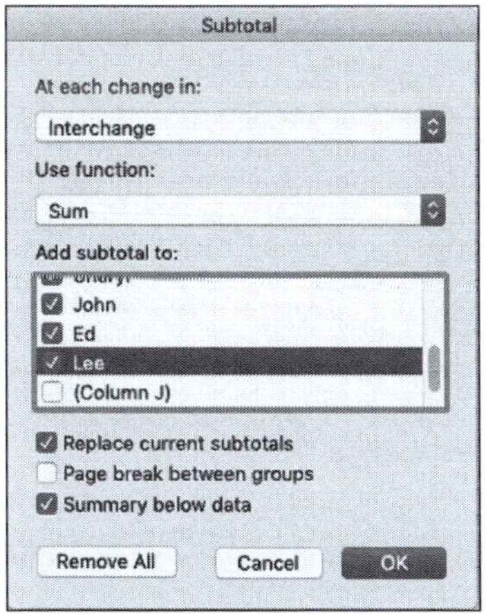

Figure 8.16: Setting up subtotals in Excel.

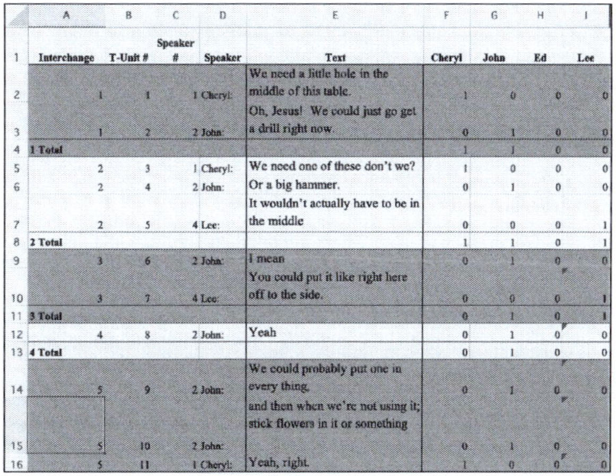

	A	B	C	D	E	F	G	H	I
1	Interchange	T-Unit #	Speaker #	Speaker	Text	Cheryl	John	Ed	Lee
2	1	1	1	Cheryl:	We need a little hole in the middle of this table.	1	0	0	0
3	1	2	2	John:	Oh, Jesus! We could just go get a drill right now.	0	1	0	0
4	1 Total					1	1	0	0
5	2	3	1	Cheryl:	We need one of these don't we?	1	0	0	0
6	2	4	2	John:	Or a big hammer.	0	1	0	0
7	2	5	4	Lee:	It wouldn't actually have to be in the middle	0	0	0	1
8	2 Total					1	1	0	1
9	3	6	2	John:	I mean	0	1	0	0
10	3	7	4	Lee:	You could put it like right here off to the side.	0	0	0	1
11	3 Total					0	1	0	1
12	4	8	2	John:	Yeah	0	1	0	0
13	4 Total					0	1	0	0
14	5	9	2	John:	We could probably put one in every thing.	0	1	0	0
15	5	10	2	John:	and then when we're not using it; stick flowers in it or something	0	1	0	0
16	5	11	1	Cheryl:	Yeah, right.	1	0	0	0

Figure 8.17: Subtotals inserted for the aggregate units in Excel.

Continued . . .

Excel Procedure 8.6: Subtotaling by Aggregate Unit (continued)

https://goo.gl/Bk9wHv

As shown in Figure 8.17, new lines are inserted at the bottom of each aggregate, with subtotals for each of the coding columns.

Notice that a new area has appeared to the left of your data representing the aggregate levels.

7. To see only the aggregates, click on the **Level 2** icon at the top of the level bar.

As shown in Figure 8.18, this will collapse the data, showing only the subtotals.

	A	B	C	D	E	F	G	H	I
1	Interchange	T-Unit #	Speaker #	Speaker	Text	Cheryl	John	Ed	Lee
4	**1 Total**					1	1	0	0
8	**2 Total**					1	1	0	1
11	**3 Total**					0	1	0	1
13	**4 Total**					0	1	0	0
17	**5 Total**					1	2	0	0
20	**6 Total**					1	1	0	0
25	**7 Total**					0	4	0	0
32	**8 Total**					0	5	1	0
39	**9 Total**					1	3	2	0

Figure 8.18: Collapsing the data to show only subtotals in Excel.

8. To reveal all of the data, click on the **Level 3** icon at the top of the **Level** bar.
9. To inspect a single aggregate, click on the + sign next to the aggregate unit.

Excel Procedure 8.7: Making an Aggregate Temporal Graph in Excel

https://goo.gl/Bk9wHv

1. Make sure the coding columns you want to graph are in numeric form (see Excel Procedure 8.1: Giving a Numeric Value to Codes) and that only your aggregates are visible (see Excel Procedure 8.6).
2. Select the values in the coding columns to be graphed. Make sure not to select the Grand Total row.

For the aggregate temporal graph shown in Figure 8.13, we selected the columns for the four speakers as shown in in Figure 8.19.

	A	F	G	H	I
1	**Interchange**	**Cheryl**	**John**	**Ed**	**Lee**
4	**1 Total**	1	1	0	0
8	**2 Total**	1	1	0	1
11	**3 Total**	0	1	0	1
13	**4 Total**	0	1	0	0
17	**5 Total**	1	2	0	0
20	**6 Total**	1	1	0	0
25	**7 Total**	0	4	0	0
32	**8 Total**	0	5	1	0
39	**9 Total**	1	3	2	0

Figure 8.19: Selecting the data to be graphed for the aggregate temporal graph shown in Figure 8.13.

3. On the **Insert** tab, click on **Insert Line Chart**.
4. In the pop-up window, click on the **2-D Area** chart.

MAXQDA Procedure 8.4: Marking the Aggregate Borders in MAXQDA

https://goo.gl/Bk9wHv

1. Make a copy of your original document.
2. **Right click** in the **Coding Strip** to the left in the **Document Browser**.
3. Select **Only activated codes** in the dialogue box as show in Figure 8.20.
4. Click **OK.**
5. Locate the beginning of an aggregate unit and drag to select the entire aggregate.
6. Click on one of the **Highlight Coding** icons.
7. Select the next aggregate unit and click on a second **Highlight Coding** icon**.**
8. Repeat steps 5–6 for the remainder of the data.

As shown in Figure 8.21, your data will now be highlighted by aggregate with alternating colors.

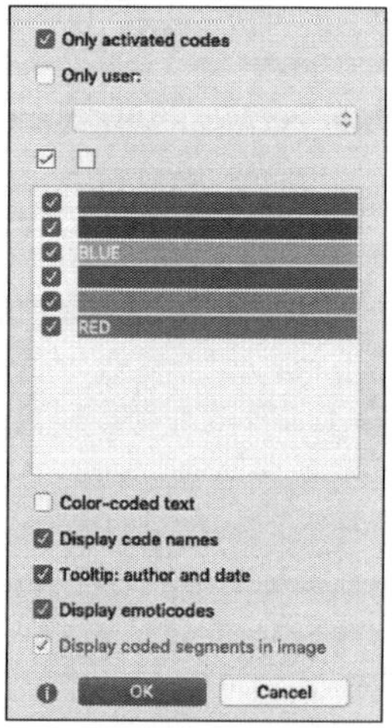

Figure 8.20: Showing only activated codes in MAXQDA.

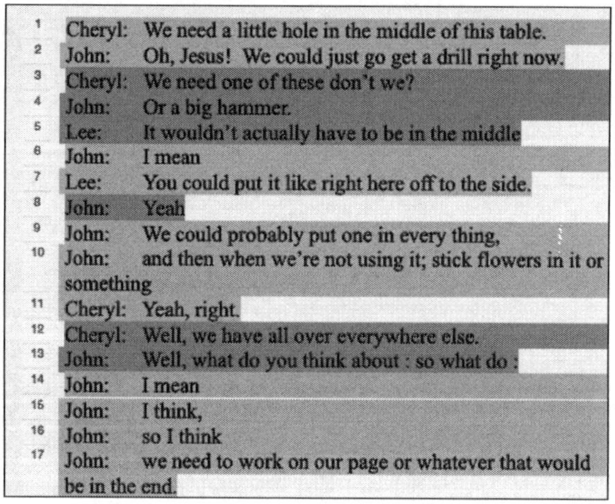
1 Cheryl: We need a little hole in the middle of this table.
2 John: Oh, Jesus! We could just go get a drill right now.
3 Cheryl: We need one of these don't we?
4 John: Or a big hammer.
5 Lee: It wouldn't actually have to be in the middle
6 John: I mean
7 Lee: You could put it like right here off to the side.
8 John: Yeah
9 John: We could probably put one in every thing,
10 John: and then when we're not using it; stick flowers in it or something
11 Cheryl: Yeah, right.
12 Cheryl: Well, we have all over everywhere else.
13 John: Well, what do you think about : so what do :
14 John: I mean
15 John: I think,
16 John: so I think
17 John: we need to work on our page or whatever that would be in the end.

Figure 8.21: Aggregate units with highlight coding in MAXQDA.

MAXQDA Procedure 8.5: Creating and Moving the MAXQDA codeline into Excel

https://goo.gl/Bk9wHv

To make an aggregate temporal graph with MAXQDA data, we need to move the codeline data into Excel and then create the graph there.

1. In MAXQDA, create a codeline for the data by selecting the **Codeline** command from the **Visual Tools** menu.
2. Leave the defaults in the dialog box and click **OK**.
3. Move the codeline into Excel by clicking on the **Excel** icon.

The codeline will now open in an Excel workbook.

MAXQDA Procedure 8.6: Moving the MAXQDA codeline into a new Excel worksheet

https://goo.gl/Bk9wHv

Next we create a copy of the codeline data and move it into a new worksheet were we can reformat it in order to make the aggregate temporal graph.

1. Place your cursor inside the table and type **Control-A** to select it.
2. Copy the selected table and move to a new worksheet
3. Place your cursor in A1 and issue the **Paste Special** command under the **Edit** menu.
4. As illustrated in Figure 8.22, in the dialog box, select **Transpose**.

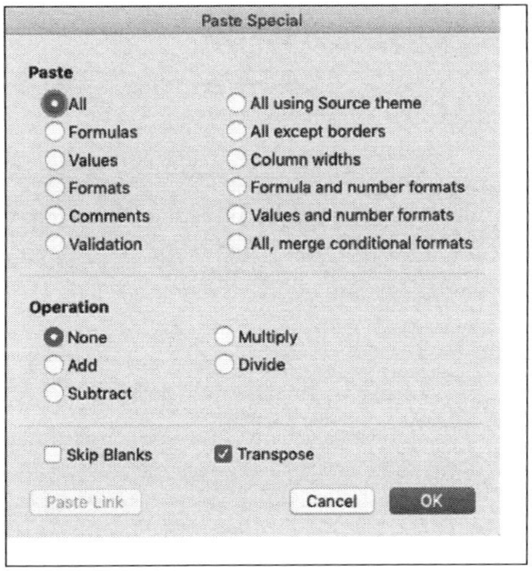

Figure 8.22: Transposing codeline data from MAXQDA in Excel.

Continued . . .

MAXQDA Procedure 8.6: Moving the MAXQDA codeline into a new Excel worksheet (continued)

https://goo.gl/Bk9wHv

5. Click **OK.**
6. If you have a warning symbol next to the numbers in your first column, select all of the column values and choose **Convert to Number** under the warning symbol as shown in Figure 8.23.

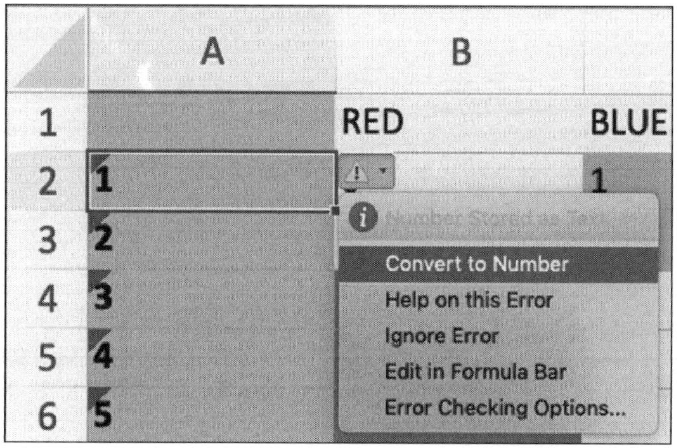

Figure 8.23: Converting t-units from a MAXQDA codeline to numeric values in Excel.

MAXQDA Procedure 8.7: Marking the Aggregate Borders in Excel

https://goo.gl/Bk9wHv

1. Insert a new column to the left of the original segmenting unit.
2. In the aggregate column, next to the first data point, type a zero.
3. Next to the second data point, type the following formula

   =IF(OR(X3>X2,Y3>Y2),0,"")

   where X is the column with your first highlight color and Y is the column with your second highlight color.

Continued . . .

MAXQDA Procedure 8.7: Marking the Aggregate Borders in Excel (continued)

https://goo.gl/Bk9wHv

In Figure 8.24, for example, we have used the following formula to locate the beginning of the aggregates

=IF(OR(C3>C2,D3>D2),0,"")

where Column C contains the red highlight and Column D contains the blue highlight.

	A	B	C	D	E	F	G	H
1	Aggregate	T-Units	RED	BLUE	Cheryl	John	Ed	Lee
2	0	1	0	1	0	0	0	0
3		2	0	1	0	1	0	0
4	0	3	1	0	1	0	0	0
5		4	1	0	0	1	0	0
6		5	1	0	0	0	0	1
7	0	6	0	1	0	1	0	0
8		7	0	1	0	0	0	1

Figure 8.24: Marking the beginning of the highlighted aggregate units from a MAXQDA codeline.

MAXQDA Procedure 8.8: Reformat the MAXQDA codeline in Excel

https://goo.gl/Bk9wHv

1. Filter the column so only the zeroes are visible.
2. In the first data cell of the new column, replace the zero with the following formula:

   =MAX($A$1:AX)+1

   where AX is the the name of the cell above the current cell.

   In the worksheet shown in Figure 8.24, for example, the formula in cell A2 would be

   =MAX($A$1:A1)+1

3. Drag the formula down to fill the column.
4. Remove the filter.
5. Select the column and **Paste Special** in place for **Values only**.
6. Within each aggregate unit, drag the unit number down as show in Figure 8.15.

MAXQDA Procedure 8.9: Subtotaling by Aggregate Unit

https://goo.gl/Bk9wHv

1. Place your cursor anywhere in the data for which you want subtotals.
2. Click on the **Subtotal** icon on the **Data** ribbon.
3. As shown in Figure 8.16, In the field **At Each change in:** choose the column with your aggregate unit numbering.
4. In the field **Use function:** choose **Sum**.
5. Under **Add subtotal to:** check off the columns for which you want subtotals.
6. Click **OK**.

As shown in Figure 8.17, new lines are inserted at the bottom of each aggregate with subtotals for each of the columns chosen.

Notice that a new area has appeared to the left of your data representing the aggregate levels.

7. To see only the aggregates, click on the **Level 2** icon at the top of the **Level** bar.

As shown in Figure 8.18, this will collapse the data, showing only the subtotals.

8. To reveal all of the data, click on the **Level 3** icon at the top of the **Level** bar.
9. To inspect a single aggregate click on the + sign next to the aggregate unit.

MAXQDA Procedure 8.10: Making an Aggregate Temporal Graph in Excel

https://goo.gl/Bk9wHv

1. Make sure that only your aggregates are visible (see MAXQDA Procedure 8.9).
2. Select the values in the coding columns to be graphed. Make sure not to select the Grand Total row.

For Figure 8.13, we selected the columns for the four speakers as shown in in Figure 8.19.

3. On the **Insert** tab, click on **Insert Line Chart**.
4. In the pop-up window, click on the **2-D Area** chart.

■ Interpreting Aggregate Patterns

Aggregate temporal graphs like that in Figure 8.13 help you to understand the relative contribution of each of the coding categories to the total activity in an interchange. In Figure 8.13, for example, we can see that the activity starting roughly at Conversational Sequence 16 and continuing through Conversational Sequence 28 was lively and involved all the three major participants. Interaction between Interchange 33 and 40, by contrast, though somewhat lively, took place between just Cheryl and John. Such patterns can send us back into the data itself to explore what was going on.

To see how aggregate temporal graphs differ from temporal indices, compare the graph in Figure 8.13 with the one in Figure 8.1. Figure 8.1 does a better job of pinpointing the exact locations of contribution from each speaker and the relatively infrequency of participation by Lee and Ed. It is for this reason we call it an index—there is a one-to-one relationship between each point on the graph and each segment of the data.

The aggregate temporal graph in Figure 8.13 does a better job, however, of helping us to see who is interacting with whom over more extended periods and gives us a much better sense of the level of activity in any given period. All this information is, of course, very useful is pulling together a complete description of the way that the stream of verbal data plays itself out over time across the categories in your coding scheme.

Exercise 8.4 Try It Out

In Figure 8.17, you will find an aggregate temporal graph of the agents talked about by a student during an interview about a writing project on paternalism, aggregated by turn. Each turn represents the student's response to a question by the interviewer. These were the six questions asked:

- At what point did you stop today?
- Why did you stop?
- Can you sort of describe to me generally what you put in the introduction?
- Can you summarize what you put in that paragraph too?
- Can you summarize what you put in that paragraph too?

- Do you feel better now that you've gotten those first two paragraphs written?

Given the pattern of activity and attention to agency shown in Figure 8.25, what kinds of questions would you ask to elicit attention by a writer to agents others than the writer herself? What kind of questions would you ask to elicit a lot of discussion? What kinds seem to elicit attention only to the writer herself?

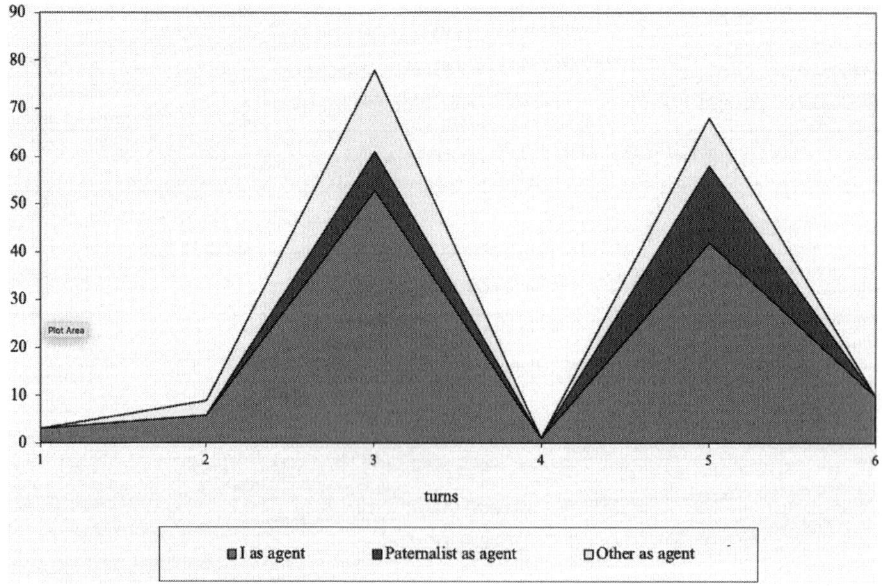

Figure 8.25: Aggregate temporal graph of the data shown in Figure 8.2, aggregated by turn.

For Discussion: What aspects of the verbal data are clearer in Figure 8.25 than in 8.2? What aspects of Figure 8.2 are less clear in Figure 8.25?

Memo 8.3: Aggregate Temporal Graph

Construct a temporal aggregate graph for each piece of your data across your built-in contrast.

Note overall differences in temporal shape among them. What differences do you see in how they unfold over time?

Are there specific sequences that you find interesting. Explore them further by using the temporal indices to look at the verbal data itself.

What might you conclude from looking at the temporal aggregates?

Selected Studies Examining Temporal Patterns

Geisler, C. & R. Munger, R. (2001). Temporal analysis: A primer exemplified by a case from prehospital care. In E. Barton & G. Stygall (Eds.), *Discourse Studies in Composition*. NY: Hampton Press.

Geisler, C. (2003). When management becomes personal: An activity-theoretic analysis of Palm technologies. In C. Bazerman & D. R. Russell (Eds.), *Writing selves / writing societies: Research from activity perspectives* (pp. 125–158). Fort Collins, CO: The WAC Clearinghouse and Mind, Culture, and Activity. Retrieved from: https://wac.colostate.edu/books/perspectives/selves-societies

For Further Reading

Kelly, A. R., Autry, M. K., Mehlenbacher, B. (2014). Considering chronos and kairos in digital media rhetorics. In G. Verhulsdonck & M. Limbu (Eds.), *Digital rhetoric and global literacies: Communication modes and digital practices in the networked world*. Hershey, PA: IGI-Global.

Chapter 9. Evaluating Significance

With Emily H. Griffith, Ph.D.
Department of Statistics
NC State University

Over the last four chapters you have been looking at ways of seeing patterns in verbal data. In particular, you have been asking how the distribution of data into coding categories varied across contrast and across dimension. In some cases, you may have found small variations; in some cases, large variations. In this chapter, we turn to considering the issue of evaluating the significance of those variations.

Significance and Surprise

Generally speaking, we call something "significant" if it is *important*, if it has a bearing on what we will do. But statistical significance is better thought of as *surprising* rather than *important*. If something surprises us that means it seems outside of our expectations. It's unusual. As this definition suggests, evaluating statistical significance involves making a comparison between what we have observed and what we would usually expect to observe if nothing much was going on.

The comparison of observations and expectations guides our evaluation of significance in all kinds of everyday activities. We judge, for example, the significance of Jenna's not returning our morning greeting against our expectations for what Jenna would do if nothing much were going on. If our model of expectations is that she always returns our greeting, her failing to do so this morning can seem highly significant. If, however, she is often lost in thought on days when she has a lot of work to do, her failure to return our greeting will be seen as far less significant.

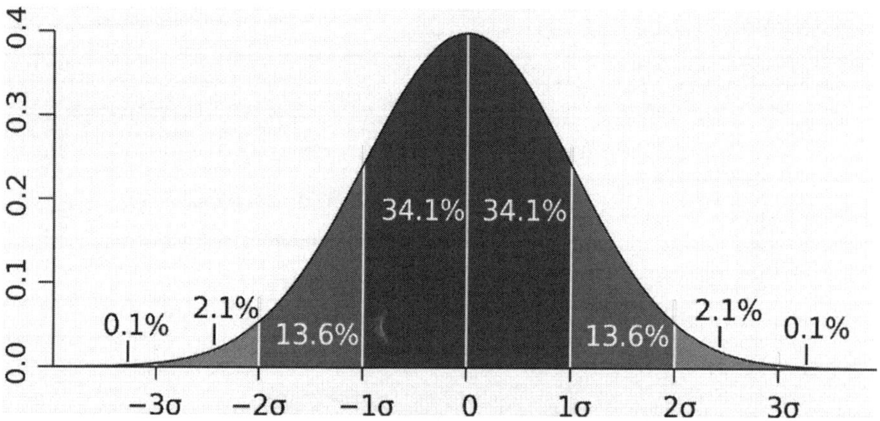

Figure 9.1: A normal distribution.[7]

For many of us, the most familiar tests of statistical significance involve comparing what was actually observed to expectations represented in a normal curve like that shown in Figure 9.1. With a normal curve, just by knowing the values of two parameters, the mean (or the average) and the standard deviation, you can draw the curve. The standard deviation is a measure of the degree to which the data is spread out around the mean. It is calculated by subtracting the mean from each data point, squaring the results (to make sure that none of them are negative numbers), taking their average, and then taking the square root of the result (to reverse the effects of the earlier squaring).

7 Graphic by M. W. Toews and used under the Creative Commons Attribution license 2.5 Generic (retrieved from https://commons.wikimedia.org/wiki/File:Standard_deviation_diagram.svg)

Statistics that use a normal curve shape our expectations about our observations using this mean and standard deviation. Graphically, one standard deviation is located at the graph's inflection points, where the slope changes from curving down to curving up. With a normal curve, we expect most of our observations to cluster symmetrically around the center or average, with fully 34.1% of the data lying evenly on either side of this mean. Within the further boundaries of two standard deviations from the mean we expect to find 95% of our observations. And we expect almost all of our observations (99.7%) to lie within the further boundaries of three standard deviations.

In many statistical methods, we imagine drawing a number of random samples from the expected model—100 samples, 1,000 samples, even 10,000 samples—and ask, how often would one of them look like what I've observed? In terms of Jenna's greetings—and assuming we had perfect memory—we might examine her morning behavior over the last three years when we know everything was OK between us and ask, how many times did she not return our greeting? If it just one time in 1,000, we might say the chances that this morning's behavior was expected was one in 1,000 or, written in statistical language, $p < .01$.

The assumption that an appropriate underlying model of expected distribution follows a symmetrical normal curve works very well for some phenomena. The number of times a coin turns up heads in a set of tosses, for example, follows a normal distribution, assuming the coin is not dinged up in a way that favors one side or the other. Many phenomena are not normally distributed however. If we ask about the distribution of household income in a country, for example, we often find that a few individuals have a net worth far greater than the average household. These high-income households, when averaged in with everyone else positively skew the mean household income as shown in Figure 9.2, not a normal curve.

Many researchers evaluate significance without understanding that they are implicitly making a choice about how to model their underlying expectations for the data. If the assumption of normalcy is inappropriate, such tests will tell you little about how you should evaluate the outcome of your analysis. It would be as if you had taken Jenna's behavior and inappropriately compared it to your model of expectations for Ralph: Ralph always returns my greeting, we might think, so Jenna's silence must be highly significant. As this example is meant to indicate, using the wrong model of underlying expectations can warp your evaluation of significance.

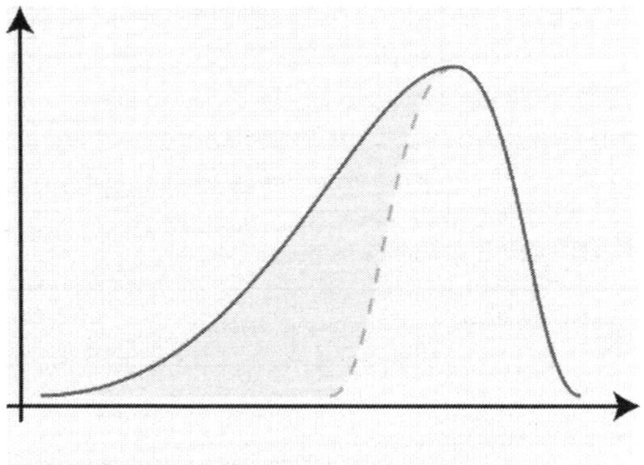

Figure 9.2: A skewed distribution.[8]

Exercise 9.1 Test Your Understanding

Decide whether you would expect the following distributions to be normal if nothing much were going on. Think about where the average might be, and then consider whether you would expect values above and below that average to be evenly distributed and increasingly less common the further from the average.

- The number of times heads arise in 150 coin tosses.
- The length of essays written in a timed writing assessment.
- The number of students who pass and who fail as the result of a writing assessment.
- The number of times a computer user checks email in an average day.
- The number of personal and work-related emails a computer user receives.

For Discussion: What aspects of the data seem to be important to consider in choosing a significance test?

8 Graphic by Rodolfo Hermans and used under the Creative Commons Attribution-Share Alike 3.0 Unported license. Retrieved from https://commons.wikimedia.org/wiki/File:Negative_and_positive_skew_diagrams_(English).svg.

Significance Tests for Coded Verbal Data

For the kind of analyses we have been discussing in this book—the analysis of verbal data gathered from a number of different cases (different speakers, different classrooms, different disciplines)—the normal curve is inappropriate as a model of underlying expectations. Verbal data coded into categories—categorical data—can never expected to approach a normal distribution because a normal distribution is continuous while categorical data is, well, categorical.

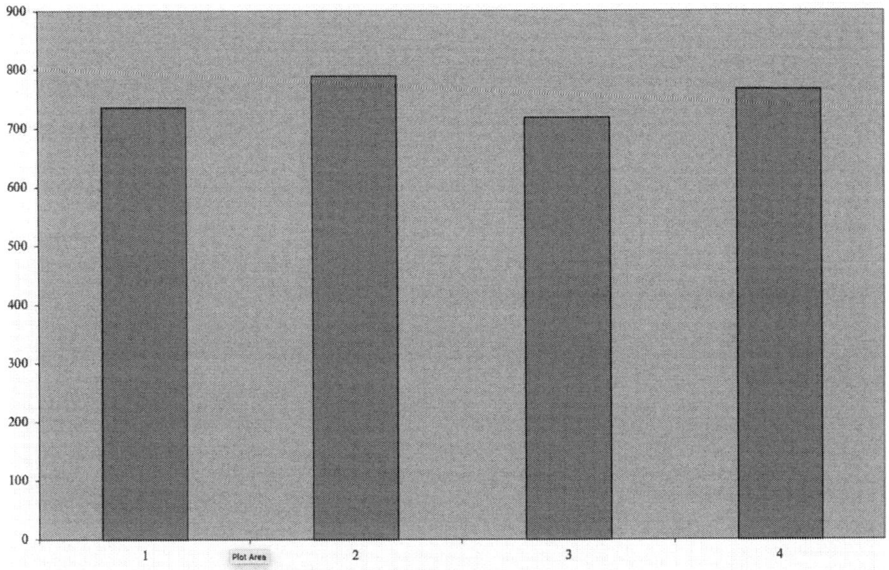

Figure 9.3: Expected distribution of categorical data with a 4-code coding scheme.

To see the difference, imagine a data set that has values up to 4. If this data were continuous, the values might include .01, 3.3, 1.2, 1.27, and so on. But if the data were categorical with only four categories, the values would always be 1, 2, 3, or 4. To see the difference, imagine we put a set of four buckets on the floor and randomly toss coins into them. Each toss is going to go into the 1 bucket, the 2 bucket, the 3 bucket, or the 4 bucket. And if our toss was truly random, after a while the buckets would have about the same number of coins in them with the kind of flat distribution shown in Figure 9.3. Indeed, if one bucket had more or fewer coins than expected, we might suspect that our tosses had not been truly random.

When evaluating the significance of a pattern of coded verbal data, the underlying model of distribution is usually the kind of flat distribution shown in Figure 9.3 where the probability of each category is equal to every other category. The most frequently used significance test for coded verbal data is the χ^2 test. χ^2 is pronounced chi-square. A second and less commonly used test is the multinomial logistic regression with a case effect. Both tests are designed to work with categorical data and both can tell us something about the extent to which the patterns in coded data are surprising. In the rest of this section, we explain how each of these tests work. Then, in the second half of this chapter, we introduce procedures for using them.

How the χ^2 test works

The χ^2 test measures the level of association among the categories of a frequency table like the one shown in Figure 9.4. An association occurs when the values along one of the dimensions generally co-occur with certain values along the other dimension. In Figure 9.4, an association would mean that one or more of the categories in the Frame dimension (*Identity, Object, Practice*) would co-occur with one or more of the categories of the Alignment dimension (*Professional, Social, Technical*). That is, they would occur more or less than we would expect. They would be surprising.

	Identity	object	practice	
Professional	9	0	4	13
Social	23	12	14	49
Technical	5	63	80	148
	37	75	98	210

Figure 9.4: Sample frequency table showing the distribution of Frame (Identity, Object, Practice) by Alignment (Professional, Social, Technical).

Whether the distribution of the data in Figure 9.4 is surprising is what a χ^2 test is designed to tell us. It does so by comparing the actual distribution of coded data like what we see in Figure 9.4 with a model of the expected distribution if nothing much was going on, like the one shown in Figure 9.5.

Let's examine the model in Figure 9.5 in more detail. First, you may have noticed that its marginal sums are the same as we saw in the actual data. This is no coincidence. The χ^2 model works by saying, "if we keep the totals in each row and column the same, what would we expect the distribution in the cells to be by random chance?" For instance, overall, *Identity* occurs about 18% of the time in the actual data, *Object* about 36%, and *Practice* about 47%, all adding up to 210 or 100%. For any other row in the table in Figure 9.5, these percentages remain true throughout. That is, in every row, about 18% of the data are *Identity*, 36% *Object*, and 47% *Practice*.

	identity	object	practice	Total
Professional	2	5	6	13
Social	9	18	23	49
Technical	26	53	69	148
Total	37	75	98	210
	18%	36%	47%	100%

Figure 9.5: Expected distribution of the data shown in Figure 9.4.

Another way to understand expected model is to see it in terms of a visualization like the block chart on the bottom in Figure 9.6, where all three planes of the chart have the same shape. Moving from the front with *Professional* to the back with *Technical*, values increase from the left. Everything is proportional.

Compare this with a block chart for the actual data, shown at the top of Figure 9.6. The front plane, the data with *Professional* alignment, shows a shallow U curve. The second plane, the data with *Social* alignment, is also shaped like a U, although a little less shallow. And the back plane, the data with *Technical* alignment, the curve slopes sharply to the right. None of these shapes looks particularly similar to each other.

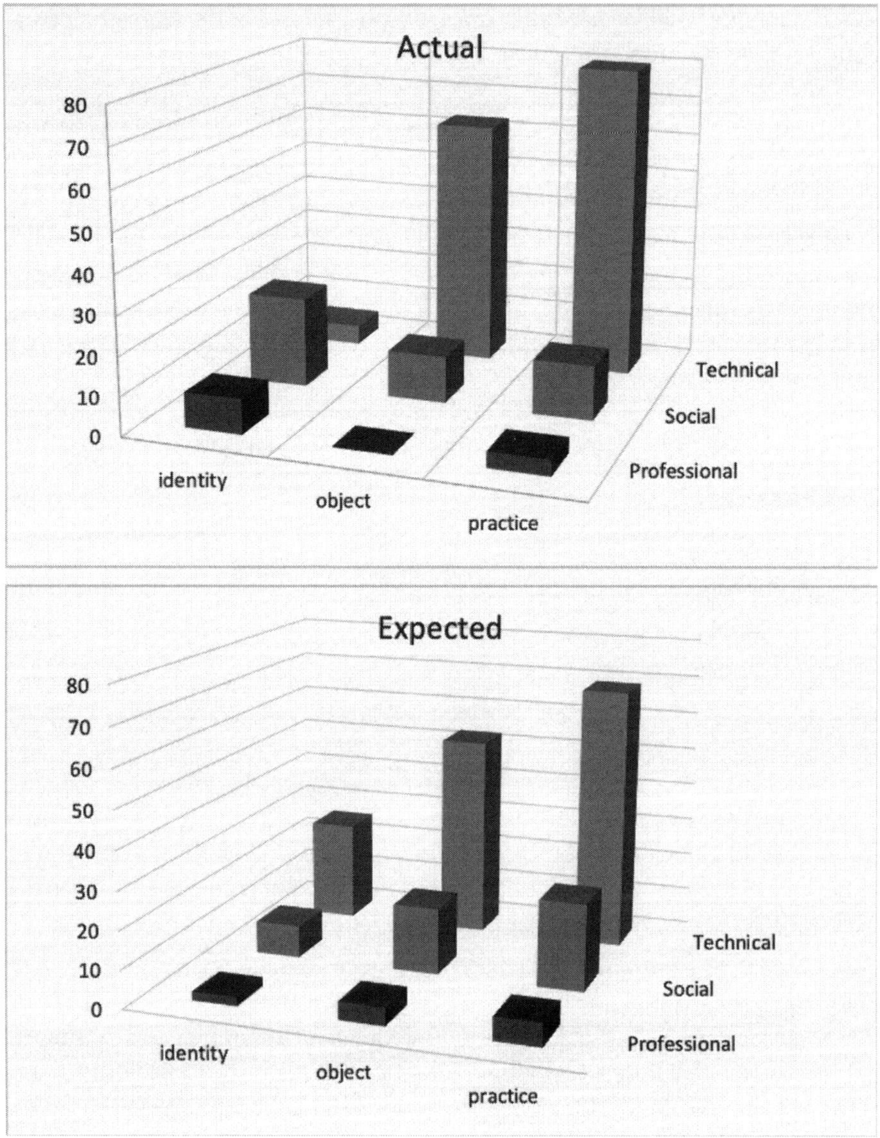

Figure 9.6: Visual representations of the actual (top) and expected (bottom) distributions from Figures 9.3 and 9.4.

The χ^2 test works by comparing these two distributions, one for the actual data and the other for the expected data using the following formula:

$$\chi^2 = \text{sum of} \left[\frac{(O-E)^2}{E} \right]$$

Translated into English, this formula means that χ^2 equals the sum of the squares of the differences between the observed and expected values for each cell in your frequency table, each difference having been divided by the expected value for that cell. The greater the sum of differences between two, the more surprising or statistically significant the result is. This decision-making rule parallels our example with Jenna's morning greeting: the more that her behavior on a given day doesn't fit with our understanding of her usual behavior, the more we find her behavior surprising or significant.

How Multinomial Logistic Regression Works

Multinomial logistic regression works in nearly the opposite way from the χ^2 test. Whereas surprise and significance for the χ^2 test lies in the lack of fit between the actual distribution and the model, for multinomial logistic regression, as we shall see, surprise and significance lies in an increasing fit.

Furthermore, unlike the model used in a χ^2 test, which uses the categorical sums in a frequency table, a multinomial logistic regression uses all of the data points, not just their sums. As shown in Figure 9.7, for example, the model created by a multinomial logistic regression tries to predict what the coding for Alignment would be, given a coding for Frame.

In this way, rather than looking for an association among dimensions as the χ^2 test does, multinomial logistic regression seeks to determine the predictive power of one factor—such as the dimension of Frame—for a dimension—such as Alignment. The first of these is often called the predictor variable and the second the outcome variable.

Unit	Year	User	Content	Frame	Alignment
1	Year1	irunepan	I'm a student of a Biomedical Engineering Master of Barcelona,	Identity	Professional
2	Year1	irunepan	and I'm doing my Master Thesis about virtual endoscopy.	Identity	Professional
3	Year1	irunepan	Specifically I'm trying the endoscopy module of the 3D slicer in the Abdominalatlas2011 data set.	Practice	Technical
4	Year1	irunepan	First I'm testing the navigation mode,	Practice	Technical
5	Year1	irunepan	I create a Fiduacil list and Fly through,	Practice	Technical
6	Year1	irunepan	but I wanted to know if it possible to record	Practice	Technical
7	Year1	irunepan	and make a video of the navigation.	Practice	Technical

Figure 9.7: Data points as modeled by a multinomial logistic regression.

In the verbal data coding dealt with in this book, predictor variables are usually one of two types. The first, as we illustrate with Figure 9.7, is a value on a first coding dimension and would answer the question: given this value, what do we predict would be the value on a second dimension?

The second possibility for a predictor variable is the contrast we have built into our data collection. In the data shown in Figure 9.7, for example, the data have been labeled by the year in which the content was produced. With this data, we could seek to answer the question: given that a piece of data was produced in *Year1*, what do we predict would be its alignment? With a well-fitted regression model, we should be able to predict with better than chance accuracy the answers to questions like these. The ability to make such a prediction would be surprising—and significant.

Like all regressions, multinomial logistic regression works by fitting lines to actual data. In a simple linear regression like that shown in Figure 9.8, a straight line is drawn to minimize the distance between the actual data points shown in blue and the line shown in red. A multinomial logistic regression fits a more complicated line like that shown in Figure 9.9. In this logistic curve, the values are limited to a range between 0 and 1, making it a good model for categorical data.

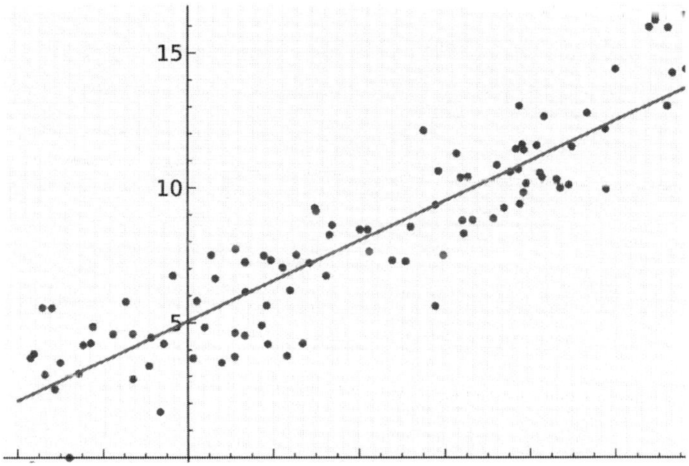

Figure 9.8: Fitting a line in simple linear regression.[9]

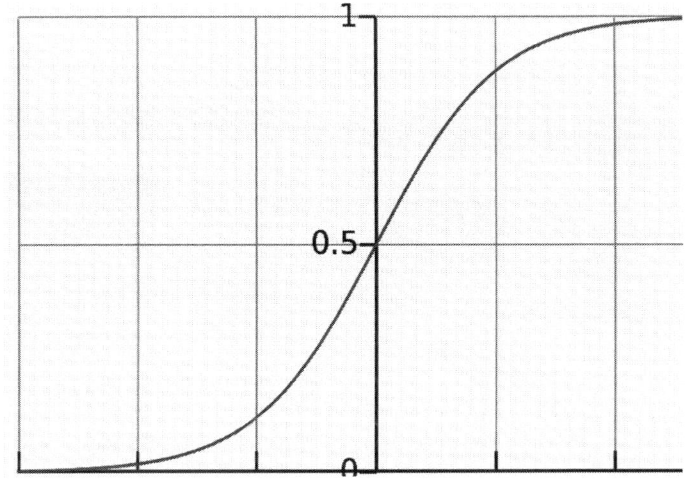

Figure 9.9: A logistic curve used by a multinomial logistic regression.[10]

---

9 Graphic by Sewaqu and released into the public domain (retrieved from https://commons.wikimedia.org/wiki/File:Linear_regression.svg).

10 Graphic by Qef and released into the public domain Retrieved from https://commons.wikimedia.org/wiki/File:Logistic-curve.svg

As we saw earlier, a χ^2 test works by using probabilities. Probabilities in verbal data analysis can be defined as the frequency of segments in a given category divided by the total number of segments in all categories. So, as illustrated on the right in Figure 9.10, if we have a three-category scheme with equal probabilities applied to nine pieces of data, the probability of the category *Social* is 3 divided by 9 or .33. Probabilities like these are key in a χ^2 test where they are used to model the expected values.

With multinomial logistic regression, the key is the slightly different concept of odds. Odds compare the probability of a category being used to the probability of it not being used. In verbal data, odds can be defined as the frequency of segments in a given category divided by the frequency of segments in all other categories. As illustrated on the left in Figure 9.10, the odds of the category *Social* are 3 divided by 6 or .5. In gambling contexts, this can be expressed as an odds of 2 to 1 against being coded as *Social.*

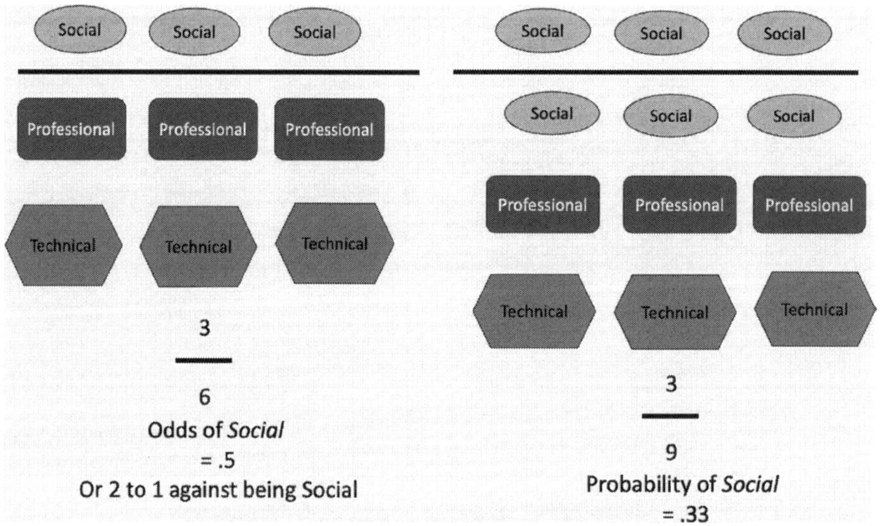

Figure 9.10: The difference between probability and odds. Modeled after Doliner (2014).

A multinomial logistic regression makes a comparison between two models, a baseline model without the value of interest and a model with the value of interest added. Thus, it begins by choosing a baseline category from a categorization scheme. It doesn't matter which category is chosen as the baseline, but the app developed for this book generally chooses the first category it encounters in the worksheet. So for coding the data shown in Figure 9.7, the baseline would be the category *Professional* as it is the first coding category used for Alignment.

Next, the multinomial logistic regression makes a series of comparisons between the odds of each of the other categories in the categorization scheme and the odds of this baseline. To do so, it computes the log odds as the comparison.[11] So with our data, for example, it computes the log odds of being coded as *Social* compared to being coded as *Professional*. Then it will compute the odds of being coded as *Technical* compared to being coded as *Professional*. If the additional information provided by the model with the added category provides a better fit than the baseline model, then we find the category to be significant predictor.

Note here that, as we said earlier, significant doesn't mean important. A variable might be significant in improving a fit between the line and the data by making a relatively small but stable improvement. In other words, our chance of being correct might be better than chance with this additional information, but it might still be relatively poor. So with this and all significance testing judging whether a significant result is an important result requires assessing the patterns you discovered using the techniques outlined in chapters 6 and 7.

Assessing Your Data

As we have just seen, all significance testing builds one or more models against which to evaluate the distribution of our actual data. To better understand which significance test (if any) to use with a given data set, we need to review the structure of our data set and then check to see whether and how it is appropriate for the significance testing we describe in this chapter.

11 Log odds are the natural logarithm of the odds ratio between the category of interest and the baseline category. If you remember from high school what a logarithm is, that's fine, but otherwise, don't worry about it.

Data Points

We begin by counting the total number of data points in our data set. We can count up the number of data points or, if we have built a frequency table, we can find the total in the bottom right-hand of the marginals. In the frequency table in Figure 9.4, for example, the total number of data points is 210. Most statistical tests are more accurate with more data points. If you have just a few data points, you may not be able to evaluate significance.

Independent Cases

Next, we count the number of independent cases in our data set. If you have followed earlier chapters, you may have put each independent case—each interview, each text, etc.—in a separate worksheet or a separate document, even though you may now have combined them to do statistical analysis. For our combined data, as shown in Figure 9.7, the cases come from different users like irunepan. In fact, our data set includes verbal data from 11 such users, or 11 cases. Some statistical tests are designed to take into account the way that a data set is structured by cases.

Keep in mind that cases should be more or less independent from one another. In our example, independence means that what irunepan says is not influenced in any direct way by what another user says. If speakers are in the same conversation, their contributions are likely to be influenced by one another and probably should not be considered separate cases. But if their contributions are from separate interviews, then they could be considered independent. In your data, you may find that you have multiple independent cases, or, if you are studying one focus group, for example, you may only have one case.

Built-In Contrast

We may have one or more built-in contrasts in the design of our data set. A built-in contrast in a data set means that we have deliberately sampled our data from different areas in the universe of our phenomenon. Perhaps we gathered transcriptions of both Design and Managerial meetings. Perhaps we have essays from students who did above and below average in their composition course. Perhaps we have scraped web texts from political discussions and from discussions about gardening. In any of these cases, we have a built-in contrast that needs to be taken into account in choosing a statistical test. In our sample data, we have data from four years so we could use Year as a possible built-in contrast.

Coding Dimensions

Much of the data we analyze has only one coding dimension. That is, we have used only one coding scheme with our data set. But, as we see in Figure 9.7, it is not uncommon to use two different dimensions such as Frame and Alignment. Knowing how many dimensions we have is important to deciding which kind of significance testing to use.

Choosing Your Significance Test(s)

Some Preliminaries

The analytic techniques introduced in this book are primarily focused on producing a descriptive analysis of verbal data. That is, they are designed to describe the data set you have collected. Some researches want to take their analysis an additional step to produce an analysis that is inferential. An inferential analysis uses a description of a data set to make inferences about the larger population from which the data set was taken. In our description of Design and Managerial meetings, we have focused largely on trying to describe what was going on in those meetings in terms of speaker participation; this is a descriptive purpose.

If we wanted to draw inferences about other meetings, we would need to consider the kind of sample we had drawn from the larger population of possible meetings. In general, inferences are only valid if the sample is drawn using random sampling, a sampling method we reviewed in Chapter 2. So if we wanted to make inferences about other Managerial and Design meetings, we would have had to collect and analyze a random sample of such meetings. In many cases with verbal data, such random sampling is neither possible nor desirable.

All statistical methods do require, however, that you have enough data. If your frequency table is sparse, the statistics will yield results that are not to be trusted. In general, a sparse frequency table is one where:

- One or more of the cells is empty.
- More than about 20% of the cells have values less than 5.

A sparse frequency table indicates that you have one or more coding categories that were not often used in coding your data. If this is the case, you may be able to combine infrequent categories into some more general category—combining some less interesting categories into a larger Miscellaneous category for example—but make sure that you maintain the categories that motivated your study in the first place.

If combining coding categories will not be possible, then you simply may not have enough data to use significance testing. Going back to our analogy with morning greetings, you may not have encountered Jenna on enough mornings to enable you to say whether her failure to greet you this morning is surprising. This doesn't mean that you cannot describe what you have seen her do, only that you cannot say if it is surprising.

Choosing Your Test

The decision about which test you use to evaluate significance depends on the structure of your data, as shown in Figure 9.11. Usually, we recommend that you always run some kind of χ^2 test first. As we shall see, such a test tells you a great deal more about your data than just its significance.

In many cases, we also recommend that you go on to run a multinomial logistic regression and compare the results. As we discussed earlier, a multinomial logistic regression is an inferential test that will tell you something about your chances of predicting a value on a second, or outcome variable, given a value on a first, or predictor variable. This is not something that a χ^2 test can do.

But there is a further and perhaps more important reason to run a multinomial logistic regression in addition to a χ^2 test. The χ^2 test assumes that each data point in your frequency table is independent. This is an assumption that is often violated with verbal data. If your data segments combine to make up continuous discourse, they are not going to be independent from one another. Furthermore, if two segments come from texts that are written by the same author, they may well not be independent. Even when segments come from essays written by students enrolled in the same writing course, they might not be independent.

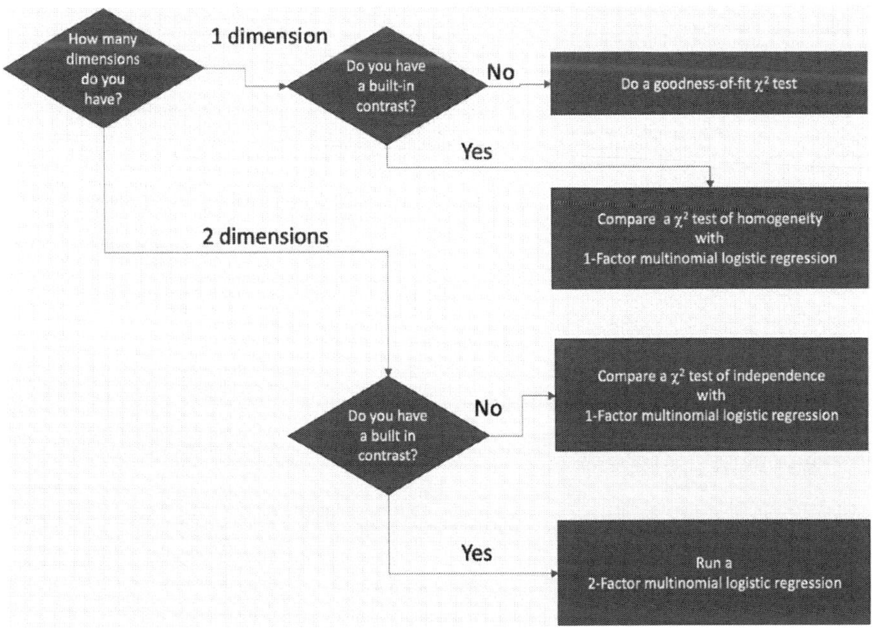

Figure 9.11: A decision tree for choosing significance test(s) for coded verbal data.

As these example are meant to indicate, it can be difficult to tell in advance whether a data set violates the requirement of independence. Sometimes the only way to tell is to run the χ^2 test. If the results suggest you need to get a more valid measure of significance, go on to multinomial logistic regression. Multinomial logistic regression can take into account the interdependency among the data points within each case, factor it out, and establish whether the remaining variation is still surprising, still significant.

Multinomial logistic regression works best when there are a lot of data points within each case. If there are few data points or something else inappropriate about the model, the regression may produce unstable results. To make sure that your multinomial logistic regression is producing stable results, we suggest you run a multinomial logistic regression at least twice. If the significance results are the same, then you can feel confident in them. If the results remain unstable, you may have too few data points for significance testing. If nevertheless you believe that you have enough data, we recommend that you consult with a statistician.

Exercise 9.2 Test Your Understanding

Use the decision tree in Figure 9.11 to make a plan for evaluating the significance of the following data sets.

1. You have gathered and coded essays from six classes, three of which were taught using the usual curriculum and three of which were taught with a new curriculum. Your coding scheme was for Engagement.
2. You have examined published journal articles from biology, physics, and medicine all dealing with the same phenomenon. You have coded the citations for Function and for Source.
3. You have coded a set of published articles for Genre.
4. You are trying to understand the patterns of interaction among students and their teachers in your program. You have coded classroom transcripts for Speaker and Contribution.

For Discussion: What is the impact on evaluating significance of adding a second dimension to your coding? What is the impact of including a built-in contrast?

■ Additional Notes on Procedures for Significance Testing

Some additional notes on our procedures for the statistical analyses. First, all of the procedures for χ^2 analysis start with the assumption that you have created a frequency table for your data using methods introduced in Chapter 6. If you don't yet have a frequency table, you may want to turn to this chapter.

Second, we have provided procedures for doing all of the statistical analysis using both online apps and, for the χ^2 analysis, using Excel. We have not provided any procedures using MAXQDA because the standard package does not support significance testing.

Third, multinomial logistic regression with a case effect is a relatively recent development in statistical methods and its application can be tricky. The online app for conducting a multinomial logistic regression we direct you to has been developed for us by Dr. Emily Griffith of North Carolina State University. We are grateful to Dr. Griffith for this contribution to the analysis of coded verbal data.

Memo 9.1: Plan for Significance Testing

Record your assessment of your dataset, its size, contrast, cases, and coding dimensions. What significance test(s) do you plan to use and why?

The χ^2 Test of Goodness of Fit

Although we have emphasized the value of using a built-in contrast to code your data, you may find that you want to look at a set of data that has been coded along one dimension without contrast to ask the question:

How likely is it that my segments have been coded randomly?

Answering such a question can assure you—and your readers—that the coders were coding by something more than chance.

Calculating the χ^2 Test of Goodness of Fit

The six steps shown in Figure 9.12 and discussed in Excel Procedure 9.1 will take you through the χ^2 test for goodness of fit. You can download a template for your calculations at https://wac.colostate.edu/books/practice/codingstreams/. Directions for an app to do this calculation are provided in Procedure 9.1.

Step 1. Observed	Identity	Object	Practice	Total
Observed	37	75	98	210
Total	37	75	98	210
Step 2. Expected	identity	object	practice	Total
Expected	70	70	70	210
	70	70	70	210
Step 3. O-E	identity	object	practice	Total
0	-33	5	28	0
	-33	5	28	0
Step 4. $(O-E)^2/E$	identity	object	practice	Total
0	15.56	0.36	11.20	27.11
	15.56	0.36	11.20	**27.11**
Step 5. DF				
Number of categories	3			
Number of categories - 1	2			
df	2			
Step 6. Table Lookup	http://www.z-table.com/chi-square-table.html			
The sume of Chi Square equals	27.11	df & probability	df = 2 p<.005	

Figure 9.12: The six-step calculation of the goodness-of-fit χ^2 test.

■ Interpreting the Results of the χ^2 Test of Goodness of Fit

The final step in the computation of the Goodness of Fit χ^2 test—looking up the values on the table—tells you what the chances are that the distribution of your data over categories is surprising. Generally speaking, we think of any probability of less than .01 as significant, less than .001 as highly significant, and less than .05 as somewhat significant. See Excel Procedure 9.1 and Procedure 9.1.

Such numbers do not tell you how your observed data is departing from the expected model in such a fashion as to lead to a significant outcome for the χ^2 test. For this, we need to compare the observed values with the expected distribution. Then we will be able to see that some observed values lay closer to their expected counterparts and some are more distant. The greater the difference between the pairs, the more they contribute to a large sum of χ^2 value.

Thus, interpreting a significant χ^2 result involves pinpointing the greatest differences in the values making up the χ^2 value. To see these, you must return to examine the table in Step 4 where you computed (O-E)2/E for each cell. Since these are the numbers that you added up to get the final sum of χ^2, extremely high values tell you what is so unexpected in the distribution of your data. In Step 4 in Figure 9.12, for example, we see that almost all of the value for the significant sum of χ^2 comes from the values for *Identity* (15.56) and *Practice* (11.20). The value for *Object* is nearly zero (.36).

Having pinpointed the cells that make the greatest contribution to your significant χ^2 value, you next try to understand what makes the observed values in these cells so different from the expected values. You can do this by looking at differences between the observed and expected values, comparing Steps 1 and 2. For example, looking at the tables in Figure 9.12, we see that the observed value for *Identity* is much lower than expected and the observed value for *Practice* is much higher than expected. This means that our coders have been using the code *Identity* much less than we would have expected had they been coding by chance, and they are using the code *Practice* much more than we would have expected by chance.

Excel Procedure 9.1: Calculating a Goodness of Fit χ^2 Test in Excel

https://goo.gl/Hx5Ay7

1. Create a frequency table holding the categories of your coding scheme, as shown in Step 1 of Figure 9.12. Make sure to include the marginal sums.
2. Create 3 more tables in the same way. Label them as shown in Figure 9.12. You may also use the Excel template at https://wac.colostate.edu/books/practice/codingstreams/ that will automatically do the calculations for steps 3–5.
3. For Step 2, Expected, divide the total number of segments by the number of categories and put the result in each cell of this table.
4. For Step 3, O-E, subtract the expected frequencies from the observed values and put the result in each of the cells.

In Figure 9.12, we used a formula like the following to accomplish this calculation in each cell:

```
=B18-B22
```

5. In Step 4, $(O\text{-}E)^2/E$, for each cell, square the value from Step 3 and divide the result by the expected value from Step 2.

In Figure 9.12, we used a formula like the following to accomplish this calculation in each cell:

```
=(B26*B26)/B22
```

The sum of χ^2 will be the grand total in the table.

6. Calculate the degrees of freedom by subtracting 1 from the number of categories in your coding scheme.
7. Use a chi-square calculator like the one at https://www.socscistatistics.com/pvalues/chidistribution.aspx to calculate the p-value for your sum of chi-squares with your degrees of freedom.

Procedure 9.1: Calculating a Goodness of Fit χ^2 Test with an Online App

https://goo.gl/Hx5Ay7

1. Create a frequency table holding the categories of your coding scheme. Make sure to include the marginal sums.
2. Create a table in the same way to hold your expected values. To calculate your expected values, divide the total number of segments by the number of categories.
3. Go to the online app at http://vassarstats.net/csfit.HTML and enter the data for the observed and expected values as showin in Figure 9.13.
4. Click **Calculate**.
5. The app will return the degrees of freedom, the sum of χ^2 and the probability value as shown in Figure 9.14.

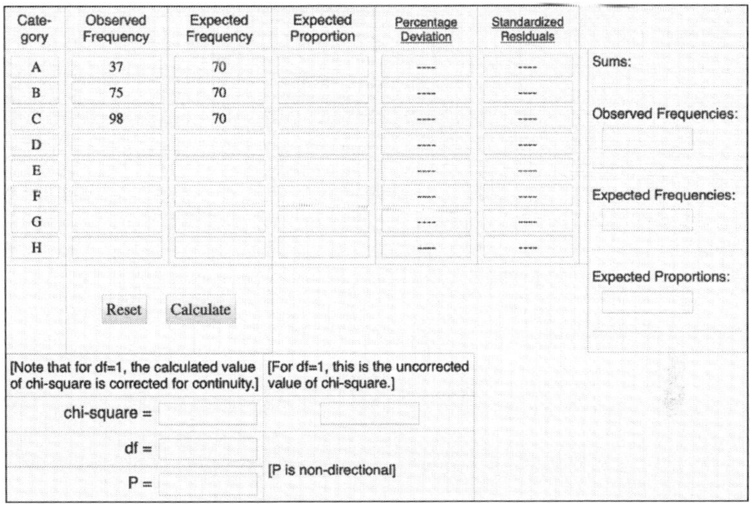

Figure 9.13: Calculating the goodness-of-fit χ^2 test online.

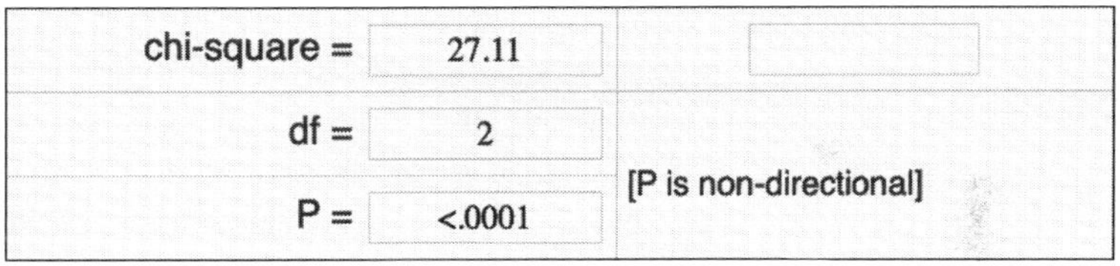

Figure 9.14: Results of the online calculation for the goodness-of-fit χ^2 test (http://vassarstats.net/csfit.HTML).

Overall then, the Goodness of Fit χ^2 test can give us a way to see the coding preferences that our coders used in coding the data. Unfortunately, the results of our example χ^2 test cannot take us much further than this because the sum of χ^2 appears inflated. This suggests that the test has not given us a valid measure of significance. As discussed earlier, inflated sums of χ^2 can result from a lack of independence among the data segments.

So while the χ^2 test gives us a way of seeing what is going on in our coders' use of the coding categories, if you find a lack of independence, the results cannot be relied on as a measure of significance. If the sum of χ^2 appears inflated, you should not infer anything about the coding patterns of the larger population from which your data set was drawn. In reporting an analysis that yields inflated sums of χ^2, then, you can point out to readers what the distribution of coding preferences was, but you should not report the results of the χ^2 test.

■ The χ^2 Test of Homogeneity

The χ^2 test of homogeneity works with data coded along one dimension which has a built-in contrast. It is a way of answering the question:

> How likely is it that two or more groups in my study share the same distribution across the categories in my coding scheme?

Answering such a question can help you to evaluate the significance of differences across your built-in contrast. Such a test is often called a test of homogeneity because we are asking whether the distribution in one sample of data is similar to—or homogeneous with—the distribution in another sample.

■ Computing a χ^2 test of homogeneity

The six steps shown in Figure 9.16 and discussed in Excel Procedure 9.2 will take you through the χ^2 test. You can download a template for your calculations at https://wac.colostate.edu/books/practice/codingstreams/. Directions for an app to do this calculation are provided in Procedure 9.2.

Excel Procedure 9.2: Calculating a χ^2 Test of Homogeneity in Excel

https://goo.gl/Hx5Ay7

1. Create a frequency table holding the categories of your coding scheme and the values of your contrast as shown in Step 1 of Figure 9.15. Make sure to include the marginal sums.
2. Create 3 more tables in the same way. Label them as shown in Figure 9.16. You may also use the Excel template available at https://wac.colostate.edu/books/practice/codingstreams/ that will automatically do the calculations for steps 3–5.

In Figure 9.15, we used the following formula to accomplish this calculation in each cell:

=($E15*B$19)/$E$19

3. For Step 3, O-E, subtract the expected frequencies from the observed values and put the result in each of the cells.

Step 1. Observed	Identity	Object	Practice	Total
Year1	25	45	53	123
Year2	8	25	23	56
Year3	0	0	2	2
Year4	4	5	20	29
Total	37	75	98	210
Step 2. Expected	Identity	Object	Practice	Total
Year1	22	44	57	123
Year2	10	20	26	56
Year3	0	1	1	2
Year4	5	10	14	29
Total	37	75	98	210
Step 3. O-E	Identity	Object	Practice	Total
Year1	3.33	1.07	-4.40	0.00
Year2	-1.87	5.00	-3.13	0.00
Year3	-0.35	-0.71	1.07	0.00
Year4	-1.11	-5.36	6.47	0.00
Total	0.00	0.00	0.00	0.00
Step 4. $(O\text{-}E)^2/E$	Identity	Object	Practice	Total
Year1	0.51	0.03	0.34	0.87
Year2	0.35	1.25	0.38	1.98
Year3	0.35	0.71	1.22	2.29
Year4	0.24	2.77	3.09	6.10
Total	1.46	4.76	5.02	11.24
Step 5. DF				
Number of rows -1	4			
Number of categories	3			
Number of rows -1	3			
Number of categories - 1	2			
df	6			
Step 6. Table Lookup	http://www.z-table.com/chi-square-table.html			
The sume of Chi Square equals	11.24	df & probability	df=6. p<.10	

Figure 9.15: Calculating χ^2 of homogeneity.

Continued . . .

Excel Procedure 9.2: Calculating a χ^2 Test of Homogeneity in Excel (continued)

https://goo.gl/Hx5Ay7

In Figure 9.15, we used a formula like the following to accomplish this calculation in each cell:

=($E15*B$19)/$E$19

4. For Step 3, O-E, subtract the expected frequencies from the observed values and put the result in each of the cells.

In Figure 9.15, we used a formula like the following to accomplish this calculation in each cell:

=B15-B22

5. In Step 4, (O-E)2/E, for each cell, square the value from Step 3 and divide the result by the expected value from Step 2.

In Figure 9.15, we used a formula like the following to accomplish this calculation in each cell:

=(B29*B29)/B22

The sum of χ^2 will be the grand total for the table.

6. Calculate the degrees of freedom by subtracting 1 from the number of rows in your contrast and 1 from the number categories in your coding scheme. Multiple these 2 numbers together

For Figure 9.15, we multipled together (4-1) and (3-1) to get degrees of freedom equal to 6.

7. Use a chi-square calculator like the one at https://www.socscistatistics.com/pvalues/chidistribution.aspx to calculate the p-value for your sum of chi-squares with your degrees of freedom.

Procedure 9.2: Calculating a χ^2 Test of Homogeneity with an Online App

https://goo.gl/Hx5Ay7

1. Go to the online app at http://turner .faculty.swau.edu/mathematics /math241/materials/contablecalc/ and enter the number of rows and columns in the opening page of the app. Press **Continue**.
2. Enter a title, labels and data for your frequency table as shown in Figure 9.16. Leave the option to display individual χ^2 values checked and press **Compute**.

The app will return a frequency table in which each cell holds the observed value, followed by the expected value (in italics), and the individual ^{2} values as shown in Figure 9.17. The sum of χ^2, the degrees of freedom, and the probability value can be found below the table.

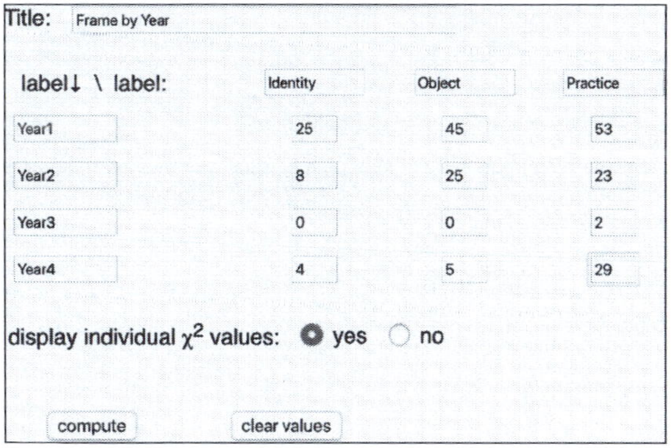

Figure 9.16: Entering data for the online app for the χ^2 test of homogeneity.

Frame by Year

	Identity	Object	Practice	
Year1	25 *20.78* (0.86)	45 *42.12* (0.20)	53 *60.10* (0.84)	**123**
Year2	8 *9.46* (0.23)	25 *19.18* (1.77)	23 *27.36* (0.70)	**56**
Year3	0 *0.34* (0.34)	0 *0.68* (0.68)	2 *0.98* (1.07)	**2**
Year4	4 *6.42* (0.91)	5 *13.01* (4.93)	29 *18.57* (5.86)	**38**
	37	**75**	**107**	**219**

χ^2 = 18.383, df = 6, χ^2/df = 3.06, P(χ^2 > 18.383) = 0.0053

warning: some observed or expected frequencies are less than 5; thus the Central Limit Theorem may not apply and the resultant χ^2 may be invalid

expected values are displayed in *italics*
individual χ^2 values are displayed in (parentheses)

Figure 9.17: Results of the calculations for the online app for the χ^2 test of homogeneity (http://turner.faculty.swau .edu/mathematics/math241/materials/contablecalc/).

Exercise 9.3 Try It Out

Perform a χ^2 test of homogeneity for the data in Figure 9.18 (and available at https://wac.colostate.edu/books/practice/codingstreams/).

	Ed	Cheryl	John	
Meeting 1	70	128	115	313
Meeting 2	104	106	104	314
	174	234	219	627

Figure 9.18: Observed frequency distribution of speakers in meetings 1 and 2.

For Discussion: What do the results tell you about the likelihood that Meetings 1 and 2 share the same distribution of speakers?

■ Interpreting the Results of the χ^2 test of Homogeneity

The final step in the computation of the χ^2 test of homogeneity tells you what the chances are that the distribution of your data over categories and across contrast is surprisingly different or not homogeneous. Interpreting a significant χ^2 result of $p < .05$ or $p < .01$ involves pinpointing the greatest differences in the values making up the χ^2 value which can be found in the table in Step 4 of Figure 9.15 or the third row in the cells of Figure 9.17 High values can tell you what is so unexpected in the distribution of your data; low values tell you what is not surprising.

Our calculations shown in Figure 9.15 suggest that there is nothing surprising about the way the distribution of data into our coding categories changes by year. The total, 11.24 with df equal to 6 show a probably of less that 1 in 10 ($p < .10$), a result that well can occur by chance. So the answer to the question with which we opened, How likely is it that two or more groups in my study share the same distribution across the categories in my coding scheme? appears to be "pretty likely."

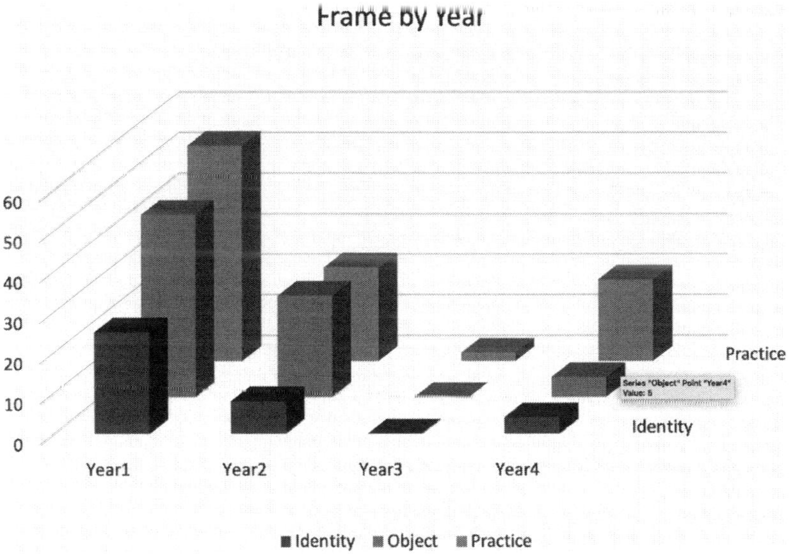

Figure 9.19: A block chart of the actual data from Figure 9.16.

A look at the individual χ^2 values shown in Step 4 of Figure 9.15 confirms that none of the values look surprisingly large. And the block chart of the same data shown in Figure 9.19 also shows homogeneity with each year's data being lower for *Identity*, medium sized for *Object* and, for the most part, highest for *Practice*. While it is the case that *Practice* shows up proportionately less in *Year2*, the difference is not large enough to reach significance.

Part of the problem with the data in our example χ^2 is that almost all of the observed values for *Year3* are very small; two are 0 and one is just 2. As mentioned earlier, scarce data can compromise the validity of a χ^2 analysis. In this case, it might be worthwhile to combine the *Year3* and *Year4* into a category like *After Year2* which we have done in the analysis shown in Figure 9.20.

The results for the analysis with combined categories yields a sum of χ^2 of 10.50. This value crosses the threshold for significance of the .05 level with df equal to 4. A look at the values in Step 4 pinpoints the After *Year2* values for *Object* and *Practice* make the largest contributions. And a comparison of the observed and expected values in Steps 1 and 2 suggests that surprise is coming from an unexpectedly low number of *Object* codes and an unexpectedly high number of *Practice* codes.

Step 1. Observed	Identity	Object	Practice	Total
Year1	25	45	53	123
Year2	8	25	23	56
After Year 2	4	5	22	31
Total	37	75	98	210
Step 2. Expected	Identity	Object	Practice	Total
Year1	22	44	57	123
Year2	10	20	26	56
After Year 2	5	11	14	31
Total	37	75	98	210
Step 3. O-E	Identity	Object	Practice	Total
Year1	3.33	1.07	-4.40	0.00
Year2	-1.87	5.00	-3.13	0.00
After Year 2	-1.46	-6.07	7.53	0.00
Total	0.00	0.00	0.00	0.00
Step 4. $(O-E)^2/E$	Identity	Object	Practice	Total
Year1	0.51	0.03	0.34	0.87
Year2	0.35	1.25	0.38	1.98
After Year 2	0.39	3.33	3.92	7.64
Total	1.26	4.61	4.64	10.50
Step 5. DF				
Number of rows -1	3			
Number of categories	3			
Number of rows -1	2			
Number of categories - 1	2			
df	4			
Step 6. Table Lookup	http://www.z-table.com/chi-square-table.html			
The sume of Chi Square equals	10.50	df & probability	df=4. p<.05	

Figure 9.20: A χ^2 analysis with data combined over scarce categories.

The fact is, however, that the surprise arises only in the *After Year2* category for which we have relatively little data. As a consequence, we would be somewhat conservative in making claims about the way that the data changes after *Year2*. At best, these results suggest that we should go on to do a One-Factor Multinomial Logistic Regression.

So while the χ^2 test of homogeneity gives us a way of seeing what is going on across our built-in contrast, scarce data may mean the results cannot be relied on as a measure of significance. If you have any cell values of 0 or many cell values of less than 5, you should consider combining categories.

In addition, inflated sum of χ^2 may affect a χ^2 test of homogeneity just as it did with the χ^2 test for goodness of fit. For this reason, we always recommend that you go on to do a One-Factor Multinomial Logistic Regression to confirm any significant results from a χ^2 analysis.

The χ^2 Test of Independence

The χ^2 test of independence works with data coded along two dimension without a built-in contrast. It is a way of answering the question, "*How likely is it that two dimensions in my study are independent of one another?*" Answering this question can help you to see whether there is a relationship between the way your data is coded along one dimension with the way it is coded along a second dimension.

Computing a χ^2 test of Independence

The six steps shown in Figure 9.21 and discussed in Excel Procedure 9.3 will take you through the χ^2 test of independence. You can download a template for your calculations at https://wac.colostate.edu/books/practice/codingstreams/. Directions for an app to do this calculation are provided in Procedure 9.3.

Interpreting the Results of a χ^2 test of Independence

The final step in the computation of the χ^2 test of independence tells you the chances that the two dimensions of coding are associated with one another.

Excel Procedure 9.3: Calculating a χ^2 Test of Independence in Excel

https://goo.gl/Hx5Ay7

1. Create a frequency table holding the categories of your first and second coding schemes shown in Step 1 of Figure 9.21. Make sure to include the marginal sums.
2. Create three more tables in the same way. Label them as shown in Figure 9.21. You may also use the Excel template available at https://wac.colostate.edu/books/practice/codingstreams/ that will automatically do the calculations for steps 3–5.
3. For Step 2, Expected, for each cell, multiple the row total by its column total and then divide the result by the table's grand total.

In Figure 9.21, we used the following formula to accomplish this calculation in each cell:

=($E19*B$22)/$E$22

4. For Step 3, O-E, subtract the expected frequencies from the observed values and put the result in each of the cells.

Step 1. Observed	Identity	Object	Practice	Total
Professional	9	0	4	13
Social	23	12	14	49
Technical	5	63	80	148
Total	37	75	98	210

Step 2. Expected	identity	object	practice	Total
Professional	2	5	6	13
Social	9	18	23	49
Technical	26	53	69	148
	37	75	98	210

Step 3. O-E	identity	object	practice	Total
Professional	6.71	-4.64	-2.07	0.00
Social	14.37	-5.50	-8.87	0.00
Technical	-21.08	10.14	10.93	0.00
	0	0	0	0

Step 4. $(O-E)^2/E$	identity	object	practice	Total
Professional	19.65	4.64	0.70	25.00
Social	23.91	1.73	3.44	29.07
Technical	17.03	1.95	1.73	20.71
	60.60	8.32	5.87	**74.79**

Step 5. DF	
Number of rows	3
Number of columns	3
Number of rows -1	2
Number of columns - 1	2
df	4

Step 6. Table Lookup	http://www.z-table.com/chi-square-table.html		
The sume of Chi Square equals	74.79	df & probability	df=4. p<.005

Figure 9.21: Results of a χ^2 test of independence.

Continued . . .

Excel Procedure 9.3: Calculating a χ^2 Test of Independence in Excel (continued)

https://goo.gl/Hx5Ay7

In Figure 9.21, we used the following formula to accomplish this calculation in each cell:

=B19-B25

5. In Step 4, $(O-E)^2/E$, for each cell, square the value from Step 3 and divide the result by the expected value from Step 2.

In Figure 9.21, we used the following formula to accomplish this calculation in each cell:

=(B31*B31)/B25

The sum of χ^2 will be the grand total for the table.

6. Calculate the degrees of freedom by subtracting 1 from the number of rows in your contrast and 1 from the number categories in your coding scheme. Multiple these 2 numbers together

For Figure 9.21, we multipled together (3-1) and (3-1) to get degrees of freedom equal to 4.

7. Use a chi-square calculator like the one at https://www.socscistatistics.com/pvalues/chidistribution.aspx to calculate the p-value for your sum of chi-squares with your degrees of freedom.

Procedure 9.3: Calculating a χ^2 Test of Independence with an Online App

https://goo.gl/Hx5Ay7

1. Go to the online app at http://turner.faculty.swau.edu/mathematics/math241/materials/contablecalc/ and enter the number of rows and columns in the opening page of the app. Press **Continue**.
2. Enter a title, labels and data for your frequency table. Leave the option to display individual χ^2 values checked and press **Compute**.

The app will return a frequency table like that shown in Figure 9.22 in which each cell holds the observed value, followed by the expected value (in italics), and the individual χ^2 values. The sum of χ^2, the degrees of freedom, and the probability value can be found below the table.

	Frame x Alignment			
	Identity	**Object**	**Practice**	
Professional	9 *2.29* (19.65)	0 *4.64* (4.64)	4 *6.07* (0.70)	**13**
Social	23 *8.63* (23.91)	12 *17.50* (1.73)	14 *22.87* (3.44)	**49**
Technical	5 *26.08* (17.03)	63 *52.86* (1.95)	80 *69.07* (1.73)	**148**
	37	**75**	**98**	**210**

χ^2 = 74.787, df = 4, χ^2/df = 18.70 , P(χ^2 > 74.787) = 0.0000

warning: some observed or expected frequencies are less than 5; thus the Central Limit Theorem may not apply and the resultant χ^2 may be invalid

Figure 9.22: Results of the calculations for the online app for the χ^2 test of independence (http://turner.faculty.swau.edu/mathematics/math241/materials/contablecalc/).

That is, to what extent will values on the first dimension co-occur with values on a second dimension.

In the example shown in Figures 9.21 and 9.22, we see a very high sum of χ^2 (74.79 with 4 degrees of freedom) which could suggest that there is a very strong relationship between *Frame* and *Alignment*. A χ^2 calculator (https://www.socscistatistics.com/pvalues/chidistribution.aspx) shows that this is highly surprising.

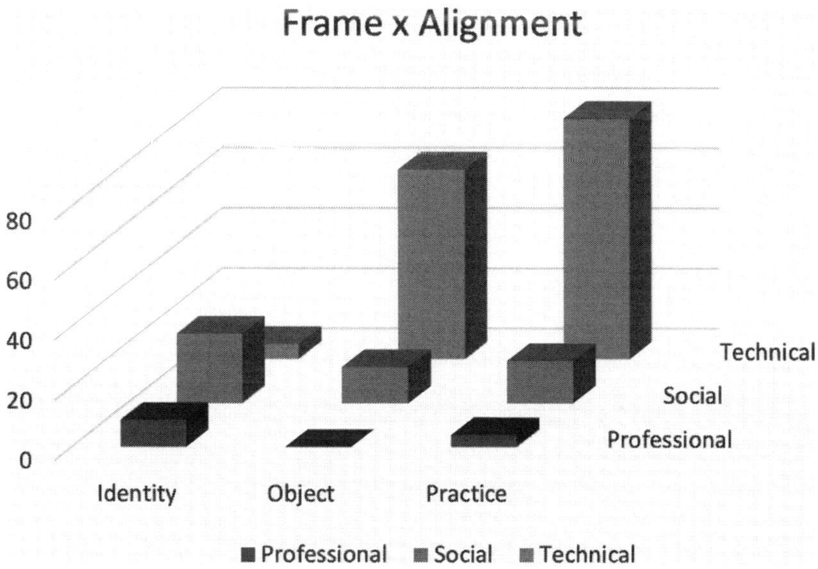

Figure 9.23: Block chart of the observed data from Figure 9.20.

A look at the block chart for the observed data in Figure 9.23 provides more detail about these surprises. In general, the observed values of *Technical* varies considerably depending on the *Frame* used. With *Object* and *Practice*, it is the most common category, but with *Identity*, it is the least common category. In fact, as we see in Step 4 of Figure 9.21, the individual χ^2 value for *Technical* with *Identity* is a high 17.03. The values of the other categories for *Identity* are also matters of surprise with high individual χ^2 values (19.65 for *Professional* and 23.91 for *Social*).

When we use Steps 1 and 2 to compare the observed and expected values in these three cells we can see that *Professional* and *Social* are both higher than expected (9 vs. 2 for *Professional* and 23 vs. 9 for *Social*) while *Technical* is lower than expected (5 vs. 26). Clearly, there is a surprising relationship between these two dimensions.

Unfortunately, because of the inflated sum of χ^2, we cannot draw any conclusions about the significance of this relationship. As discussed earlier, a high sum of χ^2 is often the result of a lack of independence among the data points. To get a clearer picture of what is going on here, we would turn to a One-Factor Multinomial Logistic Regression.

The χ^2 test of independence gives us a way of seeing a relationship between two coding dimensions. But just as with our earlier χ^2 tests, scarce data can compromise it as a measure of significance. If you have any cell values of 0 or many cell values of less than 5, you should consider combining categories.

In addition, as we have just seen, inflated sum of χ^2 may affect a χ^2 test of independence. Thus, we always recommend that you go on to do a One-Factor Multinomial Logistic Regression to confirm any significance results from a χ^2 analysis.

Memo 9.2: Your χ^2 Analysis

Record the frequency table that you used as input to the χ^2 test. Record the results: your degrees of freedom, the sum of χ^2 and the probability level. Check for an inflated χ^2 value that would limit your ability to draw conclusions about significance.

If significant, use the individual χ^2 values to determine which values are making the largest contribution. For these cells, compare the observed frequencies to the expected frequencies. Put into plain language what these comparisons mean in terms of what is surprising in your data.

One-Factor Multinomial Logistic Regression

One-factor multinomial logistic regression is an analytic tool designed to examine the impact of a predictor variable on an outcome variable. With coded verbal data, the outcome variable is always the coding along a given dimension.

The predictor variable may be the values on the contrast built into the design of the data. In this case, it is designed to answer the question:

> What is the likelihood of a given code given a value on the built-in contrast?

In this first form, we recommend you use this test as a follow-up analysis to the χ^2 test of homogeneity.

The predictor variable may also be the values on a second coding dimension. In this case, one-factor multinomial logistic regression is designed to answer the question:

> What is the likelihood of a given code along a second coding dimension given a value on a first coding dimension?

In this second form, we recommend you use this test as a follow-up analysis to the χ^2 test of independence.

Running a One-Factor Multinomial Logistic Regression

The one-factor multinomial logistic regression works with the individual data points in your data set. Prepare your data for the app as detailed in Excel Procedure 9.4 paying particular attention to the labels of your columns. Then run the app using Procedure 9.5.

Interpreting a One-Factor Multinomial Logistic Regression

The first step in interpreting the results of a one-factor multinomial logistic regression is ensuring your results are stable. This involves comparing the results of the two runs you have made. For the sample data the results for our two runs are shown in Figure 9.27.

Procedure 9.4: Preparing the Data for a One-Factor Multinomial Regression

https://goo.gl/Hx5Ay7

1. Combine the coded data from individual data worksheets into a single worksheet, keeping track of which data comes from which worksheet.
2. Creating a new column in the combined worksheet. Label it as **Case**.
3. In this column, next to each segment, enter the name of the data worksheet from which the segment was copied.
4. Determine which column is to be used as the predictive factor and change its heading to **Factor1**.

	A	B	C	D	E
1	**Unit**	**Year**	**Case**	**Factor1**	**Dimension**
2	1	2011	irunepan	Identity	Professional
3	2	2011	irunepan	Identity	Professional
4	3	2011	irunepan	Practice	Technical
5	4	2011	irunepan	Practice	Technical
6	5	2011	irunepan	Practice	Technical
7	6	2011	irunepan	Practice	Technical
8	7	2011	irunepan	Practice	Technical
9	8	2011	irunepan	Identity	Technical
10	9	2011	irunepan	Practice	Technical
11	10	2011	pieper	Practice	Technical
12	11	2011	pieper	Object	Technical
13	12	2011	pieper	Practice	Technical
14	13	2011	pieper	Object	Social
15	14	2011	haehn	Object	Technical

Figure 9.24: Worksheet arrangement for a one-factor multinomial logistic regression.

The Factor1 column may be the one holding the values of your built-in contrast or it may be the one holding the values of your first coding dimension, depending on which variety of the one-factor multinomial logistic regression you are preparing for.

5. Determine which column is to be used as the outcome dimension and label it **Dimension**.
6. Delete the column holding the actual verbal data.

The online app will not work properly if the verbal data is left in the worksheet. Your worksheet should look something like the one shown in Figure 9.24.

Save this worksheet in a CSV (comma separated values) format using the **File** > **Save As** command.

Procedure 9.5: Running a One-Factor Multinomial Regression

https://goo.gl/Hx5Ay7

1. Navigate to the online app at https://wac.colostate.edu/books/practice/codingstreams/.
2. The interface should look like that shown in Figure 9.25.

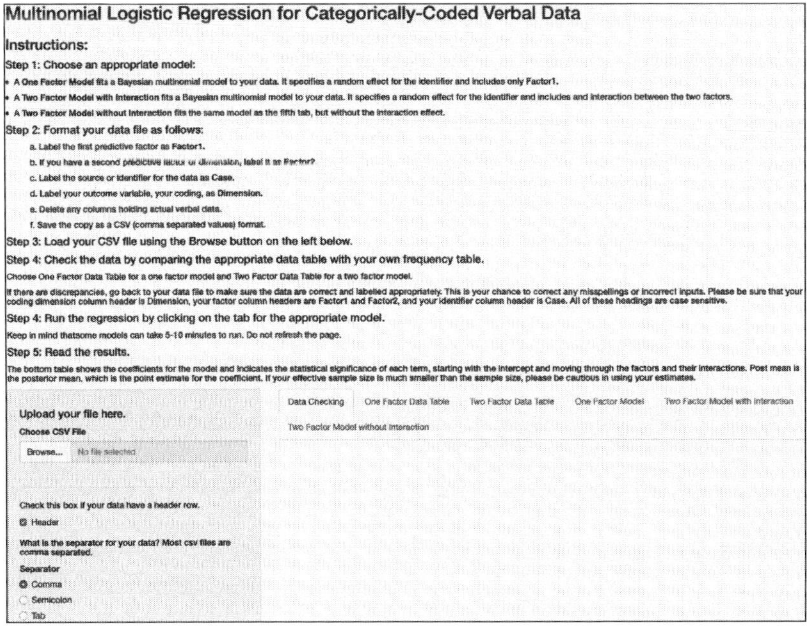

Figure 9.25: Interface for the online app for multinomial logistic regression.

3. Click on the **Browse button** on the left. Navigate to and choose the CSV file holding your data.

The data should load.

4. Click on the tab labeled **One Factor Data Table**.

If the app returns an error, check your data setup following Procedure 9.4.

5. Compare the frequency table on the tab with the frequency table you created for your earlier χ^2 analysis.

Continued . . .

Procedure 9.5: Running a One-Factor Multinomial Regression (continued)

https://goo.gl/Hx5Ay7

If the frequency table does not match a frequency table you generated earlier, check that you are using the correct data file and that the columns are labeled appropriately.

6. To get the results of the regression, click on the tab labeled **One Factor Model**.
7. Wait until the calculation is completed.

The output will look like that shown in Figure 9.26.

```
 Iterations = 10001:99901
 Thinning interval  = 100
 Sample size  = 900

 DIC: 272.2726

 G-structure:  ~idh(trait):Case

                              post.mean l-95% CI u-95% CI eff.samp
traitDimension.Social.Case       1.3330  0.04435   3.1674   142.31
traitDimension.Technical.Case    0.2383  0.01739   0.7477    53.71

 R-structure:  ~us(trait):units

                                                      post.mean l-95% CI
traitDimension.Social:traitDimension.Social.units       0.31406  0.02240
traitDimension.Technical:traitDimension.Social.units    0.01242 -0.42167
traitDimension.Social:traitDimension.Technical.units    0.01242 -0.42167
traitDimension.Technical:traitDimension.Technical.units 0.21119  0.02234
                                                      u-95% CI eff.samp
traitDimension.Social:traitDimension.Social.units       0.9841    83.77
traitDimension.Technical:traitDimension.Social.units    0.3651   116.27
traitDimension.Social:traitDimension.Technical.units    0.3651   116.27
traitDimension.Technical:traitDimension.Technical.units 0.6290   124.27

 Location effects: Dimension ~ -1 + trait + Factor1

                         post.mean l-95% CI u-95% CI eff.samp   pMCMC
traitDimension.Social      0.09732 -0.82864  1.01817   334.82 0.78444
traitDimension.Technical   1.23417  0.47790  1.97048   209.19 < 0.001 **
Factor1Object              2.17303  0.81538  3.49232    22.53 < 0.001 **
Factor1Practice            1.39528  0.38909  2.49851    92.42 0.00889 **
---
Signif. codes:  0 '***' 0.001 '**' 0.01 '*' 0.05 '.' 0.1 ' ' 1
```

Figure 9.26: Output of a one-factor multinomial logistic regression.

8. Make a copy of the output and place it in a worksheet along with your data worksheet. Label it Run 1.
9. Reload the app page in your browser to clear the data.
10. Click on the **Browse button** and load the same CSV file.
11. Click on the tab labeled **One Factor Model**.
12. Copy the output into a second worksheet labeled Run 2.

```
                          post.mean l-95% CI u-95% CI eff.samp   pMCMC
traitDimension.Social       0.09732 -0.82864  1.01817   334.82 0.78444
traitDimension.Technical    1.23417  0.47790  1.97048   209.19 < 0.001 **
Factor1Object               2.17303  0.81538  3.49232    22.53 < 0.001 **
Factor1Practice             1.39528  0.38909  2.49851    92.42 0.00889 **
---
```

Run 1

```
                          post.mean l-95% CI u-95% CI eff.samp   pMCMC
traitDimension.Social        0.1394  -0.8573   1.0766   180.34 0.75333
traitDimension.Technical     1.2388   0.5671   2.0205   198.42 0.00222 **
Factor1Object                1.9628   0.6942   3.1814    55.05 < 0.001 **
Factor1Practice              1.4305   0.4198   2.1984    74.85 < 0.001 **
---
Signif. codes:  0 '***' 0.001 '**' 0.01 '*' 0.05 '.' 0.1 ' ' 1
```

Run 2

Figure 9.27: Comparing the results of two runs of the app for one-factor multinomial logistic regression.

In our analysis, the code of *Professional* serves as the baseline for the outcome dimension of Alignment. The first two lines in the two outputs shown in Figure 9.25 give the results for the other two Alignment codes, *Social* and *Technical*, compared with this baseline.

The next two lines in the output give the results for the Frame dimension. Here the category of *Identity* serves as the baseline, and these two lines give the results for the other two Frame codes, *Object* and *Practice*, compared with this baseline.

On each line, the first and last columns are your main focus. In the first column, labeled post.mean (posterior mean), you find the critical log odds values computed by the multinomial logistic regression. In the last column, labeled pMCMC, you find an estimate of the probability that the log odds could have occurred by chance. Asterisks mark those that may be considered significant. P values of less than 1 in a thousand ($p < .001$) are labeled with a triple asterisk (***). Those with p values of less than 1 in a hundred ($p < .01$) are labeled with a double asterisk (**). Those with p values of less than 5 in a hundred ($P < .05$) are labeled with a single asterisk (*).

When you compare the two runs for stability, you want to see that they have the same results in terms of significance levels and somewhat similar log odds values. When we compare the significance values of the two runs shown in Figure 9.27, for example, we see that they both show significance values at

$p < .001$ for *Technical*, for *Object*, and for *Practice* and we see that the log odds are somewhat similar. This assures us that the results are stable.

To understand these results, we take a closer look at the log odds. Looking at Run 1, Figure 9.26, we see that the log odds listed for traitDimension.Social is .09732. In other words, log-odds for being coded as *Social* relative to being coded as *Professional* is .09732. The fact that this number is positive shows that any segment is more likely to be coded as *Social* than *Professional* regardless of how it was coded for Frame. If we refer back to the frequency table of observed values repeated in Figure 9.28, we can confirm that the frequencies for the *Social* row are all larger than the *Professional* row. But the small log odds from the multinomial logistic regression tells us that this difference is not large enough to be surprising.

We look next at the results for traitDimension.Technical. Here the results are suggesting that the log odds for being coded as *Technical* relative to being coded as *Professional* are 1.23417, which is significant at $p < .001$. That is, any segment is significantly more likely to be coded as *Technical* than *Professional* regardless of how it was coded for Frame. Again, a look at the frequency table in Figure 9.28 confirms that the values for *Technical* are generally much higher than those for *Professional*. That is, there is less than one chance in a thousand that this would have occurred by chance if there were no true difference.

The next two lines show the impact of the Frame dimension, our predictor variable, on Alignment, our outcome variable. For Factor1Object, the log odds for being coded as *Object* relative to being coded as *Identity* are 2.17303, which is significant at $p < .001$. This means that if a segment were to change coding from *Identity* to *Object* along the Frame dimension, the multinomial log-odds for being coded as something other than *Professional* along the Alignment dimension would be expected to increase by 2.17303 units while holding all other variables in the model constant. In other words, the impact of coding a segment as *Object* along the Frame dimension increases its chances of being coded as something other than *Professional* along the Alignment dimension. That is, when people wrote about objects, they did not often talk about the professional contexts for those objects.

Step 1. Observed	Identity	Object	Practice	Total
Professional	9	0	4	13
Social	23	12	14	49
Technical	5	63	80	148
Total	37	75	98	210
Step 2. Expected	identity	object	practice	Total
Professional	2	5	6	13
Social	9	18	23	49
Technical	26	53	69	148
	37	75	98	210
Step 3. O-E	identity	object	practice	Total
Professional	6.71	-4.64	-2.07	0.00
Social	14.37	-5.50	-8.87	0.00
Technical	-21.08	10.14	10.93	0.00
	0	0	0	0
Step 4. $(O-E)^2/E$	identity	object	practice	Total
Professional	19.65	4.64	0.70	25.00
Social	23.91	1.73	3.44	29.07
Technical	17.03	1.95	1.73	20.71
	60.60	8.32	5.87	**74.79**

Figure 9.28: Frequency tables from the χ^2 test of independence for the same data used to produce the output shown in Figure 9.24.

For Factor1Practice, the log odds for being coded as *Practice* relative to being coded as *Identity* are 1.39528, which is also significant at $p < .001$. This means that if a segment were to change coding from *Identity* to *Practice* along the dimensions of Frame, the multinomial log-odds for being coded as something other than *Professional* along the dimension of Alignment would be expected to increase by 1.39528 units while holding all other variables in the model constant. In other words, the impact of coding a segment as *Practice* along the Frame dimension also increases its chances of being coded as something other than *Professional* along the Alignment dimension. That is, when people wrote about practices they did not often talk about the professional contexts for those practices.

These results are generally consistent with those of our earlier χ^2 test of independence, where we found a very high sum of χ^2 (74.79) but were unsure of how to interpret this inflated result. With the significant results of the multinomial logistic regression, we can have greater confidence in this earlier finding and see some further patterns that are indicated by color in Figure 9.28. In gold, we see the three frequencies identified in the χ^2 analysis as being unexpectedly different from their expected values. And in shades of orange we have marked those values that have been identified by the multinomial logistic regression as significant.

As we noted in our earlier discussion, the χ^2 analysis suggested that something surprising is going on with the predictor variable of *Identity*. And, as we just noted, the significant log odds for Factor1Object and Factor1Practice also suggest something going on with this category: as coding on the Frame dimension moves out of the *Identity* category into the other two categories, the chances of being coded as *Professional* decrease significantly. In Figure 9.28, this is indicated by the light orange and medium orange cells in the *Object* and *Practice* columns compared to the uncolored cells in the *Professional* row. That is, when people wrote about practices and objects they did not often talk about them in their professional contexts.

The results of the multinomial logistic regression also tell us something else: the value for *Technical* compared to *Professional* is surprisingly high on the Alignment dimension. Though not examined by the earlier χ^2 test for independence, this result is consistent with our frequency table of observed values. The dark orange cell in Figure 9.28 pinpoints an overall frequency of 148 for *Technical* compared to the overall frequency of 13 for *Professional*. The log odds for traitDimension.Technical tell us that this is significant. And it might appear that the frequency of 49 for *Social* compared to the frequency of 13 for *Professional* would also be significant. But the log odds for traitDimension.Social tell us this is not the case.

Two-Factor Multinomial Logistic Regression

Two-factor multinomial logistic regression is an analytic tool designed to examine the impact of two predictor variables on an outcome variable. With coded verbal data, the outcome variable is always the coding along a given dimension.

The predictor variables will be the values on a build-in contrast and the values on a second dimension. It is designed to answer the question, "*Given a value on a built-in contrast, what is the likelihood of a given code along a second coding dimension given a value on a first coding dimension?"* This is the test to use when you have data coded along two dimensions as well as a built-in contrast, a complex analysis that cannot be handled by a χ^2 test.

In addition to looking for the main effects of the two predictor variables, a two-factor multinomial logistic regression can also look for a significant interaction between them. An interaction between two variables means the effect of one of those variables on a third variable is not constant—the effect differs at different values of the other. For the sample data we will be using show in Figure 9.29, an interaction would mean that the effect of Factor2 (the Frame dimension) on Dimension (the Alignment dimension) would be different depending on the built-in contrast of Year. As we noted earlier in Chapter 7, a pattern of association between two dimensions may not hold true on both sides of a contrast; this is an interaction. A two-factor multinomial logistic regression will tell us if this interaction is significant.

Adding an interaction to a two-factor model may improve the fit of the model, but it is also possible that it does not improve it. For this reason, in the following procedures, we suggest that you run a two-factor multinomial logistic regression both with and without an interaction and then determine which is the better fit.

Running a two-factor multinomial logistic regression

The two-factor multinomial logistic regression, like its one-factor counterpart, works with the individual data points in your data set. Prepare your data for the app as detailed in Procedure 9.6 and then run a two-factor multinomial logistic regression both with and without interaction using Procedures 9.7 and 9.8.

Interpreting a Two-factor multinomial logistic regression

The first step in interpreting the results of a two-factor multinomial logistic regression is choosing between the two tests you have run, one with interaction and one without. In most cases, you will choose to use the one with the interaction as it will give you more information. But occasionally, the model

Procedure 9.6: Preparing the Data for a Two-Factor Multinomial Regression

https://goo.gl/Hx5Ay7

1. Combine the coded data from individual data worksheets into a single worksheet, keeping track of which data comes from which worksheet.
2. Create a new column in the worksheet. Label it as **Case**.
3. In this column, next to each segment, enter the name of the data worksheet from which the segment was copied.
4. Change the name of the column holding your built-in contrast to **Factor1**.
5. Change the name of the column with your first dimension to **Factor2**
6. Change the name of the column with your second dimension to **Dimension**.
7. Delete the column holding the actual verbal data.

The online app will not work properly if the verbal data is left in the worksheet. Your worksheet should look something like the one shown in Figure 9.29.

Obs	Case	Factor1	Factor2	Dimension
1	irunepan	Year1	Identity	Professional
2	irunepan	Year1	Identity	Professional
3	irunepan	Year1	Practice	Technical
4	irunepan	Year1	Practice	Technical
5	irunepan	Year1	Practice	Technical
6	irunepan	Year1	Practice	Technical
7	irunepan	Year1	Practice	Technical
8	irunepan	Year1	Identity	Technical
9	irunepan	Year1	Practice	Technical
10	pieper	Year1	Practice	Technical

Figure 9.29: Worksheet arrangement for a two-factor multinomial logistic regression.

Save this worksheet in a CSV (comma separated values) format using the **File** > **Save As** command.

Procedure 9.7: Running a Two-Factor Multinomial Regression with Interaction

https://goo.gl/Hx5Ay7

1. Navigate to the online app at https://wac.colostate.edu/books/practice/codingstreams/. The interface should look like that shown in Figure 9.25.
2. Click on the **Browse button** on the left. Navigate to and choose the CSV file holding your data.

The data should load.

3. Click on the tab labeled **Two Factor Data Table**.

If the app returns an error, check your data setup following Procedure 9.6.

4. Check the frequency table on the tab to make sure that the values look right.

If the frequency table does not look right, check that you are using the correct data file and that the columns are labeled appropriately.

5. To get the results of the regression with interaction, click on the tab labeled **Two Factor Model with Interaction**.
6. Wait until the calculation is completed.

The output will look like that shown in Figure 9.30.

```
 Iterations = 5001:79971
 Thinning interval  = 90
 Sample size  = 834

 DIC: 271.2435

 G-structure:  ~idh(trait):Case

                              post.mean l-95% CI u-95% CI eff.samp
traitDimension.Social.Case       1.5550  0.03869   4.2242    97.84
traitDimension.Technical.Case    0.2024  0.01506   0.6315   130.28

 R-structure:  ~us(trait):units

                                                    post.mean l-95% CI
traitDimension.Social:traitDimension.Social.units      0.36178  0.02382
traitDimension.Technical:traitDimension.Social.units   0.03881 -0.40194
traitDimension.Social:traitDimension.Technical.units   0.03881 -0.40194
traitDimension.Technical:traitDimension.Technical.units  0.22481  0.02148
                                                    u-95% CI eff.samp
traitDimension.Social:traitDimension.Social.units      1.2215    62.45
traitDimension.Technical:traitDimension.Social.units   0.6138    52.70
traitDimension.Social:traitDimension.Technical.units   0.6138    52.70
traitDimension.Technical:traitDimension.Technical.units  0.6334    76.31

 Location effects: Dimension ~ -1 + trait + Factor1 + Factor2 + Factor1 *
Factor2

                            post.mean l-95% CI u-95% CI eff.samp  pMCMC

traitDimension.Social         0.02296 -0.97040  1.04654   260.56 0.9616

traitDimension.Technical      1.15934  0.39163  1.96202   156.16 0.0024 *
*
Factor1Year2                  0.47757 -0.60851  1.70344   196.56 0.3717

Factor2Object                 2.14273  0.85537  3.36889    71.84 <0.001 *
*
Factor2Practice               1.19465  0.07297  2.32849   105.64 0.0384 *

Factor1Year2:Factor2Object    0.52472 -1.08910  2.25891    94.08 0.5755

Factor1Year2:Factor2Practice  0.24464 -0.97286  1.77297   118.38 0.7434

---
Signif. codes:  0 '***' 0.001 '**' 0.01 '*' 0.05 '.' 0.1 ' ' 1
```

Figure 9.30: Output from a two-factor multinomial logistic regression with interaction.

Procedure 9.8: Running a Two-Factor Multinomial Regression without Interaction

https://goo.gl/Hx5Ay7

1. Navigate to the online app at https://wac.colostate.edu/books/practice/codingstreams/.

The interface should look like that shown in Figure 9.25.

1. Click on the **Browse button** on the left. Navigate to and choose the CSV file holding your data.
2. The data should load.
3. To get the results of the regression without interaction, click on the tab labeled **Two Factor Model without Interaction**.
4. Wait until the calculation is completed.

The output will look like that shown in Figure 9.31.

```
 Iterations = 7001:89901
 Thinning interval  = 100
 Sample size  = 830

 DIC: 272.0983

 G-structure:  ~idh(trait):Case

                              post.mean l-95% CI u-95% CI eff.samp
traitDimension.Social.Case       1.6330  0.04846   4.6775    44.73
traitDimension.Technical.Case    0.2491  0.01519   0.8326    57.51

 R-structure:  ~us(trait):units

                                                     post.mean l-95% CI
traitDimension.Social:traitDimension.Social.units      0.34472  0.02647
traitDimension.Technical:traitDimension.Social.units   0.03253 -0.43202
traitDimension.Social:traitDimension.Technical.units   0.03253 -0.43202
traitDimension.Technical:traitDimension.Technical.units 0.24841 0.02532
                                                     u-95% CI eff.samp
traitDimension.Social:traitDimension.Social.units      1.1345   125.12
traitDimension.Technical:traitDimension.Social.units   0.5842    66.05
traitDimension.Social:traitDimension.Technical.units   0.5842    66.05
traitDimension.Technical:traitDimension.Technical.units 0.7774   72.76

 Location effects: Dimension ~ -1 + trait + Factor1 + Factor2

                         post.mean l-95% CI u-95% CI eff.samp   pMCMC
traitDimension.Social     -0.02805 -1.05551  0.91618   323.53 0.98072
traitDimension.Technical   1.07304  0.34776  1.84195   238.52 0.00482 **
Factor1Year2               0.67048 -0.36824  1.77548    60.91 0.20723
Factor2Object              2.04976  0.99334  3.25079    59.85 < 0.001 **
Factor2Practice            1.43713  0.44051  2.62174    62.19 0.01205 *
---
Signif. codes:  0 '***' 0.001 '**' 0.01 '*' 0.05 '.' 0.1 ' ' 1
```

Figure 9.31: Output from a two-factor multinomial

with interaction will be a poorer fit for the data. To check for this, compare the DIC numbers at the top of the two outputs.

With our sample data, we see that the DIC for the run with interaction, shown in Figure 9.30, is 271.2435. Without interaction, the DIC, shown in Figure 9.31, is 272.0983. In general, the run with the smaller DIC is a better fit. These two DICs are pretty close to one another, so it may not make much difference, so we choose to work with the results with interaction.

To understand the results, we take a closer look at the log odds. Looking at Figure 9.30, we see that the log odds listed for trait Dimension.Social are .02296. In other words, log-odds for being coded as *Social* relative to being coded as *Professional* are .02296. The fact that this number is positive shows that any segment is more likely to be coded as *Social* than *Professional* regardless of how it was coded for Frame or Year, although this difference is not big enough to be significant.

We look next at the results for traitDimension.Technical. Here the results are suggesting that the log odds for being coded as *Technical* relative to being coded as *Professional* are 1.15934, which is significant at $p < .01$. That is, any segment is significantly more likely to be coded as *Technical* than *Professional* regardless of how it was coded for Frame or Year.

The next line shows the impact of Year, the first of our predictor variables, on Alignment, our outcome variable. For Factor1Year2, the log odds for being *Year2* relative to being coded as *Year1* are .47757, which is not significant. This means that if a segment were to change coding from *Identity* to *Object* along the built-in contrast of Year, the multinomial log-odds for being coded as something other than *Professional* along the Alignment dimension would be expected to increase by .47757 unit while holding all other variables in the model constant. In other words, the impact of being *Year2* rather than *Year1* along the built-in contrast of Year does not have much effect on how it is coded along the Alignment dimension.

The next two lines show the impact of the Frame dimension, our second predictor variable, on Alignment. For Factor2Object, the log odds for being coded as *Object* relative to being coded as *Identity* are 2.14273, which is significant at $p < .01$. This means that if a segment were to change coding from

Identity to *Object* along the Frame dimension, the multinomial log-odds for being coded as something other than *Professional* along the Alignment dimension would be expected to increase by 2.14273 units while holding all other variables in the model constant. In other words, the impact of coding a segment as *Object* along the Frame dimension increases its chances of being coded as something other than *Professional* along the Alignment dimension.

For Factor2Practice, the log odds for being coded as *Practice* relative to being coded as *Identity* are 1.19465, which is also significant at $p < .01$. This means that if a segment were to change coding from *Identity* to *Practice* along the dimensions of Frame, the multinomial log-odds for being coded as something other than *Professional* along the dimension of Alignment would be expected to increase by 1.19465 units while holding all other variables in the model constant. In other words, the impact of coding a segment as *Practice* along the Frame dimension also increase its chances of being coded as something other than *Professional* along the Alignment dimension.

Our final results concern the interactions between Year and Frame. For Factor1Year2:Factor2Object, the log odds for being coded as *Object* relative to being coded as *Identity* under a coding of *Year1* or *Year2* are .52472, which is not significant. For Factor1Year2:Factor2Practice, the log odds for being coded as *Practice* relative to being coded as *Identity* under a coding of *Year1* or *Year2* are .24464, which is also not significant. This means that neither being coded as *Object* nor *Practice* are significantly affected by Year.

We note that the data used here are slightly different than that used for the earlier χ^2 test of homogeneity because here we only have two values for the built-in contrast of Year.

Memo 9.3: Interpreting Your Multinomial Logistic Regression

Record the results of a multinomial logistic regression on your data. What are the log odds of each category? Which ones are significant at which level? Also record a frequency table for the data set.

For each result, write a sentence describing what each result means. Refer to the frequency tables for details. Overall, which predictor variables seem to have an impact on the way your data was coded?

For Further Reading

Dolinar, S. (2014). *Statistics—Probability vs. odds*. Retrieved from https://stats.seandolinar.com/statistics-probability-vs-odds/.

Grace-Martin, K. (2019a). *Chi-square test vs. logistic regression: Is a fancier test better?* The Analysis Factor. Retrieved from https://www.theanalysisfactor.com/chi-square-test-vs-logistic-regression-is-a-fancier-test-better/.

Grace-Martin, K. (2019b). *The difference between interaction and association?* The Analysis Factor. Retrieved from https://www.theanalysisfactor.com/interaction-association/.

Kiernan, K. (2018). Insights into using the GLIMMIX procedure to model categorical outcomes with random effects. *SAS Global Forum Proceedings*. Retrieved from https://www.sas.com/content/dam/SAS/support/en/sas-global-forum-proceedings/2018/2179-2018.PDF.

Kleinbaum, D. G. & Klein, M. (2010). *Logistic regression: A self-learning text*. New York: Springer.

Miller, S. V. (2014). *Reading a regression table: A guide for students*. Retrieved from http://svmiller.com/blog/2014/08/reading-a-regression-table-a-guide-for-students/.

Papageorgiou, G. & Hinde, J. (2012). Multivariate generalized linear mixed models with semi-nonparametric and smooth nonparametric random effects densities. *Stat Comput* 22, 79–92.

UCLA: Statistical Consulting Group.Multinomial logistic regression: Stata annotated output. Retrieved September 8, 2019, from https://stats.idre.ucla.edu/stata/output/multinomial-logistic-regression-2/.

Chapter 10. Writing the Analysis

> In this chapter, you will develop the details necessary to support the analyses you developed in earlier chapters and throughout your memoing process. By sorting, reflecting on, and ordering your memos, you will develop an emerging understanding of your phenomenon to demonstrate and argue through the presentation of details from your data. You will learn to detail codes, patterns, and discrepancies in a way that will make your findings come alive for yourself and your readers.

Over the course of this book, we have taken you from your thoughts and intuitions about a phenomenon in the world through increasingly abstract ways of seeing and thinking about that phenomenon. By coding the data according to contents and themes, you reduced the phenomenon from its three-dimensional realness to a simpler set of codes that described some salient aspect for closer study. In the chapters on distributions, analyses across dimensions, and temporal analysis we asked you to abstract your phenomenon further by turning descriptive codes into numbers and visualizations of the relationships between those numbers. All of these moves make our phenomena easier to handle and easier to understand. Your phenomenon will not fit on a spreadsheet or in MAXQDA without first reducing the complexity and increasing the abstraction, but it is our engagement with the phenomenon in the world that initially impels our research and it is to that phenomenon, in all of its richness and detail, that we must return.

We want to return to the living phenomenon in the world and use what we have learned in the abstract to discuss and demonstrate something meaningful about the phenomenon. This is the process of writing your results, which consists of five different activities: sorting, reflecting, ordering, detailing the results, and then writing the draft.

Sorting

The result of all the coding and tabulating that you have done will be scads of data, multiple spreadsheets with coding passes, coding summaries, distributions across data streams and contrasts, and correlations between coding passes. Admit to yourself now that not everything you produced over the course of this analysis has yielded true insight. Some of the analyses led to dead ends. Others might have shown marginal results. Some results might have shown that something is going on but in an area unrelated to your current investigation. Amid this data and analysis will be a fair number of insights and a whole lot of chaff. The first step in writing up the results of your study is to learn to recognize the difference between what adds value to your study and what does not.

One source of information to rely upon when deciding where to focus your analysis is the significance testing (see Chapter 9). Whether you used a chi square test or the multinomial logistic regression to find relationships of interest, you can use any significant relationships that emerged to focus your attention for further analysis.

If you have been keeping memos of your planning, thinking, insights, and analysis along the way, those memos will be valuable to you now as a way to look back on what seemed important at the time and on how that sense of importance shifted or became more refined through the analysis. Your memos tell a story of the analysis and the connections that you have been making.

MAXQDA has a built-in function that allows you to sort your memos into an overview and select memos for further study (see MAXQDA Procedure 10-1). Unfortunately, Excel does not have similar capabilities that would allow you to collect and review memos stored as comments. Instead, review your memos one by one. You may find it useful to copy these memos to a text file for future reference and use them in your write up of the results (see Excel Procedure 10.1 and MAXQDA Procedure 10.1).

Begin comparing memos to each other. Look at some of the first memos that you wrote and recall your expectations. Consider how many of those expectations have held up in your investigations of the data. Sort out those memos that no longer hold up and save them for another time. Just because an expectation was not borne out in the approach that you took through the data or in the patterns revealed through your coding does not mean that your expectation was wrong, necessarily; it might become the basis of a future study that attempts to get at that expectation in a different way.

Next, select the memos that reveal key insights about your coding or that build upon and elaborate codes that have proven significant to your data analysis. These memos will help you make sense of those codes and connect them to each other, to theory, and to the literature to which you want to make a contribution.

The result of sorting through your memos should be at least two piles: memos that will help you propel the current study and memos that will not. The memos that will not support the current analysis might still be meaningful, so this pile could be further sorted into memos that are dead ends and memos that offer intriguing or compelling insights that might be right for a different study.

Excel Procedure 10.1: Viewing Memos in Excel

https://goo.gl/8mQssf

1. Open a sheet in Excel and select **View** > **Comments** to reveal all the memos.

Review memos and decide whether to retain memos in Excel or copy to a word processor. Delete any memo that is no longer pertinent to the analysis.

2. **Right click** and choose **Delete Comment** to delete.

MAXQDA Procedure 10.1: Selecting Memos in MAXQDA

https://goo.gl/8mQssf

1. To see all your memos in MAXQDA, click on the **Overview of Memos** icon in the top toolbar.

The **Overview of Memos** window will open with a list of all your memos as shown in Figure 10.1. This will include your memos with code definitions, your free memos, and any other memos you might have created.

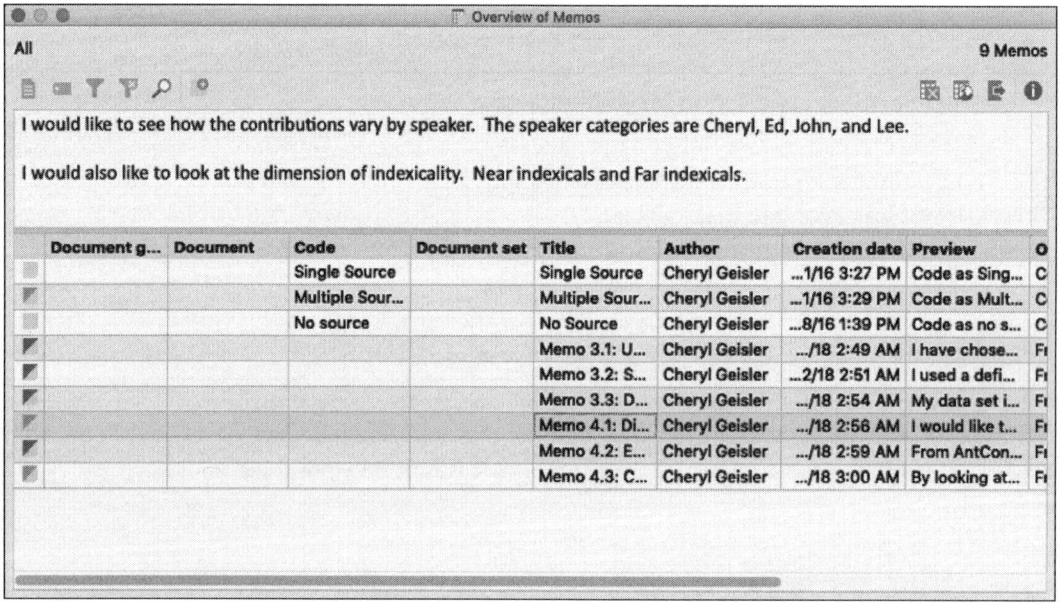

Figure 10.1: Overview of memos in MAXQD.

2. To view the contents of a specific memo, click on its row. The contents will appear in the upper pane of the window.

In Figure 10.1, we have clicked on Memo 4.1 and see its contents in the top pane.

3. To open and edit a memo, double click on its icon.
4. To mark memos you want to consult for your current analysis, double click to open and then mark it with an icon you reserve for this purpose.

Continued . . .

MAXQDA Procedure 10.1: Selecting Memos in MAXQDA (continued)

https://goo.gl/8mQssf

In Figure 10.2, we have used the red shaded icon to mark those we wish to examine further.

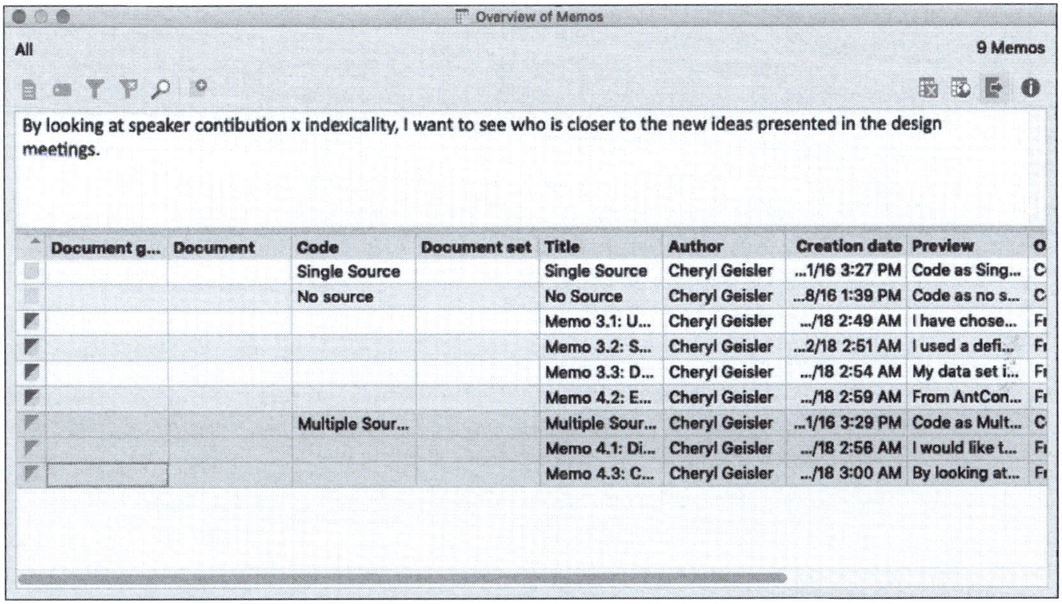

Figure 10.2: Selecting memos to export for further consultation.

5. To sort memos into a group of those you want to consult further, click in the top of the icon column.

The memos will be sorted by icon type.

6. To export specially marked memos, click the first memo, then shift click the last memo to select them.
7. Then click on the **Export** icon and choose an appropriate name for this set of memos, and save them in Rich Text Format (rtf).
8. To review these selected memos, you can open the files in Microsoft Word.

■ Reflecting

Use the memos that you have retained as pertinent to the analysis to begin reflecting on the meaning of your coding categories as they relate to the descriptive framework that you started with at the beginning of your study. Where do your memos create insight about the descriptive framework?

The memos might lead to insights about the actors in the descriptive framework. For example, if we are looking at the interactions between instructors and teams of students in a classroom, perhaps the memos point to differences in the composition of those teams that might explain how they interact with each other and how they approach their team meetings. The memos might suggest something about the instructors and how they differ in terms of pedagogical philosophies. Perhaps the memos point to the importance of other actors that never made it into the descriptive framework: actors like technologies, texts, or other non-humans that have some significant impact on the phenomenon. What are these actors and what makes them significant?

The memos might suggest something about the interactions implied in the descriptive framework. For example, if the descriptive model of the classroom suggests that the important interactions are between students within a team and between the instructors and the teams, find out what your memos suggest those main interactions might be. Which interactions appear to be prominent and most likely associated with qualities of the phenomenon you want to discuss? Do the interactions appear in a particular order? Do they layer on top of one another? Do they co-occur? Perhaps your memos point to interactions that you had not anticipated or seen in the initial descriptive framework. For example, perhaps the interactions among instructors are meaningful and have some impact on how the instructors then interact with teams. Perhaps the teams interact with each other. Perhaps there are interactions between team members and actors that had not appeared in the initial descriptive framework.

The memos might also provide insight about the environments in which the phenomenon takes place. Are there codes and interactions showing that it matters where actors engage with each other? Do actors interact with different aspects of the environment? Does the arrangement of actors in space (e.g., where in a room actors are located) or time (e.g., when actors contribute to the phenomenon and then stop) have some bearing on the activity?

At each step along the way in this reflection, work back through the distributions and codes to the underlying data, grounding your reflections on the abstract in the concreteness and rhetorical richness of your data. Eventually, upon enough reflection, the memos will start to reveal to you themes or concepts that begin to posit a relationship between your understanding of the phenomenon, the descriptive framework where the phenomenon occurs, the coding that you have done, and the literature that has been quietly guiding how you see the data. Reflection can take you to this point, but it does not end. Although your memos might suggest these interpretations, they were not written to elaborate those interpretations. Use this opportunity to revise your descriptive framework to reflect your developing understanding of the phenomenon. Also use the opportunity to write new memos that offer a synthesis of what you learn from reading across the memos.

Memo 10.1: Memos

Examine the memos that you have retained as pertinent to your analysis. Reflect on and write down interpretations that these memos suggest of your data. Are any of these findings expected or surprising?

Ordering

The next preliminary stage to writing your results is to begin drawing connections across memos and the concepts that they help reveal. Specifically, we will be focusing on the coding that you have done. Given how you are now thinking about your phenomenon of study and given the revisions to your descriptive framework, consider how to link codes together. It may be the case that your coding dimensions still adequately reflect the point that you want to discuss. However, you may find that there are connections between codes across different dimensions that are just as meaningful as the original code dimensions. These groupings of codes may reflect meaningful qualities of your phenomenon that only became visible through analysis. Cluster these codes together to see if a pattern emerges. These recurring patterns may be evidence of a theme.

As an example, consider a study of user interactions on an open source software forum. One coding dimension looks at development decisions when community members appear to reach a decision about what the software does do or should do. Another coding dimension looks at contexts users rely on to articulate software issues. Independently, these coding dimensions may show when and how often development decisions are made and they may show the ways that users describe the issues that they encounter. If we look at how these coding categories intersect, however, we might find that development decisions frequently appear to follow certain kinds of contextualizing statements. Perhaps the pattern that emerges is that development decisions occur around discussions that move back and forth between contextualizing statements about the user's social/professional setting and the technological context of the software's interface and operating logic. Earlier memos might comment on the patterns of coding distribution within the dimensions but memos that synthesize across those dimensions might help identify this pattern of codes that point to, in this case, a conversational circumstance that is associated with development decisions.

This process of ordering and looking across coding dimensions will help you make a selection of codes and find any patterns that link those codes together to say something about your phenomenon. The better these patterns, and the themes they represent, are tied to the descriptive framework and your sense of the phenomenon, the closer they get you back to the realm of living discourse and actors. These themes can then become the focus of your analysis. Moreover, because the themes are directly connected to the coding that you have been doing, you will have a way to filter and sort your data to pull out examples of the themes as well as a way to understand what those examples mean in terms of your overall argument.

Detailing

After you have reflected on your coding, sorted your memos, and ordered them to see what theory might be emerging, it is time to make another move back to the lived discourse by detailing examples of those codes and themes. Charmaz describes this move as the process of turning one's concepts into actors (2014, p. 285). By turning concepts and themes into actors, we allow them to be the agents through which the story of your phenomenon is told and your theory is elaborated.

Not surprisingly, the final stage in this analytic process brings you back to the details of language that drew you to your project in the first place. These details can illuminate your analysis both for yourself and your readers. And it is in this process of detailing the results that you can use the analytic connections and structures that became apparent to you through the processes of coding and analysis to give meaning to the raw data.

Defining Detail

For our purposes, detail can be defined as selections from a stream of verbal data chosen to provide specific examples of more general patterns. Detail can range in size from a single word or phrase to extended passages of interaction selected for its relevance to a point you want to make. Here, for example, is how a paragraph from a writer's text has been used to detail the concept of a "problem case in paternalism" (Geisler, 1994):

> A prototypic problem case in the issue of paternalism, taken from Roger's final draft, is as follows:
>
>> Mister N, a member of a religious sect which strictly forbids blood transfusions, is involved in a serious automobile accident and loses a large amount of blood. On arriving at the hospital, he is still conscious and informs the doctor that his religion forbids blood transfusions. Immediately thereafter he faints from loss of blood. The doctor believes that if Mister N is not given a blood transfusion he will die. Thereupon, while Mr. N is still unconscious, the doctor arranges for and carries out the blood transfusion.

Details like this one can be presented in many contexts. Methodologically, details can show how your coding scheme works. But the same details could be used in a results section to give an example of a prevalent verbal data phenomenon or to illustrate an example of a theme that emerges from the coding.

What makes something a detail is its relationship to the larger patterns you have already established by earlier analyses:

- Details can add nuance and significance to abstract patterns of code distributions. You may have found, for example that Cheryl talked more in design meetings than in management meetings. Detail can help you understand what she was talking about in both meetings.
- Details can help you and your readers understand what patterns of association might mean across coding categories. You may have found, for example, that Cheryl tended to use more indexical language in design meetings. Detail can help you understand what points Cheryl was making about the design and why those points were more highly indexed.
- Details can also help illustrate patterns of code change over time. You may have found, for example, that Cheryl didn't begin making significant contributions in a design meeting until more than half way through. Detail can help you to understand what changed at that half way point that lead to her increased contributions.

Detail does more than illustrate the general patterns found through analysis: it enriches your understanding of those patterns, allows you to explore potential explanations for these patterns and can even become the source of schemes and codes that launch a second wave of analysis or the design of a further study.

The Value of Detail

The value of details lies in their ability to link the abstract analysis captured in coding tables, distribution graphs, block charts, and temporal indices with the emerging theory that comes from your organized reflections, curated through your memos. Our codes have done their work, allowing us to take a messy, unwieldy phenomenon in the lived world of language use and to reduce it to numbers on a spreadsheet that we can combine with other numbers to see relationships that might not have been apparent while observing our verbal data phenomena in the wild. To paraphrase Bruno Latour, by losing the verbal phenomenon itself, we gain knowledge of it as a data object (1999, p. 38). Details allow us to reverse that process by taking what knowledge we have gained about the verbal data phenomenon to see the verbal phenomenon in a new light.

When you return from analysis to the detail of language, you return as a different person. Analysis has given you both articulated concepts with which to understand phenomenon and important understandings of the overall patterns. In other words, having gone through analysis, your intuition is now better prepared to interpret detail. Coming back to detail, then, can be understood as the "big payoff" for the entire analytic process. You now see the verbal data through the lens of intuitions tutored by the analytic process.

Detail also functions as a key component of the interpretive processes in which your reader will engage with your analysis. Some readers in some forums will be willing to engage fully with your study—following the intricacies of your coding and reaching for the abstractions of your analysis. Many, however, will not. Instead, they will rely on you to use details to make your results both concrete and meaningful.

Details can help these readers in the meaning-making process in three ways. First, detail helps readers with understanding. Anchoring generalizations in concrete instances helps readers better understand what you are talking about—how you define the phenomenon, how you saw the associations. Second, detail helps readers to evaluate the credibility of your analysis—weighing it against their own intuitions and experience to see if it makes sense. And, finally, detail helps readers to see the significance of your results—to recognize applications to the contexts in which they operate.

■ Areas for Detailing

Opportunities for detailing are associated with nearly every component of analysis. In this section, we provide examples of some of these opportunities.

Introducing the Phenomenon

Just as a picture is worth a thousand words, so too is a well-chosen detail worth a thousand vague descriptions of the phenomenon you are studying. Here, for example, is the opening of an article that distinguishes between the use of reading and writing by academic experts and academic novices in terms of authority (Penrose & Geisler, 1994):

> By early March, Janet is ready to set aside the notecards she's been laboring over since midwinter. She begins to write:
>
> > This paper will define paternalism and discuss its justification. Paternalism is the action of one person interfering with another person's actions or thoughts to help him. The person who interferes, called the paternalist, breaks moral rules of independency because he restricts the other person's freedom without that person's consent. He does it, however, in a fatherly, benevolent way, and assumes that the person being restrained will appreciate the action later.
>
> Across town a few days later, Roger makes a similar decision. Setting aside his scrawled pages of notes, he, too, begins his text:
>
> > Consider the following situations:
> >
> > Situation One: Mister N, a member of a religious sect which strictly forbids blood transfusions, is involved in a serious automobile accident and loses a large amount of blood. On arriving at the hospital, he is still conscious and informs the doctor that his religion forbids blood transfusions. Immediately thereafter he faints from loss of blood. The doctor believes that if Mister N is not given a blood transfusion he will die. Thereupon, the doctor arranges for and carries out the blood transfusion. Is the doctor right in doing this? [Two more cases are presented.) . . .

> Sometimes paternalistic actions seem justified, and sometimes not; but always, paternalism seems at least to be a bit disquieting. . . . The authors whose efforts will be reviewed here have undertaken the task of trying to spell out conditions which must be satisfied for paternalistic actions to be justified . . . [S]o a preliminary task is that of giving an account of what are paternalistic actions; that of settling on a definition in order to gain a clearer notion of what we are talking about, and of what, if anything, has to be justified.

> The contrast between these two introductions is striking. Though they share a common focus on the definition and justification of paternalism, Janet's text views the definition and justificatory conditions as established truths, while Roger introduces them as matters yet to be resolved.

Notice here how the extended and contrasting detail from different texts is used to help the reader understand what differences in authority amount to. Good detail often works in this way to introduce a reader to a phenomenon. Your readers may find it helpful if you label passages with the codes that you applied. Sometimes seeing the codes that apply can help reinforce the connection between a passage and the emerging theory through which you are reading it.

Illustrating Segmentation

The next opportunity for using detail is for describing the kinds of segments that you have used to break up the verbal stream. Often, such segments do not need to be explained because they represent well-known choices (sentences, t-units, etc.). At other times, however, you may anticipate that the segment will be unfamiliar to readers. In these cases, detail will help readers understand, as in the following case (Geisler, Rogers & Haller, 1998):

> We expected that the lists these participants produced would be indicative of the kinds of issues to which they normally attend in a software engineering design task. They produced such issues as the following:

- "How should system respond if a credit card transaction is declined by the issuer? If credit card was reported stolen?" [Last of nine issues listed by a software engineering expert.]
- "Can user query how much charges they've run up?" [Eighth of nine issues listed by an advanced technical communication student.]
- "Can the user select a bus any time that it runs or must they take the next available bus?" [Fourth of nine issues generated by an advanced software engineering student.]
- "If the machine doesn't work, you can't get to where you want to go." [First of five issues generated by an advanced chemistry student.]

The four details used in this example not only clarify the nature of the segment "issue," but also represent the range of issues produced by the four groups in the study. These details, then, not only serve their current purpose (illustrating segmentation), but also prepare the reader for later findings.

■ Understanding Codes

As noted in Chapter 4, a good coding scheme will provide not only definitions of coding categories but also sample segments that would be coded in that category. These sample segments, you may now realize, can become details that help readers to understand what your coding scheme really amounts to, as in the following example (Geisler, 1994):

> To analyze participants' use of the construct of authorship, I examined the protocol data for the presence of *author mentions*, which were defined to include: (a) names of specific authors (e.g., "Childress"), (b) nominals standing for an aggregate of authors (e.g., "these guys"), (c) nominals standing for roles of authors (e.g., "a moral philosopher"), and (d) pronouns standing in for any of the aforementioned ("she"; "they").

Illuminating Patterns

The greatest opportunity for detail comes in the service of understanding the overall patterns revealed by your analysis. Good detail here will be linked to the overall patterns as in the following example, where details are directly referenced to patterns in the graphs shown in Figure 10.3a and 10.3b (Geisler, 2004):

> Actions "to say" are foundational verbs of articulation. Some of them were literal:
>
> "Jamie and I talked about this at great length."
>
> But most were metaphorical, describing giving voice in text:
>
> "that I . . . I said was impurely paternalistic."
>
> "Say" was the preferred action for Janet who used it in more than half (54%) of her public accounts. The figure suggests that she used it both to describe her own actions and the actions of the authors that she read, and that "saying" occurred in accounts throughout her sessions. Roger portrayed himself and authors as "saying" things a lot less often (11%). Figure 6 suggests that, for Roger, "saying" was a minor part of periods of generally high activity on the public stage.

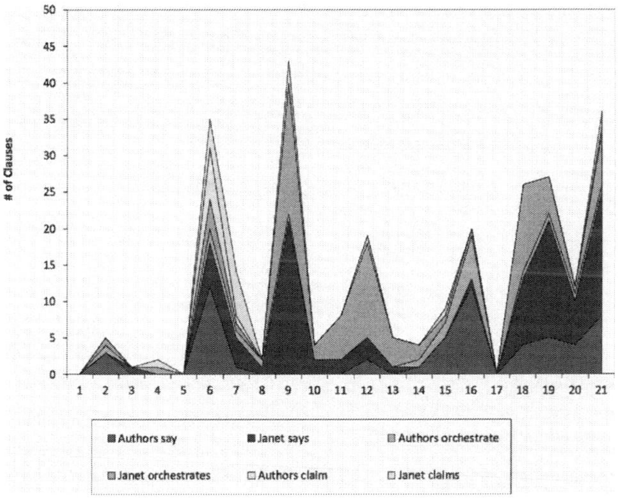

Figure 10.3a: Actions in Janet's 22 sessions. Adapted from Geisler, 2004.

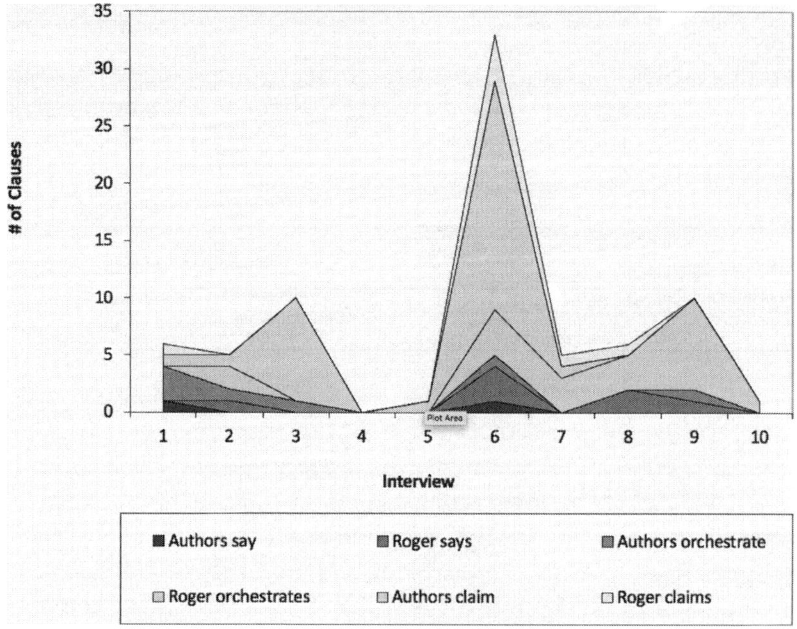

Figure 10.3b: Actions in Roger's 10 sessions. Adapted from Geisler, 2004.

As this example shows, details can help to provide a more intuitive understanding to the otherwise dense abstractions represented in graphs.

Exercise 10.1 Test Your Understanding

In the excerpts below (and available at https://wac.colostate.edu/books/practice/codingstreams/), underline the details that have been added. Rewrite the text to eliminate the details.

> *Sample Segment 1.* Before 1988, I used the still-common academic year calendar, Week-at-a-Glance, available from most university bookstores. A little bigger than the PalmPilot (4 x 6.5), it offered seven days in a 2-page spread as diagrammed in Figure 10.4. Monday through Friday provided 7 full blank lines; the weekend (on which I would presumably be loafing) provided 7 half-lines per day. A sample week, that of Dec 7, 1987, showed that I recorded four kinds of information in the Week-at-a-Glance. First, I listed

daily appointments by writing a time followed by the name of the appointment: "9:30 Graduate Review Committee." Second, I noted deadlines such as "Final project due." Third, I created numbered task lists like the following:

- Annenberg
- Book revision plans

And finally, I recorded untimed events that, nevertheless, were scheduled to occur on specific days: "David Phillips visits, New Zealand." As might be expected with all of these kinds of entries, the seven lines provided for each day often made space tight in my Week-at-a-Glance.

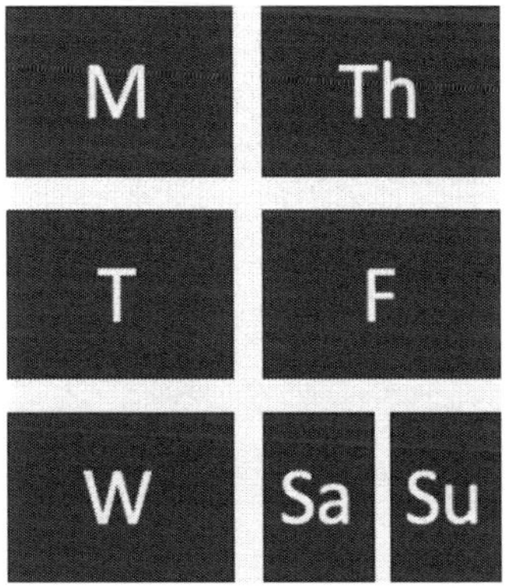

Figure 10.4: Figure for Exercise 10.1 Test Your Understanding, Sample Segment 1. Adapted from Geisler, 2003.

Sample Segment 2. Activity theory requires us to understand how a tool builds upon the user's prior tools, responds to her desires and dissatisfactions, and, through its affordances, extends the capacity of the user in unexpected directions. We can see all of these factors at work with my use of the Day-Timer. The same kinds of information that we noted in the Week-at-a-Glance—daily appointments, deadlines, task lists, and untimed events—found their place in the new Day-Timer technology. In addition, my desire for better control over project tasks and a mechanism through which to assure that I did not neglect my scholarship lead me to develop new mediating means built on tool affordances: not only task lists created in a space whose label ("To Be Done Today") invited such use, but also time-keeping notes ("9:30–12:30") in spaces (Diary Record) designed for other purposes (billable hours). (From Geisler, 2003)

Sample Segment 3. The largest of these activities could be characterized as "doing email," though the work accomplished through this activity was broader than might be expected. In its simplest form, as shown in the activity graph in Figure 10.5, doing email involved reading messages and taking one of a number of simple actions in response to messages received:

- archiving many (action sequences 17, 19, 29, 22, 23, 25, 27, 30),
- replying to one (action sequence 21),
- trashing a couple (action sequences 18 & 26),
- holding one for later reply (action sequence 37), and
- responding to one by modifying an earlier reply (action sequence 24).

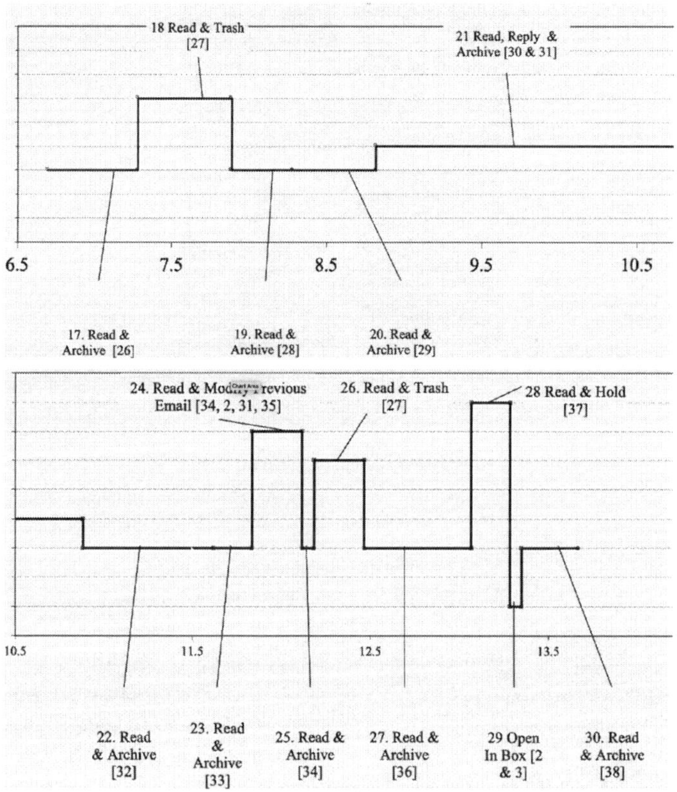

Figure 10.5: Figure for Exercise 10.1 Test Your Understanding, Sample Segment 3. Adapted from Geisler, 2003.

For most of these actions sequences, texts were processed serially in the order in which they were encountered. Only two new texts were created: Text 31 which served as a reply to Text 30; and Text 35 which became an addition to that same reply later on in action sequence 24.

Sample Segment 4. While "doing email," I invoked Palm Technologies when messages were linked to task management issues. As shown in Figure 10.6, for example, I responded to one email message (Text 12) in three different ways, all involving the Palm:

- First, I created the event (Text 19) mentioned in the message by going to my daily calendar for today (Text 1), moving forward 3 weeks (Texts 13, 14, and 15) and 3 days (Texts 16, 17, and 18) to the date of the event.
- Second, in the course of replying (Text 20) to the message, I sought to confirm the time for an upcoming meeting—going back to my Palm (Text 17), returning to the daily calendar for today (Text 1), changing to the weekly view (Text 21), and then checking the start time I had listed for the appointment (Text 22), which I then included in my reply (Text 23).
- Third, while viewing my weekly schedule, I also decided to cancel another meeting (Text 24) earlier in the week, deleted it from the Palm, and then added a note about this (Text 25) to my email reply (Text 40).

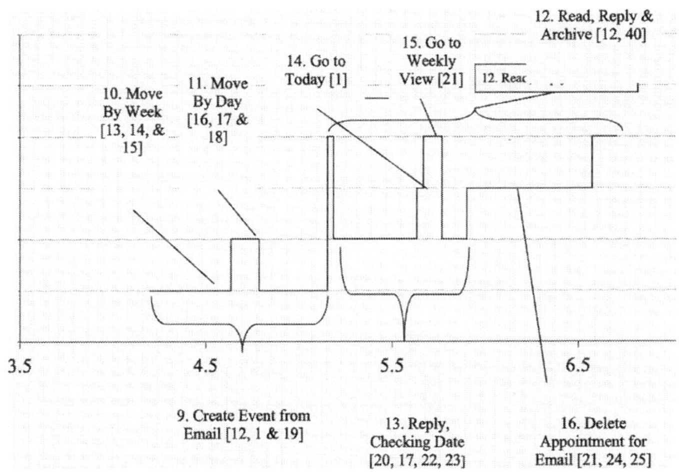

Figure 10.6: Figure for Exercise 10.1 Test Your Understanding, Sample Segment 4. Adapted from Geisler, 2003.

Sample Segment 5. "Planning work" involved the use of a special purpose task management tool, the Project Inventory, created in a spreadsheet and shown in Figure 10.7. Calendar-like in structure, each week provided room to array three kinds of texts: deadlines such as that for the "NSF ITR" shown for Tuesday, January 16; events such as "Tucson" shown for the week of February 20; and work such as "Palm Tech" shown for Monday, February 5. To the right of the week's array and off screen in Figure 10.7, texts represented a variety of projects, unscheduled but waiting my attention. Weeks that represented time past were usually grayed out though this was not true at the start of this session.

Deadlines						
Work						
Events						
	M	T	W	Th	F	S
	15-Jan	16-Jan	17-Jan	18-Jan	19-Jan	20-Jan
Deadlines						
Work		NSF-IT Proposal	NSF-IT Proposal	NSF-IT Proposal	NSF-IT Proposal	
Events						
	M	T	W	Th	F	S
	22-Jan	23-Jan	24-Jan	25-Jan	26-Jan	27-Jan
Deadlines			NSF-IT			
Work						
Events						
	M	T	W	Th	F	S
	29-Jan	30-Jan	31-Jan	1-Feb	2-Feb	3-Feb
Deadlines				JBTC		
Work	JBTC	JBTC	JBTC	Palm Tech	Palm Tech	
Events						
	M	T	W	Th	F	S
	5-Feb	6-Feb	7-Feb	8-Feb	9-Feb	10-Feb
Deadlines					JBTC	
Work	Palm Tech	Palm Tech	Palm Tech	Palm Tech	Palm Tech	
Events						
	M	T	W	Th	F	S
	12-Feb	13-Feb	14-Feb	15-Feb	16-Feb	17-Feb
Deadlines						
Work	Palm Tech	Palm Tech	Palm Tech	Palm Tech	Palm Tech	
Events						
	M	T	W	Th	F	S
	19-Feb	20-Feb	21-Feb	22-Feb	23-Feb	24-Feb
Deadlines						
Work						
Events			Tuscon	Tuscon	Tuscon	Tuscon
	M	T	W	Th	F	S
	26-Feb	27-Feb	28-Feb	1-Mar	2-Mar	3-Mar

Figure 10.7: Figure for Exercise 10.1 Test Your Understanding, Sample Segment 5. Adapted from Geisler, 2003.

For Discussion: How does the rewrite change the meaning and impact of the text?

Locating Detail

In large data sets, finding details can seem an easy task since details are, if anything, overly abundant. Yet finding the right detail to do the work can be a challenge. As we have seen, good details don't simply illustrate; they illuminate and persuade. Based on work that you have done to sort, reflect on, and order your thoughts via memos, you can use several strategies to select appropriate details.

Using the Descriptive Framework

In the process of reflecting on your analytic memos, we asked you to return to your descriptive framework in order to verify details or revise them on the basis of your emerging analysis. The descriptive framework reveals some of the key relationships between participants in the verbal phenomenon, their tools, their settings, and their motivations for interacting. Through the descriptive framework, you can see the contrast used to highlight the phenomenon of interest. Now you can go back to those participants and settings and contrasts to find details that both show those details while also using them as points of comparison to isolate what is meaningful about the data.

In a study of five classrooms, for example, if you had found that teachers contributed more ideas about content than students did you might look for details by focusing on participants in the classroom framework and the different conversation activities that occupy them:

- Teachers' talk about content in each of the five classrooms—are they doing similar things when they all talk about content?
- Students' talk about content in each of the five classrooms—what do students talk about when they actually talk about content? Is there something in this talk that shows why it doesn't happen more often?
- Teachers' talk about other things in each of the five classrooms—is teacher's talk about content distinctive from other kinds of teacher talk?
- Students' talk about other things in each of the five classrooms—is students' talk about other things more compelling for students?

- Students' talk in response to teachers' talk about content—When teachers talk about content, why aren't students responding on the same topic? What topics do they respond to?
- Teachers' talk in response to students' talk about content—is there something about the way that teachers respond to students' talk about content that keeps them from pursuing it further?

As this partial list of questions illustrate, a single overall result can lead to a whole host of follow-up inquiries that can be addressed and illuminated by detail.

Filtering Data by Codes

Once you have decided which parts of the descriptive framework to illuminate through detail, you can use the filtering techniques to pick out segments that meet these criteria (see Excel Procedure 10.2 and MAXQDA Procedure 10.2). If, for example, you wanted to look at teachers' comments about content, you could filter a data file first by speaker, choosing teacher as speaker code, and then by topic, choosing content as your topic code. The resulting selection would show you all segments that might serve as details.

If you are simply picking out individual segments for details, a simple filter like the one just described will work. If, as is more often the case, you want to look at these segments in context, you will want to see more than a filtered list shows you.

Exercise 10.2 Try it Out

Download the datasheet found at https://wac.colostate.edu/books/practice/codingstreams/, and apply filters that will allow you to focus on the segments in which participants are talking about their objects of work (coded as *Object* in the Frame dimension) but attempt to align that discussion to a technical context (coded as *Technical* in the Alignment dimension). Select details that would allow you discuss the range of technical objects that the participants discuss.

For Discussion: What do the segments of data coded *Object* do in the context of the conversation in which they are embedded? After additionally filtering the *Object* codes by *Technical*, consider how those segments differ from the other segments coded as *Object*.

Excel Procedure 10.2: Exploring Detail in Full Context

https://goo.gl/8mQssf

1. To filter data by a specific code, place a filter on the coding column.
2. Use the drop down menu to select the specific code you want to explore.

Alternatively, to search the data for segments using a specific phrase, select the data column and use the search box to type in the phrase.

3. Once you have found relevant segments either by filtering or searching, change their font color to something noticable, like red.
4. Remove the filter if there is one in place

You will then be able to see selected segments in full context.

MAXQDA Procedure 10.2: Exploring Detail in Full Context

https://goo.gl/8mQssf

1. To filter data by a specific code, activate the document(s) you want to explore in the **Document** window
2. Activate the code(s) you want to explore in the **Code System** window.

The segments that match your criteria will appear in the **Retrieved Segments** window.

3. To see a segment in full context, click anywhere in the identifying information to the left of the segment.

The segment will appear in full context in the **Document Browser**.

4. Alternatively, to search for segments using a specific phrase, select **Analysis** > **Lexical Search** from the menu and type in the phrase.
5. Click **Run Search**.

A search results window of segments using this phrase will appear.

6. To see a specific phrase in full content click on its row.

The segment will appear in full context in the **Document Browser**.

Memo 10.2: Detail

Use filtering or searching to locate five details on either side of your built-in contrast that illustrate what you take to be the major differences you have found in your analysis. Write one to two sentences characterizing them for the rest of your classmates.

Using a Temporal Index

A third technique for locating good detail involves the use of a temporal index. If you have constructed a temporal index, you can use it to locate specific interesting details. In the temporal index shown in Figure 10.8, for instance, we see that Lee did very little talking. To find those places where he did talk, we can simply hold our cursor over the point in the graph where he is talking and Excel will give us the information about that point. In this case, we see that one point of Lee's talk is associated with x-coordinate of 101 and y-coordinate of 4. Returning to the data sheet from which this graph was constructed, we can easily find point 101, shown in red at the bottom of Figure 10.8, and begin our interpretive process.

Using Memory

One final way to find details to illuminate overall patterns is through the use of memory. After coding and analysis, many analysts find that certain passages in the data stand out in their memories, are striking for what they show, and even haunt them as they develop the overall picture. Picking details for their salience can lead to serious mischaracterization of the data if done *without* the kind of systematic analysis described in this book. But picking out such details after analysis insures that you can place them in the big picture of what was going on generally. Using memory to find your details in this kind of situation can be one of your most powerful techniques.

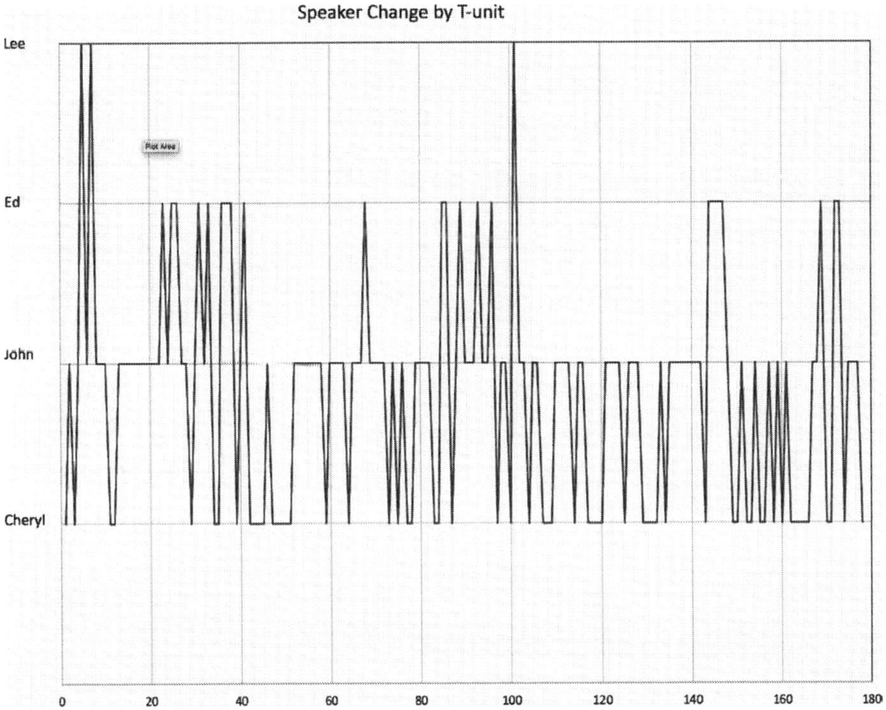

103	100 Cheryl:	pairings ...
104	101 Lee:	... if you have power for them ...
105	102 John:	... you could have two dozen

Figure 10.8: Using a temporal index to locate detail.

Writing the Draft

When you have selected the details that best help you illuminate your phenomenon of study and present an argument that illustrates your emerging theoretical understanding of that phenomenon, you are ready to start organizing your thoughts into a conventional written presentation.

We begin with the literature review; move to define the phenomenon; describe the data; survey the analysis; present the patterns; elaborate with detail; provide a discussion, and conclude with significance. Whether you use this particular ordering will depend upon the genre conventions of a specific journal. In any case, when a full accounting of your analysis is called for, these topics will be covered.

The Literature

What is the state of the art in the literature to which your analysis aims to contribute? What have been the relevant issues? The previous findings? The controversies? The missing links?

Your work began with the survey of the literature in Chapter 2 to anchor your project. As you have carried out your analysis, you probably added to your reading and developed a more focused interpretation of the state of the art. In presenting your results, then, you provide readers with a revised picture of this literature and its current state so that they may better understand the contribution your study makes.

The Phenomenon

What is the phenomenon examined in your analysis? In what context does it arise? Of what importance is it? Does it create problems for us? Does it present us with opportunities?

Your definition of the phenomenon of interest is critical to your readers' being able to understand and take an interest in your work. Sometimes the phenomenon is a well-established topic in the literature. At other times, you must work to get your readers to see something they may not have thought much about before.

Occasionally, striking details can be used to call attention to a phenomenon and provide the basis for analyzing its characteristics. Because different audiences have different interests and level of familiarity, the way you define a phenomenon can vary from one publication venue to another. But you must always make sure that your readers know what phenomenon you are examining and why it is important.

The Design

By what design did you structure your analysis? What contrasts were built in to it? How does this contrast relate to the phenomenon in general? What categories of phenomenon did you sample? What questions were you seeking answers to?

A full accounting of a research project includes a description of the entire design that structured your data gathering and analysis. You present some version of your descriptive framework and well as your research questions as described in Chapter 2. Through these, you set up readers' expectations for a discussion of the results of both the analyses that were illuminating and those that were less interesting.

Sometimes, aspects of your descriptive framework turn out to be uninteresting. Some research questions may not have answers; some analyses lead nowhere. In these situations, many accounts of research do not review the full set of analyses conducted. Rather, they review only those that make a contribution to the literature. The conventions of your discipline, your readers' expectations, and your own intentions will guide your decision on how fully to describe your initial design and questions.

The Data

What data did you collect? Where did it come from? How did you select it? How is it related to the phenomenon in general? Did you analyze all of it? If not, how did you make your selection?

A full accounting of your data makes clear what data you collected and/or analyzed and your reasons for selecting it. A data table can provide an economical way of giving a full accounting. It can be included in a table in the body of the paper for a full accounting or moved to an appendix for a more abbreviated account.

Always make sure to describe how you selected your data samples. Many studies using verbal data do not make selection clear enough. This can leave readers without an understanding of the criteria by which you selected the data and, therefore, without a way to assess how well your results represent the phenomenon. If, on the other hand, you show that you had a process for selecting data and reasons for using that process, you enhance your credibility.

Data collection and selection is always described in a full accounting. For a more abbreviated account, some details can be moved to endnotes. It is also not uncommon to see authors referring readers to other published papers for more complete descriptions of data collection and selection.

The Analysis

How was the data segmented? How was it coded? What reliability was achieved between coders? What is the relationship of your analytic procedures to the phenomenon under investigation and to the research questions you have asked?

The bulk of the technical detail in a full accounting rests in the description of the analytic methods. As you now understand, the devil is in these details. They represent a significant investment of a researcher's time and the merit of the study rests on quality of these procedures.

Nevertheless, most readers are less interested in these analytic details than in other aspects of your research. Even those with the competence to evaluate your methods will often not have the interest—at least initially. Readers often focus first on results and only later may begin to pick apart your analytic process. Peer reviewers in research journals do, of course, look carefully at the analysis. Other readers, in fact, count on them to do so. In fact, many readers assume that if a study has made it into print, the analytic methodology must be sound. For this reason, even technical readers feel free to skim your analytic methods.

In a more abbreviated accounting, the analytic methodology is often the first thing to go from the body of the text. Segmentation may not be described. Coding schemes may not reproduced in full. Reliability figures may not be mentioned. Nevertheless, as a responsible researcher, you should make sure that information about these topics is available in some peripheral way. Otherwise it will be impossible for others to assess and build on your work.

The Patterns

What patterns has the analysis revealed? How has the built-in contrast actually played out? How does what you actually observed compare to what we might have expected had nothing really been going on?

The patterns you find through an analysis of verbal data are the heart of a presentation of results. It is here that the "news" of your presentation should be found. As you have already learned, such patterns can be complex. In presenting them, you need to decide how to orchestrate their presentation. Some of your options include:

> BY QUESTION: If your research questions have addressed several different aspects of the phenomenon, you may want to adopt an organization that takes up and reviews the answer to each research question in turn.
>
> BY CONTRAST: If your analysis has confirmed significant differences across your built-in contrast, you may want to begin with the overall evidence of this difference and then move to characterize each side of the contrast in turn.
>
> BY DIMENSION: If your analysis has involved multiple dimensions, you may want to review the basic results in each dimension first and then turn to their interrelationship.
>
> BY STREAM: If your analysis has suggested a basic pattern with lots of variation by data stream, you may want to begin with the basic pattern and then present the individual variations.

Other organizational patterns do exist and can be imagined. The important point is this: Your results are complex and you need to find the best way to present them simply for a full accounting.

If you want to give a more abbreviated account of results, focus on the main results, the ones with the greatest significance in terms of theory or practice. Abbreviated accounts may also reduce the presentation of graphs and tables in favor of more discursive descriptions of patterns.

The Discussion

How do you interpret the patterns found? What is the nature of the phenomenon under investigation? What meaning do they have in terms of the issues raised in the literature? What answers can be given to your research questions?

The results section presents the nitty gritty of the patterns you found and their significance compared to expectations. It is filled with tables and graphs. When you move into discussion, you are still focused on the patterns you found, but rise to a higher level of seeing the patterns in the context of the prior literature. In an abbreviated accounting, most of the presentation of results may in fact, be focused on discussing those results for readers.

The Significance

Of what significance are the findings? Why should readers care? Of what import are they theoretically? Of what import practically? If the results found here were to hold true more generally, what would be the implications? What further work needs to be done to confirm these patterns?

The final section of a canonical presentation of results concerns itself with assessing the significance of the contribution made by the study. This significance may lie in the realm of theory, of practice, of methodology, or in all three. The contribution may be in a single field or across several fields. The study may answer questions or raise them. It may confirm existing claims about a phenomenon or raise doubts about them. The study may put to rest an issue or set the stage for a continuing line of work. All of this should be made clear in a discussion of significance.

Selected Studies Using Details

Geisler, C. (1994). *Academic literacy and the nature of expertise: Reading, writing, and knowing in academic philosophy.* Mahwah, NJ: Lawrence Erlbaum Associates.

Geisler, C. (2003). When management becomes personal: An activity-theoretic analysis of Palm technologies. In C. Bazerman & D. R. Russell (Eds.), *Writing selves / writing societies: Research from activity perspectives* (pp. 125–158). Fort Collins,

CO: The WAC Clearinghouse and Mind, Culture, and Activity. Retrieved from https://wac.colostate.edu/books/perspectives/selves-societies.

Geisler, C. (2004). Upon the public stage: How professionalization shapes accounts of composing in the academy. In B. Couture & T. Kent (Eds.), *The private, the public, and the published: Reconciling private lives and public rhetoric* (pp. 112–126). Logan, UT: Utah State University.

Geisler, C., Rogers, E. H. & Haller, C. (1998). Disciplining discourse: Discourse practice in the affiliated professions of software engineering design. *Written Communication, 15*(1), 2–24.

Penrose, A. M. & Geisler, C. (1994). Reading and writing without authority. *College Composition and Communication, 45*(4), 505–520.

Swarts, J. (2004). Technological mediation of document review: The use of textual replay in two organizations. *Journal of Business and Technical Communication, 18*(3), 328–360.

Swarts, J. (2007). Mobility and composition: The architecture of coherence in non-places. *Technical Communication Quarterly, 16*(3), 279–309.

Swarts, J. (2011). Technological literacy as network building. *Technical Communication Quarterly, 20*(3), 274–302.

For Further Reading

Charmaz, K. (2014). *Constructing grounded theory* (2nd ed.). Thousand Oaks, CA: SAGE Publications.

Latour, B. (1999). *Pandora's hope: Essays on the reality of science studies.* Cambridge, MA: Harvard University Press.